S0-EHH-479

THE ARDEN SHAKESPEARE
GENERAL EDITOR: UNA ELLIS-FERMOR

LOVE'S LABOUR'S LOST

THE ARDEN EDITION OF THE WORKS OF WILLIAM SHAKESPEARE

LOVE'S LABOUR'S LOST

Edited by

RICHARD DAVID

BASED ON THE EDITION OF

H. C. HART

METHUEN AND CO. LTD. LONDON

36 Essex Street, Strand, W.C.2

The original editor of the Arden Shakespeare was W. J. Craig (1899-1906), succeeded by R. H. Case (1909-1944). Present editor, Una Ellis-Fermor
H. C. Hart's edition of Love's Labour's Lost first published 1906
It was reprinted twice
Fourth Edition (Richard David), revised and reset, December 1951
Fifth Edition, 1956

5·1

CATALOGUE NO. 4731/U

PRINTED IN GREAT BRITAIN AT THE UNIVERSITY PRESS ABERDEEN
AND BOUND BY JAMES BURN & CO. LTD., ESHER

TO

MY MASTERS

G. H. W. R.

H. G. B.

J. D. W.

CONTENTS

GENERAL EDITOR'S PREFACE

THE first volumes of the original series of the Arden edition of Shakespeare's works appeared in 1899, fifty years before the first volume in the present series. It has not, until now, been possible to alter what was originally set up except by the addition of such footnotes and brief appendices as were supplied at successive revisions by the editors themselves or the general editors. Some of the latest volumes in the original series were not gravely affected by this, as they already had the solid body of twentieth-century scholarship behind them when they were first produced. But the earliest of that series, even if edited by the most distinguished scholars of their day, have inevitably become to varying degrees outmoded by investigations that have followed their publication. It was to remedy this that the publishers proposed a new revision, of which the first volumes were to appear in 1949.

Two facts governed the nature of this revision, as, indeed, of the original edition. The first was the need to offer to the senior pupils of schools and to university students as much as could be presented in brief and intelligible form of the immense body of scholarship which the first half of the twentieth century has contributed to the field of Shakespeare studies. The second was the need to present a reliable text within the limits imposed by modernization, with its inevitable effects upon spelling, punctuation [1] and, less directly, upon collation.

Working within these conditions, the revising editors have adopted in general the following methods of treating text, collations and annotations.

The modernized text which formed the basis of the original series was that of the Cambridge edition of 1891-3.

[1] Some change is unavoidable in substituting modern, grammatical punctuation for the pointing of Elizabethan dramatic texts. This is more generally understood now than in the early years of this century, but comments on the problems of individual passages or plays will be found in the separate volumes.

For the present edition we have reached the following agreement:

(1) To follow the substantive text (if that was easily determined, as in the case of "Folio only" plays), except for obvious and agreed errors, spelling variants, mispunctuation and mislineation. (It will be at once recognized that the connotations of the words "obvious" and "agreed" admit a wide solution and allow of some dispute.)

(2) To follow, in cases where there was divergence between a F. and a good Q. text (or between a F., good Q. and bad Q.), the generally accepted blend of the two which had been used by the Cambridge editors, except where fresh light had since been thrown on the relative validity of the source texts.[1] It has rested with the individual editors to determine when changes were necessary. There has been a tendency to interpret this in the direction of a return to F. or Q. readings in place of traditional emendations.[2]

The collations were affected by the use of a modernized text, as in all such editions of the work of Elizabethan dramatists, but, with due allowance for this, they have been arranged in the customary way. Sometimes this has meant little alteration of those of the original Arden volume, but sometimes, where a subsequent textual discovery has modified the evidence, complete recasting has been necessary.

The annotations have been designed to cover, as before, description of specific textual problems including classical emendations, the elucidation of obscure passages with comments on syntax and vocabulary, explanation of references to customs and events that are no longer familiar to modern readers, quotation of illustrative parallels from

[1] As, for example, in the case of certain good Quartos, whose reputation has improved during the past fifty years.

[2] A minor example may be given from *Macbeth*, the first volume in the new series. At II. iv. 4, all former editors followed Rowe in the slight alteration involved in emending *Ha,* to *Ah!* The present editor restores the reading of the Folios.

other sixteenth- and seventeenth-century writers, and brief comments, if the editors so wished, on a few aspects of the thought or dramatic technique. These subjects necessarily receive different emphases in different volumes. The extent to which individual editors have found themselves able to adopt or obliged to modify the work of their predecessors in this section has varied so widely that it is left to each editor to indicate in his own introduction the nature of his indebtedness.

In the appendices each revising editor has included as full representation as possible of source material and in the introductions (in necessarily varying proportions) description of the text of each play and its problems, discussion of the evidence for its date, some critical comment on the play as a work of art and in relation to its sources and any further comment which, in the view of that editor, is proper to a full understanding of the lines along which the student may most profitably continue his work.

UNA ELLIS-FERMOR

London, 1949

PREFACE TO FIFTH EDITION

THE occasion of reprinting allows me to correct some errors (many of my own, a few of the printers') and to add notes on two or three discoveries and interpretations made since the previous edition appeared. There has been no change in the general plan or substance of the book.

18 August 1955 R. D.

ADDITIONAL NOTES

I. i. 48. *Not to see ladies*] In *Gesta Grayorum*, 1594, " the sixth Counsellor, persuading pass-time and sport ", says : " What, nothing but tasks ? nothing but working days ? No feasting, no music, no dancing, no triumphs, no comedies, no love, no ladies ? Let other men's lives be as pilgrimages, but Princes' lives are as Progresses, dedicated only to variety and solace " (Nichols' *Progresses*, iii. 295). The previous counsellors had recommended War, Fame, State, Virtue and philosophy.

I. ii. 28. *an eel is quick*] See also William Bullein, *A Dialogue* against the Fever Pestilence, 1564 (E.E.T.S., p. 91) : " *Vxor*. There is also painted a lustie young man, stouping downe to a vessell, in which swimmeth bothe Eles and Snakes ; he seemeth to catche one of them : what meaneth that ? *Ciuis*. Ha, ha, ha ! it is merrily handled ; forsothe, it is one that is ouer come either with loue or coueteousnesse. [of a wower how he sped] He goeth a woyng, my dyng, dyng ; and if he spedeth, my dearlyng, what getteth he, my swetyng ? Forsoth, either a serpente that will styng hymn all his life with cruell words, or els a swete harte with pleasant speache, that when hee thinketh her moste sure, hee hath but a quicke Ele : you knowe where. [Ha, ha, ha ! well fished]"

INTRODUCTION

1. The Play

" If we were to part with any of the author's comedies it should be this," wrote Hazlitt of *Love's Labour's Lost*, and his opinion was shared by most critics between Shakespeare's day and our own. Their reason was partly the belief that this was one of the earliest of Shakespeare's plays, if not the very earliest, a beginner's clumsy effort, full of stilted rhyming couplets and over-elaborate puns, the characters unlifelike and the action constantly held up for skirmishes of what the uneducated countryman from Stratford mistakenly took for wit. Pope found the comic scenes so generally barren that he cut whole pages of them out of his text, printing them at the page-foot for those curious archæologists who might wish to see what blunders Shakespeare made before he learnt his business. Actors took it for granted that the play could not be " good theatre " ; the general reader gave thanks that here at least was one work of Shakespeare which it was not considered necessary to read.

Recently there has been a change of feeling. Scholars have come to the conclusion that, in spite of some misleading signs, *Love's Labour's Lost* is not one of Shakespeare's earliest plays, but belongs rather with *Richard II*, *Romeo and Juliet*, and *A Midsummer Night's Dream*, a group written in the same heat as Shakespeare's essays in pure poetry, *Venus and Adonis*, *Lucrece*, and perhaps the sonnets, and with the same sheer lyrical power carrying off occasional unpractised crudities in the action. At the same time a number of revivals on the stage, both professional and amateur, have shown that as entertainment and as drama *Love's Labour's Lost* is still very much alive ; the fault is rather too much exuberance—individual characters are lost in the sparkle of quirks and comicalities and personal touches, and the jokes are crammed into the dialogue four deep. Yet this excess of high spirits and invention has its own charm. Shakespeare, it is clear, hugely enjoyed writing the play, and his gusto, his drive, his delighted discovery of the buoyancy of his own genius, carries his audience away with him. It is fascinating, too, to recognize here, so tightly packed on each other that they have no space to develop, the seeds of so many characters and situations to which Shakespeare in later plays was to give full elbow room. Rosaline is clearly a portrait of his own Dark Lady, but from her, and her fellows in the Princess's retinue, stems a whole race of heroines, Portia and Nerissa, Beatrice, Rosalind. Berowne, likewise, is "father to a line" of gallants. The clowns' mistaking of words reappears in Dogberry and Verges, their play of the Nine Worthies in Bottom's Pyramus and Thisbe. Holofernes is a great-uncle of Dr. Caius, and even the mighty Falstaff has a trick of accent and gesture that proclaims him a direct descendant of Armado. Dr. Johnson, no kinder than other critics to the play as a whole, is compelled to admit that there is no work that has "more evident marks of the hand of *Shakespeare*."

If this were all, if the play were interesting only in the light of the better use to which Shakespeare was later to put some of its material, it might well be left to scholars and to dramatic societies with antiquarian tastes. But *Love's Labour's Lost* stands firmly in its own right. No play of Shakespeare is more distinct, has more a character and "aura" of its own, and in few is the spell of personality so strong. The attraction springs from an unique combination of formality and actuality, fantastication and common sense. This quality, or balance of qualities, has been admirably characterized by Granville Barker in one of the best of all his *Prefaces to Shakespeare* (*First Series*, 1927, pp. 1-50). He points to "style" as the quality above all that a production of this play must achieve if it is to be successful, and "style" as the essence of the play itself. The situations, for all their flippancy and extravagance, are designed with admirable economy and dovetail with perfect precision. What could be neater than the main plot, with the young men's pious resolutions inviting their discomfiture, the ladies and their suit held off at arm's length, and then the tables turned? What more telling single effects than Jaquenetta's sudden appearance with the letter that pricks the bubble of Berowne's self-righteousness, Costard's interruption, which finally takes the wind out of Armado, or Marcade's, which in a moment swings the play from farce to earnest? Old stage-tricks and gags are used, but with the bravado of genius that can change a damp squib into a rocket—as when the stock eavesdropping scene is multiplied by three and becomes not, as sublunary arithmetic would make it, just trebly boring, but a star of mirth. The dialogue, too, has always the controlled energy of fine musical phrasing, whether it be the elegant banter of Navarre and his peers, the quicksilver repartee of the "mocking wenches," or the fine flights of Armado's and Holofernes' disordered fancies; and the characters, for all that many of them are fantastic, have a method in their madness, a consistency in their exaggeration, which is again the mark of "style."

This play then has, like opera, its conventions, which we must accept at the outset if we are not to be merely bewildered and antagonized by their apparent unreality; but having accepted them we start at once on a higher plane, from which we can proceed to explore the remoter ranges of imagination and feeling and are spared the laborious climb up from the jungle of everyday trivialities. The comparison between *Love's Labour's Lost* and a work of music is inescapable. To quote again from Granville Barker, the play is "never very far from the actual formalities of song and dance. The long last act is half mask and half play; and in song and dance the play ends." And in another passage he says that "the actor, in fine, must think of the dialogue in terms of music; of the time and rhythm of it as at one with the sense—in telling him what to do and how to do it, in telling him, indeed, what to be."

It is this musical quality, evident in both construction and language, that gives the play its buoyancy, its coherence, and its feeling of release, but this must not be taken to suggest that its effect is of a purely formal and artificial beauty. If it is likened to an opera, it must be to one of Mozart's Italian comedies in which perfection of form is combined with shrewdness of characterization and humanity of feeling: to *Figaro*, or to that *Cosi fan Tutte* for so long misjudged by those who missed the understanding that fills out the modish satire of the plot and the tenderness that informs the elegant melodic line. Armado, like his countryman, Don Quixote, inspires affection as well as mirth. Even Holofernes, conceited, misguided, intolerant, cannot fail to win our sympathy with his final "This is not generous, not gentle, not humble"; and Nathaniel, bowler or no bowler (see 2.53), has it from the start, though practically he is no more than an ineffectual toady. It is usual to dismiss the secondary heroes and heroines as indistinguishable shadows and reflections one of another, but this is to disregard the delicate touches with which Shakespeare has established a definite personality and even physical character for each: the over-tall and slightly quizzical Longaville, Dumain, impetuous but not quite sure of himself, the red and gold charm of Katharine, and the brusquer Maria. As for Berowne and his Rosaline, there is nothing to touch their genuineness, their completeness as human beings, and their "high seriousness" till we come to *As You Like It*.

As You Like It, again, is the only Shakespearean comedy earlier than the late romances that in total impression can match this for imaginativeness and variety of mood, or so strongly suggest that beneath the shimmering surface the waters are deep. Anyone who has seen *Love's Labour's Lost* acted will admit the powerful effect of Marcade's entrance in Act v, Scene ii, not only as a superb *coup de théâtre* but as setting up an ever present pressure of reality throughout the rest of the play until it fades out in bird-calls. And yet this sudden enrichment of the texture has been anticipated again and again in earlier scenes, as in the tale of Katharine's sister or in Berowne's set speeches. In a flash we are back to earth, and it is all the more solid and immediate for our absence and for the suddenness of our return.

There is perhaps another reason, less reputable, for the revival of interest in *Love's Labour's Lost*. In this age of detective stories, who does not enjoy a good "mystery"? And not only is this, of the men behind the masks of Armado and Holofernes, one of the best, but it is linked more or less directly with the series of unsolved puzzles that makes the literary history of the early 1590s sound like a collection of Father Brown's cases: the elusive Martin Marprelate, the lost years of William Shakespeare, the secret society of Sir Walter Ralegh, the stabbing of Christopher Marlowe, the riddle of Willobie and his Avisa, to say nothing of the ubiquitous Francis Bacon and other such unhistorical mystifications. This is the attraction that has brought cranks swarming about *Love's Labour's Lost* and strange indeed is some of the honey they have distilled from it. Behind this, however, lies a more genuine interest. Of all Shakespeare's plays this is the most personal; a solution of the puzzle he has set here (and I had better say at once that I cannot provide it), would not only satisfy the most rabid detective ardour but illuminate Shakespeare's own early life and the conditions that shaped his career and his first plays—an essential background of which at present absolutely nothing is known.

2. The Text

2.1. **The Quarto of 1598.** The earliest surviving text of the play is the edition in Quarto dated 1598. The title page reads: *A*/PLEASANT/Conceited Comedie/CALLED, /Loues Labors lost./ As it vvas presented before her Highnes /this last Christmas./Newly corrected and augmented/ *By W. Shakespere.*/[ornament]/Imprinted at London by *W. W.*/for *Cutbert Burby.*/1598.

The phrase "newly corrected and augmented" reappears on the title-page of the "good" Quarto of *Romeo and Juliet*, also published by Burby (1599) and, like *Love's Labour's Lost*, never entered on the Stationers' Register. The "good" Quarto of *Romeo and Juliet* was evidently issued to supplant the "bad" Quarto printed by Danter in 1597, and no doubt it was the existence of this earlier edition that made registration, for licensing purposes, unnecessary. Since Burby's *Love's Labour's Lost* appears so similar to his *Romeo and Juliet* it is likely that it was issued with the same purpose, to replace a "bad" Quarto of which no copy has survived.

2.2. **The Printing of the Quarto.** The printer of the 1598 Quarto was William White. Dover Wilson's researches, the results of which are given in his Note on the Copy in the New Cambridge edition of the play, have established a remarkably clear picture of what went on in the shop of this printer, and have presented succeeding editors with all the evidence they need to judge how closely White's text is likely to have followed Shakespeare's original.

White had in 1598 only just set up as a printer, and *Love's Labour's Lost* must have been one of the very first books he printed. His compositor was obviously very inexperienced. Misprints abound, mostly "literals"—one letter used for another, either because the compositor's hand was not sufficiently practised to go to the right compartment of his "case" for the letter required (as a bungling typist will hit the wrong key), or because the case was "foul," the type used for an earlier printing and subsequently broken up having been sorted back into the wrong compartments. Many letters again are "turned," i.e. they were placed the wrong way up in the composing-stick, very much a beginner's blunder. The punctuation is chaotic; not even the most advanced theories of Elizabethan "rhetorical punctuation" can make it consistent even with itself. Most significant of all, the compositor had not learnt to "lock up" his type properly, so that when it was shaken, either in being carried to the press, on being rubbed with the inking pads, or under the stress of the actual impression, the letters tended to fall apart from each other or were even jerked out altogether. There are frequent blanks in the Quarto where letters have disappeared; and it is clear that the type became looser and looser as printing proceeded, since in the Bodleian copy and in those held by the British Museum and Trinity College, Cambridge, these blanks become progressively more extensive. (For a note on the status of the "Devonshire" copy see IV. iii. 180.)

2.3. **The Folio of 1623.** It is this peculiarity that provides the proof that the First Folio text of the play was set up not, as Hart supposed, from an independent (and more authoritative) manuscript, but from a copy of the 1598 Quarto ; for the word " venew " (v. i. 57) appears in the Quarto as two words, " vene we," the type having fallen apart in the middle, and this error is exactly reproduced in the Folio. Now it is inconceivable that the same accident should have happened in the same place of the same work in two independent printings ; and, besides, Jaggard's compositors were experienced men who did not allow their type to remain loose. Clearly they were merely following what was in the Quarto (which they must therefore have been using as " copy "), without realizing that it was a misprint.

True, the Folio occasionally improves on the Quarto, correcting " literals," replacing turned letters, making good the obvious gaps ; but none of these improvements is beyond the scope of an experienced printer, and several are quite clearly honest, but weak, patchwork which could never have come from the author (see v. ii. 806). Of the two major alterations, the Folio's " That were to climb o'er the house to unlock the gate " (I. i. 109) is ill-fitting and flat beside the Quarto's " Climb o'er the house to unlock the little gate " ; and the extra line, " You that way ; we this way," at the end of the play has presumably been added to make possible an orderly *Exeunt.* It has charm—it may be Shakespeare's ; but, like the other improvements, it is well within the capacity of an intelligent prompter or stage-manager.

2.4. **The Copy for the Quarto.** Dover Wilson believed that the 1598 Quarto was set up from a manuscript of Shakespeare's, whose oddities of spelling and handwriting are reflected in the printed text (see notes on I. i. 165, II. i. 34, IV. ii. 36, IV. ii. 54, and IV. iii. 13). Miss Greta Hjort has argued (*Modern Language Review*, XXI, 1926) that the " good " Quarto of *Romeo and Juliet* was set up from a corrected copy of the " bad " Quarto, and that the same procedure is likely to have been followed with

Love's Labour's Lost. But the peculiarities and corruptions that can only be due to a manuscript original are surely too many to be explained either (*a*) as originating entirely from the mere MS. *corrections* made in the margin of the "bad" Quarto to bring that corrupt version up to standard, or (*b*) as a reflection of the eccentricities of the MS. copy for the "bad" Quarto which, to survive two printings, must have been more pronounced even than Shakespeare's, and in the same kind.

2.5. **Evidence of Revision.** A decision on this point is vital. If Dover Wilson is right, the two distinct kinds of material evident in the play, and at times conflicting with each other, can only be Shakespeare's original version and a later revision of it. The words on the title-page are then to be taken at their face value: some years ("newly") after first writing the play, Shakespeare revised and augmented it. If on the other hand Miss Hjort is right, the phrase is merely the normal indication that the text that bears it is a "good" Quarto, i.e. a text authorized by its proprietor and with those passages restored that were garbled or cut in the corrupt version. The two strands in the play would then be Shakespeare's re-established text and surviving traces of the "bad" Quarto.

I find it impossible to accept Sir Walter Greg's contention (*The Editorial Problem in Shakespeare*, 1942, p. 127) that the two elements represent first and second thoughts in Shakespeare's original draft, and that the Quarto preserves both because it was set up, deletions and all, from his "foul papers." As will be seen, the differences not only in style but in intention are too great to be included in a single act of composition.

2.51. *Doublets.* The most striking instances of the double nature of the play are those first noticed by Capell in IV. iii. 287-362 and a similar passage at V. ii. 806, where alternative versions of an identical speech are retained side by side. It is a matter of opinion whether the shorter version of Berowne's speech in IV. iii. is best explained as an early draft of Shakespeare's on the basis of which he later elaborated the longer version, or merely as a pirate's corruption of this. Dover Wilson makes much of the meaningless fragment, "with ourselves," which appears in early texts tacked on at the end of the shorter version (line 313). To explain it he produces the plausible theory that Shakespeare marked the earlier version for deletion not by scoring it through, but by enclosing it in a bracket, the lower arm of which cut into the last line. The compositor could not miss the mutilated line, and duly omitted all but the two words that had escaped Shakespeare's reckless stroke; he did miss the main span of the bracket running up the margin and failed to realize that all the lines embraced by it should have been omitted too. This agrees well with Shakespeare's known carelessness, the compositor's known lack of experience, and the undoubted existence of more than one passage that should have been deleted but was not. To Miss Hjort, however, the fragment "with ourselves" is one of the loose ends and misunderstandings with which all "bad" Quartos abound.

It is noteworthy that a passage constantly quoted as parallel to this of Berowne's, namely, the speech with which Theseus opens Act v of *A Midsummer Night's Dream*, appears to have undergone a precisely similar expansion. Theseus' speech in its original version clearly dealt only with lover and madman. The poet is an afterthought, and the lines that describe him are purple patches, of a later and richer material, added to the original, which makes connected sense even if these are detached (see New Shakespeare edition, pp. 80-3). The joins in Berowne's speech are less obvious, but we can guess that it was constructed on the same principle.

The fuller treatment of Berowne's exchange with Rosaline in v. ii. shows a change of intention as to how the scene is to develop and can surely only be due to author's revision. Supporters of Miss Hjort's view would still point to passages in the *Contention* and in the "bad" Quarto of *Hamlet* as equally radical perversions of the Shakespearean scenes.

2.52. *The "Katharine-Rosaline tangle"* in II. i. Failure to cancel a rejected draft must also be responsible for this famous puzzle. At II. i. 114 begins a conversation between

Berowne and a lady who is designated Katharine in the Quarto, Rosaline in the Folio. Editors, with the exception of Capell, have followed the Folio, and it certainly looks as if Berowne should be skirmishing with his own lady at this point. Yet it is odd that he should have another encounter with her at line 180, while the other pairs of lovers are never given a turn to speak; and the situation is further complicated by both Quarto and Folio reading Rosaline at line 195 where we should expect Dumain to be told of his own lady, Katharine, and Katharine at line 210, where Berowne's inquiry should surely be for his Rosaline.

This muddle has been variously put down to printers' errors (that easy cutting of every Gordian Knot), and to an early version of the play in which there were only three pairs of lovers, Berowne's opposite being the fair Katharine who, by an oversight of the reviser, still usurps Rosaline's place in this scene and elsewhere sometimes lends her her attributes (e.g. the "white hand" of III. i. 164 and "whitely" complexion of III. i. 193—see notes). This theory is developed at length by H. D. Gray in *The Original Version of "Love's Labour's Lost"* (Stanford University, 1918), and on rather different lines, with a dark Katharine, by Dr. Janet Spens (*Review of English Studies*, vii. 1931).

It was Capell who suggested that this scene was originally one of cross-purposes, the ladies wearing masks (which still persist at line 124) and each lover being put off with the wrong opposite. On this assumption Berowne first tackles Katharine thinking she is Rosaline, discovers his mistake, and leaves her; next approaches Rosaline, who succeeds in hiding her identity, so that, convinced again that he has hit on the wrong person, Berowne leaves her too; finally he asks Boyet who the third lady is and, on being told "Katharine," sees he has been made game of, and goes off in a huff. In the same way Dumain and Longaville, inquiring after their ladies, are given misleading answers.

That this was originally the intention of the scene is clear from the survival of the allusion to masking, but Capell's explanation still does not account for the Rosaline in line 195 (line 61 has already established that it *must* be Katharine who is associated with Alençon) and he too is forced to attribute this to a printer's error. Nor can it be that in the scene as it stands now the lovers are intended to be left mystified, since in IV. iii. they have no difficulty in addressing their sonnets to the right ladies.

The most satisfactory solution is that put forward by H. B. Charlton in *The Library*, 8 (1917), p. 355, and elaborated by Dover Wilson (New Shakespeare edition, pp. 120 ff.). It is that in revising the play Shakespeare decided to transfer his comedy of mistaken identities, originally placed here in II. i, to Act V. Scene ii., where it becomes the fooling of the "Muscovites." To transform the present scene into one of straightforward exposition certain adjustments were necessary: Berowne's exploratory conversations with Katharine at line 114 and with Rosaline at line 180 had to be cut out, and at the end of the scene each lover must be made to inquire after and be informed of his own lady. Shakespeare, however, scrawled his cancellation so roughly, as in IV. iii. and V. ii, that the compositor missed the indication that the passages were to be deleted, and set them both up in his text; and the vital change of Katharine to Rosaline was made in the wrong line (195 instead of 210).

2.53. *The recasting of the "Worthies."* Traces of a change of plan can also be found in the pageant of the Nine Worthies and in the winding up of the action. In first casting his players (V. i. 122) Holofernes gives the parts of Joshua and Judas to actors who do not in the event play them, and apparently leaves his own role undecided; and it has been suggested by H. D. Gray (*op. cit.*) that Alexander was originally played by Dull, a more likely person than Nathaniel to be commended by Costard for his skill at bowls and his neighbourliness, and to possess that strong smell always associated by Shakespeare with "the base vulgar." Furthermore the Princess's reference (V. ii. 729) to her "great suit so easily obtain'd" seems inexplicable in the play as we have it. Did Marcade originally bring the Princess not the news of her father's death but the missing document required to establish her claim? And did the play end

Berowne. Our wooing doth not end like an old play;
  Jack hath not Jill: these ladies' courtesy
  Might well have made our sport a comedy.
King. Come, sir, it wants a twelvemonth and a day,
  And then 'twill end.
Berowne. That's too long for a play?

2.54. *A lost Armado scene.* Again, at the end of IV. i. Costard's words (lines 143-7) suggest that he and the audience have recently been watching some comic business performed by Armado and his page; but these two characters do not appear at all in the scene as it stands now.

2.55. *Variant speech-headings.* The speech-headings also suggest two different drafts. Their variations have been studied at length by Dover Wilson (New Shakespeare edition, pp. 109-13). Certain characters, including Navarre but particularly the group of comics—Armado, Moth, Costard, Dull, Holofernes, Nathaniel—appear sometimes under their personal names, sometimes with the generic titles of King, Braggart, Boy, Clown, Constable, Pedant, and Curate. For the most part the names, generic or personal, remain constant for any one scene: Navarre is Navarre (or Ferdinand) for the first two acts, King for the rest of the play; Armado and Moth his Page are so called in I. ii. and the second half of III. i. but appear as Braggart and Boy for the first sixty-eight lines of that scene and for the whole of Act V. There are, however, scenes in which both types of heading are used indiscriminately. Dover Wilson's analysis of these shows that speeches essential to the structure and continuity of the scene are invariably headed by personal names; the speeches, and parts of speeches, headed by type-names might all be additions to the original material. This sounds more like a man touching up and expanding his own first draft than the correction of another's garbled version. It also suggests that some time had elapsed between the writing and the re-writing, so that the author had come to remember his *dramatis personæ* by their general characters and not by the particular names he had given them.

2.56. *Variations in typography.* Peculiarities of typography and lining may imply that the printer's copy was not uniform. We have seen (2.2) that the compositor was a beginner but, perhaps for that very reason, he seems (except in the matter of punctuation) to have followed his copy slavishly. Hence Armado's letter in I. i., set in italic with an ornament at the head, may represent an original elaborately written out in Italian hand. The letter in IV. i. is in roman like the rest of the text; here Shakespeare cannot have bothered to distinguish the inset letter from the dialogue, but wrote all out in his normal English script. The change of practice, supported by a difference in the spelling of Armado's signature, suggests a lapse of time between the writing of the two scenes.

In several places, notably V. ii. 1-4 and 15-17, the Quarto prints verse-speeches as prose. These are all points at which revision is suspected on other grounds, and Dover Wilson suggests that the new material was written crabbedly in the margin, so that the compositor was unable to distinguish any line-division.

2.57. *Conflicting allusions.* Finally, it is difficult to reconcile with a single date of composition the various allusions to contemporary events that have been detected in the play. The Navarre setting must belong to some date earlier than 1594, by which time the real King of Navarre had ceased to be an ally of Elizabeth and the doings of a Navarrese court would no longer arouse friendly interest in England; the hunting scene appears very close to the account of Elizabeth's entertainment at Cowdray, published in 1591; and if, as has been suggested, the play is partly ridicule of Ralegh and his "school" of mathematicians and atheists, it cannot be much later than Ralegh's disgrace in 1592, and the official inquiry into the school held in 1594. On the other hand the scene of the masque of Muscovites in V. ii. if, as seems probable, it bears a reference to the Gray's Inn Revels of Christmastide 1594, cannot have been written earlier than the summer of 1595. We may therefore expect to find indications of two distinct dates for the writing of *Love's Labour's Lost.*

3. The Date of Composition

3.1. **External evidence.** The *terminus ante* is given by the first Quarto, dated 1598 and carrying a reference to a performance at Christmas. Since the year in the old style ran from March to March, this performance may have been either at Christmas 1598 or Christmas 1597, and the play in its present form completed autumn 1598 or 1597. The earlier dates are more probable. References to the play by name occur in Francis Meres' *Palladis Tamia* (published 1598, probably in October) and in Robert Tofte's *Alba* (also dated 1598). The wording of the latter is

> Loues Labour Lost, I once did see a Play
> Ycleped so, so called to my paine.

The "once" suggests some time long before the time of writing, but it is just possible that it means "on one occasion only."

It has been suggested that Robert Southwell's poem, *St. Peter's Complaint*, with its play, in stanzas 56 and 57, on eyes and stars, borrows from *Love's Labour's Lost.* It was published in 1595, but Southwell had been kept a close prisoner since 1592 and can hardly have read, much less seen the play after that date. It is, of course, arguable that Shakespeare borrowed from Southwell, or that the similarity is pure coincidence.

The joke about "remuneration" and "guerdon" (III. i. 166) appears in the anonymous *A Health to the gentlemanly profession of serving-men* (1598), where it is said to have been told to the author "not long since by a friend." It may have been taken from *Love's Labour's Lost;* but may equally well have been traditional.

3.2. **Internal evidence.**

3.21. *Style.* According to the metrical tests invented by Fleay, whose ranging of the plays in chronological order by this means has been largely confirmed by other evidence, *Love's Labour's Lost* is the earliest of the series. The proportion of rhymed lines, end-stopped lines, and doggerel metres is very high. The play has, however, a highly artificial theme to which these metrical devices are particularly appropriate; for the special subject-matter Shakespeare may well have revived a technique which he had otherwise discarded.

The same considerations apply to the play's structure. T. W. Baldwin, in *Shakspere's Five-Act Structure*, 1947, argues that this is the most primitive, the least classical in form of all Shakespeare's plays, and therefore the earliest. Its peculiarities of construction may just as well be due to a special purpose for which it was designed. They are certainly not such overwhelming proofs of early date as to justify Baldwin's, to my mind, petulant refusal to study the other evidence impartially.

Love's Labour's Lost is intensely lyrical and teems with echoes of the non-dramatic poems of Shakespeare, particularly *Lucrece*, and of the sonnets. The most striking resemblances, involving both thought and expression, are those between the "Dark Lady" sonnets (especially 127 and 132) and Berowne's praise of "blackness" in IV. iii.; and between Sonnet 21 and several passages in the play similarly decrying flattery (II. i. 13-16, IV. iii. 237). Other examples are given in the notes, and a long list has been collected by C. F. McClumpha in *Modern Language Notes*, XV, no. 6 (1900). The date of composition of individual sonnets is of course not known, but *Venus and Adonis* was printed in 1593 and *Lucrece* in 1594. Until Hotson brings forward weightier evidence than appears in *Shakespeare's Sonnets Dated* (1949) for the ante-dating of Shakespeare's non-dramatic (and with it much of his dramatic) work, it is to 1593-4 that the stylistic affinities of *Love's Labour's Lost* would seem to attach it.

3.22. *Allusions.*

3.221. *Navarre.* It was Joseph Hunter who first suggested that the characters of the play are historical, though he failed to realize that they were Shakespeare's contemporaries. There was a real King of Navarre, very much in the Elizabethan news, who possessed many of the characteristics of the King in the play, though his name was Henri and not Ferdinand. The Duc de Biron and the Duc de Longueville were his faithful supporters; and though the Duc de Mayenne was not a supporter, but his bitterest enemy, this name too was constantly linked with the King's (see particularly 4.2 below), and may also have been confused with that of d'Aumont, a trusted general of the King's who was especially well known to Englishmen. Gossip about life at the court of Navarre might have been available to an English author at any time after 1586, or even earlier, but the period in which it would be appreciated with sympathy by an English audience is more limited. The question has been carefully explored by H. B. Charlton (*Modern Language Review*, XIII, 1918). He recalls that it was in October 1589 that English troops, under Lord Willoughby, were first sent openly to help the Protestant Henri to enforce, in the face of the Catholic League, his claim to the throne of France; that Henri's popularity in England was at its height in August 1591 (when Essex played a flamboyant but not very effective part in the campaign for the capture of Rouen), but was forfeited in July 1593 when, coming to terms with the League, Henri renounced his Protestantism and was received into the Catholic church; and that the English troops supporting him were finally withdrawn in November 1593. A playwright would therefore be most tempted to write a play about Navarre in 1591-3, when Englishmen were fighting with his troops as allies in a popular cause.

3.222. *Anti-alien riots.* The same dates fit the other apparent references to historical events. Moth's joke at III. i. 6 about a "French brawl" has been taken as referring to the London riots against foreign refugees, many of them Huguenots, whose competition for the city's accommodation, food, and employment was much resented. These riots recurred at intervals in the 'eighties and 'nineties. There was an abortive anti-alien plot in September 1586, and more open demonstrations in May 1593. The serious outbreak of June 1595, followed by a savage execution of the ringleaders, seems to have been directed more against profiteering tradesmen than against aliens.

3.223. *Plague.* The plague, to which much reference is made in v. ii. 419 ff., was also particularly violent in the years 1591-4, but it was many years earlier that the phrase "Lord have mercy upon us" (quoted at v. ii. 419) was first widely used as the sign, painted on house doors, that those within were infected. See note on the passage.

3.224. *Morocco.* The "dancing horse" of I. ii. 51 is usually taken to be Banks' famous "Morocco." The earliest certain reference to him is dated 1591, but there was a performing horse, Morocco or another, at the Cross Keys theatre as early as 1588 (see note on the passage) and Banks' animal was still doing tricks in 1600. In view of this long span of activity, no precise date can be deduced for Moth's allusion.

3.225. *Cowdray.* Hart believed that the unnecessarily elaborate treatment of the hunting-scene (Act IV. i, ii) owed something to the publication in 1591 of an account of the *Queen's Entertainment at Cowdray.* The details of the erection of "stands," the shooting with cross-bows, the use of hounds, etc., are certainly similar to those in the play, but the methods may well have been those generally accepted for ceremonial hunting parties of this kind. As Sir Edmund Chambers acidly remarks (*William Shakespeare,* I. 335), "There is no reason whatever to suppose that Elizabeth shot a deer with a cross-bow for the first or the last time at Cowdray in 1591."

3.226. *Pierce Penilesse.* Hart was also responsible for calling attention to the echoes in *Love's Labour's Lost* of the pamphlet war between Gabriel Harvey and Thomas Nashe, of which more below (5.22). The battle proper began with the appearance of Robert Greene's *A Quip for an Upstart Courtier*, Nashe's *Pierce Penilesse his Supplication to the Divell*, and Harvey's answer to both in *Foure Letters . . . especially touching Robert Greene*, all in the autumn of 1592. The probable references are to *Pierce Penilesse* and to Harvey's second major pamphlet, *Pierce's Supererogation*, almost certainly published in October 1593; but some ears have detected faint echoes of Nashe's rejoinder, *Have Wit*

You to Saffron Walden, which was not ready until spring 1596.

3.227. *Ralegh.* Allusions have also been suspected (see 5.23) to Sir Walter Ralegh's fall from favour on account of his liaison with the Queen's maid of honour, Elizabeth Throgmorton (afterwards Lady Ralegh); to his circle of mathematicians and philosophers whose "atheism," notorious for several years before, could only be openly investigated after the disgrace had removed Ralegh's protection; and to the poem, *The Shadow of Night*, written by George Chapman apparently in honour of this circle. Now Ralegh was sent to the Tower in July 1592, the investigation into his atheistical associates was set on foot in March 1594, and Chapman's poem, published in 1594, had been entered on the Stationers' Register in December 1593 and probably seen in manuscript by Marlowe before his death in June.

3.228. *Gray's Inn.* Many have wondered why the lords should choose in Act v, Scene ii. to appear in *Russian* disguises. Russia, like Navarre, had been in the news during the 'eighties and 'nineties. The voyages of Richard Chancellor and the Burroughs had opened up trade with Russia and a trading company, the Company of Muscovy Merchants, was formed in 1584. There had been an exchange of ambassadors between England and Russia and in 1583 a special envoy was sent by Czar Ivan the Terrible to ask for the hand of Lady Mary Hastings in marriage. The lady was nicknamed at court the "Empress of Muscovia" and was much teased about the wooing, which was conducted with elaborate and, on the part of the English, mock ceremony. Sir Sidney Lee was convinced that this incident lay behind the scene in the play. In 1591 appeared Giles Fletcher's detailed account of Russia and Russian customs, *Of the Russe Common Wealth;* and it was perhaps the reading of this work that inspired a remarkable "revel" at Gray's Inn during the Christmas season of 1594-5. Attention was first drawn to this by E. K. Chambers in his *William Shakespeare*, and it has been independently studied in detail by R. Taylor (*The Date of Love's Labour's Lost*, 1932). There are two main points of contact with the masque in *Love's Labour's Lost* over and above the fact that a mock embassy of Muscovites appears in both. The " Russians " of the present play are accompanied, rather strangely, by blackamoors, who *may* be a reflection of the " Negro Tartars " of the Gray's Inn revel ; and Rosaline's jibe at v. ii. 393, " sea-sick, I think, coming from Muscovy " may be an echo of the excuse made by the Prince of Purpoole (the director of the Christmas merry-making elected each year by the benchers) who, on his return from a " visit " to Russia, declared that he must forego certain ceremonies on account of his exhaustion " by length of my Journey, and my sickness at Sea." Shakespeare may have had particular reason to bear this Gray's Inn revel in mind. During the same Christmas festivities the benchers put on, as the climax to an evening's rag, a " play of Errors." On that day, 28 December 1594, Shakespeare's company performed his *Comedy of Errors* before the Queen at Greenwich ; and it is generally assumed that it was a repeat performance of this play that was given at Gray's Inn that night, with the same actors, among whom may well have been Shakespeare himself.

3·3. **Conclusions.** The occurrence in *Love's Labour's Lost* of many ideas and images from Shakespeare's poems, here wrought into the very fabric of the play, suggest that it was written at the same time as they were, viz. 1593-4. The historical events which are also found woven into the pattern belong, with the exception of the Gray's Inn revel, to the same years ; the interest in Navarre would be cold before 1594, but on the other hand Shakespeare could hardly have seen *Pierce's Supererogation* or *The Shadow of Night* before the autumn of 1593. To that season, then, the date of composition of the main body of the play is best assigned.

The reference to the Gray's Inn revel, if it is accepted, must be a later touch added to the original play, and the doublets in the text, the apparent reshaping of certain scenes, and the variations in speech-headings also point to a revision. The date of this must fall between February 1594-5 (the date of the revel) and Christmas 1597 (the presumed date of the performance before the Queen). Since this introduction was first written, Mr. J. W. Lever's discovery in Gerard's *Herball* (see note on v. ii. 885-6) has come to support a revision of the play in 1597.

4. The Sources

4.1. **A hypothetical source.** No written source is known from which the plot might have been borrowed; there is, however, some reason to think that such a source did exist but is now lost. For every other play Shakespeare is known to have used some documentary original. Moreover the description on the title-page of the 1598 Quarto—"newly corrected and augmented"—suggests the existence of an earlier printed edition, and it would appear that such a "bad" Quarto might sometimes be compiled on the basis of an earlier "non-copyright" version of the play. This discarded piece would be brought into some sort of conformity with the modern work that had superseded it by the addition of scenes and dialogue supplied either by actors willing to give away their parts in the new play or by the writer's own memory of performances he had attended. The foundation can be clearly traced in other "bad" Quartos. If then there was a "bad" Quarto of *Love's Labour's Lost*, it may be that this too was constructed on a similar basis, viz. an earlier play with the same plot.

It is possible also that such things as the confusion between the Princess' ladies, and the doggerel of Costard (IV. i. 139-47) and Nathaniel (IV. ii. 24-33)—surprising even in such a confirmed experimenter as Shakespeare—go back not to an early Shakespearean draft but to this pre-Shakespearean play.

4.2. **The historical basis.** Shakespeare's play follows historical fact remarkably closely. The real King of Navarre received two embassies from France, either of which might have served as a model for that in *Love's Labour's Lost*. In one the ambassador was indeed a Princess of France, Marguerite de Valois (daughter of Catherine dei Medici and herself married to Henri), who came with her mother in 1578; in the other it was the Queen of France, Catherine herself (and in several places the Quarto reads "Queen" for "Princess") who met Henri at Saint Bris in 1586. In both discussions probably, and certainly in the earlier one, an important topic was Marguerite's dowry, which included Aquitaine (compare II. i. 129 ff.). On both occasions the royal envoy, reinforcing diplomacy by coquetry, was supported by that famous bevy of ladies-in-waiting who for their grace and flightiness were known as "l'escadron volant." Abel Lefranc, who first drew attention to the earlier embassy (*Sous le Masque de William Shakespeare*, 1918), points out that negotiations were conducted at Nerac in an atmosphere of pageantry, gallantry, and continual entertainment which is strikingly similar to that of *Love's Labour's Lost*. Sully wrote of the occasion: "On se livra au plaisir, aux festins et aux fêtes galantes, ne nous amusant tous qu'à rire, danser et courir la bague." In the years immediately preceding this visit, Marguerite had made journeys exactly corresponding to those referred to by the Princess and her ladies in Act II, Scene i. of the play: to Alençon (Marguerite's brother François was Duc d'Alençon) in 1578 and to Liége (Brabant) in 1577. It was at Liége that Hélène de Tournon, daughter of one of Marguerite's ladies-in-waiting, died of love for a young nobleman, the Marquis de Varembon. The Marquis was not in Liége at the time of her death, and only learnt of it when, returning, he met the funeral procession. It is highly probable that this incident suggested not only the decline of Katharine's sister (V. ii. 14) but the story of Ophelia in *Hamlet*.

The King's "Achademe" is also a reflection of history. In 1583 the English ambassador to the court of France reported to Walsingham that Navarre "has furnished his Court with principal gentlemen of the Religion, and reformed his house"; and in the autumn of 1582 Marguerite herself had written to Henri: "Si vous etiez honete homme vouz quitteriez l'agriculture et l'humeur de Timon pour venir vivre parmi les hommes." Navarre had in fact followed a widespread fashion and become royal patron of an academy. Miss F. A. Yates, in her *French Academies*

(1947), has described how the example of Plato first fired renaissance scholars in Italy to found these, in essence, philosophical debating societies; how the vogue spread to France and was there fostered by the Medicis, who no doubt remembered how their ancestors had been patrons of the movement in its cradle, Florence; and how Navarre was inspired (probably through the Huguenot poet d'Aubigné, a member of the Palace Academy) to emulate his brother-in-law Henri III. It is perhaps significant that Henri III's academy had extended its field of interest to philology and music, and the poets and artists who composed it were largely responsible for the court entertainments. In such elaborate masques as, for instance, those devised for the wedding of Henri of Navarre and Marguerite, Catholic and Huguenot nobles met on an equal footing. The only *milieu* in which Navarre and de Mayenne might have been found side by side was one, like that of the play, closely associated with both masquing and academies. It is, however, extremely unlikely that Shakespeare had any direct knowledge of Navarre's academy, of which neither the Duc de Biron nor the Duc de Longueville were members. His idea of it most probably came from Pierre de la Primaudaye's *L'Académie françoise*, a generalized account of the French movement which was translated in 1586 and became very popular. The model academy described is composed by *four* young idealists of Anjou.

A great many other correspondences are listed in Professor Lefranc's book: the King's impetuous riding (IV. i. 1-2) and his covering of the whole sheet, "margent and all," in his letter-writing (V. ii. 8) were actual habits of Henri of Navarre; and the names Boyet, Marcadé, and de la Mothe appear in contemporary registers of court officials. Other of these examples are not so convincing, and we can smile at the contention that Armado's fixing of the position where he caught Costard and Jacquenetta—"north north-east and by east from the west corner of thy curious-knotted garden"—is navigationally correct. In his anxiety to prove that *Love's Labour's Lost* was written by someone with intimate and first-hand knowledge of

Navarre and its court, Lefranc overstates a case already established by the Hélène de Tournon story, which was not published until it appeared in Marguerite de Valois' own memoirs (1628). A suggestion has been made, and is noted in 5.25 below, as to the channel through which even Shakespeare may have obtained it, together with the rest of the Navarre material which any unbiassed reader of Lefranc must recognize as a source of the play.

4.3. **Dramatic Models.**

4.31. *John Lyly.* That *Love's Labour's Lost* is an imitation of Lyly's plays is as much a commonplace of criticism as that it is a satire on Lyly's affected language, his " Euphuism." It is constantly repeated that Armado and Moth are copied from Sir Thopas and his page Epiton in *Endymion.* But in fact there is no real similarity between Shakespeare's play and those of Lyly, which belong to an older and more courtly *genre* even than *Love's Labour's Lost*, Shakespeare's most courtly play ; the ridiculous language of Armado and Holofernes is much nearer to Sidney's *Arcadia* than to Lyly's *Euphues*, and the resemblance between Armado and Sir Thopas exists not because one is an imitation of the other but because both can be traced back, though by different channels, to a common source.

4.32. *The Commedia dell' Arte.* Lyly's plays derive from the academic *Commedia Erudita* (itself based on classical originals), with its formalized plot and characters, and its simplified staging in which a separate " house " (though all are set together on the same stage) symbolizes the location of each group of characters. Shakespeare's play lacks this stylization altogether, but it does owe something to the *Commedia dell' Arte*, which replaced the *Commedia Erudita* on the popular stages. The distinguishing mark of the *Commedia dell' Arte* was the entirely improvised dialogue in which the stock plots, of much the same character as those of the " learned " plays, were elaborated. The professional actors who in Italy developed this form of drama specialized each one in the presentation of a particular figure from among the group of conventional types that formed the *dramatis personæ*. Thus Francesco Andreini, chief of the Gelosi company which visited France and possibly England in the last quarter of the sixteenth century, was famous for his Braggart. This character, derived from the Miles Gloriosus of Plautine comedy, had already been transformed in Italian comedy into a Spanish soldier of fortune, a familiar figure in an Italy much of it garrisoned by Spanish armies. The role was played by Andreini in a multitude of different plays, but always under the same name, Capitano Spavento del Vall' Inferno ; and he built up the character by a series of highly elaborate set speeches, which took infinite study and pains to compose and which were so popular that Andreini published two collections of them.

Armado would have been impossible without the Captain and his kin ; and in the same way Holofernes, with his scraps of languages, his false etymologies, and his blunders over technical terms, is an English version of the pedant, Doctor Graziano, as Costard of the rustic servant Zanni and the yes-man Nathaniel of the parasite. The line of descent is not always direct. Armado, in love with a bumpkin, and finding classical precedents for his predicament, is nearer Doctor than Captain ; but though the family characteristics may be mixed the Italian parentage of all the comic supporting characters in *Love's Labour's Lost* cannot be denied. For a detailed analysis of the debt see O. J. Campbell's *Love's Labour's Lost Restudied* (University of Michigan Studies in Shakespeare, Milton and Donne, 1925).

4.33. *The Queen's Progresses.* Professor Campbell has also described another probable influence in the make-up of Shakespeare's play—the elaborate entertainments, often prolonged over several days, which were presented to the Queen at the rich houses which she visited on "progress." These entertainments were made up of a number of dissimilar but largely standardized elements. Among them constantly figure masques of courtiers, disputations both serious and burlesque, dancing and song, and a play presented in all earnestness by local talent (often led by the schoolmaster) to be duly mocked by the Queen and her retinue with all the brutality accorded here to Holofernes' pageant. No doubt Shakespeare, as Campbell suggests, in devising a suitable entertainment for the reception of a Princess of France would naturally turn to what was provided *de rigueur* for her English counterpart. Hence the episodical nature of the play and the accumulation of set pieces that so prolong its final section. Bookish critics have called it a lack of proportion, but it is precisely this, with its recollection of Elizabeth's *al fresco* diversions, that gives the play its delightful air of formal informality.

5. The Topical Context

5.1. **Evidences of hidden meaning.** Neither the historical events on which the play is based nor the dramatic models by which it is shaped can provide the full explanation of its purpose and point ; and that these must lie deeper than the superficial import of the words, often vapid and sometimes completely senseless, is clear from the indefinable impression of a coherent intention with which the reader of the play is left. The more he enjoys the play the more (in the words of " Q ") " he will be teased by afterthoughts of meanings missed, and will long to go back and solve them." There are, for example, nine passages which *must* embody some contemporary joke now lost to us. These are :

(*a*) Armado and Moth's play with the words " tender Juvenal " (I. ii. 8 ff.).

(*b*) Armado's resentment of Moth's allusion to an eel (I. ii. 29).

(*c*) The constant punning on " penny " and " purse " (III. i. 26, V. i. 70) and particularly the flourish on the phrase " piercing a hogshead " (at IV. ii. 86).

(*d*) The doggerel on the Fox, the Ape, and the Humblebee (III. i. 83).

(*e*) The reference (if it is not a misprint) to a " Schoole of Night " (IV. iii. 252).

(*f*) Armado's pronunciation of " Sirrah " as " Chirrah " (V. i. 33).

(*g*) The reference to a "charge-house" on a "mountain," where Holofernes teaches (v. i. 78).

(*h*) The unorthodox inclusion of Hercules and Pompey among the Nine Worthies (v. i. 124-5).

(*i*) The connection of Holofernes with Judas Iscariot (v. ii. 588 ff).

Any key to the general mystery we may think we have found must be tested on these nine locks.

5.2. **Suggested explanations.** Incidental suggestions go back almost within reach of Shakespeare's own day, but it is only recently that connected explanations of the play's meaning have been put forward.

5.21. *Individual identifications.* The first note (1747) comes from Warburton, who stated bluntly, without citing any authority, "By *Holofernes* is designed a particular character, a pedant and schoolmaster of our author's time, one *John Florio*, a teacher of the *Italian* tongue in *London*, who has given us a small dictionary of that language under the title of *A world of words*." This derivation for Holofernes was blown upon by Dr. Johnson, but scholars have continued to canvass it. Even anagrams have been rushed to its support, but the arguments brought against it are hardly less feeble. It has been said, for instance, that Shakespeare would hardly have risked offending his patron Southampton by attacking Florio, a member of the Earl's household; but in fact he may have hoped to curry favour by doing just this, since Florio was almost certainly placed in that household by Burghley, presumably to keep a severe and Protestant eye on his young Catholic ward. It is certainly curious that, in the preface to the 1598 edition of his dictionary, Florio combines abuse of his chief detractor H(ugh) S(anford), with a savage sneer at "*Aristophanes* and his comedians" who "*make plaies, and scowre their mouthes on Socrates*." This looks like a reference to an actual attack by a playwright on that famous teacher, John Florio. In connecting it specifically, as he does, with *Love's Labour's Lost*, Warburton may be following an old and authentic tradition. If so, crux (*g*)—the "charge-house on the mountain" might be explained as a pun on Florio's work on *Montaigne;* but there are perhaps better solutions of this puzzle.

Some of these incidental suggestions, as that Holofernes is a caricature of the schoolmaster who taught Shakespeare at Stratford, spring too plausibly from the facts. Others are too fanciful. Lefranc's contention, that Holofernes must be one Richard Lloyd, the pedantic tutor of the sixth Earl of Derby, rests on the fact that Lloyd actually composed a pageant of the Nine Worthies, in which each character introduces himself with the words "I am," and the arms of Alexander are described as in *Love's Labour's Lost*. J. H. Roberts has shown (*Modern Philology*, XIX, 1921-2) that this formula of introduction is common to a host of sixteenth-century didactic poems including the *Mirrour for Magistrates*, and that Alexander's arms are those generally given for him in the heraldic text-books of the period. Equally lacking in solid foundation is Fleay's identification of the comic characters of the play with the protagonists in the pamphlet-war between the Puritans, their unauthorized and unidentified champion "Martin Marprelate," and the defenders of the established church. The Marprelate scandals, as Fleay justly points out, would be a likely subject for a topical play in the early 'nineties. There may indeed be something in the general suggestion, though nothing in Fleay's detailed correspondences.

5.22. *Harvey and Nashe.* Fleay had maintained that Moth represents Thomas Nashe, the young "University wit" whose part in the tracts written against Martin, though never yet clearly defined, is generally recognized to have been extensive. In the first Arden edition of *Love's Labour's Lost* H. C. Hart confirmed that there were traces of Nashe in the play, but detailed investigation appeared to show that these led back not to the Marprelate controversy but to its sequel, Nashe's long-drawn battle with the Cambridge don, Gabriel Harvey. This conclusion was awkward for Hart who, like Fleay, held the then orthodox view that the play must be dated about 1590; now that we believe it was written in 1593 Hart's findings are just what we should expect.

The Harvey-Nashe quarrel, then, is a solid foundation, the first to be offered to theory-builders. For this reason, and for its complication, it deserves examination in some detail. In origin it goes back to 1580, when the Earl of Oxford quarrelled violently (on the tennis-court) with Sir Philip Sidney. Gabriel Harvey was a protégé of the Earl of Leicester and his nephew Sidney (both of Puritan sympathies) and now wrote a lampoon which might be construed as an attack on Oxford's Italianate airs, his political trickery, and his irreligion, though Harvey afterwards denied this interpretation. The poem was brought to Oxford's attention through the malice of his secretary, John Lyly, the dramatist and novelist, and Harvey had an unpleasant time of it until he had made his peace.

Nine years later Lyly was one of the hacks hired on behalf of the bishops of the established church to answer Marprelate in his own vein ; and in his pamphlet, *Pappe with an Hatchet*—out of sheer devilment it seems—he dared his old victim to undertake the Puritan defence. Harvey prepared his reply but for some reason kept it by him and did not publish it. Instead he preferred (or so Lyly and his friends believed) to make his contribution to the controversy by collaborating with his brother Richard in the writing of *Plaine Percevall* and *The Lambe of God*, two pamphlets in which impartial rebuke of Martinists and anti-Martinists is coupled with specific condemnation of Nashe and of the playwright Robert Greene. (Both had probably had a hand in the anti-Martinist tracts though the connection is never made explicit.)

Greene and Nashe took two years to mature their answers, but in 1592 came Greene's *A Quip for an Upstart Courtier* in which he managed to insert a sneering passage about the whole Harvey family and their humble origin. Gabriel Harvey threatened physical and legal reprisals and Greene, now on his deathbed, was frightened into cancelling the libellous passage and almost certainly into printing a warning to his young friend Nashe against the danger of being "too bitter against scholars." Nashe, however, disregarded it and his *Pierce Penilesse his Supplication to the Divell* carried a withering retort to the criticisms that had appeared in *Plaine Percevall* and *The Lambe of God.* This induced Harvey to expand the pamphlet he had in hand against the dead Greene, and his *Foure Letters* eventually included a severe sermon to Nashe as well.

The battle was now joined. In April 1593 Nashe brought out his *Strange Newes of the intercepting Certaine Letters*, or *The Four Letters Confuted*, an uproarious and outrageous guying of Harvey and all his works. Friends of both sides then tried to bring about a reconciliation and Nashe was even persuaded to print an apology to Harvey in the preface to his *Christ's Teares* (September 1593) ; but that only gave Harvey an opportunity to get his own back. In *A New Letter* he pounced with ridicule on Nashe's apology, and followed this up with a lengthy, circuitous and obscure attack on Nashe and his allies, *Pierce's Supererogation*, into which he worked the unpublished reply to Lyly's *Pappe*, written four years before.

In the spring of 1594 *Christ's Teares* was reprinted with, of course, a violent onslaught on Harvey in place of the apology ; but Nashe's full rejoinder was delayed till 1596 and in any case *Pierce's Supererogation* is the last of this series of pamphlets to contain any striking parallel to a passage in *Love's Labour's Lost.*

Shakespeare's echoes of the controversy are manifold and are catalogued (many of them are harder to catch than a bat's squeak) in R. Taylor's *The Date of Love's Labour's Lost.* Two major ones, about which there can be no doubt, should be enough to prove that Harvey and Nashe are behind some of the fooling in the play. In III. i. Armado addresses Moth as " tender juvenal," and this is elaborated in a long interchange. Now " gallant young juvenal " was to be the title given to Nashe by Francis Meres in his catalogue of writers, *Palladis Tamia* (1598) ; and it is all but certain that Nashe again is the " Young Iuvenall, that byting Satyrist," whom Greene in his deathbed tract, *Greene's Groatsworth of Wit* (1592), warned against baiting scholars, i.e. Harvey. Moth, therefore, here is Nashe. Furthermore, it is Moth who is perpetually the centre of the puns about purses and pennies, many of them close echoes of those which Harvey and Nashe himself made about the title of Nashe's first anti-Harvey pamphlet, *Pierce Penilesse.* As evidence, the cumulative effect of these parallels seems to me overwhelming, even though we must now perhaps discount the reference to "piercing a hogshead," which has for long seemed the most striking of all (see note on IV. ii. 82-6).

This disposes of two of the test cruces, (*a*) and (*c*); it may also explain (*d*), the Fox and Ape rhyme. Dover Wilson has already suggested (privately) that this jingle may have something to do with the Marprelate controversy, in the course of which such motto-rhymes were freely adopted by both sides. Compare this, from the title-page of the anti-Martinist *Martin's Months Minde*

Martin the ape, the dronke, and the madde
The three Martins are, whose workes we have had,
If Martin the fourth comes, after Martins so euill
Nor man, nor beast comes, but Martin the devill.

"Martin" was, incidentally, Elizabethan slang for a monkey or ape.

I believe that the connection between the Fox and the Ape and Marprelate is at one remove, through Nashe who, in his *Pierce Penilesse*, inserted a mysterious fable which can best be explained as another anti-Martinist tract in disguise. In it (after some satire on the Bear, Leicester, who favoured Puritans) he describes the conspiracy of the Bear's creatures, the Fox and the Chameleon, the second of whom had an especial aptitude for intrigue since he could vary his colour and shape and, indeed, for a large part of the story puts on the form of an Ape. These evil beasts try to persuade the Husbandman that he can have good honey without keeping bees—at a pinch wasps will do as well. The allegory is surely transparent, with the Husbandman standing for authority, honey for true religion, the bees for the bishops and the wasps for the "presbyters" the Puritans would substitute for them. The Chameleon can only be Martin in his various disguises; while the Fox I presume is some Puritan dignitary like Thomas Cartwright who, not himself Martin, was thought by many to be directing the campaign.

Shakespeare's rhyme plays on this : the Puritan party, Marprelate, and the Bishops were quarrelling ; how could they be anything but " at odds," since there were three of them? The appearance of a fourth party to the controversy " stays the odds." I return to Dover Wilson for the suggestion that the Goose is Gabriel Harvey, who with his brother Richard had in *Plaine Percevall* advocated a middle way and sought to reconcile the quarrellers. For is it not precisely Goose that Harvey is called in Nashe's *Have With You to Saffron Walden*, in a passage which, like Shakespeare's, caricatures " envoys," a form of composition to which Harvey was partial ?

> Gabriel Harvey, fames duckling,
> hey noddie, noddie, noddie :
> Is made a gosling and a suckling,
> hey noddie, hey noddie.

Here is merely a suggestion ; let no scepticism about this conclusion affect the earlier proof that Moth in some ways reflects Thomas Nashe. Who then is to be cast for Harvey? Both Armado and Holofernes (but particularly Armado) have some of his affectations of language, both have the wizened mahogany face so praised by the Queen (she took Harvey for an Italian) and so cruelly mocked by Nashe in *Have With You*. It is Armado to whom Moth is more particularly attached in the play, Holofernes whom he more unmercifully mocks—and indeed the very name Holofernes might be one of the distortions to which Nashe subjects that of Harvey. Holofernes is attended by an obsequious clerical shadow, just as Gabriel was by his parson brother Richard. Armado pawns his linen, as Harvey was said to have done to pay his printer, and is as stingy as Harvey to his dependants. The objections to each identification are equally extensive, not the least being the strength of the rival claim. To note only single difficulties in addition, Holofernes' precise pronunciation seems as remote from Harvey (who wrote " dettor " and was all for modernity) as does Armado's romantic passion for

Jacquenetta. In *Love's Labour's Lost* Harvey is still to seek.

5.23. *Ralegh and the "Schoole of Night."* To Arthur Acheson is largely due the discovery of a second clue that seems to lead some way into the labyrinth. Professor Minto had suggested, in his *Characteristics of the English Poets* (1885), that Chapman was the "rival poet" of Shakespeare's sonnets, and Chapman's *Shadow of Night* (published 1594), the poem whose "proud full sail" challenged Shakespeare's. Following this hint, Acheson was struck by a curious opposition between the theme of this *Shadow of Night* and that of *Love's Labour's Lost.* Chapman's poem is a eulogy of contemplation, study, knowledge (often symbolized as astronomy) as opposed to the life of pleasure and practical affairs. It appears that in composing it Chapman hoped to curry favour with a group of noblemen—"most ingenious Darby, deep-searching Northumberland, and skill-embracing heir of Hunsdon"—and with this end in view addressed an introductory letter to Matthew Roydon, a minor poet who had connections with the group. The central theme of *Love's Labour's Lost* is ridicule of the academic affectations of a group of noblemen, and the words

> Never durst poet touch a pen to write
> Until his ink were temper'd with Love's sighs

with which Berowne dissolves the academy and turns its members back to real life, might well be a specific answer to Chapman's

> No pen can anything eternal write
> That is not steep'd in humour of the Night.

Now Roydon's particular patron was Sir Walter Ralegh. With Ralegh himself and others of his protégés, such as Marlowe and the mathematician Thomas Harriot (both "soul-loved friends" of Chapman), Roydon made up a little "academy" for philosophical and scientific discussion which in 1592 was branded by a pamphleteer as "Sir Walter Rauley's Schoole of Atheisme" and in 1594, after Ralegh's disgrace, subjected to the attentions of a special commission appointed by the Privy Council to investigate its heresies. Harriot, with Walter Warner and Thomas Hughes, two other mathematicians of the group, later transferred his service to a close friend of Ralegh's, the very Earl of Northumberland mentioned by Chapman in his dedication of *The Shadow of Night;* another indication that the circle which Chapman sought to approach through Roydon, and which he hoped to flatter by praise of the studious and contemplative life, was Ralegh's circle.

The dedication to Roydon contains the following sentences:

"How then may a man stay his marvailing to see passion-driven men, reading but to curtail a tedious hour, and altogether hide-bound with affection to great men's fancies, take upon them as killing censures as if they were judgment's butchers, or as if the life of truth lay tottering in their verdicts.

"Now what a supererogation in wit this is, to think Skill so mightily pierced with their loves, that she should prostitutely show them her secrets, when she will scarcely be looked upon by others but with invocation, fasting, watching."

This may be a general censure of uninstructed critics, but it looks rather more like resentment at a particular attack, made by an uneducated hack in the payment of a rival group, upon Chapman's own poem before publication. This attack, says Acheson, is no other than *Love's Labour's Lost*, the hack is Shakespeare, and the rival group that of Southampton and his friend Essex, who was in perpetual rivalry with Ralegh at court. The attack on *The Shadow of Night* is essentially an attack on Ralegh; the over-serious academe is Ralegh's "schoole," and it is his three famous mathematicians that are mocked in the comic characters who, as Dover Wilson has pointed out, are so hopeless at sums.

It is even possible that Ralegh's circle is explicitly named in the play. What could the mysterious "schoole of night" (crux (*e*)) of IV. iii. 252 more fitly be than the "Schoole of Atheisme" in whose honour had been written *The Shadow of Night?* And does the sneer (II. i. 16) in

"Beauty . . . not utter'd by base sale of *chapmen's* tongues" pun on the name of that poem's author? Acheson believed that Chapman himself figured in *Love's Labour's Lost*, as Holofernes, but it is hardly Chapman's style that is parodied in the poem on the pricket, nor Chapman's pronunciation (he rhymed "debtor" with "better") in Holofernes' orthographical pedantries. With more probability Dover Wilson puts forward Thomas Harriot himself as Holofernes' original. He was a schoolmaster, he was for a long time living at Sion House, Northumberland's residence at Isleworth (perhaps the "mountain" of crux (*g*)), he scribbled doggerel poems, full of mathematical puns, upon his scientific papers, and he was attended by a clerical toady whose name was the reverend *Nathaniel* Torporley.

5.24. *John Eliot and the Earl of Northumberland.* A synthesis of the Harvey-Nashe and the School of Night theories was attempted by Miss F. A. Yates in *A Study of Love's Labour's Lost* (1934), still the most complete summary of the researches and speculations that have been devoted to this play. She introduces two new elements. The first is a certain John Eliot, a teacher of French and compiler for the printer Wolfe of a London news-letter on French affairs. In dudgeon at the challenge to his livelihood offered by refugees who set up as language teachers, he published in April 1593 his *Ortho-Epia Gallica*, superficially another French phrase-book in dialogue form but also a satire on the foreigners and a parody of the method of teaching favoured by such noted educationalists among them as Florio and, earlier, Vives.

There appears to be a reference to the preface of this book in Harvey's *Pierce's Supererogation* (printing at the same time and at the same printers) in connection with an acquaintance Harvey had recently met and of whom he quotes a long speech. This acquaintance, Miss Yates believes, was therefore Eliot himself; the speech, which praises Nashe, the champion of "real life," at the expense of more academic writers, agrees with Eliot's line in *Ortho-Epia Gallica*, and incidentally with Shakespeare's in *Love's Labour's Lost.* Furthermore it may be noticed that

Chapman, in the passage from the dedication of his *Shadow of Night* quoted in 5.23 above, drags in the words "supererogation" and "pierced," and it is impossible not to believe that this must be a deliberate reference to Harvey's pamphlet, particularly as the argument of Harvey's anonymous friend there reproduced is precisely the view Chapman is concerned to refute. The two camps thus become more clearly defined; on the one side the practical writers, the "reporters," Eliot, Nashe, Shakespeare; on the other the conscious artists, the academicians, Harvey, Chapman (with the School of Night behind him) and (if Harvey's acquaintance *is* Eliot) Florio and Vives.

Miss Yates' second link is more certain and more far-reaching. It lies in an essay, discovered by Miss Yates in the Record Office, and written by Ralegh's friend the Earl of Northumberland to prove to his lady the infinite superiority of the attractions of learning over those of any female whatsoever. The essay cannot be dated, but it sums up Northumberland's attitude (which we know from contemporary reports) to his own wife Dorothy Devereux, whom he married about the year 1594. Dorothy was of course the sister of the Earl of Essex and of the more famous Penelope Devereux, Lady Rich, whose identity with the "Stella" of Sidney's sonnet-sequence is now confirmed. "Stella" had already suffered, from another academician, the same insult now offered to her sister by Northumberland's essay; for in 1585 the Italian astronomer Giordano Bruno, who had connections with the French Palace Academy and was at that time in England on secret business for the French King, dedicated to Sidney his *De gli eroici furori*, a bitter condemnation of romantic love (and in particular sonnet-writing) as standing in the way of the pursuit of higher knowledge. The slight to the object of Sidney's own love and love-poems was hardly redeemed by Bruno's perfunctory conclusion, in which he added that English women were exceptions to his rule, being celestial creatures, stars (with perhaps a pun on the name "Stella"). Bruno's strictures on women were revived, significantly enough, by Florio, his friend and housemate during his London visit, in his *Second Fruits*

(1591), one of the very dialogues directly parodied by Eliot's *Ortho-Epia Gallica*.

Here, then, is the plot of *Love's Labour's Lost* as Miss Yates sees it; Essex is insulted by Ralegh, his sisters, famous beauties, by Ralegh's friends, the members and correspondents of Ralegh's pretentious study-circle; their defence is undertaken by Shakespeare, protégé of Essex's friend Southampton. "Women *are* stars" is the theme of the play; "men derive more light, warmth, and inspiration from them than from the cold and distant objects to which these astronomers devote themselves."

5.25. *Conclusions.* Some of Miss Yates' evidences are shaky. In particular the convenient ubiquity of Eliot is suspect for there is hardly a corner of all this intrigue in which his traces have not been seen—he might, for instance, have so easily provided Shakespeare with the French gossip on which *Love's Labour's Lost* is founded. The very words "Schoole of Night" may be an invention not of Shakespeare's but of his commentators (see note on IV. iii. 252). Yet even the loss of this piece of corroborative evidence would not annul either the fact that Ralegh's "school" existed, or the apparent links between school and play brought out by Acheson. There can be little doubt that Shakespeare's butts are the superior persons who exalt art and learning above nature and common sense, and that among them he intended his audience to recognize some living people of the time—Harvey, Chapman, Florio, Thomas Harriot's "schoole," and its patron, Sir Walter Ralegh. If these are the enemy, it is clear on whose behalf the play must have been written: Essex, and the young noblemen of his party, Bedford, Rutland, and Southampton.

The key to many of the interrelations of these two groups, if we could only grasp it, is, I am sure, that elusive and engaging person Thomas Nashe. Just as Moth has an equivocal position in the play, attached to Armado and yet twitting him and Holofernes as openly as do the King and his lords, so Nashe shifted between the two parties in real life. It is not known who was his patron before the summer of 1592; *Pierce Penilesse* was then dedicated to "Amyntas," presumably the same as the Amyntas of Spenser's *Colin Clout's Come Home Again*, that is Ferdinando, Lord Strange, later the "ingenious Darby" mentioned by Chapman in his dedication of *The Shadow of Night*, and so connected with the Ralegh group. The "Lord S.," of Lancastrian blood, for whom Nashe's *The Choise of Valentines* was written, can only be the same person. In 1593 Nashe had passed under the protection of Sir George Carey who, as Hunsdon, is named by Chapman in the same breath as Ferdinando Stanley and Northumberland, but was later to be the Lord Chamberlain who gave his name and his protection to Shakespeare's company of actors. While with Carey, Nashe was persuaded by the "motive inspiration" of some person unnamed to write a tract significantly called *The Terrors of the Night*, which ridicules the pretensions of "conjurers" (the name had been applied to Harriot), reproves the follies of atheists, and rails at the neglect of patrons who are more interested in being accounted *Gloriosos* at court than in rewarding real merit. In the next year Nashe finally crosses the dividing line between the two camps and dedicates his *Unfortunate Traveller* to Southampton, although it appears that the overture was not well received since the dedication was dropped from later editions of the book.

Does Nashe's conscientious renunciation of the properties of the Night suggest that he had been more closely connected with its School than has been suspected? It is odd how the memory of an unkind and vainglorious patron is associated in his mind with atheism—not only in the *Terrors*, but in *Pierce Penilesse* and *Christ's Tears* as well. Was Nashe's first patron Ralegh himself?

Confirmation of this guess would strengthen our appreciation of the general sense of the play, but it would not be likely to help much in revealing exact correspondences. It is doubtful if any discovery could do this, since it is highly probable that they do not exist. Navarre and his friends are not actual portraits of Ralegh, Derby, Northumberland and Hunsdon any more than the Princess's ladies, for all the punning on "rich" at v. ii. 158-9, number among them the real Stella. It is tempting to see something of Ralegh in Armado. The "Chirrah" of v. i. 33 *may* be a gibe at the Wessex accent that Ralegh kept all his life, and Armado's predicament with Jacquenetta is exactly that which brought about Ralegh's disgrace in 1592—the taunt "the eel is quick" that so upsets him in Act I may be only a variant of Costard's "the party is gone," which repeats the process in Act v. It would be tidy if it were so, but the Elizabethans were not tidy. It is clear from Spenser's *Faerie Queene* that they were capable of assimilating a multiple allegory, in which a fictional character can stand simultaneously for two persons in real life, themselves exemplars of an abstract virtue. It may well be that Shakespeare ridiculed Ralegh's academic pretensions by presenting him as the pedant Harvey, himself disguised as Armado; and Holofernes may be all the "masters" of Ralegh's school, Bruno, Florio, Harriot, Chapman, rolled into one. It does not matter. Though odd lines may puzzle us and some of our nine locks remain unopened, the point of the play is clear, and it is a point worth writing a play about.

6. The Occasion

All the evidence then goes to show that *Love's Labour's Lost* was a battle in a private war between court factions. This confirms the indications, from other sources, that it was written for private performance in court circles. The artificiality of its form and tone, though not immediately borrowed from Lyly, are clearly directed at Lyly's audience. The large number of parts for which boy-players would be required—the Princess and her ladies, Jacquenetta, Moth—points away from the regular actors' companies to some great household where a troupe of choristers was maintained; for the professional children's companies were out of action between 1590, when the combined company under Giles and Lyly was suppressed, and 1599-1600, when Evans and Giles were granted licences to reconstitute the Paul's and Chapel children respectively.

Austin K. Gray, in *Publications of the Modern Language Association*, xxxix (September 1924), has put case for a first performance of the play in Southampton's house at Tichfield on the occasion of the Queen's visit "on progress" in 1591; but, as has been seen, the writing of the play as we have it must be later than this date, and a more likely occasion would be an entertainment in a private house at Christmas 1593, when the regular theatres were all closed because of the plague.

Though the title-page of the second Quarto (1631) declares that it was publicly acted "at the Blacke-Friers and the Globe," *Love's Labour's Lost* retained its peculiar connection with the court. The first Quarto title-page bears witness to a performance before Queen Elizabeth in 1597 or 1598. In 1604, when Southampton, who for three years had been imprisoned in the Tower for his part in Essex' rebellion, was released by James I and wished to entertain the royal party at his house, the play chosen for their delight was *Love's Labour's Lost.* We have already guessed at the personal associations that may have induced Southampton to put the play on; the reasons given by Burbage to the Chamberlain of the exchequer are more lasting and more essential—that "for wytt and mirthe" it would "please exceedingly."

Acknowledgments

There is nothing new or startling in this Introduction, nor in the recension of the text and the notes that follow. I believe that an edition of this kind, intended in the first place for students, should not parade new theories, though it should contain a summary of any genuinely fruitful work in this kind that has been done by previous editors. For the same reason my text is conservative. As a devoted disciple of McKerrow, I have kept to the only primary text we have, the 1598 Quarto, wherever a conceivable explanation can be made out for its reading, while recording as fully as possible the emendations and elucidations that have been suggested by more adventurous editors as solutions of the undoubted difficulties.

In accordance with the general style of the Arden edition, spelling and punctuation are modernized throughout, and this means that sometimes a definite sense must be given to a passage that Shakespeare left ambiguous. Thus the spelling "loose" was used by the Elizabethans for both "loose" and "lose," and the question mark did duty equally for the exclamation; an editor who uses modern spelling must make up his mind which of the two meanings Shakespeare intended by such symbols, for example at I. i. 72, I. ii. 4, IV. iii. 71 and V. ii. 224.

My debts are enormous and obvious. The greatest is to Dr. Dover Wilson, and it is a double one—a general, shared with all other editors who may succeed to his masterly investigation into text and copy, and a personal, for his typical generosity not only in answering all my questions but in putting at my disposal unpublished notes prepared for his own edition.

The second debt I owe is to my predecessor in the editing of this play for the Arden series, H. C. Hart. His notes, particularly those on parallels of language and thought between *Love's Labour's Lost* and other Elizabethan writings, are still of the highest value, and I have not hesitated to take advantage of the Arden tradition and preserve much of his work verbatim. For anything so reprinted I take, of course, full responsibility, and in those instances where I do not entirely share Hart's view, I have made it quite clear where his opinion ends and mine begins.

Finally, I should like to say how grateful I am to the general editor for setting an inspiring standard of thoroughness; to Mr. John Crow for a wealth of references and examples that have saved my notes from at least some indiscretions; to Miss Agnes Latham, to Miss F. A. Yates, and to Professor F. P. Wilson for helping me in my chase of various quarries—eels, libbards, and, I fear, wild geese; to Professor J. A. K. Thomson for coaching me in the Latin of Elizabethan schools; to George Rylands for patiently correcting at least some of my errors in the use of English, as well as one in entomology; and to my wife for cheerfully supporting both the natural grumblings of an editor and the theorisings that this play inevitably provokes.

R. D.

JULY, 1951.

LOVE'S LABOUR'S LOST

DRAMATIS PERSONÆ[1]

KING FERDINAND OF NAVARRE.
BEROWNE, LONGAVILLE, DUMAIN, } *Lords attending on the King.*
BOYET, MARCADE, } *Lords attending the Princess of France.*
DON ADRIANO DE ARMADO, *a fantastical Spaniard.*
SIR NATHANIEL, *a Curate.*
HOLOFERNES, *a Schoolmaster.*
DULL, *a Constable.*
COSTARD, *a Clown.*
MOTH, *Page to Armado.*
A Forester.
THE PRINCESS OF FRANCE.
MARIA, KATHARINE, ROSALINE, } *Ladies attending on the Princess.*
JAQUENETTA, *a country Wench.*

Officers and others, Attendants on the King and Princess.

SCENE: *The King of Navarre's park.*

[1] The *dramatis personæ* were first listed by Rowe. Their names, as given in stage-directions and speech-headings, are widely varied in the Quarto. In the directions to Act I. Scene i the King is called Ferdinand, and again in Act II. i. lines 129-67; but the name is not found elsewhere in the directions or at all in the dialogue of the play. Similarly The Princess's speeches are sometimes headed "Queen"—on her first appearance in II. i, throughout IV. i, and once in V. ii. For the variations in the speech-headings for Armado and the other comics see Introduction 2.55.

Some modern editors are at pains to correct the Quarto spellings of all the French names as being mere archaisms. It is, however, arguable that Shakespeare's intention was to *anglicise* them; certainly the original form of, e.g., Berowne, gives the clearer indication of how the name must be pronounced in the play (it rhymes with "moon" at IV. iii. 229). For "Marcade" see note on V. ii. 706.

LOVE'S LABOUR'S LOST

ACT I

SCENE I

Enter FERDINAND, *King of Navarre*, BEROWNE, LONGAVILLE, *and* DUMAIN.

King. Let fame, that all hunt after in their lives,
Live register'd upon our brazen tombs,
And then grace us in the disgrace of death ;
When, spite of cormorant devouring Time,
Th' endeavour of this present breath may buy
That honour which shall bate his scythe's keen edge,
And make us heirs of all eternity.
Therefore, brave conquerors—for so you are,
That war against your own affections
And the huge army of the world's desires—
Our late edict shall strongly stand in force :
Navarre shall be the wonder of the world ;
Our court shall be a little academe,
Still and contemplative in living art.

ACT I

Scene I

Berowne] Qq, F 1 ; *Biron*, Ff 2, 3, 4. 1. *King*] *Ferdinand* Ff, Qq, throughout the scene. 5. *Th' endeavour*] Ff ; *Thendeuour* Q 1. 13. *academe*] Q 2, F 2 ; *Achademe* Q 1, F 1 ; *Academy* Ff 3, 4.

3. *in the disgrace*] in the midst of, or in spite of, the degradation (loss of physical beauty and material honour) that death will bring us.

4. *cormorant*] ravenous. Elsewhere Shakespeare has " cormorant war " and " cormorant belly." Nashe frequently uses the noun for a rapacious person.

5. *Th' endeavour of this present breath*] Our efforts while we are alive will earn us fame after death.

6. *bate*] dull, deaden or lessen.

13. *academe*] A poetic form of " academy." The name, originally that of Plato's school at Athens, was adopted by the Medicis for the circle of poets and savants which gathered

You three, Berowne, Dumain, and Longaville,
Have sworn for three years' term to live with me,
My fellow-scholars, and to keep those statutes
That are recorded in this schedule here :
Your oaths are pass'd ; and now subscribe your names,
That his own hand may strike his honour down
That violates the smallest branch herein :—
If you are arm'd to do, as sworn to do,
Subscribe to your deep oaths, and keep it too.

Long. I am resolv'd ; 'tis but a three years' fast :
The mind shall banquet, though the body pine :
Fat paunches have lean pates, and dainty bits
Make rich the ribs, but bankrupt quite the wits.

Dum. My loving lord, Dumain is mortified :
The grosser manner of these world's delights
He throws upon the gross world's baser slaves :
To love, to wealth, to pomp, I pine and die ;
With all these living in philosophy.

18. *schedule*] *sedule* Q 1 ; *scedule* Q 2, Ff. 23. *oaths*] *oath* Steevens (1793). *it*] Qq, F 1 ; *them* Ff 3, 4. 27. *bankrupt quite*] *bancrout quite* Q 1 ; *banerout quite* Q 1 (Dev. copy), Furnivall ; *bankerout* Ff. 31. *pomp*] *pome* Q 1. 32. *living*] *lyning* Q 1 (Devon copy).

in Florence under their patronage ; and it became the standard term for the societies set up in imitation of the Medicis at other European courts for the discussion of philosophy and art. De la Primaudaye's fictional account of the movement in France, englished as the *French Academy* by Thomas Bowes in 1586, became favourite reading in fashionable Elizabethan circles ; with Sidney's *Arcadia* it was prescribed for the instruction of the "Knights of the Helmet" in the Gray's Inn rag of 1594 (*Gesta Grayorum*, Malone Society, ed. W. W. Greg, pp. 29-30). See Introduction 4.2 and, for details, Miss F. A. Yates' *French Academies* (1947).

14. *living art*] J. S. Reid thinks this is a rough translation of "ars vivendi," the crowning (ethical) study in the Stoic discipline. The threefold vow and the "still and contemplative" method certainly sound like Stoicism, which the Elizabethans knew from such Latin writers as Cicero and Seneca. But the translation is excessively rough, and the phrase may mean no more than "vital learning."

26. *Fat paunches have lean pates*] The sentiment may have come, with the rest of the academy, from De la Primaudaye who has (T. B.'s translation ch. xx) : "For (as Plato saith) . . . gluttonie fatteth the bodye, maketh the minde dull and unapt, and which is worse, undermineth reason." After Shakespeare the phrase became proverbial.

28. *mortified*] dead to worldly desires and temptations. Compare Marlowe, *Jew of Malta*, I. ii. 342 : "She has mortified herself. . . . And is admitted to the Sisterhood."

32. *all these*] his companions.

Ber. I can but say their protestation over ;
So much, dear liege, I have already sworn,
That is, to live and study here three years.
But there are other strict observances ;
As not to see a woman in that term,
Which I hope well is not enrolled there :
And one day in a week to touch no food,
And but one meal on every day beside ;
The which I hope is not enrolled there :
And then to sleep but three hours in the night,
And not be seen to wink of all the day,
When I was wont to think no harm all night,
And make a dark night too of half the day,
Which I hope well is not enrolled there.
O, these are barren tasks, too hard to keep,
Not to see ladies, study, fast, not sleep.
King. Your oath is pass'd to pass away from these.
Ber. Let me say no, my liege, an if you please.
I only swore to study with your grace,
And stay here in your court for three years space.
Long. You swore to that, Berowne, and to the rest.
Ber. By yea and nay, sir, then I swore in jest.
What is the end of study, let me know?
King. Why, that to know which else we should not know.
Ber. Things hid and barr'd, you mean, from common sense?

57. *barr'd*] *bard* Q 1 ; *hard* Q 1 (Devon copy).

37. *not to see a woman*] Greene, in *The Royal Exchange*, 1590 (Grosart, vii. 314) says that "Plato admitted no Auditour in his *Academie*, but such as while they were his schollers woulde abstaine from women : for he was wont to say that the greatest enemie to memorie, was venerie."

43. *of all the day*] in, or during all the day. Compare *Hamlet*, I. v. 60.

44. *think no harm all night*] sleep well, from the proverb "He that sleeps well thinks no harm" (Tilley, *Dict. of Prov. in Eng.*, H 169).

48. *Not to see ladies*] See p. xii.

54. *By yea and nay*] The injunction in St. Matthew, v. 37, "let your communication be, Yea, yea ; Nay, nay" came to be taken by the simple-minded as a formula for a particularly earnest oath. Both Shallow and Quickly so use it in *Merry Wives of Windsor*. Berowne is making play with its apparent equivocation.

57. *common sense*] ordinary perception, average intelligence. A parallel passage in Golding's *Ovid* (1567) suggests that Navarre's academe was in part derived from Numa, the Roman King who retired to the country to study philosophy, and "taught his silent sort . . . what shakes the earth : what law the starres doo keepe theyr courses under, and what soever other *things is hid from common sence*" (xv. 80).

King. Ay, that is study's god-like recompense.
Ber. Come on, then; I will swear to study so,
To know the thing I am forbid to know;
As thus,—to study where I well may dine,
When I to feast expressly am forbid;
Or study where to meet some mistress fine,
When mistresses from common sense are hid;
Or, having sworn too hard a keeping oath,
Study to break it and not break my troth.
If study's gain be thus, and this be so,
Study knows that which yet it doth not know.
Swear me to this, and I will ne'er say no.
King. These be the stops that hinder study quite,
And train our intellects to vain delight.
Ber. Why! all delights are vain, but that most vain,
Which with pain purchas'd doth inherit pain:
As, painfully to pore upon a book
To seek the light of truth; while truth the while
Doth falsely blind the eyesight of his look:
Light seeking light doth light of light beguile:
So, ere you find where light in darkness lies,
Your light grows dark by losing of your eyes.
Study me how to please the eye indeed,
By fixing it upon a fairer eye,
Who dazzling so, that eye shall be his heed,

59. *Come on*] *Com' on* Q 1. 62. *feast . . . forbid*] Theobald *et seq.*; *fast . . . forbid* Qq, Ff; *fast . . . forebid* Theobald conj. 65. *hard a keeping*] *hard-a-keeping* Hanmer. 72. *Why!*] *Why?* Qq, Ff; *Why,* Pope, Steevens *et seq.* *but*] Q 1, Camb., New; *and* Ff, Q 2. 77. *of light*] Qq, F 1; om. Ff 2, 3, 4.

59. *Come on*] The Quarto spelling suggests that Berowne is punning on "*common* sense."

71. *train*] allure, entice.

73. *inherit*] possess. See IV. i. 20. Berowne is condemning activities that, painful in themselves, achieve ("purchase") only more pain as their reward.

76. *falsely*] treacherously.

77. *Light seeking light*] while the eyes seek wisdom from books they lose their sight with too much reading.

80. *Study me*] Study for me (the "ethic dative").

82. *Who dazzling so*] The man who is thus dazzled. Compare *Venus and Adonis*, 1064: "her sight dazzling makes the wound seem three."

heed] explained by *N.E.D.* as "that which one heeds"; but more probably "that which takes heed of one," a guardian. Compare the

And give him light that it was blinded by.
Study is like the heaven's glorious sun,
That will not be deep-search'd with saucy looks ;
Small have continual plodders ever won,
Save base authority from others' books.
These earthly godfathers of heaven's lights,
That give a name to every fixed star,
Have no more profit of their shining nights
Than those that walk and wot not what they are.
Too much to know is to know nought but fame ;
And every godfather can give a name.

King. How well he's read, to reason against reading !

Dum. Proceeded well, to stop all good proceeding !

Long. He weeds the corn, and still lets grow the weeding.

Ber. The spring is near, when green geese are a-breeding.

Dum. How follows that ?

Ber. Fit in his place and time.

Dum. In reason nothing.

Ber. Something then in rhyme.

King. Berowne is like an envious sneaping frost
That bites the first-born infants of the spring.

Ber. Well, say I am ; why should proud summer boast
Before the birds have any cause to sing ?

Lay Folks Catechism (1357), 200 : " Our gastly fadirs that has hede of us."

86. *plodders*] Compare Nashe, *The Unfortunate Traveller*, 1594 (McKerrow ii. 251) : " Grosse plodders they were all, that had some learning and reading, but no wit to make use of it."

95. *Proceeded*] Johnson suggests here the academical sense of taking a degree in a university. Compare Ascham, *Scholemaster* (Arber, p. 24) : " untill the Scholar be made able to go to the Universitie, to procede in Logik, Rhetoricke, and other kindes of learning."

97. *green geese*] young geese of the previous autumn, fit for sale about Whitsuntide. Green Goose Fair, or Goose Fair, held on Whit Monday when they were in season, is constantly referred to by Elizabethan and Jacobean writers as a festive occasion. Berowne is perhaps hinting that his earnest companions are young fools who do not know what is in store for them.

99. *reason . . . rhyme*] The phrase " neither *rhyme* nor *reason* " was already current. It occurs in *The Comedy of Errors*, II. ii. 48.

100. *sneaping*] biting, nipping. A rare word outside Shakespeare, who always uses it of the effect of frost (compare *Lucrece*, 333, and *Winter's Tale*, I. ii. 13). N.E.D. gives this and the kindred " snaping " as forms of " snubbing."

Why should I joy in any abortive birth?
At Christmas I no more desire a rose
Than wish a snow in May's new-fangled shows;
But like of each thing that in season grows.
So you, to study now it is too late,
Climb o'er the house to unlock the little gate.

King. Well, sit you out: go home, Berowne: adieu!

Ber. No, my good lord; I have sworn to stay with you:
And though I have for barbarism spoke more
Than for that angel knowledge you can say,
Yet confident I'll keep what I have sworn,
And bide the penance of each three years' day.
Give me the paper; let me read the same;
And to the strict'st decrees I'll write my name.

King. How well this yielding rescues thee from shame!

Ber. [*reads*]. Item: that no woman shall come within a mile of my court,—Hath this been proclaimed?

Long. Four days ago.

Ber. Let's see the penalty—on pain of losing her tongue. Who devised this penalty?

Long. Marry, that did I.

Ber. Sweet lord, and why?

Long. To fright them hence with that dread penalty.

Ber. A dangerous law against gentility!
Item: if any man be seen to talk with a woman within the term of three years, he shall endure such

104. *any*] Qq, Ff; *an* Pope. 106. *shows*] Qq, Ff; *earth* Theobald; *mirth* S. Walker conj., Globe. 109. *Climb . . . gate*] Q 1; *That were to climb o'er the house to unlock the gate* Ff, Q 2. 110. *sit*] Qq, Ff 2, 3, 4; *fit* F 1. 114. *sworn*] Qq, Ff 1; *swore* Ff 2, 3, 4, Camb., New. 127. *Berowne*] Theobald; Qq, Ff assign this (as far as *devise*) to Longaville.

104. *any*] Dover Wilson suggests that the Quarto compositor caught *any* from the preceding line. This is plausible; but where the Quarto reading makes sense, it is better retained.

107. *like of*] occurs several times in Shakespeare. Hart quotes "Rosalynd's Madrigal" from Lodge's *Euphues Golden Legacie*:—

"Then sit thou safely on my knee,
And let thy bower my bosome be;
Lurke in my eies, I like of thee."

109. *Climb . . . gate*] See Intro. 2.3.

112. *barbarism*] lack of culture, philistinism. Compare Dekker, *Gulls' Horn Book*, 1609: "You shall never be good Graduates in these rare Sciences of Barbarisme and Idiotisme."

127. *gentility*] good manners.

public shame as the rest of the court can possibly devise.
This article, my liege, yourself must break ;
For well you know here comes in embassy
The French king's daughter with yourself to speak—
A maid of grace and complete majesty—
About surrender up of Aquitaine
To her decrepit, sick, and bed-rid father :
Therefore this article is made in vain,
Or vainly comes th' admired princess hither.

King. What say you, lords ? why, this was quite forgot.

Ber. So study evermore is overshot :
While it doth study to have what it would,
It doth forget to do the thing it should ;
And when it hath the thing it hunteth most,
'Tis won as towns with fire ; so won, so lost.

King. We must of force dispense with this decree ;
She must lie here on mere necessity.

Ber. Necessity will make us all forsworn
Three thousand times within these three years' space ;
For every man with his affects is born,
Not by might master'd, but by special grace.
If I break faith, this word shall speak for me,
I am forsworn on mere necessity.
So to the laws at large I write my name ;
And he that breaks them in the least degree
Stands in attainder of eternal shame :
Suggestions are to other as to me ;

130. *can*] Q 1 ; *shall* Ff, Q 2. *possibly*] Ff, Q 2 ; *possible* Q 1, New.
154. *Subscribes and gives back the Paper.*] Capell ; *Subscribes.* mod. edd.
157. *other*] Q 1 ; *others* Ff, Q 2.

145. *won as towns with fire*] i.e. destroyed in the taking.

146. *of force*] necessarily.

147. *lie*] dwell, stay.

150. *affects*] passions. Compare *Othello*, I. iii. 264 : "the young affects in me defunct."

156. *Stands in attainder of*] stands condemned and disgraced. The offender would be guilty of treason against the vows sworn to the King and so liable to the normal penalty for treason—the forfeit of all honours and all rights to property. Shakespeare here uses "attainder" almost in its technical sense. Elsewhere it stands for "disgrace" or "stain" generally.

157. *Suggestions*] temptations. The usual sense in Shakespeare.

But I believe, although I seem so loath,
I am the last that will last keep his oath.
But is there no quick recreation granted?

King. Ay, that there is. Our court, you know, is haunted
With a refined traveller of Spain;
A man in all the world's new fashion planted,
That hath a mint of phrases in his brain;
One who the music of his own vain tongue
Doth ravish like enchanting harmony;
A man of complements, whom right and wrong
Have chose as umpire of their mutiny:
This child of fancy, that Armado hight,
For interim to our studies shall relate
In high-born words the worth of many a knight
From tawny Spain, lost in the world's debate.
How you delight, my lords, I know not, I;

162. *refined*] Qq, F 1; *conceited* Ff 2, 3, 4. 165. *One who*] F 1; *On who* Q 1; *One whom* Ff 2, 3, 4.

161. *haunted with*] frequented or visited by. Compare Sidney's *Arcadia*, bk. i. (Feuillerat, i. 12): "a man who for his hospitalitie is so much haunted that no newes sturre but comes to his eares."

162. *refined*] delicate, cultivated. The metaphorical sense is unusual at this date; Shakespeare generally uses the word literally, as in "refined gold."

165. *One*] regularly spelt "on" by Harvey, and perhaps by Shakespeare too.

167. *complements*] This word did duty both for "fulfillment" (as now) and for "courtesy," until the late seventeenth century when the French "compliment" was introduced to carry the second meaning. The sense here probably inclines towards "affected manners," and the modernized spelling "compliments" might be justified, as in IV. ii. 142; but it may be merely "accomplishments" as in Jonson's *Every Man Out of his Humour* (1600), I. ii.: "All the rare qualities, humours and complements of a Gentleman."

169. *hight*] is named.

170. *interim*] interval of relaxation, interlude. Compare Ben Jonson, *Cynthia's Revels*, I. i. (1600): "in which disguise, during the interim of these revels, I will get to follow some one of Diana's maids."

171. *high-born*] *high-borne* may be correct. "Born" is usually spelt *borne* at this time, so that the choice lies between high-birth and high-bearing.

172. *tawny Spain*] the colour of the people given to their country, sunburnt clime. Compare Greene, *Never Too Late* (Grosart, viii. 200): "Flora in tawnie hid up all her flowers . . . upon the barren earth." Elsewhere Greene applies the epithet to autumn leaves, and to eyes.

world's debate] warfare. Lyly employs the word *debate* with the same meaning in *The Woman in the Moone*, II. i. (*ante* 1595): "What telst thou me of love. . . . Fyre of debate is kindled in my hart."

But I protest I love to hear him lie,
And I will use him for my minstrelsy.

Ber. Armado is a most illustrious wight,
A man of fire-new words, fashion's own knight.

Long. Costard the swain, and he, shall be our sport,
And so to study three years is but short.

Enter DULL *with a letter, and* COSTARD.

Dull. Which is the duke's own person?

Ber. This, fellow. What would'st?

Dull. I myself reprehend his own person, for I am his grace's farborough: but I would see his own person in flesh and blood.

Ber. This is he.

Dull. Signior Arm—Arm—commends you. There's villany abroad: this letter will tell you more.

Cost. Sir, the contempts thereof are as touching me.

King. A letter from the magnificent Armado.

Ber. How low soever the matter, I hope in God for high words.

Long. A high hope for a low heaven: God grant us patience!

177. *fire-new*] *fire, new* F 1. *Enter . . . Costard*] Malone; *Enter a Constable with Costard with a letter* Qq, Ff. 180. *duke's*] Qq, Ff; *King's* Theobald. 183. *farborough*] Q 1; *tharborough* Ff. 192. *heaven*] *having* Theobald.

177. *fire-new*] fresh from the mint. The expression appears again in *Richard III.*, *Twelfth Night* and *King Lear.* It appears to be a Shakespearean coinage.

179. *and so to study*] i.e. with these provisions for our recreation. Many editors make it an exhortation: "And so to study! Three years is but short."

182. *reprehend*] represent. Dull's "mistaking of words" anticipates Dogberry's in *Much Ado about Nothing.*

183. *farborough*] thirdborough; a petty constable. In Blount's *Glossographia* (1656) the term is used interchangeably with "headborough." But Ben Jonson in his *Tale of a Tub* (1633) discriminates these officers, high constable, headborough, petty constable and thirdborough. He places these on the stage, the lowest in rank being the thirdborough, a tinker.

188. *contempts*] Slender is credited with a similar confusion in *The Merry Wives of Windsor*, I. i. 258.

189. *magnificent Armado*] This form of the magnificent Armada of Spain occurs twice in Greene's *Spanish Masquerado*, 1589; and in the second part of Marlowe's *Tamburlaine*, I. ii.

Ber. To hear? or forbear hearing?

Long. To hear meekly, sir, and to laugh moderately; or to forbear both.

Ber. Well, sir, be it as the style shall give us cause to climb in the merriness.

Cost. The matter is to me, sir, as concerning Jaquenetta. The manner of it is, I was taken with the manner.

Ber. In what manner?

Cost. In manner and form following, sir; all those three: I was seen with her in the manor-house, sitting with her upon the form, and taken following her into the park; which, put together, is in manner and form following. Now, sir, for the manner,—it is the manner of a man to speak to a woman; for the form,—in some form.

Ber. For the following, sir?

Cost. As it shall follow in my correction; and God defend the right!

King. Will you hear this letter with attention?

Ber. As we would hear an oracle.

Cost. Such is the simplicity of man to hearken after the flesh.

King. [*Reads*]. Great deputy, the welkin's vicegerent, and sole dominator of Navarre, my soul's earth's God, and body's fostering patron.

194. *hearing*] Qq, Ff, Steevens (1793); *laughing* Capell and some modern edd.

200. *taken with the manner*] more properly "mainour," i.e. hand-work, an old form of "manoeuvre." Taken in the act. Palsgrave's *Lesclaircissement* (1530) has "I take with the maner, as a thefe is taken with the thefte, or a person in the doyng of any other acte, *Je prens sur le faict.*" A legal expression.

205, 206. *in manner and form following*] Another set expression of the time. Craig refers to Nashe's *Unfortunate Traveller* (McKerrow, ii. 248), 1594. There is an earlier example in the *New Eng. Dict.* from T. Washington's trans. of *Nicholay's Voyage*, 1585: "Over their shoulders in the fourme and maner as the picture following doth shew." And see Lyly's *Mydas*, v. ii. (? 1589): "you shall have the beard, in manner and form following."

210. *correction*] punishment.

210, 211. *God defend the right*] See *Richard II.* I. iii. 101; *2 Henry VI.* II. iii. 55; the formal prayer made before a trial by combat. Costard is quite ready with his defence.

216. *welkin*] sky. See IV. ii. 5.

vicegerent] seems to have been a term affected by Philip of Spain. Greene in *The Spanish Masquerado*, 1589 (Grosart, v. 245, 281), refers twice to his "Vicegerentes of his

Cost. Not a word of Costard yet.

King. So it is,—

Cost. It may be so; but if he say it is so, he is, in telling true, but so.

King. Peace!

Cost. Be to me and every man that dares not fight.

King. No words!

Cost. Of other men's secrets, I beseech you.

King. So it is, besieged with sable-coloured melancholy, I did commend the black oppressing humour to the most wholesome physic of thy health-giving air; and, as I am a gentleman, betook myself to walk. The time when? About the sixth hour; when beasts most graze, birds best peck, and men sit down to that nourishment which is called supper: so much for the time when. Now for the ground which? which, I mean, I walked upon: it is ycleped thy park. Then for the place where? where, I mean, I did encounter that

222. *true, but so*] *true: but so* Qq, Ff; *true, but so so* Hanmer.

Indies." In the transferred sense here it is used by Stubbes, *Anatomie of Abuses*, ii. 104: "The Devill himselfe, whose Vice-gerent . . . he showes himselfe to be" (1583).

217. *dominator*] lord, ruler. The word occurs again in *Titus Andronicus*, II. iii. 31, in an astrological sense. The only example of the word prior to Shakespeare, in the *New Eng. Dict.*, is from *Mirour Saluacioun* (*circa* 1450), applied to the Deity. Shakespeare is likely to have met it in Puttenham's *Arte of English Poesie*; chap. xvi. is headed "In what forme of Poesie the great Princes and dominators of the world were honored."

221. *It may be so; but if he say it is so*] This recalls the jingle in *Much Ado About Nothing*, I. i. 219: "Like the old tale, my lord; it is not so, nor 'twas not so, but indeed God forbid it should be so."

222. *but so*] indifferent, not worth much. Equivalent to our "but so so," which occurs frequently in Shakespeare. The phrase "no more but so" was a favourite with Marlowe.

229. *as I am a gentleman*] frequent in Shakespeare. It occurs twice in *The Merry Wives of Windsor*.

230-235. *The time when . . . the place where*] An early example of this classical mode of speech is in Gabriel Harvey's celebrated *Judgement of Earthquakes* (Grosart, i. 63), 1580: "We are to judge of as advisedly and providently, as possibly we can, by the consideration and comparison of circumstances, the tyme when: the place where: the qualities and dispositions of the persons, amongst whom such." Compare Wilson's *Art of Rhetorique* (1553): "Seven circumstances whiche are to be considered in diverse matters. . . . Who, what, and where, by what helpe and by whose: Why how and when, doe many thinges disclose" (1562 ed., fol. 9). This was also the standard form for a legal indictment. Hotson (*Shakespeare's Sonnets Dated*, 1949, p. 55) quotes the model indictment for theft given in William West's

obscene and most preposterous event, that draweth from my snow-white pen the ebon coloured ink, which here thou viewest, beholdest, surveyest, or seest. But to the place where: it standeth north-north-east and by east from the west corner of thy curious-knotted garden: there did I see that low-spirited swain, that base minnow of thy mirth,—

Cost. Me?

King. that unlettered small-knowing soul,—

242, 244, 246. *Me? . . . Me? . . . me?*] Ff, Q 2; *Me? . . . me? . . . me* Q 1, New; *Me . . . Me . . . me.* Hanmer, Steevens, Craig.

Symboleographie (1590): "*Quis.* The person with his name, surname, addicion of the Towne, Countie, Arte, and degree. *Quando.* The day and yeare. *Ubi.* The place, Towne, and Countrie. *Quid.* The thing taken, the colour, the marke, the price and value. *Cuius.* The owner of the thing and whose it was. *Quomodo.* The manner of the doing and how. *Quare.* The entent, which is comprised in this word (*Felonicè*)." The proximity of Costard's play on "manner and form following" suggests that Armado's rigmarole is also a skit on legal phraseology.

236. *preposterous*] entirely out of place, highly improper. Compare *Othello*, I. iii. 62: "For nature so preposterously to err . . . Sans witchcraft could not."

237. *ebon-coloured*] Compare Greene, *Tullies Love* (Grosart, vii. 146), 1589: "Hir eyes like Ariadnes sparklng Starres Shone frome the Ebon Arches of hir browes."

240. *curious-knotted garden*] labyrinths and intricate patterns amongst the flower beds were the glory of early gardeners. Bacon, *Essay of Gardens*, writes: "for the *Making of Knots*, or Figures, with Diuers Coloured Earths . . . they be but Toyes: You may see as good sights, many times in Tarts" (1625). And compare Shirley, *Gentleman of Venice*, I. ii.:

"When I am digging, he is cutting
unicorns,
And lions in some hedge, or else
devising
New knots upon the ground,
drawing out crowns,
And the duke's arms, castles and
cannons in them:
Here gallies, there a ship giving a
broadside:
Here out of turf he carves a
senator
With all his robes, making a
speech to Time
That grows hard by, and twenty
curiosities,—
I think he means to embroider
all the garden."

240. *low-spirited*] base. Armado corrects here the modern use.

241. *minnow*] A contemptible little person, a shrimp. Nashe, speaking of Gabriel Harvey, says: "Let him denie that there was another Shewe made of the little Minnow his Brother. . . . Whereupon Dick came and broke the Colledge glasse windowes" (*Have With You to Saffron Walden* [McKerrow, iii. 80], 1596).

243. *unlettered*] illiterate, ignorant. See Sonnet lxxxv. 6, and again in this play, IV. ii. 18; and *Henry V.* I. i. 55, where the company kept by Prince Hal is described as "unletter'd, rude and shallow." Nashe uses the term in *A Wonderfull Prognostication* (McKerrow, iii. 390), 1591: "insomuch that sundrie unlettered fooles should creepe into the ministerie."

Cost. Me?

King. that shallow vassal,—

Cost. Still me?

King. which, as I remember, hight Costard,—

Cost. O! me.

King. sorted and consorted, contrary to thy established proclaimed edict and continent canon, which with—O! with—but with this I passion to say wherewith,—

Cost. With a wench.

King. with a child of our grandmother Eve, a female; or, for thy more sweet understanding, a woman. Him, I, as my ever-esteemed duty pricks me on, have sent to thee, to receive the meed of punishment, by thy sweet grace's officer, Anthony Dull, a man of good repute, carriage, bearing, and estimation.

Dull. Me, an't shall please you; I am Anthony Dull.

King. For Jaquenetta—so is the weaker vessel called—which I apprehended with the aforesaid swain, I keep her as a vessel of thy law's fury; and shall, at the least of thy sweet

250. *which*] *with*, Theobald. 254. *sweet*] omitted in Ff 2, 3, 4. 260. *keep*] Qq, Ff 2, 3, 4; *keeper* F 1. 261. *vessel*] *vassal* Theobald.

245. *vassal*] a country bumpkin, or clown. Collier's "Corrector" would read "vessel" here, which Dyce adopted. Compare Lodge's *Euphues Golden Legacie* (*Shakes. Lib.*, 1875, p. 21), 1590: "In this humour was Saladyne making his brother Rosader his foote boy . . . as if he had been the sonne of any country vassal."

249. *sorted*] associated.

250. *continent canon*] restraining canon; or canon enforcing restraint. This is the usual explanation, or choice of explanations, of Armado's words. But he may mean merely, in his pedantic way, the edict and the law contained therein. Ben Jonson uses the word similarly in *Every Man out of his Humour*, Induction: "So in every human body, The choler, melancholy . . . flow continually In some one part and are not continent."

251. *passion*] grieve, as in *Venus and Adonis*, 1059. Compare Nashe, *The Unfortunate Traveller*, 1594: "Having passioned thus a while, she hastely ranne and lookt herselfe in her glasse."

259. *weaker vessel*] See 1 Peter iii. 7 for the expression applied to a wife. But the term was proverbial for any woman earlier than the time of this play. Greene has it twice in *Mamillia* (Grosart, ii. 95, 255), 1583: "They say a woman is the weaker vessel, but sure in my iudgement it is in the strength of her body, and not in the force of her minde"; and "women sure, whom they count the weake vessels, had more neede to be counselled than condemned." Lyly has it also in *Euphues* (Arber, p. 78): "men are always laying baites for women, which are the weaker vessels"; and again, in *Sapho and Phao*, I. iv. (1584): "I cannot but oftentimes smile to myselfe to heare men call us weaker vessels."

notice, bring her to trial. Thine in all compliments of devoted and heart-burning heat of duty,

DON ADRIANO DE ARMADO.

Ber. This is not so well as I looked for, but the best that ever I heard.

King. Ay, the best for the worst. But, sirrah, what say you to this?

Cost. Sir, I confess the wench.

King. Did you hear the proclamation?

Cost. I do confess much of the hearing it, but little of the marking of it.

King. It was proclaimed a year's imprisonment to be taken with a wench.

Cost. I was taken with none, sir: I was taken with a demsel.

King. Well, it was proclaimed damsel.

Cost. This was no damsel neither, sir: she was a virgin.

King. It is so varied too, for it was proclaimed virgin.

Cost. If it were, I deny her virginity: I was taken with a maid.

King. This maid will not serve your turn, sir.

Cost. This maid will serve my turn, sir.

264. *Adriano*] Qq; *Adriana* Ff. 276. *demsel*] Q 1; *damosell* Ff, Q 2. 277, 278. *damsel*] Q 1; *damosel* Ff, Q 2.

267. *the best for the worst*] Compare Dekker's *Strange Horse-Race* (Grosart, iii. 364): " The Masquers . . . not needing any Vizards (their owne visages beeing good enough because bad enough)." But Lyly gives the best parallel: " [*Perim danceth*] How like you this; doth he well? *Diog.* The better, the worse " (*Campaspe*, v. i.). Greene quotes this in *Tritameron* (Grosart, iii. 88), 1584: " I thinke of lovers as Diogenes did of dancers . . . the better the worse."

276. *demsel*] Costard's malapropisms are better credited to Shakespeare's art than to the compositor's blunder. Compare this play below, v. ii. 500, and note on Holofernes' quotations at IV. ii. 92. The word " damsel " was in ordinary use earlier than this time; the Folio spelling need not be taken as implying a specialized meaning.

279. *varied*] diversified in language. Compare Sonnet cv. 10, and see this play below, IV. ii. 9.

283. *Serve my turn*] satisfy me. Costard twists the King's sentence—" This play with the letter of the law will not provide the excuse you need "—to a bawdy sense.

King. Sir, I will pronounce your sentence: you shall fast a week with bran and water.

Cost. I had rather pray a month with mutton and porridge.

King. And Don Armado shall be your keeper.
My Lord Berowne, see him deliver'd o'er:
And go we, lords, to put in practice that
Which each to other hath so strongly sworn.

[*Exeunt King, Longaville, and Dumain.*

Ber. I'll lay my head to any good man's hat,
These oaths and laws will prove an idle scorn.
Sirrah, come on.

Cost. I suffer for the truth, sir: for true it is I was taken with Jaquenetta, and Jaquenetta is a true girl; and therefore welcome the sour cup of prosperity! Affliction may one day smile again; and till then, sit thee down, sorrow! [*Exeunt.*

293. Given to Dull in the Collier MS. 297. *affliction*] *afflicio* Q 1 (Devon copy).

285. *bran and water*] Compare *Measure for Measure*, IV. iii. 160; and Nashe, *Summer's Last Will* (McKerrow, iii. 260), 1592: "Thou witholdest both the mault and flowre, And giv'st us branne, and water, (fit for dogs)."

286. *mutton and porridge*] mutton-broth. "Porridge" and "pottage" were used synonymously, the former probably formed in imitation of the latter from *purée*. Cotgrave has "*La purée de pois:* Pease strained, Pease pottage"; and "Potage: Pottage, porridge." Nashe speaks of this good nourishment: "Amongst all other stratagems . . . to pumpe over mutton and porridge into Fraunce? this coolde weather our souldirs . . . have need of it, . . . they have almost got the colicke and stone with eating of provant" (*Foure Letters Confuted* [McKerrow, i. 331], 1593). "Mutton" was also a cant term for a whore, and Costard may be punning on this.

291. *lay*] offer a bet. "I take six to one saies the Gripe, I lay it saies the vincent, and so they make a bet" (Greene, second part of *Conny-catching* [Grosart, x. 84], 1592). On the title-page of the same tract Greene has: "if you reade without laughing, Ile give you my cap for a noble"; and in *A Looking Glass for London and England* (1594) he has: "I hold my cap to a noble." See v. ii. 556 (note), and Beaumont and Fletcher, *Knight of the Burning Pestle*, III. ii.: "I hold my cap to a farthing he does."

295. *true*] honest.

297, 298. *sit . . . sorrow*]. The source of this saying is not known, It occurs again at IV. iii. 4.

SCENE II

Enter Armado *and* Moth.

Arm. Boy, what sign is it when a man of great spirit grows melancholy?

Moth. A great sign, sir, that he will look sad.

Arm. Why! sadness is one and the self-same thing, dear imp.

Moth. No, no; O Lord, sir, no.

Arm. How canst thou part sadness and melancholy, my tender juvenal?

Moth. By a familiar demonstration of the working, my tough Signor.

Arm. Why tough Signor? why tough Signor?

Moth. Why tender juvenal? why tender juvenal?

Scene II

Scene II.] Capell; *Scene* III. Pope. *Enter Armado . . .*] *Enter Armado a Braggart* F 2. 3. *Moth*] Rowe *et seq.* and throughout scene; *Boy.* Q 1, F 1. 4, 7, 11, etc. *Arm(ado)*] Qq; *Brag.*, *Bra.* or *Br.* Ff. 5. *Why!*] *Why?* Qq, Ff. 10, 11, 16. *signor*] *signeor* Q 1; *signeur* Ff.

Scene II

5. *imp*] primarily a sapling, a young shoot; then a child, especially of noble origin; and, commonly, any child, though now chiefly limited to a "child of the devil." Compare *Euphues* (Arber, p. 108): "This is therefore to admonish all young Imps and novices in love, not to blow the coales of fancy with desire."

6. *O Lord, sir*] surely, certainly. Compare Ben Jonson, *Every Man out of his Humour,* II. i.; "His lady! what, is she fair, splendidious, and amiable? *Gent.* O Lord, sir!" The ejaculation here may merely express impatience; compare Jonson's *Cynthia's Revels*, Induction: "*Child.* What shall I do with it? *Child.* O Lord, Sir! will you betray your ignorance so much?" It might serve almost any purpose; see also v. ii. 485 ff.

8. *juvenal*] youth. It is possible that this term, with a pun on the name of the Roman satirist, was commonly used as a nickname for Nashe: "As Acteon was worried of his owne hound: so is Tom Nash of his *Isle of Dogs*. *Dogges* were the death of Euripides, but bee not disconsolate gallant young Iuvenall, Linus the sonne of Apollo died the same death" (Meres, *Wits Treasurie*, 1598); and Greene speaks of "young Iuvenal that byting Satyrist" in a well-known passage in his *Groatsworth of Wit* (Grosart, xii. 143), which probably (in spite of Dyce) refers to Nashe. Shakespeare has this word for a youth again in this play (III. i. 64) and in *1 Henry IV*. I. ii. 22, and *A Midsummer Night's Dream*, III. i. 97, with no reference to the proper name.

9. *working*] operation.

10. *Signor*] To emend the title, so clearly indicated in both Quarto and Folio, to "Senior," as many editors do, is to emphasize the obvious half

Arm. I spoke it, tender juvenal, as a congruent epitheton appertaining to thy young days, which we may nominate tender.

Moth. And I, tough Signor, as an appertinent title to your old time, which we may name tough.

Arm. Pretty, and apt.

Moth. How mean you, sir? I pretty, and my saying apt? or I apt, and my saying pretty?

Arm. Thou pretty, because little.

Moth. Little pretty, because little. Wherefore apt?

Arm. And therefore apt, because quick.

Moth. Speak you this in my praise, master?

Arm. In thy condign praise.

Moth. I will praise an eel with the same praise.

Arm. What! that an eel is ingenious?

Moth. That an eel is quick.

Arm. I do say thou art quick in answers: thou heat'st my blood.

Moth. I am answered, sir.

Arm. I love not to be crossed.

13. *epitheton*] Ff 2, 3, 4; *apethatoa* Q 1; *apethaton* Q 1 (Devon copy); *apathaton* F 1, Q 2. 27. *ingenious*] Q 1, F 4; *ingenuous* Q 2, Ff 1, 2, 3.

of the pun at the expense of the less apparent. The joke, and the editorial blunder, are repeated at III. i. 177.

13. *congruent*] suitable. Ben Jonson uses the word in *Discoveries* (p. 131): "*De Stylo.* The congruent and harmonious fitting of parts in a sentence." We have this word again from Holofernes, V. i. 87. See note for other examples.

epitheton] an adjective indicating some characteristic quality or attribute (*New Eng. Dict.*). The earliest form of the word "epithet." Compare Greene, *Planetomachia* (Grosart, v. 101), 1585; "which naturall and proper qualitie in my judgement caused the auncient Poets to attribute this Epitheton unto *Venus: Alma.*"

16. *appertinent*] belonging. See *2 Henry IV.* I. ii. 194: "the other gifts appertinent to man."

25. *condign*] well-merited. Commonly used as here at this time. "Condigne thankes" occurs in Greene's *Planetomachia* (Grosart, v. 85). 1585.

28. *an eel is quick*] There must be a topical hit here since Armado so much resents it ("thou heat'st my blood"). John Crow suggests that the reference is to the proverb "to get a woman by the waist or a quick eel by the tail," and that Moth means to imply that Armado is always running after women. This seems to me a very long way round, even for *Love's Labour's Lost.* See Introduction, 5.25, and p. xii.

Moth. He speaks the mere contrary: crosses love not him. [*Aside*

Arm. I have promised to study three years with the duke.

Moth. You may do it in an hour, sir.

Arm. Impossible.

Moth. How many is one thrice told?

Arm. I am ill at reckoning; it fitteth the spirit of a tapster.

Moth. You are a gentleman and a gamester, sir.

Arm. I confess both: they are both the varnish of a complete man.

Moth. Then I am sure you know how much the gross sum of deuce-ace amounts to.

Arm. It doth amount to one more than two.

Moth. Which the base vulgar do call three.

Arm. True.

Moth. Why, sir, is this such a piece of study? Now here is three studied ere ye'll thrice wink; and how easy it is to put years to the word three, and study three years in two words, the dancing horse will tell you.

33. *mere contrary*] Qq, F 1; *clean contrary* Ff 2, 3, 4. 35. *three*] Q 1; *iii* Ff 1, 2, Q 2; *3* Ff 3, 4. *duke*] *King* Theobald. 39. *fitteth*] Q 1; *fits* Ff, Q 2. 46. *do*] Q 1; omitted Ff. Q 2.

33. *crosses*] coins, from many kinds bearing the representation of a cross. A venerable and threadbare pun. Perhaps the commonest form is "The devil may dance in his pocket for he has never a cross there." It occurs in Hoccleve (*circa* 1420). Nashe (McKerrow, i. 305), 1593, says it "hath been a graybeard Proverbe two hundred yeares before Tarlton was borne."

35. *duke*] See above, I. i. 180. The king. The term was commonly used of a sovereign prince, as in *The Tempest*, I. ii. 54, 58, etc. Sidney, in *Arcadia* (bk. v.), calls King Basilius "the duke."

39. *tapster*] a "tapster's arithmetic" is mentioned again in *Troilus and Cressida*, I. ii. 123. A "tapster" was regarded as a very ignorant person. Nashe, in his Introduction to Greene's *Menaphon* (1589), speaks of "tapsterly terms" as befitting the "mind of the meanest." See Introduction, 5.23.

40. *gamester*] player, gambler. So in Cooke's *Greene's Tu Quoque*: "Primero! why I thought thou hadst not been so much gamester as to play at it."

46. *vulgar*] the common people. Compare Henry Porter's *Two Angry Women of Abingdon* (Malone Soc., ed. Greg, lines 401 ff.): "*Comes.* Faith sir like a poore man of service. *Philip.* Or servingman. *Comes.* Indeed so called by the vulgar. *Philip.* Why where the divell hadst thou that word?" There is also a hint of the meaning "vernacular speech." Compare IV. i. 69.

51. *dancing horse*] The description fits Morocco, Banks' trick-performing horse, which is famous in Elizabethan literature and on down to the middle

Arm. A most fine figure !

Moth. To prove you a cipher. [*Aside*

Arm. I will hereupon confess I am in love ; and as it is base for a soldier to love, so am I in love with a base wench. If drawing my sword against the humour of affection would deliver me from the reprobate thought of it, I would take Desire prisoner, and ransom him to any French courtier for a new-devised courtesy. I think scorn to sigh : methinks I should

of the seventeenth century. Halliwell quotes from an MS. diary kept by a native of Shrewsbury : " September, 1591. This yeare . . . Master Banckes, a Staffordshire gentile brought into the town of Salop a white horse which would doe wonderfull and strange things, as thease—wold in a company or prese tell how many peeces of money by hys foote were in a mans purce . . . many people judgid that it were impossible to be don except he had a famyliar, or don by the arte of magicke." A tract with an illustration (reproduced by Chambers, *Book of Days*, i. 225) was published in 1596, under the title of "*Moroccus Exstaticus :* or Bankes Bay Horse in a Traunce" (in the diary the animal is said to be white). The cut shows the horse on his hind legs, and at his feet two dice, one of which has ace uppermost, the other the deuce to the front. Evidently what his master had taught him was to beat out with his hoof any suggested number ; and this talent was used in what would now be called a thought-reading act. The entry in the Shrewsbury diary for September 1591 is the first certain reference to this accomplished animal and this has been taken by several editors as evidence that *Love's Labour's Lost* could not have been written earlier than that year ; but William Clowes, in *A Prooued Practise for all Young Chirurgians* (1588) speaks of a quack being "as cunning, as the Horsse at the Crosse Keyes," which may have been the same. There may also have been other dancing horses. Morocco was still going strong in 1600, when his master took him on to the roof of St. Paul's and caused a sensation—as the author (? Dekker) of the *Owle's Almanack* has it (1606) : " The dancing horse stood on the top of Powles whilst a number of asses stood braying below." According to Jonson (*Epigram 133*) Banks and his horse were eventually burned together beyond sea for one witch, but the date of this is not given.

52. *figure*] A turn of rhetoric or of logic. See v. ii. 408.

53. *cipher*] a nothing, a nonentity.

59, 60. *French courtier for a new-devised courtesy*] a bow or complimentary acknowledgment after any of the new French fashions. Compare *Richard III.* I. iii. 39 : " French nods and apish courtesy " ; and Ben Jonson's *Case is Altered*, II. iii. (1598) : " And she should make French court'sies so most low That every touch should turn her over backward." Montaigne (1580-1588) refers to our " kissing the hands . . . our low-lowting courtesies " (Book II, chapter xii in Florio's translation).

60. *think scorn*] scorn, disdain. A frequent expression in Shakespeare, Ben Jonson (*Cynthia's Revels*, v. ii.) and others of the time. So Lyly in *Euphues and his England* (Arber rep. p. 424), 1580 : " Hee that never

outswear Cupid. Comfort me, boy. What great men have been in love?

Moth. Hercules, master.

Arm. Most sweet Hercules! More authority, dear boy, name more; and, sweet my child, let them be men of good repute and carriage.

Moth. Samson, master: he was a man of good carriage, great carriage, for he carried the town-gates on his back like a porter; and he was in love.

Arm. O well-knit Samson! strong-jointed Samson! I do excel thee in my rapier as much as thou didst me in carrying gates. I am in love too. Who was Samson's love, my dear Moth?

Moth. A woman, master.

Arm. Of what complexion?

tooke the oare in his hand must not thinke scorn to bee taught"; and Sir Philip Sidney's *Arcadia*, bk. i.: "thinking foule scorne willingly to submit my selfe to be ruled."

61. *outswear Cupid*] "surpass in swearing," according to some commentators and *New Eng. Dict.*; "conquer by swearing," Schmidt. I prefer the latter sense, i.e. forswear. Compare II. i. 104, where the expression "sworn out housekeeping" obviously means forsworn, renounced.

65. *sweet my child*] The inversion is common; so "good my knave," III. i. 149.

68. *carried the town-gates*] A passage in Middleton's *Family of Love*, I. iii. (1607), recalls this about Samson: "from what good exercise come you three? *Gerardius.* From a play where we saw most excellent Sampson excel the whole world in gate-carrying . . . Believe it we saw Sampson bear the town-gates on his neck from the lower to the upper stage, with that life and admirable accord, that it shall never be equalled, unless the whole new livery of porters set their shoulders." Henslowe paid for the book of a play called *Samson* (now lost) in July 1602. See W. W. Greg, *Henslowe's Diary*, i. 169, and ii. 223. This may be referred to by Middleton as Greg points out.

71. *my rapier*] This was becoming the fashionable weapon, introduced, along with the dress and manners of the continent, by the "Italianate" fops so often satirized by Elizabethan writers. Though the models for this fashion were largely French or Italian the rapier seems to have been regarded as peculiarly Spanish. Giles du Guez, *Introductione . . . for to speke Frenche*, c. 1530, has "the Spanische sworde, la rapiere." Cotgrave (1611) gives "Espa Espagnole—A Rapier or Tuck."

75, 76. *complexion? Of all the four*] The commonest sense of "complexion" in Shakespeare is the colour of the skin; but the word can also mean either a "humour" (Phlegm, Blood, Choler, or Melancholy) or the peculiar mixture of them in an individual that determined his character. For Moth's quibbling compare Dekker: "*Bellafront.* Is my glass there? and my boxes of complexion? *Roger*, Yes forsooth: your boxes of complexion are here I thinke: yes 'tis here: here's your two complexions, and if

Moth. Of all the four, or the three, or the two, or one of the four.

Arm. Tell me precisely of what complexion.

Moth. Of the sea-water green, sir.

Arm. Is that one of the four complexions?

Moth. As I have read, sir; and the best of them too.

Arm. Green indeed is the colour of lovers; but to have a love of that colour, methinks, Samson had small reason for it. He surely affected her for her wit.

Moth. It was so, sir, for she had a green wit.

Arm. My love is most immaculate white and red.

Moth. Most maculate thoughts, master, are masked under such colours.

87. *maculate*] Q 1, Pope *et seq.*; *immaculate* Ff, Q 2.

I had all the foure complexions, I should nere set a good face upon't, some men I see are borne under hard-favoured planets" (*Honest Whore* [Pearson, ii. 25]).

79. *sea-water green*] Holland has this expression (our "sea-green") in Pliny's *Naturall History*, trans. 1601 (bk. xxxvii. chap. v. p. 613): "Beryls . . . which carrie a sea-water green." In Ben Jonson's *Part of the King's Entertainment*, 1604, Tamesis has "a mantle of sea-green or water-colour." The name lives in the "Aquamarine," a gem, which is mentioned in Stow's *Survey* (1598) as being "of a sea-water green colour." It is mentioned as an artist's colour in Rider's *Bibliotheca Scholastica*, 1589: "A certain medly colour, made of hony, rain water, and sea water."

82. *Green . . . colour of lovers*] This statement is supported by a reference to "Green sleeves"; not only does the lady wear green but the lover puts his men in green for her sake. Green was commonly the colour of hope and of rejoicing. If Moth is Nashe, there may well be a pun here on Robert Greene, author of love-romances and, until his death in 1592, chief adversary of the Harveys. Nashe uses the quibble to sneer at writers "who with Greene colours seeke to garnish such Gorgonlike shapes" (McKerrow, I. 16), i.e. "gloss over Woman's natural deformity by describing her in the romantic terms invented by Greene"; and Gabriel Harvey has it often.

85. *green wit*] Grant White saw an allusion here to the green withes with which Samson was bound. But "Green wit" was a common expression, bound to be suggested by the context. Compare Greene's *Never Too Late* (Grosart, vii. 44), 1590: "his grave wisdome exceedes thy green wit"; and his *Mamillia* (1583): "your talk . . . sheweth surely but a green wit, not so full of gravity, as . . . age requires" (p. 46); and again on pp. 49, 79, in the same tale. In Lyly's *Euphues* "green" is used of a wit that remains fresh in spite of age.

86. *white and red*] Compare *A Twelfe Night Merriment* (*Narcissus*), 1602 (ed. M. Lee, p. 12): "Leave off to bragg thou boy of Venus breadd, I am as faire as thou for white and red." See *Pericles*, IV. vi. 27: "flesh and blood, sir, white and red."

Arm. Define, define, well-educated infant.

Moth. My father's wit and my mother's tongue assist me!

Arm. Sweet invocation of a child; most pretty and pathetical!

Moth. If she be made of white and red,
Her faults will ne'er be known,
For blushing cheeks by faults are bred,
And fears by pale white shown:
Then if she fear, or be to blame,
By this you shall not know,
For still her cheeks possess the same
Which native she doth owe.

A dangerous rhyme, master, against the reason of white and red.

Arm. Is there not a ballad, boy, of the King and the Beggar?

Moth. The world was very guilty of such a ballad some three ages since; but I think now 'tis not to be found; or, if it were, it would neither serve for the writing nor the tune.

Arm. I will have that subject newly writ o'er, that I may example my digression by some mighty precedent.

95. *blushing*] Ff 2, 3, 4; *blush-in* Qq, F 1. 110. *precedent*] Johnson; *president* (or *prescedent*) Qq, Ff.

89. *define*] explain your meaning.

92. *pathetical*] touching. An early form of "pathetic" introduced by Gabriel Harvey, with the original meaning of "passionate." He has it several times in his *Letters to Spenser*: "Dionisius . . . is reported in a certain Patheticall Ecstasie to haue cryed out" ("Earthquake Letter") (Grosart, i. 57), 1580; and earlier, in 1573, *Letter-Book* (Camden Soc.). Chapman has "pretty and pathetical" twice, in *An Humourous Day's Mirth*, I. i. 36, of the posy engraved on an agate, and in *Widow's Tears*, III. i. 129. Shakespeare uses it, each time colloquially or playfully, again in *As You Like It*, IV. i. 196, as well as later in this play (IV. i. 147).

100. *owe*] own. Compare II. i. 6.

102. *white and red*] Alluding to the two "complexions" or cosmetics, as in the quotation from Dekker above (line 75); the "Ceruse and Vermillion" of the same author in his *Gull's Horn Book*. Ceruse was known as "Spanish white."

103, 104. *King and the Beggar*] See note at IV. i. 66, 67.

107, 108. *serve . . . tune*] The song is out of date, says Moth; neither words nor music would pass muster now.

110. *digression*] deviation from the proper course; transgression. See *Lucrece*, 202. Ben Jonson has the word in a similar sense in *Cynthia's Revels*, I. i., in a speech full of affectations by Amorphus. N.E.D. has an early example from Hawes (1509).

Boy, I do love that country girl that I took in the park with the rational hind Costard: she deserves well.

Moth. To be whipped; and yet a better love than my master. [*Aside.*

Arm. Sing, boy: my spirit grows heavy in love.

Moth. And that's great marvel, loving a light wench. [*Aside.*

Arm. I say, sing.

Moth. Forbear till this company be past.

Enter DULL, COSTARD, *and* JAQUENETTA.

Dull, Sir, the duke's pleasure is that you keep Costard safe: and you must suffer him to take no delight nor no penance, but a' must fast three days a week. For this damsel, I must keep her at the park; she is allowed for the day-woman. Fare you well.

Arm. I do betray myself with blushing. Maid.

Jaq. Man.

Arm. I will visit thee at the lodge.

Jaq. That's hereby.

115. *love*] Ff 2, 3, 4; *loue* Qq; *ioue* F 1 *Enter . . .*] (Steevens (1793); *Enter Clown, Constable, and Wench* Qq, Ff. 120. *Suffer him to*] Q 1; *let him* Ff, Q 2. 121. *a'*] Q 1; *hee* Ff. 127. *hereby*] Qq; *here by* Ff.

112. *rational hind*] intelligent clown. Theobald suggested a quibble on the two senses of *hind*, rustic and stag.

116. *light*] wanton.

121. *penance*] Perhaps Dull was thinking of "pleasance," a Shakespearian word.

three days a week] In 1580-1 Elizabeth re-enacted certain Acts (1549 and 1564) relating to fishing and fishermen. They prescribed that Wednesday and Saturday in every week (except Christmas week and Easter week) should be observed as "Fish Days." Those who failed to make fish the main item of their diet on these days were subject to the penalties laid down for a similar offence on Friday, the official fast-day of the Church, although the new Fish Days were expressly dissociated from religious observances, being instituted for "the maintenance and increase of the navy," and the preservation of young cattle. Costard's penance is doubtless a reflection of these regulations, though the Wednesday had been remitted in 1585.

123. *allowed for the day-woman*] admitted or passed as dairymaid. Under *day-woman* (correctly *dey*) and *dey-wife*, *N.E.D.* gives examples of this variant of dairy-woman as early as 1398 and as late as Scott (*Fair Maid of Perth*, 1828). It is in a list of Gloucester dialect words dated 1890.

127. *That's hereby*] No doubt Jaquenetta has some vulgar wit here, such as "over the left shoulder" or "the left-hand way," but confirmation is

Arm. I know where it is situate.
Jaq. Lord, how wise you are !
Arm. I will tell thee wonders.
Jaq. With that face ?
Arm. I love thee.
Jaq. So I heard you say.
Arm. And so farewell.
Jaq. Fair weather after you !
Dull. Come, Jaquenetta, away! [*Exeunt Dull and Jaquenetta.*
Arm. Villain, thou shalt fast for thy offences ere thou be pardoned.
Cost. Well, sir, I hope when I do it I shall do it on a full stomach.

131. *that*] Q 1, Ff 2, 3, 4 ; *what* F 1, Q 2. 136. *Dull.*] Q 1 gives this to *Clown*.

lacking. Schmidt (with no authority) says " that as it may be." He adopted it from Steevens. For this scene between Jaquenetta and Armado there is a close parallel in one between Silena and Candius in Lyly's *Mother Bombie* (about 1589), ii. 3. Silena has " rackt together all the odde blinde phrases that help them that know not how to discourse, but when they cannot answer wisely, either with gybing cover their rudenesse, or by some new coined by word bewray their peevishnesse."

131. *With that face ?*] A piece of slang equivalent to " you don't mean it ! " " you're not the man," etc. Steevens, Dyce and Craig refer to Fielding's *Joseph Andrews*, rather a long way down the time. Steevens says it has no meaning and was still in use. Compare Heywood, *Fair Maid of Exchange* (Pearson, p. 11), 1607 : " Come, come, leave your jesting, I shall put you downe. *Mall.* With that face ! away, you want wit " ; and Killigrew's *Parson's Wedding* (Hazlitt's *Dodsley*, xiv. 532), 1663 : " *Parson.* Sir, my business is praying, not epilogues. *Captain.* With that face ? " There is a sidenote to the line " Despatch him, therefore, while we are alone," of Woodes' *Conflict of Conscience* (Hazlitt's *Dodsley*, vi. 53), 1581 : " Hipocrisy [aside] On your face, sir," which is the same expression slightly altered.

133. *So I heard you say*] Another rural witticism. It occurs in Jonson's *Bartholomew Fair* Act iii : " *Waspe.* Yet these will serve to pick the pictures out of your pockets, you shall see. *Cokes.* So I heard them say. Pray thee mind him not, fellow." The meaning may be paraphrased by our " you don't say so."

134, 135. *farewell. Fair weather after you*] Jaquenetta, who has been very ill-treated by the commentators, completes the rustic saw. Compare *Arden of Faversham*, iv. 3 (1592) : " See you follow us. . . . *Michael.* So. Fair weather after you ! " ; and *Wily Beguiled* (Malone Soc., ed. Greg, lines 607-9), 1606 : " Come, follow us, good Wench. *Peg.* I, farewell, faire weather after you." It occurs also in Middleton. Silena in *Mother Bombie*, ii. 3, has another form, " farewell frost."

139, 140. *on a full stomach*] There is a quibble between the literal meaning and the sense " proudly," " courageously," which can be seen

Arm. Thou shalt be heavily punished.

Cost. I am more bound to you than your fellows, for they are but lightly rewarded.

Arm. Take away this villain: shut him up.

Moth. Come, you transgressing slave: away!

Cost. Let me not be pent up, sir; I will fast, being loose.

Moth. No, sir, that were fast and loose: thou shalt to prison.

Cost. Well, if ever I do see the merry days of desolation that I have seen, some shall see—

Moth. What shall some see?

Cost. Nay, nothing, Master Moth, but what they look upon. It is not for prisoners to be too silent in their words, and therefore I will say nothing: I thank God I have as little patience as another man, and therefore I can be quiet. [*Exeunt Moth and Costard.*

Arm. I do affect the very ground, which is base, where her shoe, which is baser, guided by her foot, which is basest, doth tread. I shall be forsworn, which is

146. *fast*] *be fast* Ff 2, 3, 4. 153. *not*] omitted Q 2. *be too silent*] Q 1; *be silent* Ff, Q 2. 154. *words*] *wards* Johnson conj. 156. *Exeunt . . . Costard*] Exit Q 1.

in Palsgrave's *Lesclaircissement*, p. 230 (1530), "*Full-stomacht.*" "Full-stomacht" occurs in Greene and Nashe; and compare *Captain Smith* (Arber, p. 864), 1629: "Excellent, swift, stomack full, Tartarian horse." With a good heart.

142. *fellows*] servants. See *1 Henry IV.* IV. ii. 68: "Tell me, Jack, whose fellows are these that come after? *Falstaff.* Mine, Hal, mine."

147. *fast and loose*] a cheating trick. Most of the early examples refer it to the gipsies, as in *Antony and Cleopatra*, IV. x. 41. Compare Whetstone, *Promos and Cassandra* (pt. i.), ii. vi (Hazlitt, *Sh. Lib.*, vi. 226), 1578: "At fast or loose, with my Giptian, I meane to have a cast: Tenne to one I read his fortune by the Marymas fast" (spoken by a hangman); and Lyly, *Euphues and his England*, 1580: "Thus with the Ægyptian thou playest fast or loose" (Arber, p. 326). And Ben Jonson assigns it to a gipsy in his *Masque of the Metamorphosed Gipsies*.

157-159. *base . . . baser . . . basest*] This toying with a word is a characteristic of Sir Philip Sidney's *Arcadia*, rather than of Lyly, who repeats the letter and the sound, not the word itself. Hart quotes one or two passages from bk. iii.: "so terrible was his force, and yet was his quicknes more forcible then his force, and his judgement more quick then his quicknes"; "and yet did the ones strength excel in nimblenes, and the others nimblenes excel in strength but now strength and nimblenes were both gone"; "exceedingly a great argument of falsehood, if I love. And how can that be true love which is falsely attempted? Love is a familiar; Love is a devil: there is no evil angel but Love. Yet was Samson so tempted, and he had an excellent strength; yet was Solomon so seduced, and he had a very good wit. Cupid's butt-shaft is too hard for Hercules' club, and therefore too much odds for a Spaniard's rapier. The first

163. *was Samson*] *was Sampson* Q 1; *Sampson was* Ff, Q 2.

sory for Pamela, but exceedingly exceeding that exceedingnes in feare for Philoclea." See again Armado's letter, IV. i. 64-65; and compare Puttenham, p. 213: "Then have ye a figure which the Latines call *Traductio*, and I the tranlacer: which is when ye turne and tranlace a word into many sundry shapes as the Tailor doth his garment, and after that sort to play with him in your dittie." This is Arcadianism exactly, but Armado does not go the whole length.

160. *argument*] proof.

162. *familiar*] an attendant spirit; as in *1 Henry VI.* III. ii. 122 and *2 Henry VI.* IV. iii. 114. "Behold there is a woman that hath a familiar spirit at Endor" (1 Samuel xxviii. 7).

165. *Cupid's butt-shaft*] "strong unbarbed arrows used in the field exercises of the day" (Gifford). They hit hard but were easily extracted, so that they were suitable for Cupid's quiver. Compare *Romeo and Juliet*, II. iv. 15: "The very pin of his heart cleft with the blind bow-boy's butt-shaft." No other example has been adduced by the authorities, save Hart's from Ben Jonson's *Cynthia's Revels*, V. iii. (again in Cupid's possession): "I fear thou hast not arrows for the purpose. *Cupid.* O yes, here be of all sorts—flights, rovers and butt-shafts." See note at "bird-bolt," IV. iii. 23.

167. *Spaniard's rapier*] See note on line 71 above.

167, 168. *first and second cause*] Compare *As You Like It*, V. iv. 52, 69, and *Romeo and Juliet*, II. iv. 26. Halliwell quoted Vincentio Saviolo's *Practise*, (*Of . . . honorable Quarrels*, 1594): "I will onely treate of that which I shall judge meetest by a generall rule to be observed, and include all combats under two heads. First, then, I judge it not meet that a man should hazard himselfe in the perill of death, but for such a cause as deserveth it, so as if a man be accused of such a defect as deserve to be punished with death, in this case combate might bee graunted. Againe, because that in an honourable person, his honor ought to be preferred before his life, if it happen him to have such a defect laid against him, as in respect thereof he were by lawe to be accounted dishonorable, and should therefore be disgraced before the tribunall seate, upon such a quarrell my opinion is that hee be not able by lawe to clere himself thereof." Later critics have felt that some other source must be sought, giving the two causes more definitely and concisely, and in *M.L.R.*, xii. 76, H. B. Charlton claimed to have found it in a passage from *The Book of Honor and Armes*, attributed to Sir William Segar (1590), which is clearly the germ of Saviolo's dissertation: "I say then

and second cause will not serve my turn; the passado he respects not, the duello he regards not: his disgrace is to be called boy, but his glory is to subdue men. Adieu, valour! rust, rapier! be still, drum! for your manager is in love; yea, he loveth. Assist me, some extemporal god of rhyme, for I am

169. *duello*] *duella* Q 1. 172. *manager*] *Armiger* Collier MS.(!)

that the causes of all quarrell whereupon it behoueth to use the triall of Armes, may be reduced into two: for it seemeth to me not reasonable, that any man should expose himselfe to the perill of death, save onelie for such occasions as doo deserue death. Wherefore whensoeuer one man doth accuse another of such a crime as meriteth death, in that case the Combat ought to be graunted. The second cause of Combat is Honor, because among persons of reputation, Honor is preferred before life." Yet Armado speaks of the "causes" not precisely, as the reasons for embarking on a quarrel, but generally, as part of the regulations for its conduct. Unlike Touchstone, Cupid will not fight "by the book." I think, despite Charlton's discovery, that the reference is not a particular one to Segar but a general one to Saviolo and Caranza (*De la Filosofia de las Armas*, 1569) whose prescription of an exact etiquette of duelling is constantly ridiculed by Jonson as well as by Shakespeare. A better parallel is Jonson's *Alchemist*, IV. i. (1610): Subtle instructs Kastrill on the "grammar and logic and rhetoric of quarrelling," and tells him "You must render causes, child, Your first and second intentions, know your causes."

169. *passado*] See *Romeo and Juliet*, II. iv. 26, and III. i. 88. "A forward thrust with the sword one foot being advanced at the same time" (*New Eng. Dict.*). From the Spanish *pasada*. Jonson gives it *passada* in *Every Man in his Humour*. Howell's *Vocabulary* (1659) gives the different forms: "To make a pass, *Far' una passata; Faire une passade; Hazer passada*," in Italian, French and Spanish. Marston, quoting from Saviolo apparently, has "sly passatas, Stramazones, resolute stocatas" (*Scourge of Villainy*, Sat. xi. [1598]).

169. *duello*] the correct practise of duelling. Both this word and "duellist" (Harvey's *Pierce's Supererogation*, 1592) preceded "duel" in English use. Ben Jonson has it in *Cynthia's Revels*, I. i. (1600): "one that . . . was your first that ever enriched his country with the true laws of the duello." Compare *Gesta Grayorum*, 1594 (Malone Soc., ed. Greg, p. 28): "Item, no Knight of this Order shall, in point of Honour, resort to any Grammar-rules out of the Books *De Du*[*e*]*llo*, or such like." This is perhaps a direct reference to Caranza's work.

172. *manager*] The earliest example of this word in *New Eng. Dict.* Compare Jonson, *Every Man in His Humour*, I. iv. (1598): You do not manage your weapon with any facility or grace to invite me." "Manage arms" occurs five times in Marlowe's *Tamburlaine*, part i. Armado's mock-dignity here becomes the true thing in *Othello*, III. iii. 350-4.

173. *extemporal*] Compare G. Harvey (Grosart, i. 111), 1579: "To his very unfriendly frende that procurid the edition of his so slender and extemporall devises."

sure I shall turn sonnet. Devise, wit ; write, pen ; for I am for whole volumes in folio. [*Exit.*

174. *sonnet*] Ff, Qq ; *sonneteer* or *sonneter* Hanmer, etc. ; *a sonnet* Amyot ; *sonnets* Verplanck, Halliwell ; *sonnet-maker*, *sonnet-monger*, *sonnetist* various modern editors.

174. *turn sonnet*] It is odd that editors have boggled at the absence of article here, while remaining unmoved by IV. iii. 132—" did never sonnet for her sake compile." For *turn* in this sense, compare " turn his merry note Unto the sweet bird's throat " (*As You Like It*, II. v. 3). Furness thinks that Armado means he will become an abstract sonnet, he is so saturated with love. Hart is surely wrong to take as a parallel the " turn a song " in Thos. Brewer's (prose) *Merry Devil of Edmonton*, 1608 (1631 text ed. Abrams, p. 263) : " M. Parson turned his song," and " they turned it to his mind " (*ibid.*) where the word means " changed." At IV. i. 87 we find the sonnet Armado turns. The expression in *As You Like It* occurs earlier in Hall's *Satires*, VI. i. (1598) : " Whiles threadbare Martiall turns his merry note."

174, 175. *Devise . . . in folio*] Compare G. Harvey, *Foure Letters* (Grosart, i. 200), 1592 : " a famous deviser in folio."

ACT II

SCENE I

Enter the PRINCESS *of France,* MARIA, KATHARINE, ROSALINE, BOYET, *Lords, and other Attendants.*

Boyet. Now, madam, summon up your dearest spirits :
Consider who the king your father sends,
To whom he sends, and what's his embassy :
Yourself, held precious in the world's esteem,
To parley with the sole inheritor
Of all perfections that a man may owe,
Matchless Navarre ; the plea of no less weight
Than Aquitaine, a dowry for a queen.
Be now as prodigal of all dear grace
As Nature was in making graces dear
When she did starve the general world beside,
And prodigally gave them all to you.
Prin. Good Lord Boyet, my beauty, though but mean,
Needs not the painted flourish of your praise :
Beauty is bought by judgment of the eye,
Not utter'd by base sale of chapmen's tongues.
I am less proud to hear you tell my worth

ACT II

Scene I

Enter . . .] Rowe ; *Enter the Princesse of France with three attending Ladies and three Lordes* Qq, Ff. 13. *Prin.*] Ff 2, 3, 4 ; *Queene* Qq, F 1. *Lord*] *L.* Qq, Ff.

1. *summon up your dearest spirits*] bring forward your best wits. Compare " muster your wits," v. ii. 85 ; an expression used by Dekker (Grosart, ii. 95).

5. *inheritor*] owner. Compare Dekker, *Belman of London* (Grosart, iii. 74) : " The admiration of these Bewties made mee so enamoured, and so really in love with the inheritor of them."

6. *owe*] own ; as at I. ii. 100 ; and commonly.

7. *plea*] that which is pleaded for.

14. *flourish*] ornamentation.

16. *chapmen*] merchants, dealers. See Introduction, 5.23.

Than you much willing to be counted wise
In spending your wit in the praise of mine.
But now to task the tasker: good Boyet,
You are not ignorant all-telling fame
Doth noise abroad Navarre hath made a vow,
Till painful study shall outwear three years,
No woman may approach his silent court:
Therefore to's seemeth it a needful course,
Before we enter his forbidden gates,
To know his pleasure; and in that behalf,
Bold of your worthiness, we single you
As our best-moving fair solicitor.
Tell him the daughter of the King of France,
On serious business craving quick dispatch,
Importunes personal conference with his grace.
Haste, signify so much; while we attend,
Like humble-visag'd suitors, his high will.

Boyet. Proud of employment, willingly I go.

Prin. All pride is willing pride, and yours is so. [*Exit Boyet.*
Who are the votaries, my loving lords,
That are vow-fellows with this virtuous duke?

First Lord. Lord Longaville is one.

Prin. Know you the man?

Mar. I know him, madam: at a marriage-feast,
Between Lord Perigort and the beauteous heir

19. *your wit in the praise*] Qq, F 1; *thus your wit in praise*, Ff 2, 3, 4. 21. *You . . .*] Princ. *You . . .* F 1, Q 2. 32. *Importunes*] *Importuous* Q 1. 34. *visag'd*] *visage* Q 1; *visaged* Ff, Q 2. 36. [*Exit Boyet*] Dyce; *Exit* Qq, Ff (after previous line). 37, 38. Prose in Qq, Ff; verse Rowe (ed. 2) *et seq.* 39. First Lord. *Lord Longaville*] Capell; Lor. *Longavill* Qq, Ff. 40. *Mar.*] Rowe; *1 Lady.* Qq, Ff. 40-43. *madam: at . . . solemnized In*] Capell; *madame at . . solemnized. In* Qq, Ff.

20. *task the tasker*] task him who tasks; like the old "the guiler is beguiled" in Gower.

23. *outwear*] wear away, pass (the time). Compare Spenser, *Faerie Queene* (1590), III. xii. 29: "All that day she outwore in wandering."

28. *Bold*] confident.

29. *fair*] just, equitable.

34. *humble-visag'd*] Elsewhere Shakespeare has *grim-visaged*, *pale-visaged*, *tripe-visaged*. "Sable-visaged night" occurs in the Prologue to *The Merry Devil of Edmonton* (*circa* 1600); Jonson speaks of the "brass-visaged monster Barbarism" (*Every Man in his Humour*). The Quarto "visage" may be due to e : d confusion, so easy in English script (see Introduction, 2.4).

42. *solemnized*] The second syllable bears the accent.

Of Jaques Falconbridge, solemnized
In Normandy, saw I this Longaville:
A man of sovereign parts he is esteem'd,
Well fitted in arts, glorious in arms;
Nothing becomes him ill that he would well.
The only soil of his fair virtue's gloss,
If virtue's gloss will stain with any soil,
Is a sharp wit match'd with too blunt a will;
Whose edge hath power to cut, whose will still wills
It should none spare that come within his power.

Prin. Some merry mocking lord, belike; is't so?

Mar. They say so most that most his humours know.

Prin. Such short-liv'd wits do wither as they grow.
Who are the rest?

Kath. The young Dumain, a well accomplish'd youth,
Of all that virtue love for virtue lov'd:
Most power to do most harm, least knowing ill,
For he hath wit to make an ill shape good,
And shape to win grace though he had no wit.
I saw him at the Duke Alençon's once;

44. *of sovereign parts*] Ff, Q 2; *of sovereign peerelsse* Q 1. 45. *in arts*] Qq, F 1; *in the arts* Ff 2, 3, 4. 47, 48. *gloss*] *glose* Q 1. 56. *Kath.*] Rowe; 2. *Lad.* Qq, Ff. 60. *he*] *she* F 1, Q 2. 61. *Alençon's*] *Alansoes* Qq, F 1.

44. *sovereign parts*] Dover Wilson says the Q 1 "peerelsse" is probably "pertes" misread as "perles"; taken in isolation it looks like a simple misprint for "peerlesse" (one letter transposed). This suggests that Shakespeare wrote "sovereign," crossed it out and substituted "peerless" with a noun following; and that the compositor, who we know from IV. iii. 313 and V. ii. 807 was apt to blunder over erasures, did so here. The missing noun may well have been the "parts" of the Folio; certainly we cannot now make any better guess.

46. *would well*] intends kindly. His intention is too often malicious.

54. *Short-liv'd wits*] Ascham, in *The Scholemaster* (Arber, pp. 32-34), has much about quick wits: "Quicke wittes commonlie be apte to take, unapte to keepe . . . like over sharpe tooles, whose edges be verie soone turned. . . . In youthe also they be readie scoffers, privie mockers, and ever over light and merry. . . . They be like trees that shewe forth faire blossoms . . . but bring out small and not long lasting fruite . . . amongest a number of quicke wittes in youthe, fewe be found in the end . . . but decay and vanish, men know not which way." Compare Harvey's *Foure Letters* (Grosart, i. 193): "Flourishing M. Greene is most wofully faded, and whilest I am bemoaning his overpiteous decay; and discoursing the usuall success of such ranke wittes, loe, his sworne brother, M. Pierce Penni-lesse (still more paltery)," etc.

And much too little of that good I saw
Is my report to his great worthiness.

Ros. Another of these students at that time
Was there with him, if I have heard a truth,
Berowne they call him ; but a merrier man,
Within the limit of becoming mirth,
I never spent an hour's talk withal.
His eye begets occasion for his wit ;
For every object that the one doth catch
The other turns to a mirth-moving jest,
Which his fair tongue (conceit's expositor)
Delivers in such apt and gracious words
That aged ears play truant at his tales,
And younger hearings are quite ravished ;
So sweet and voluble is his discourse.

Prin. God bless my ladies ! are they all in love,
That every one her own hath garnished
With such bedecking ornaments of praise ?

First Lord. Here comes Boyet.

Re-enter BOYET.

Prin. Now, what admittance, lord ?

Boyet. Navarre had notice of your fair approach ;
And he and his competitors in oath
Were all address'd to meet you, gentle lady,
Before I came. Marry, thus much I have learnt ;
He rather means to lodge you in the field,

64. *Ros.*] Rowe ; *3 Lad.* Qq, Ff. 65. *if*] Q 1 ; *as* Ff, Q 2.
80. *First Lord*] *Lord* Q 1 ; *Ma.* Ff, Q 2. 84. *much*] omitted Ff 2, 3, 4.

66. *Berowne . . . but a merrier*] Is there a pun on *brown*, meaning sombre?

74. *play truant*] leave their work, in order to listen.

76. *voluble*] fluent. See again III. i. 64 ; *The Comedy of Errors*, II. i. 92 ; and *Othello*, II. i. 242. In Cotgrave, 1611. Dekker uses it in his *Lanthorne and Candle-Light* (Grosart, iii. 188), 1609 : " the high and ratling Dutch ; the unfruitfull crabbed Irish, and the voluble significant Welch." Puttenham, in his *Arte of English Poesie* (published 1589), says " The utterance in prose is not of so great efficacie, because . . . not so voluble and slipper on the tongue " (p. 24) ; and at p. 156 : " a broad and voluble tong, thinne and movable lippes, teeth even." And p. 111, speaking of the sphere : " he is even and smooth . . . most voluble and apt to turne." These last examples suffice to illustrate III. i. 64.

80. *admittance*] permission to enter.

82. *competitors*] associates, partners. Cf. *Two Gentlemen of Verona*, II. vi. 35.

83. *address'd*] made ready.

Like one that comes here to besiege his court,
Than seek a dispensation for his oath,
To let you enter his unpeopled house.
Here comes Navarre.

Enter KING, LONGAVILLE, DUMAIN, BEROWNE, *and Attendants.*

King. Fair princess, welcome to the court of Navarre.
Prin. Fair I give you back again ; and welcome I have not yet : the roof of this court is too high to be yours, and welcome to the wide fields too base to be mine.
King. You shall be welcome, madam, to my court.
Prin. I will be welcome then : conduct me thither.
King. Hear me, dear lady ; I have sworn an oath.
Prin. Our Lady help my lord ! he'll be forsworn.
King. Not for the world, fair madam, by my will.
Prin. Why, will shall break it will, and nothing else.
King. Your ladyship is ignorant what it is.
Prin. Were my lord so, his ignorance were wise,
Where now his knowledge must prove ignorance.
I hear your grace hath sworn out house-keeping :

88. *unpeopled*] Ff, Q 2 ; *unpeeled* Q 1, Cambridge (1863). 89. [*The Ladies mask*] Capell. 90. *King*] *Navar.* Qq, Ff. 100. *it will*] Qq, Ff ; *it ; will* Capell *et seq.*

88. *unpeopled*] Dover Wilson takes the unique " unpeeled " of Q 1 as a misprint for " unpeepled." I agree. Compare *As You Like It*, III. ii. 134 : " Why should this a desert be? For is it unpeopled ? " and *Richard II.* I. ii. 69 : " empty lodgings and unfurnish'd walls, Unpeopled offices." The term here has the sense of without servants or attendance suitable for such guests. " People," meaning retinue, servants, is very commonly found in Shakespeare, and the King has forsworn hospitality and womankind.

99. *by my will*] willingly.

100. *it will*] The Q 1 punctuation is far from infallible ; Capell's version makes good sense (that making and breaking an oath are actions equally arbitrary) and echoes Berowne's speech on necessity (I. i. 148). But " it will " is good Shakespearean baby-talk (see *Lear*, I. iv. 239 and, for the tone, *Troilus and Cressida*, IV. ii. 30). The Princess treats the King as a wilful child—compare the " Don't-care was *made* to care " of nurseries.

104. *sworn out house-keeping*] sworn house-keeping at an end, sworn it away, outsworn it, as in I. ii. 60. The Princess is alluding to the deadly sin of forgoing and banishing hospitality, another sense of the word " house-keeping." This was

'Tis deadly sin to keep that oath, my lord,
And sin to break it.
But pardon me, I am too sudden-bold :
To teach a teacher ill beseemeth me.
Vouchsafe to read the purpose of my coming,
And suddenly resolve me in my suit.
King. Madam, I will, if suddenly I may.
Prin. You will the sooner that I were away,
For you'll prove perjur'd if you make me stay.
[*Ber.* Did not I dance with you in Brabant once ?
Ros. Did not I dance with you in Brabant once ?
Ber. I know you did.
Ros. How needless was it then to ask the question !
Ber. You must not be so quick.
Ros. 'Tis long of you that spur me with such questions.
Ber. Your wit's too hot, it speeds too fast, 'twill tire.
Ros. Not till it leave the rider in the mire.
Ber. What time o' day ?
Ros. The hour that fools should ask.
Ber. Now fair befall your mask !

106, 107. *And . . . sudden-bold*] one line Q 1. 106. *And*] *Not* Hanmer, Dyce. 110. *Gives a paper.*] Collier MS. 115, 117. etc., to 125. *Ros.*] *Kather.* Q 1. 116-118. Two lines ending *then, quick.* Capell.

one of the cries of the people, especially the " poor players," against the rich at the time.

106. *And sin*] Hanmer's emendation is quite unwarranted. The King is in a quandary : he must commit one or other deadly sin—against charity if he keeps his oath, against good faith if he breaks it.

110. *suddenly*] immediately.

114-128. *Did not I . . . be gone*] The reasons for considering this, and the parallel interchange at 180-193 below, as accidental survivals from an early draft are given in the Introduction, 2.52. The omission of the passage, however, does not leave much time for the King to study the paper setting out the French claim.

118. *quick*] sharp.

119. *long of you*] owing to you. Common provincially. Compare Palsgrave, 1530 : " I am longe of this strife : *je suis en cause de cest estrif.*"

spur . . . questions] " Spur " puns on the northern word " speer," to put a question. The complete phrase occurs in J. Rainoldes, *Overthrow of State Plays* (ed. 1629, p. 60), 1593 : " You were disposed to spurre him idle questions."

119, 120. *spur . . . wit's . . . speeds*] *spur* and *speed* come together naturally—both are frequently applied to wit. As " Fresh wits need no spur " (Ben Jonson, *Case is Altered*, II. iii. [1598]) ; and " fooled you up In a new suit with the best wits in being, And kept their speed."

124. *fair befall*] A very old phrase occurring in Langland's *Piers the Plowman* (1377), and a favourite with Shakespeare. Craig refers to Burns'

Ros. Fair fall the face it covers !
Ber. And send you many lovers !
Ros. Amen, so you be none.
Ber. Nay, then will I be gone.]
King. Madam, your father here doth intimate
The payment of a hundred thousand crowns ;
Being but the one half of an entire sum
Disbursed by my father in his wars.
But say that he, or we, as neither have,
Receiv'd that sum, yet there remains unpaid
A hundred thousand more ; in surety of the which,
One part of Aquitaine is bound to us,
Although not valued to the money's worth.
If then the king your father will restore
But that one half which is unsatisfied,
We will give up our right in Aquitaine,
And hold fair friendship with his majesty.
But that, it seems, he little purposeth,
For here he doth demand to have repaid
A hundred thousand crowns ; and not demands
On payment of a hundred thousand crowns
To have his title live in Aquitaine ;
Which we much rather had depart withal,
And have the money by our father lent,
Than Aquitaine, so gelded as it is.

129. *King*] Ff. ; *Ferd.* Q 1. The heading persists until the business discussion is concluded (it last appears before line 167). 135. *A*] Q 1 ; *An* Ff, Q 2. 143. *repaid*] *repaie* F 1, Q 2. 145. *On*] Theobald ; *One* Qq, Ff.

Lines to a Haggis : " Fair fa' your honest sonsy face." For the *mask* see Introduction, 2.52.

129. *intimate*] informs us of. Joseph Hunter (*New Illustrations*, 1845) was the first to claim an historical basis for this incident. He referred it to an engagement by Charles VI, about 1420, to pay Charles of Aragon, King of Navarre, 200,000 crowns. Sidney Lee suggested the more nearly contemporary negotiations (1586) between Catherine de Médicis and Henri of Navarre which partly concerned Aquitaine. An even more exact parallel has been traced by Abel Lefranc (*Sous le Masque de Shakespeare*, II. p. 90) with the embassy of Marguerite de Valois to her husband, Henri, in 1579, to settle disputes that had arisen over her dowry. See Introduction, 5.21.

147. *depart withal*] part with, surrender.

149. *gelded*] impaired, reduced in power or value. The term was commonly applied to livings where the patron put in the incumbent, pocketing most of the income himself. Nashe says that " he that first

Dear princess, were not his requests so far
From reason's yielding, your fair self should make
A yielding 'gainst some reason in my breast,
And go well satisfied to France again.

Prin. You do the king my father too much wrong,
And wrong the reputation of your name,
In so unseeming to confess receipt
Of that which hath so faithfully been paid.

King. I do protest I never heard of it;
And if you prove it I'll repay it back,
Or yield up Aquitaine.

Prin. We arrest your word:
Boyet, you can produce acquittances
For such a sum from special officers
Of Charles his father.

King. Satisfy me so.

Boyet. So please your grace, the packet is not come
Where that and other specialties are bound:
To-morrow you shall have a sight of them.

King. It shall suffice me: at which interview
All liberal reason I will yield unto.
Meantime, receive such welcome at my hand
As honour, without breach of honour, may
Make tender of to thy true worthiness.
You may not come fair princess, within my gates;

168. *I will*] Q 1; *would I* Ff, Q 2. 172. *within*] Q 1; *in* Ff, Q 2.

gelt religion of Church-livings . . . was Cardinal Wolsey" (*Unfortunate Traveller* [McKerrow, ii. 238]), 1594. "A vicarige . . . gelded" is in *Return from Parnassus* (ed. W. D. Macray, p. 98), 1602; "gelded chapel" in Hall's *Satires*, IV. ii. (1598); "gelded vicarage" in Marston and Shirley; and "gelded bishoprick" in Sir John Harington (*Nugae Antiquae*, i. 101).

160. *arrest your word*] seize your word as security. The expression occurs again in *Measure for Measure*, II. iv. 134. The *New Eng. Dict.* has these two and no other instances. Shakespeare may have found this uncommon expression in Sidney's *Arcadia*, bk. i. (Feuillerat, i. 99), *ante* 1586: "She tooke the advauntage one daye, uppon Phalantus unconscionable praysinges of her, and certaine castawaie vows, howe much he would doo for her sake, to arrest his woord assoone as it was out of his mouth, and by the vertue thereof to charge him to goe with her."

172. *fair princess, within*] Dover Wilson suspects that "queen" stood for "princess" in the first draft and that Shakespeare corrected the word without adjusting the metre. If to write smoothly was really an aim of

But here without you shall be so receiv'd
As you shall deem your self lodg'd in my heart,
Though so denied fair harbour in my house.
Your own good thoughts excuse me, and farewell :
To-morrow shall we visit you again.

Prin. Sweet health and fair desires consort your grace !

King. Thy own wish wish I thee in every place ! [*Exit.*

Ber. Lady, I will commend you to mine own heart.

Ros. Pray you do my commendations ; I would be glad to see it.

Ber. I would you heard it groan.

Ros. Is the fool sick ?

Ber. Sick at the heart.

Ros. Alack ! let it blood.

Ber. Would that do it good ?

Ros. My physic says, ay.

Ber. Will you prick't with your eye ?

Ros. No point, with my knife.

Ber. Now God save thy life !

Ros. And yours, from long living !

Ber. I cannot stay thanksgiving.] [*Retiring.*

175. *fair*] Q 1 ; *farther* Ff, Q 2. 177. *Shall we*] Q 1 ; *we shall* Ff, Q 2. 180. *mine own*] Q 2 ; *my none* Q 1 ; *my own* Ff. 180, 183, 185, 187, 189, 191, 193. *Ber.*] Q 1 ; *Boy.* Ff, Q 2. 184. *fool*] Q 1 ; *soul* Ff, Q 2. 190. *No point*] *No poynt* (italics) Qq, Ff. 193. [*Retiring*] Capell ; [*Exit. Enter Dumain* Qq, Ff.

Shakespeare's at this date, such carelessness would be more than Shakespearean ; if not, need we boggle at such roughnesses here or elsewhere ?

184. *fool*] The word is a favourite with Shakespeare, who uses the phrase " poor fool " where we should say " poor thing." Compare the Nurse's use of " pretty fool " in *Romeo and Juliet*, I. iii. 31 ; and *Much Ado*, II. i. 328.

186. *let it blood*] bleed him. An expression of the time, as in Lyly's *Mydas*, II. i. : " Hee is the man, that being let blood, carries his arme in a scarfe of his mistresse favour."

190. *No point*] (i) it's blunt, (ii) not at all. Florio (*World of Words*, 1598) has : " *Punto*, . . . never a whit, no jot, no point as the frenchmen say." Stock repartee, used even by Journeyman Firk (Dekker, *Shoemaker's Holiday*, IV. iv. 96). The repetition of both tag and pun at V. ii. 277 supports the view that the present passage is an early draft left uncancelled.

193. *I cannot stay thanksgiving*] This appears to trouble commentators. Berowne's rejoinder to Rosaline's unkind wishes is that he cannot spare the time to return proper thanks for them.

Dum. Sir, I pray you, a word : what lady is that same ?
Boyet. The heir of Alençon, Katharine her name.
Dum. A gallant lady. Monsieur, fare you well. [*Exit.*
Long. I beseech you a word : what is she in the white ?
Boyet. A woman sometimes, an you saw her in the light.
Long. Perchance light in the light. I desire her name.
Boyet. She hath but one for herself ; to desire that were a shame.
Long. Pray you, sir, whose daughter ?
Boyet. Her mother's, I have heard.
Long. God's blessing on your beard !
Boyet. Good sir, be not offended.
She is an heir of Falconbridge.
Long. Nay, my choler is ended.
She is a most sweet lady.
Boyet. Not unlike, sir ; that may be. [*Exit Long.*
Ber. What's her name in the cap ?
Boyet. Rosaline, by good hap.
Ber. Is she wedded or no ?
Boyet. To her will sir, or so.
Ber. O you are welcome, sir. Adieu.
Boyet. Farewell to me, sir, and welcome to you. [*Exit Ber.*
Mar. That last is Berowne, the merry mad-cap lord :

195. *Katharine*] Singer (Capell conj.) ; *Rosaline* Qq, Ff. 198. *an*] *and* Q 1 ; *if* Ff, Q 2. 203. *on*] Qq, *a* Ff. 210. *Rosaline*] Singer ; *Katharine* Qq, Ff. 213. *O you*] Q 1 ; *You* Ff, Q 2. 214. [*Exit Berowne*] Q 1 ; *Exit.* Ff, Q 2.

195. *Katharine*] See Introduction, 2.52.

198. *light*] wanton, quibblingly. A very common sense in Shakespeare.

203. *blessing on your beard*] Longaville, serious before, shows his irritation in mocking the waggish Boyet. Satirical references to one's beard were very common forms of chaff, and were generally summed up in the phrase " to play with one's beard," i.e. to insult, belittle. It occurs in Jonson's *Bartholomew Fair*, IV. iii. Johnson says : " may you have sense more proportionate to your beard," but he often takes gibes too seriously.

212. *or so*] " a mere expletive " (Schmidt, who collects ten examples in Shakespeare). Rather, as Craig says, " or something of that sort." See again v. i. 147. Compare Lyly's *Mother Bombie*, iv. 2 : " He would never tire—it may be he would be so weary hee would goe no further, or so."

213. *O you*] see note, III. i. 144.

214. *Farewell . . . and welcome*] You are welcome to go. Hardly obsolete.

215. *mad cap*] The earliest example of the word in the *New Eng. Dict.* Compare " mad wenches," line 257 below, and again at v. ii. 264. I reject the always violent senses of

Not a word with him but a jest.
Boyet. And every jest but a word.
Prin. It was well done of you to take him at his word.
Boyet. I was as willing to grapple as he was to board.
Kath. Two hot sheeps, marry !
Boyet. And wherefore not ships ?
No sheep, sweet lamb, unless we feed on your lips.
Kath. You sheep, and I pasture : shall that finish the jest ?
Boyet. So you grant pasture for me.
Kath. Not so, gentle beast :
My lips are no common, though several they be.
Boyet. Belonging to whom ?
Kath. To my fortunes and me.
Prin. Good wits will be jangling ; but, gentles, agree :

219. *Kath.*] *La. Ka.* Q 1 ; *La. Ma.* F 1. 222. [*Offering to kiss her*] Capell.

" mad " in this place as given in the *New Eng. Dict.* The word has a playful use, nearly our " droll." Greene has " crue of Popish madcaps " in *The Spanish Masquerado* (Grosart, v. 265), which is probably earlier. There, and again in his *Orlando Furioso*, the word means madman, but not here. The word " mad-cap " occurs in Lyly's *Endymion*, v. ii. : " O *lepidum caput*, O mad-cap master ! You were worthy to winne Dipsas were she as olde againe."

217. *take him at his word*] take him up, or talk to him in his own strain. Not our sense of adopting a suggestion, which occurs in *The Comedy of Errors*, I. ii. 17.

219. *ships*] pronounced like " sheeps " at this time, and affording quibbling again in *The Two Gentlemen of Verona*, I. i. 73, and in *The Comedy of Errors*, IV. i. 94, two of Shakespeare's earliest plays. So engrained was this pun that the saying " lose not the sheep for a halfp'orth of tar " was sometimes written " ship," which serves as well.

220. *feed on your lips*] Malone appropriately cites *Venus and Adonis :* " Feed where thou wilt, on mountain or on dale ; Graze on my lips " (Steevens, 1793).

223. *common, though several*] " fields that were enclosed were called severals, in opposition to commons ; the former belonging to individuals, the latter to the inhabitants generally " (Halliwell). Katharine says : " no doubt my lips are good pasturing, but they are private and reserved," with quibbling on " several." Boyet immediately sees her meaning and asks for whom. Nares and Steevens give several examples, but the best is Johnson's : " Of a lord that was newly married, one observed that he grew fat ; ' Yes,' said Sir Walter Raleigh, ' any beast will grow fat, if you take him from the common and graze him in the several.' " Malone, Nares and others make a difficulty out of the use of " though " here quite needlessly. But should they insist upon it, the reply is easy : Shakespeare, like other writers of the time, gave " though " the meaning " since," " inasmuch as." See *Othello*, I. i. 70, and III. iii. 146.

225. *Good wits*, etc.] Lyly has " Good wits will apply " (*Sapho and Phao*, III. ii. [1581]). Dekker put in

This civil war of wits were much better us'd
On Navarre and his book-men, for here 'tis abus'd.

Boyet. If my observation, which very seldom lies,
By the heart's still rhetoric disclosed with eyes
Deceive me not now, Navarre is infected.

Prin. With what?

Boyet. With that which we lovers entitle affected.

Prin. Your reason?

Boyet. Why, all his behaviours did make their retire
To the court of his eye, peeping thorough desire:
His heart, like an agate, with your print impress'd,
Proud with his form, in his eye pride express'd:
His tongue, all impatient to speak and not see,
Did stumble with haste in his eyesight to be;
All senses to that sense did make their repair,
To feel only looking on fairest of fair:
Methought all his senses were lock'd in his eye,
As jewels in crystal for some prince to buy;

234. *did*] Q 1; *doe* Ff, Q 2.

"Good wits love good wine" (*The Honest Whore*, part ii.); and "Good wits jump" became proverbial later (*Wits Recreations*, 1640).

227. *book-men*] scholars. See below, IV. ii. 34, for the only other use of the word in Shakespeare. Compare Greene's *Looking-Glass for London*, 1143-4, (Grosart, xiv. 53): "And though the Sailer is no booke-man held, He knowes more Art than ever booke-men read." Nashe uses the expression in *Summer's Last Will*, line 1421 (McKerrow, III. 278).

229. *still rhetoric*] Malone compares Daniel, *Complaint of Rosalind* (1594): "Sweet silent rhetorick of persuading eyes; Dumb eloquence."

234. *all his behaviours*] all his powers of expression were concentrated in his eye, and shared in the longing look he gave you.

235. *thorough*] an old form of "through," as in *thoroughfare*.

236. *like an agate*] Figures and mottoes were commonly cut in agate and worn as rings, the lineal descendants of the engraved gems of the ancients. Compare *Doctor Dodypoll* (Bullen's *Old Plays*, iii. 111): "See there (my Lord) this agget that containes The image of that Goddesse and her sonne Whom auncients held the sovereignes of Love"; and in Nichols' *Progresses*, ii. 52, a New Year's gift of 1576-77 is "an agathe of Neptune sett with 6 very small rubyes," etc.

237. *his form*] the form impressed on the heart—the Princess's image.

238. *His tongue . . .*] "His tongue, not able to endure the having merely the power of speaking without that of seeing" (Dyce).

241. *feel*] here used generally for the functions of all the senses. Each and every sense receives full satisfaction from the eye's contemplation of the Princess.

243. *jewels in crystal for some prince*] One of the New Year's gifts presented to Queen Elizabeth in 1573-4 is de-

Who, tend'ring their own worth from where they were glass'd,
Did point you to buy them, along as you pass'd:
His face's own margent did quote such amazes,
That all eyes saw his eyes enchanted with gazes.
I'll give you Aquitaine, and all that is his,
An you give him for my sake but one loving kiss.

Prin. Come to our pavilion: Boyet is dispos'd.

Boyet. But to speak that in words which his eye hath disclos'd.
I only have made a mouth of his eye,
By adding a tongue which I know will not lie.

Mar. Thou art an old love-monger, and speak'st skilfully.

Kath. He is Cupid's grandfather and learns news of him.

244. *where*] Q1; *whence* Ff, Q2. 245. *point you*] Q1; *point out* Ff, Q2. 254. *Mar.*] *Lad.* Q1; *Lad. Ro.* F1. 255. *Kath.*] *Lad. 2.* Q1; *Lad. Mar.* F.

scribed as "a juell, being a cristall garnished with golde; Adam and Eve enamuled white, and a cristole pendante garnished with golde, and four small perles pendaunte"; and in 1575-6: "a juell, being a cristall sett in golde with two storyes appearing on both sides with a small pendaunte" (Nichols, i. 380; ii. 1).

244. *tend'ring*] offering, proffering for acceptance. So Gabriel Harvey, *An Advertisement for Papp-hatchett* (1589): "fayre offer of preferment handsomely tendered unto some."

from where] In his defence of the Folio "from whence," Hart noted that the expression occurs at least nine times in Shakespeare's early plays and poems. "From where" seems to be "absent."

glass'd] enclosed in glass, referring to the crystal glass the jewels were placed in.

245. *point*] direct, with a hint of urging. This is nearest to sense 12 in the N.E.D., which quotes Andrew Boorde's *Fyrst boke of the Introduction of Knowledge* (?1550), ch. xxxii oddly enough an account of Navarre): "I hauynge pitie they [some pilgrims] should be cast away poynted them to my hostage [i.e. lodgings]." Compare *Hamlet*, I. v. 129: "as your business and desire shall point you"; and *Winter's Tale*, IV. iv. 524. The concentrated interest in Navarre's face cries out to be noticed.

246. *margent*] Parallel passages, references and comments were commonly printed in the margins of books at this time. Compare *Romeo and Juliet*, I. iii. 86, and *Lucrece*, 102. The amazement in Navarre's face draws attention to the love in his eyes.

250. *dispos'd*] inclined to be playful or merry. It occurs in Peele: "I pray let go, Ye are disposed I think" (*Edward I* Bullen's *Peele*, i. 135]). See below, V. ii. 466.

254. *love-monger*] Shakespeare has an even dozen of these compounds with *monger*. Nashe has a few others: news-monger, star-monger, devil-monger, metre-monger, complement-monger.

skilfully] knowledgeably.

Ros. Then was Venus like her mother, for her father is but grim.

Boyet. Do you hear, my mad wenches?

Mar. No.

Boyet. What then, do you see?

Mar. Ay, our way to be gone.

Boyet. You are too hard for me.

[*Exeunt.*

256. *Ros.*] *Lad. 3.* Q 1; *Lad. 2.* F 1. 257. *Mar.*] *Lad.* Q 1; *La. 1* F 1. 258. *Mar.*] *Lad.* Q 1; *Lad 3* F 1.

257. *Do you hear*] A common phrase for claiming the hearer's attention—as we to-day say "listen." Compare *Troilus and Cressida*, v. iii. 97.

mad wenches] occurs again at v. ii. 264. See note at "mad-cap" above, line 215. Compare Lodge, *Euphues Golden Legacie* (*Shakes. Lib.* 1875, p. 40): "Why then doth my Rosalynd grieve at the froune of Torismond . . . and more (mad lasse) to be melancholy, when thou hast with thee Alinda." Compare also "madman," v. ii. 338. A phrase of Lyly's, *Sapho and Phao*, I. iv. (1581): "Wee are mad wenches, if men marke our words: for when . . . we cry away, doe wee not presently say go to." And in *Mother Bombie*, II. iii.

258. *too hard for me*] See again, IV. i. 137, and *As You Like It*, I. ii. 51. More than I can manage (Sense 7 in *New Eng. Dict.*). Compare Ben Jonson, *The Magnetic Lady*, III. iv. (Chorus): "The boy is too hard for you, brother Damplay; best mark the play and let him alone."

ACT III

SCENE I

Enter ARMADO *and* MOTH.

Arm. Warble, child: make passionate my sense of hearing.

Moth. [*Sings.*] Concolinel.

Arm. Sweet air! Go, tenderness of years; take this key, give enlargement to the swain, bring him festinately hither; I must employ him in a letter to my love.

ACT III

Scene I

Enter Armado and Moth] *Enter Braggart and his boy* Q 1; *Enter Braggart and Boys. Song* Ff, Q 2.

Scene I

1. *make passionate my sense of hearing*] Puttenham, speaking "Of proportion by situation" (chap. x.), says: "This proportion consisteth in placing of every verse in a staffe or ditty by such reasonable distaunces as may best serve the eare for delight . . . which maner of situation, even without respect of the rime, doth alter the nature of the Poesie, and make it either lighter or graver, or more merry, or mournfull, and many wayes passionate to the eare and heart of the hearer" (Arber, pp. 97, 98).

2. *Concolinel*] The Folio informs us a song opens this Act, but it does not imply that this word is part of it, or even that the song is sung by Moth. The Quarto has only *Concolinel*, which perhaps has no more sense than *tirra-lirra*, etc., and merely means that Moth exercised his notes in a warble. "Warble" was the technical term for such utterances of melody. Compare Laneham's *Letter* (Furnivall's *Cox*, p. 41), 1575: "cleered his vois . . . wiped hiz lips . . . temperd a string or too with his wrast; and after a littl warbling on hiz harp for a prelude, came foorth with a sollem song." More probably *Concolinel* represents the title of Moth's song; and it was plausibly suggested by a correspondent to *Notes and Queries* (II. xi. 214, 1861) that it stands for *Can cailin gheal* (pronounced "Con colleen yal"), meaning "Sing, maiden fair." Compare Pistol's corruption of Irish song words in *Henry V*. IV. iv. 3. Collier would have it that "Con Colinel" are the first two words of a lost Italian song.

4. *enlargement*] freedom. See *1 Henry IV*. III. i. 31.

festinately] in a hurry. The adjective appears in *King Lear*, III. vii. 10; and for both uses Shakespeare is the earliest authority in *New Eng. Dict.* The word was not so rare

Moth. Master, will you win your love with a French brawl?

Arm. How meanest thou? brawling in French?

Moth. No, my complete master; but to jig off a tune at the tongue's end, canary to it with your feet, humour it with turning up your eyelids, sigh a note

6. *Master, will you*] Q 1; *Will you* Ff, Q 2. 10. *Your feet*] Q 1; *the feet* Ff, Q 2. 11. *eyelids*] Q 1; *eye* Ff, Q 2; *eyes* Dyce (2), Hudson.

perhaps. Nashe has it as a verb in *Have With You to Saffron Walden* (McKerrow, iii. 91): "he would accelerate and festinate his procrastinating ministers" (1596); and Ben Jonson uses it in *The Silent Woman*, III. ii. (1609): "Gentlemen, my princess says, you shall have all her silver dishes, festinate."

6, 7. *French brawl*] A French dance (the *bransle*) that became popular in England during the second half of the sixteenth century. In *Ancient Ballads and Broadsides* (p. 221) there is a ballad of date 1569 (or earlier) which begins: "Good fellowes must go learne to daunce, The brydeall is full nere a; There is a brall come out of Fraunce, The tryxt [trickiest] ye harde this yeare a: For I must leape, and thou must hoppe, And we must turne all three a; The fourth must bounce it lyke a toppe, And so we shall agree a. I praye thee, mynstrell, make no stoppe For we wyll merye be a." In Marston's *Pasquil and Katherine* (Act V.), 1600, one says, "what, gallants, have you ne'er a Page can entertain the pleasing time with some French brawle or song?"—which recalls Moth's position very plainly. The same dramatist describes a brawl at length in *The Malcontent*, IV. i. (1604), quoted by Steevens: "music!—we will dance. *Guer.* . . . Passa regis, or Bianca's brawl? *Aur.* We have forgot the brawl. *Fer.* So soon? 'tis wonder! *Guer.* Why, 'tis but two singles on the left, two on the right, three doubles forward, a traverse of six round: do this twice, three singles side, galliard trick-of-twenty corantopace; a figure of eight, three singles broken down, come up, meet, two doubles, fall back, and then honour." The distinctly forced introduction of the phrase here is explained by Miss F. A. Yates as a reference to the 1593 riots against Protestant refugees (Huguenots from France especially), satire of whom, in their capacity of foreign language teachers, she finds to be a major element in the topicality of the play. See Introduction, 3.222, 5.24.

9. *jig off a tune*] jerk off a tune, in the manner of a jig. The earliest use of the verb in *New Eng. Dict.*

10. *canary*] dance, as if dancing the canaries. See *All's Well that Ends Well*, II. i. 79. To "dance the canaries" became a common expression for dancing in a lively fashion, as in Beaumont and Fletcher's *Rollo*, II. ii.; Middleton's *Spanish Gipsy*, IV. iii., and see Nares for more. Compare Dekker, *The Wonderfull Yeare* (Grosart, i. 136), 1603: "a drunkard, who no sooner smelt the winde, but he thought the ground under him danced the canaries." The passage in the text is the earliest reference we have to the dance, which appears to have been derived from the aborigines of the "Fortunate Isles" by the Spaniards. It is described by Arbeau, *Orchesographie* (1589), quoted by Furness.

and sing a note, sometime through the throat as if you swallowed love with singing love, sometime through the nose, as if you snuffed up love by smelling love ; with your hat penthouse-like o'er the shop of your eyes ; with your arms crossed on your thin-belly doublet like a rabbit on a spit ; or your hands in your pocket, like a man after the old painting ; and keep not too long in one tune, but a snip and away. These are complements, these are humours, these betray nice wenches, that would

12. *as if*] Theobald ; *if* Qq, Ff. 13. *singing love, sometime*] Theobald ; *singing love sometime* Q 1 ; *singing, love sometime* Ff, Q 2. *through the nose*] Ff 2, 3, 4 ; *through : nose* Qq, F 1. 17. *thin-belly doublet*] Ff 3, 4 ; *thinbellies doblet* Q 1 ; *thin belly doublet* Ff 1, 2, Q 2 ; *thin belly-doublet* Steevens, Schmidt Craig ; *thin belly's doublet* Collier.

15. *penthouse-like*] like an overhanging shed or projecting roof. Compare *Macbeth*, I. iii. 20, and *Much Ado About Nothing*, III. iii. 100. The hat over the eyes, penthouse-like, was the correct wear for a lover, or a critic. The image is not new ; see Sir T. Elyot, *Pasquil the Plaine* (1540) A3 : " the tirfe of the cappe tourned downe afore like a pentise."

16. *arms crossed*] Compare III. i. 178 ; IV. iii. 133 ; and *The Two Gentlemen of Verona*, II. i. 20. So also Ben Jonson, *Cynthia's Revels*, III. ii : " anon, doth seem As he would kiss away his hand in kindness ; Then walks off melancholie, and stands wreathed, As he were pinned up to the arras." And in Sidney's *Arcadia*, bk. iii. : " the onely ods was that when others tooke breath, he sighed ; and when others rested, he crost his armes. For Love . . . still made him remember." And Lodge, *Euphues Golden Legacie* (*Shakes. Lib.*, 1875, p. 66), 1590 : " they saw the sodaine change of his lookes, his folded armes, his passionate sighes, they heard him often abruptly cal on Rosalynd."

17. *thin-belly doublet*] The reading of the earliest texts agrees here and is correct. " Belly-doublet " is, in fact, nonsense, as Staunton says. Some doublets were stuffed, others were not ; but the reference here is to the thinness of the belly, like a spitted rabbit's. Compare Dekker, *A Strange Horse-race* (Grosart, iii. 335), 1613 : " The third that came sneaking in was a leane, ill-faced, shotten-herring-bellied rascall."

18, 19. *like a man after the old painting*] It is not known whether Moth is referring to a particular old painting.

19. *snip*] a scrap or shred. The common phrase in Shakespeare's time was " a snatch and away," which Dekker varies to " a licke at all sorts of learning, and away " (*Gull's Horn Book* [Grosart, ii. 258], 1609). Compare Higgins, *Nomenclator* (1584). " *Prandium statarium* . . . manger de bout en pied. A standing dinner which is eaten in haste. . . . A snatch and away." And G. Harvey, *Foure Letters* (Grosart, i. 230), 1592 : " A snatch and away, with Neoptolemus, and the common sort of students." Travellers reported that the dogs of Egypt drank this way along the Nile on account of the crocodiles.

be betrayed without these ; and make them men of note (do you note, men ?) that most are affected to these.

Arm. How hast thou purchased this experience ?

Moth. By my penny of observation.

Arm. But O, but O,—

Moth. The hobby-horse is forgot.

Arm. Call'st thou my love hobby-horse ?

22. *men of note, (do you note, men ?) that*] Steevens ; *men of note : do you note men that* Qq, Ff ; *men of note—do you note me ?—that* Hanmer, Cambridge.
26. *penny*] Hanmer *et seq.* ; *pen* (or *penne*) Qq, Ff, New.

23. (*do you note, men ?*] I believe with Hart that Moth is here addressing the male members *of the audience ;* and that, in accordance with the regular clown's tradition, he is giving them a tip on how to be successful in love.

26. *penny of observation*] Compare the similar expression in the title of Greene's *Groatsworth of Wit bought with a million of repentance.* Dover Wilson supports the reading " pen " as peculiarly appropriate to a Moth who is the pamphleteer Nashe in disguise ; but " penny " (for which the Quarto " penne " may well be a Shakespearean spelling) is even more suitable to the author of *Pierce Penilesse* who was being exhorted by Harvey to publish next his *Penniworth of Discretion.* " A pennyworth of wit " is an ancient expression, and gave its name to a chapbook mentioned in Laneham's *Letter*, 1575, as *The Chapman of a peniwoorth of Wit* (Furnivall's *Cox*, p. 30). The expression occurs in *How a Merchande dyd hys Wyfe betray* (Hazlitt's *Early Popular Poetry*, i. 198), *c.* 1500 : " As thou art my trewe weddyd fere : Bye ye me a penyworth of wytt, And in youre hert kepe well hyt."

27, 28. *But O, but O,—The hobby-horse is forgot*] A frequent lament, of which this is perhaps the earliest example. Perhaps the words are a fragment of a popular song. The hobby-horse went out of fashion before the Puritanical movement against sports in general became rancorous. It was a popular adjunct of the morris-dance and other May-games, and is mentioned as early as 1557 (*New Eng. Dict.*) as a recognized village May-day sport. The words in the text occur again in *Hamlet*, III. ii. 126. See also Kemp's *Nine Daies Wonder* (Bodley Head Quarto, p. 12), 1600 : " With hey and ho, through thicke and thin, The hobby horse quite forgotten, I follow'd, as I did begin, Although the way were rotten." The lament occurs also in Ben Jonson's *Bartholomew's Fair*, v. iii., and in his *Masque of the Metamorphosed Gipsies*, and again in his *Satyr.* It is dwelt upon in Beaumont and Fletcher's *Woman Pleased* at some length. See also Cooke's *Greene's Tu Quoque* (quoted by Steevens). But the hobby-horse was by no means forgotten—it survives to-day in Cornwall—so that these words are most likely a quotation.

29. *Call'st thou my love hobby-horse ?*] i.e. drudge, hackney. Ben Jonson uses this as a term of abuse in *Cynthia's Revels*, v. ii. (1600) : " *Amorphys.* Make your play still upon the answer, sir. *Anaides.* Hold your peace, you are a hobby-horse." And of a foolish lecherous person in *The Silent Woman*, IV. ii. (1609) : " here

Moth. No, master; the hobby-horse is but a colt,—and your love perhaps a hackney [*aside*]. But have you forgot your love?

Arm. Almost I had.

Moth. Negligent student! learn her by heart.

Arm. By heart, and in heart, boy.

Moth. And out of heart, master: all those three I will prove.

Arm. What wilt thou prove?

Moth. A man, if I live; and this, by, in, and without, upon the instant: by heart you love her, because your heart cannot come by her; in heart you love her, because your heart is in love with her; and out of heart you love her, being out of heart that you cannot enjoy her.

Arm. I am all these three.

Moth. And three times as much more, and yet nothing at all.

Arm. Fetch hither the swain: he must carry me a letter.

Moth. A message well sympathized: a horse to be ambassador for an ass.

39. *and this, by*] Theobald; (*and this*) *by* Qq, Ff.

be in presence have tasted of her favours. *Clerimont.* What a neighing hobby-horse is this!" In the latter passage it is equivalent to "colt" of line 30. In *Othello*, iv. i. 157 it bluntly means "prostitute."

31. *hackney*] prostitute. Compare Nashe, *Christ's Teares* (McKerrow, ii. 184), 1593: "dormative potions to procure deadly sleepe, that when the hackney he hath payde for lyes by hym, hee may have no power to deale wyth her, but shee may steale from hym."

49. *well sympathized*] in good harmony. Lyly seems to have introduced the words "sympathia" and "sympathy" (Arber's *Euphues*, pp. 46, 236, etc.), which were both at once adopted by Greene (Grosart's *Greene*, iv. 219, vii. 41, and ix. 179). Lyly seems also first with verbs in *ize*. The word "sympathize" is perhaps due to Shakespeare. It is in Cotgrave, 1611. The minting of words in "ize" proceeded at a great rate at this time. Nashe is eloquent upon the subject in his To the Reader, *Christ's Teares* (McKerrow, ii. 184), 1594: "To the second rancke of reprehenders that complain of my boystrous compound wordes, and ending my Italionate coyned verbes all in *Ize*, thus I replie. . . . Our English tongue of all languages most swarmeth with the single money of monasillables, which are the onely scandall of it. Bookes written in them and no other seeme like Shop-keepers boxes, that containe nothing else save halfpence, three-farthings, and two-pences. Therefore what did me I, but having a huge heape of those worthlesse shreds of small English . . . had them to the compounders immediately . . . they

Arm. Ha? ha? what sayest thou?
Moth. Marry, sir, you must send the ass upon the horse,
 for he is very slow-gaited. But I go.
Arm. The way is but short: away!
Moth. As swift as lead, sir.
Arm. The meaning, pretty ingenious?
 Is not lead a metal heavy, dull, and slow?
Moth. *Minime*, honest master; or rather, master, no.
Arm. I say lead is slow.
Moth. You are too swift, sir, to say so:
 Is that lead slow which is fir'd from a gun?
Arm. Sweet smoke of rhetoric!
 He reputes me a cannon, and the bullet, that's he—
 I shoot thee at the swain.
Moth. Thump then, and I flee. [*Exit.*
Arm. A most acute juvenal; voluble and free of grace!
 By thy favour, sweet welkin, I must sigh in thy face:

56. *The*] Q 1; *Thy* Ff, Q 2. 64. *voluble*] Ff, Q 2; *volable* Q 1, New.

carrie farre more state with them than any other, and are not halfe so harsh in their desinence as the old hobling English verbes ending in R."

51. *Ha? ha?*] Armado only half hears Moth's insult. This joke is perennial; compare W. H. Auden, *Paid on Both Sides* (*Poems*, 1930, p. 24).

58. *Minime*] *Latin*, by no means. Moth gives us more evidence of his Latin in v. i. 63. It was proper for pages to know Latin. Compare Sir Thopas' attendants in Lyly's *Endymion*.

63. *Thump*] represents the sound of the cannon. Sometimes early writers used "dub a dub" for this purpose, as in Peele's *Old Wives Tale* (Bullen, i. 333) and in the ballad *Winning of Cales* (Percy Folio, iii. 454). "Bounce" was for smaller fire-arms. Halliwell says "thump" refers to the stroke of the bullet (as in IV. iii. 23) but the bullet is still on its way to the mark. The word may be noun or verb, and Moth means either "Bang, I'm off" or "Make a noise like a gun and I'll go."

64. *acute*] applied to the intellect. This is the earliest example in the *New Eng. Dict.* See below again at IV. ii. 72. The adverb occurs in *All's Well that Ends Well*, I. i. 221. Ben Jonson has early parallels for both uses: "the most divine and acute lady in court" (*Every Man in his Humour*, III. i. [1598]); and "she has the most acute ready and facetious wit" (*Every Man out of his Humour*, IV. vi. [1599]).

juvenal] See note, I. ii. 8, above.

voluble] Dover Wilson retains the Quarto reading "volable," interpreted as "quick-witted." It might be better explained as a coinage of Armado's to express Moth's quickness of movement, his bullet-swiftness in *flying* on an errand. But the word is not found elsewhere, and "voluble" is a term particularly appropriate to Moth. See note on II. i. 76 above.

65. *welkin*] See below, IV. ii. 5: "*coelo*, the sky, the welkin, the heaven."

Most rude melancholy, valour gives thee place.
My herald is return'd.

Re-enter MOTH *with* COSTARD.

Moth. A wonder, master! here's a costard broken in a shin.

Arm. Some enigma, some riddle: come, thy l'envoy; begin.

Cost. No egma, no riddle, no l'envoy; no salve in the mail, sir. O, sir, plantain, a plain plantain! no l'envoy, no l'envoy: no salve, sir, but a plantain!

66. *Most rude*] *Moist-eyed* Collier MS. (!) 68-131. *A wonder . . . let me loose*] Put in the margin by Pope. 69. *come, thy*] Qq, F 1; *no* Ff 2, 3 4. *l'envoy; begin*] Capell; *lenvoy begin* Qq, Ff.

68. *costard*] apple, or head: "here's a head broken in the shin."

broken in a shin] Hart wrote: "References to the breaking of shins are so abundant at this time that one is inclined to think they must have been even more susceptible than nowadays." The probable explanation, for which I am indebted to Mr. John Crow, is that a "broken shin" had for the Elizabethans a metaphorical as well a literal sense, and was in fact slang for a sexual disappointment. This is clearly what it means in "*A merry new Song how a Bruer meant to make a Cooper cuckold, and how deere the Bruer paid for the bargaine,*" reprinted in Henry Huth's *Ancient Ballads and Broadsides* (1867). The same sense doubtless hovers at the back of the present dialogue, which never misses a pun where one is possible.

69. *enigma*] Compare Greene, *Tritameron*, pt. ii. (Grosart, iii. 145), 1587: "she tooke it either for some propheticall Ænigma or els for a bare jest." A rare word at this time.

l'envoy] An address or send-off, usually placed at the end of a prose or poetical composition; often taking the form of a concise or obscure commendation to the readers. Common in early writers as Lydgate, etc. Gabriel Harvey places a L'Envoy at the end of his poetical *Theme upon Vertue* of which he was so proud (Grosart, i. 79), 1580. He has another at the close of his *Gorgon Sonnett* against Nashe (Grosart, i. 297), 1592; and his use of the word in this trivial manner was expressly singled out for reprehension and ridicule by Nashe in *Have With You to Saffron Walden* in his coarsest and wittiest way. See McKerrow's edition, ii. pp. 11, 113, 133, 135. Nashe makes a verb of it: "we shall l'envoy him," give him farewell. Harvey's theme, to which he appends a L'Envoy, is "*In Commendation of three most precious Accidentes, Virtue, Fame and Wealth:* and finally of the fourth, *A good tongue.*" The parallelism is striking, the goose being "the good tongue."

70. *no l'envoy; no salve*] Costard mistakes the word "salve" (as in the old salve for a sore) for *salvé*, a salute. Since the latter word was used as a verb (Chaucer, Spenser), possibly the latter syllable was occasionally slurred, but in any case the orthography warranted the pun. Greene at any rate thought so. Compare *Mamillia* (Grosart, ii. 22),

Arm. By virtue, thou enforcest laughter; thy silly thought, my spleen; the heaving of my lungs provokes me to ridiculous smiling: O, pardon me, my stars! Doth the inconsiderate take salve for l'envoy, and the word l'envoy for a salve?

Moth. Do the wise think them other? is not l'envoy a salve?

Arm. No, page: it is an epilogue or discourse to make plain
Some obscure precedence that hath tofore been sain.

70. *the mail*] *thee male* Qq, F 1; *the male* Ff 2, 3 4; *the vale* Johnson conj.; *them all* Knight (Tyrwhitt conj.). 71. *O*] Q 1, Ff, 3, 4; *Or* Q 2, Ff 1, 2. *plain*] *pline* Q. 1. 72. *no salve*] Qq, F 1; *or salve* Ff 2, 3, 4. 80. *page*] *Moth* Rowe (ed. 1). 81. *sain*] Q 1; *fain* Q 2, Ff.

1583: "so his sodaine sore had a new salve . . . he espied Mamillia . . . and after he had curteously given her the Salve." One word suggests the other. See again pp. 196, 197. Both senses are very common in Greene, and often, as in "give one a salve," only determinable by context. To an ignoramus the pun was unavoidable, when puns were desiderata. Steevens quoted the same quibble from *Aristippus, or The Jovial Philosopher*, 1630.

71. *mail*] wallet, budget. No ointment or plaster in the bag. Compare *Narcissus* (ed. M. L. Lee, pp. 9, 10), 1602: "wee may provide a plaster Of holsome hearbes to cure this dire disaster. *Tyresias.* If I should tell you, you amisse would iudge it: I have one salve, one medecine in my budgett." *Narcissus* has several echoes of Shakespeare. See "keel the pot," note, v. ii. 910.

plantain] Costard wants no high-class remedy with a foreign name, but the well-known simple, always required for the head or for the shin. Compare Tomkis, *Albumazar*, iv. 11 (1614): "Help, Armellina, help: I'm fall'n in the cellar: Bring a fresh plantane leaf, I have broke my shin"; and Ben Jonson, *The Case is Altered*, II. iv (1598): "[*Martino breaks his head. Onion.* Foh, tis nothing, a fillip, a device: fellow Juniper get me a plantain; I had rather play with one that had skill by half." According to Hart plantain leaves are still used in the north of Ireland, from their cooling properties, to apply to bruises.

73, 74. *laughter . . . spleen*] The excesses of mirth or anger were controlled, it was held, by the spleen. Compare *Measure for Measure*, II. ii. 122; and below, v. ii. 117; and Lyly, *Mother Bombie*, iv. 2: "for wee should laugh heartily, and without laughing my spleene would split."

76, 77. *Doth the inconsiderate*, etc.] The whole point of this trifling is here; and the answer, of course, is "yes." The muddle which arises in the minds of those who will not understand this may be seen in pages of notes in Steevens and in Furness.

76. *inconsiderate*] a thoughtless, ignorant person. Compare Harvey's *New Letter*, etc. (Grosart, i. 286): "the shallow breast of inconsiderate youth."

81. *precedence*] that which has preceded. Walker (*Crit.* iii. 36) suggests that these two lines may be a quotation from some old treatise on composition (Furness).

I will example it :
The fox, the ape, and the humble-bee,
Were still at odds, being but three.
There's the moral : now the l'envoy.

Moth. I will add the l'envoy. Say the moral again.

Arm. The fox, the ape, and the humble-bee,
Were still at odds, being but three.

Moth. Until the goose came out of door,
And stay'd the odds by adding four.
Now will I begin your moral, and do you follow with my l'envoy.
The fox, the ape, and the humble-bee,
Were still at odds, being but three.

Arm. Until the goose came out of door,
Staying the odds by adding four.

Moth. A good l'envoy, ending in the goose : would you desire more ?

Cost. The boy hath sold him a bargain, a goose, that's flat.
Sir, your pennyworth is good an your goose be fat.
To sell a bargain well is as cunning as fast and loose :
Let me see ; a fat l'envoy ; ay, that's a fat goose.

Arm. Come hither, come hither. How did this argument begin ?

Moth. By saying that a costard was broken in a shin.
Then call'd you for the l'envoy.

Cost. True, and I for a plantain : thus came your argument in ;

82-90. *I will . . . four*] omitted in Ff, Q 2.

83. *The fox, the ape*] For a guess at the meaning, see Introduction, 5.22.

90. *adding four*] adding a fourth. There are so many fox and goose apologues that the latter was bound to appear. "The Courtier, after travaile, tells his Lady a better tale than of a fox and a goose" (N. Breton, *An Old Man's Lesson*, 1605) i.e. homely stuff.

99. *sold him a bargain, a goose*] made a fool of him. Compare *Romeo and Juliet*, II. iv. 75 (with the same pun on goose meaning prostitute as at line 120 below) : "was I there with you for the goose? *Rom.* Thou wast never with me for anything when thou wast not there for the goose." Similar expressions, by which the speaker points out that the other is a goose, as here, are numerous. "To sell one a goose for a bargain," shortened to "sell one a bargain" later, has not been earlier found than here. Taylor, in *The Goose*, puts it : "take my goose amongst you, gentlemen" (*Works*, 1630, p. 111).

101. *fast and loose*] See note, I. ii. 147.

Then the boy's fat l'envoy, the goose that you bought ;
And he ended the market.

Arm. But tell me ; how was there a costard broken in a shin ?

Moth. I will tell you sensibly.

Cost. Thou hast no feeling of it, Moth : I will speak that l'envoy.

I, Costard, running out, that was safely within,
Fell over the threshold and broke my shin.

Arm. We will talk no more of this matter.

Cost. Till there be more matter in the shin.

Arm. Sirrah Costard, I will enfranchise thee.

Cost. O ! marry me to one Frances—I smell some l'envoy, some goose in this.

Arm. By my sweet soul, I mean setting thee at liberty, enfreedoming thy person : thou wert immured, restrained, captivated, bound.

Cost. True, true, and now you will be my purgation and let me loose.

Arm. I give thee thy liberty, set thee from durance ; and, in lieu thereof, impose on thee nothing but this : bear this significant to the country maid Jaquenetta. There is remuneration ; for the best ward of mine honour is rewarding my dependents. Moth, follow. [*Exit.*

Moth. Like the sequel, I. Signior Costard, adieu.

122. *immured*] Ff 2, 3, 4 ; *emured* Qq, F 1. 130. *honour*] Q 1 ; *honours* Ff, Q 2. 132. *adieu*] *adew* Q 1, F 1.

119. *Frances*] Nashe gives this name to the prostitute in his *Choise of Valentines*. McKerrow writes : " Possibly a typical name for women of the class ; cf. S. Rowlands' *Letting of Humorous Blood*, B5^{v}, '*Francke* in name, and Francke by nature, *Fraunics* is a most kinde creature,' and the same author's *Whole Crew of Kind Gossips*, E2, where a similar person is called '*Franke*' and ' Mistris *Francis*.' "

128. *significant*] sign, intimation, and so letter. Compare *1 Henry VI.* II. iv. 25 : " Since you are tongue-tied. . . . In dumb significants proclaim your thoughts."

129. *ward*] guard.

132. *sequel*] that which follows in a story or book. Moth continues the tone of illustration his master adopted with the *l'envoy*. Compare Nashe, *Foure Letters Confuted* (McKerrow, i. 268), 1593 : " he mist the Oratorship of the Universitie, of which, in the sequele of his booke, he most slanderously complaineth."

Cost. My sweet ounce of man's flesh ! my incony Jew ! [*Exit Moth.*

Now will I look to his remuneration. Remuneration ! O that's the Latin word for three farthings : three farthings, remuneration. 'What's the price of this inkle ?' 'One penny' : 'No, I'll give you a remuneration' : why, it carries it. Remuneration ! why it is a fairer name than French crown. I will never buy and sell out of this word.

133. *Jew*] *jewel* Warburton. 137. *inkle*] *yncle* Qq, Ff. *One penny*] *i. d* Qq, Ff 1, 2 ; *i. de.* Ff 3, 4. 138. *carries it. Remuneration!*] Theobald ; *carries it remuneration* Qq, Ff 1, 2 ; *carries it's remuneration* Ff 3, 4. 139. *French*] Q 1 ; *a French* Ff, Q 2.

133. *incony*] "darling." The earliest use of this slang term the origin of which is only guessed at. See Murray's *New Eng. Dict.* Jonson, in the latest example found (1633), accents the word on the second syllable and rhymes it with "money" (*Tale of a Tub*, IV. i.). The *New Eng. Dict.* says : "rare, fine, delicate, pretty, nice." It must be connected with "cony" (also spelt and pronounced "cunny") which was used as a term of endearment for a woman (*N.E.D. cony* sense 5a & b). In Dekker's *Shoemaker's Holiday* (Pearson, i. 60) "incony" takes on a more active sense, almost Shakespeare's "honeying"—"There" (in the Church) "they shall be knit like a paire of stockings in matrimony, there theyle be incony." Other examples of its occurrence are *Doctor Dodypoll* (Bullen's *Old Plays*, iii. 117) and Brome's *Northern Lass*, iii. The first of these is noted in Steevens' *Shakespeare*. In the early editions of Marlowe's *Jew of Malta*, Act iv., the reading is "Whilst I in thy incoomy lap do tumble."

Jew] Hart surmised that the word "Jew" might have been suggested by the Shylock association of "ounce of man's flesh" ; but it is again used as a term of endearment in *A Midsummer Night's Dream*, III. i. 97 : "most brisky Juvenal and eke most lovely Jew." That it occurs there in company with "Juvenal" (of which Dover Wilson conjectures it may be a "playful diminutive") is significant.

135. *three farthings*] A three-farthing coin, six grains, hammered, was issued at various dates from 1561 to 1581. On the obverse it bears the crowned bust, with rose behind the head. See *King John*, I. i. 143.

137. *inkle*] A kind of linen tape ; or, as in *Pericles*, v. 8 (Gower), the yarn it was made from. See also *The Winter's Tale*, IV. iv. 208. It is spelt "yncle" in Cunningham's *Revels Accounts* (Shakes. Soc. p. 119), 1576.

138. *it carries it*] it bears the prize, it wins. See *The Merry Wives of Windsor*, III. ii. 70 ; *All's Well that Ends Well*, IV. i. 30, etc. ; "Tis not thy words proud Queene shall carry it" (*The Troublesome Raigne of King John*, 1591).

139. *French crown*] A pun on the coin and on the bald crown produced by the "French disease." See *Measure for Measure*, I. ii. 52.

140. *out of this word*] using any other word but this.

Enter BEROWNE.

Ber. O my good knave Costard! exceedingly well met.
Cost. Pray you, sir, how much carnation ribbon may a
man buy for a remuneration?
Ber. O what is a remuneration?
Cost. Marry, sir, halfpenny farthing.
Ber. O! why then, three-farthing worth of silk.
Cost. I thank your worship. God be wi' you!
Ber. O stay, slave! I must employ thee:
As thou wilt win my favour, good my knave,
Do one thing for me that I shall entreat.
Cost. When would you have it done, sir?
Ber. O this afternoon.
Cost. Well, I will do it, sir. Fare you well.
Ber. O thou knowest not what it is.
Cost. I shall know, sir, when I have done it.

144. *O what*] Q 1; *What* Ff, Q 2. 146, 148, 152, 154, 170. *O*] Qq, Ff; omitted in Camb., New. 146. *three farthing worth* Q 1; *three farthings worth* Ff, Q 2.

141. *exceedingly well met*] So in Jonson's *Bartholomew's Fair*, v. iii.: "Master Cokes! you are exceedingly well met."

142. *carnation ribbon*] flesh-coloured ribbon. The colour of a man's skin or flesh. A very popular colour. Compare Dekker's *Honest Whore* (Pearson, ii. 49), 1604: "Sweetest properest gallant . . . flame-coloured doublet, red satin hose, carnation silk stockings"; and Heywood's *If you know not me*, etc., pt. ii. (Pearson, p. 259), *ante* 1605: "carnation girdles and busk-point suitable, as common as coales from Newcastle: you shall not have a kitchen maid scrape trenchers without her washt gloves"; and in *A Warning for Faire Women* (Simpson's *School of Shakespeare*, ii. 277), Act ii. (*circa* 1599): "Pray ye bestow a groat, or sixpence, of Carnation ribbin to tie my smock sleeves; they flap about my hands." It appears several times in the costumes of Jonson's masques at court.

144. *O what*] The "O" with which Berowne's lines so frequently begin was explained by the Cambridge editors as having crept into the text from the speech-heading "Bero.," which still occurs at many points in the Quarto. Two facts give some slight support to this theory: the "O" is never found beginning a speech where the heading "Bero." is retained; and it often throws out the metre. It does, however, begin lines in the middle of speeches where there can be no question of an intrusion from a heading; and metrical irregularities need not be taken too seriously (see note on II. i. 172). Hart's conclusion was that "'O' is an affectation of Berowne's, inserted purposely here and elsewhere for reasons known to the author." Whether or not we accept the view that Shakespeare is here caricaturing the mannerism of a real person, it is wiser, when in doubt, to preserve the Quarto reading. There is another heavy crop of "O's" in IV. iii.

Ber. Why, villain, thou must know first.
Cost. I will come to your worship to-morrow morning.
Ber. It must be done this afternoon. Hark, slave, it is but this :
The princess comes to hunt here in the park,
And in her train there is a gentle lady ;
When tongues speak sweetly, then they name her name,
And Rosaline they call her : ask for her,
And to her white hand see thou do commend
This seal'd-up counsel. There's thy guerdon : go.
Cost. Gardon, O sweet gardon ! better than remuneration ; a'leven-pence farthing better. Most sweet gardon ! I will do it, sir, in print. Gardon ! Remuneration ! [*Exit.*
Ber. O ! and I forsooth in love !
I, that have been love's whip ;
A very beadle to a humorous sigh ;
A critic, nay, a night-watch constable,
A domineering pedant o'er the boy,
Than whom no mortal so magnificent !

165. *go*] [*Gives him money* (or *shilling*)] inserted by some edds. 167. *a 'leven-pence*] *a levenpence* Qq, Ff. 170-175. Q 1 prints as three lines, ending *whip, constable, magnificent ;* Ff as six, ending *love, whip, criticke, constable, boy, magnificent.*

164. *white hand*] The commentators, obsessed by Rosaline's " blackness," have jibbed unnecessarily at this, the traditional attribute of a lady-love whatever her complexion.

165. *guerdon*] When Costard devotes a speech to explaining that Berowne has given him a guerdon of a shilling, surely a stage direction " gives him a shilling " is a useless excrescence ? Johnson put it in first. " Guerdon " was a common word at this time and earlier. Compare Cotgrave (1611) : " *Guerdon* guerdon, recompence, meed, remuneration, reward ; also as *Gardon.*"

168. *in print*] exactly, most carefully. See *The Two Gentlemen of Verona*, II. i. 175, and *As You Like It*, V. iv. 92. Greene uses this expression several times, as in *Farewell to Follie* (Grosart, ix. 308), 1591 : " Setting hir husbande therefore foorth in print, he tooke his waye unto the Court " ; *Mamillia* (ii. 219), 1583 ; and see earlier in Harvey (Grosart, i. 84), 1580 : " Every one A per se A, his termes and braveries in print."

170-202. *I forsooth in love*, etc.] Furnivall points out in *The Centurie of Prayse* that Golding's speech in Heywood's *Faire Maide of the Exchange* (Pearson, ii. 20) is an imitation of this. " With that face ? " (I. ii. 131) has occurred on page 11 in the same play which, besides being weak twaddle, is full of plagiarism.

175. *magnificent*] proud, arrogantly ambitious (*New Eng. Dict.*). Compare Knolles *History of the Turks*

This wimpled, whining, purblind, wayward boy,
This signor junior, giant-dwarf, dan Cupid ;
Regent of love rhymes, lord of folded arms,
The anointed sovereign of sighs and groans,
Liege of all loiterers and malcontents,

177. *signor junior*] *senior junior* Hanmer ; *Signior Junios* Qq, Ff ; *Signior Junio* Pope ; *Signior Julio's* Upton conj. *dan*] Q 1 ; *Don* Ff, Q 2.

(1621), p. 732 : "This Perenus was one of the greatest peeres of Hungarie, but of a most haughtie and magnificent mind." The line as a whole may be read either as referring to Berowne, whose pride in scorning love led to his fall ; or to imperious Cupid, avenging such slights in the high-handed manner of a tyrant. Of the two, the second perhaps best fits the humour of the speech as a whole : "magnificent boy" is another paradox to match "giant-dwarf."

176. *wimpled*] blindfold, muffled. The "wimple" was a kind of hood or tippet, used as a muffler in the Shakespearian sense. Compare *Appius and Virginia* (Malone Soc., ed. McKerrow, 969), 1575 : "Let first my wimple bind my eyes, and then thy blow assaile. Now father worke thy will on me . . . [*Here tye a handcarcher aboute hir eyes, and then strike of hir heade*]" ; and Lyly, *Mydas*, I. i. : "Justice herselfe, that sitteth wimpled about the eyes."

177. *signor junior*] Hanmer's ingenious reading is widely accepted but there is no reason why this half of the pun should be brought out rather than the other. Hart's suggestion "Signior junior" is almost exactly the old reading, the idea being to give a title to the boy Cupid. This passage is recalled by Heywood in *Love's Mistress* (Pearson, v. 112-114) : "*Clowne.* What might you call that yong gentleman that rules and raignes, revells and roares in these walkes of Arcadia. . . . 2 *Swain.* It is the god of Love they call him Cupid. . . . *Clowne.* Can any of you all give me his true title. . . . I give you his stile in Folio : Hee is King of cares, cogitations, and coxcombes ; Vice-roy of vowes and vanities ; Prince of passions, prate-apaces and pickled lovers ; Duke of disasters, dissemblers, and drown'd eyes ; Marquesse of melancholly and mad-folks, grand Signior of griefes and grones, Heroe of hie-hoes, Admirall of ay-mees, and Mounsieur of mutton-laced." Laneham has an exordium to Neptune on the same lines in his *Letter* (1575) : "the great god of the swelling seas, Prins of profundities, and soverain Segnior of al Lakes, freshwaters, Rivers, Creeks and Goolphs." These passages bear out the reading *signor*.

dan Cupid] a variant of "don," a contraction of *dominus* (or its first syllable), master, sir. A title of honour formerly. Spenser applies "dan" to Chaucer. "Dan Cupid" occurs earlier in T. Howell's *Devises* (ed. Raleigh, p. 70), 1581 : "Then you that fayne Dan Cupide is a God, Recante in tyme" ; and in lines prefixed to Greene's *Mamillia* (1583) by "Roger Portington Esquier, in Commendation of this Booke" (Grosart, ii. 11, 12). For similar raillery upon Cupid, see Sidney's *Arcadia*, Eclogues concluding bk. i. (1593 Folio) : "*Cupid* the wagg that lately conquer'd had Wise Counsellors, stout Captaines puissant Kings, And ti'de them fast to leade his triumph badd."

178-180. *folded arms . . . malcontents*] Compare *The Two Gentlemen of Verona*, II. i. 20, and in the present play, IV. iii. 133.

Dread prince of plackets, king of codpieces,
Sole imperator and great general
Of trotting paritors : O my little heart !
And I to be a corporal of his field,
And wear his colours like a tumbler's hoop !
What ! I love ! I sue ! I seek a wife !
A woman that is like a German clock,

186. *What ! I love !*] *What ? I ! I love* Malone, Steevens (Tyrwhitt), New.
187. *clock*] Ff 2, 3, 4 ; *cloak* Qq, F 1.

181. *plackets . . . codpieces*] Both terms occur several times in Shakespeare. The former was used of a petticoat, or the opening in it leading to a pocket, and hence a pocket itself, as in *King Lear*, III. iv. 100. The latter was " a bagged appendage to the front of the close-fitting hose or breeches worn by men from the fifteenth to the seventeenth century ; often conspicuous and ornamental " (*New Eng. Dict.*). As distinctive portions of female and male attire they came to stand for " women " and " men," especially in a flippant or bawdy sense, as " skirt " is used to-day. Nashe sets these two terms in similar conjunction in his fiercest raillery upon Gabriel Harvey in *Have With You to Saffron Walden* (McKerrow, iii. 129), 1596.

183. *paritors*] officers of the Ecclesiastical Courts, who served citations. Johnson says these were most frequently issued for fornication and such-like breaches. This statement is borne out by a passage in Greene's *Art of Conny-catching* (Grosart, x. 45), 1592 : " shifters and coosners, who learning some insight in the civill law, walke abrode like parators, sumners and informers, being none at all either in office or credit, and they go spying about where any marchant, or marchants prentice, . . . either accompany with anie woman familiarly, or else hath gotten some maide with childe . . . they send for him . . . telling him he must be presented to the Arches, and the scitation shal be peremptorily served in his parish church. The partie afraid to have his credit crackt . . . takes composition with this cosner for some twentie markes." They were a class much hated by the people. " Belike thou art the Divels paritor, The basest officer that lives in Hell " (*Wily Beguiled* [Malone Soc., ed. Greg, 2002]).

184. *corporal of his field*] " A superior officer of the army in the sixteenth and seventeenth century, who acted as an assistant or a kind of aide-de-camp to the sergeant-major " (*New Eng. Dict.*). He is mentioned in Gerrard, *Art of Warre*, 1591. A field-officer to a general.

185. *wear his colours like a tumbler's hoop*] a hoop decorated with ribbons, twisted round it, or coloured silks. With this the tumbler performed feats with his juggling sticks, and other buffoonery. See Chettle's account of William Cuckoe (whose hoop is not mentioned) in *Kind-Hartes Dream* (Bodley Head Quarto, 12), 1592 ; and see a picture of fourteenth century tumbling in Strutt's *Sports and Pastimes*. It was not a hoop for jumping through—which seems to be a later accomplishment. Tumbling was very popular and courtly at this time. See Laneham's *Letter* (Furnivall's *Cox*, p. 18) for " the feats of agilitiee, in goinges, turninges, tumblinges," etc., etc., shown by an Italian before Queen Elizabeth at Kenilworth (1575).

187. *woman that is like a German clock*] There can be no doubt the later Folios correct " cloak " rightly here,

Still a-repairing, ever out of frame,
And never going aright, being a watch,
But being watch'd that it may still go right !
Nay to be perjur'd, which is worst of all ;
And among three, to love the worst of all ;
A whitely wanton with a velvet brow,
With two pitch-balls stuck in her face for eyes ;
Ay and by heaven, one that will do the deed
Though Argus were her eunuch and her guard :
And I to sigh for her ! to watch for her !

193. *whitely*] Ff 3, 4 ; *whitly* Qq, Ff 1, 2 ; *wightly* Cambridge ; *witty* Collier.

since this simile was at once adopted by Shakespeare's successors. It is made use of by Ben Jonson, *The Silent Woman*, IV. ii. ; Webster, *Westward Ho*, I. i. ; Middleton, *A Mad World my Masters*, IV. i. ; Beaumont and Fletcher (" Dutch watches "), *Wit Without Money*, iii. ; and Cartwright, *Ordinary*. Dekker has a variant in *Newes from Hell*, 1606 (Grosart, ii. 106) : " their wits (like wheeles in Brunswick clocks) being all wound up so far as they could stretch, were all going, but not one going truly." There is an earlier mention of a " faire Germaine clocke " in *The Travels of Sir Jerome Horsey* (Hakluyt Society edition, p. 192). The work was never printed by Horsey, but the incident of the clock is dated 1580. It is surely a mere coincidence that Horsey's book is also the source of our knowledge of Ivan the Terrible's wooing (by proxy) of Lady Mary Hastings, which, it has been suggested, may lie behind the masque of Muscovites in Act V. See Introduction 3.227.

193. *whitely*] pale, sallow. Furness gives a passage cited by Arrowsmith (*Shakespeare's Commentators*, etc., p. 4) from Heywood's *Troja Britannica*, cant. 5, st. 74 : " That hath a whitely face and a long nose, And for them both I wonderous well esteeme her " (1609). Furness also cites Walker (*Critical Examination*, ii. 349) : " In North's *Plutarch* (*Life of Brutus*) Cassius and Brutus are called by Cæsar ' lean and whitely-faced fellows.' " These contemporary parallels are ample confirmation of Shakespeare's text, if confirmation be needed. The word has been disputed solely on the ground that Rosaline was dark. See IV. iii. 244-74. How can this be a difficulty ? There is nothing (except perhaps line 3 of Sonnet 130) to suggest that Rosaline or the Dark Lady of the Sonnets was swarthy though both had black eyes and hair. The word " whiteley " is in Johnson and several other dictionaries of recent date ; and see Cotgrave in v. *blanchastre*. For the connection with the Sonnets see Introduction 3.21.

194. *pitch-balls . . . eyes*] Paralleled by the modern " eyes like two burnt holes in a blanket " ; and compare *2 Henry IV*. II. ii. 88.

195. *do the deed*] the act of love, as in *The Merchant of Venice*, I. iii. 86, and commonly.

196. *Argus*] For the tale of Cyllenius (Mercury) closing the eyes of Argus, whom Juno had set to " duely watch and warde " Io, see Golding's Ovid's *Metamorphoses*, i. 770-900.

To pray for her! Go to; it is a plague
That Cupid will impose for my neglect
Of his almighty dreadful little might.
Well, I will love, write, sigh, pray, sue, and groan:
Some men must love my lady, and some Joan.

[*Exit.*

201. *sue, and groan*] *sue and groan* Ff 2, 3, 4; *shue, grone* Q 1, F 1.

198. *Go to*] to business. "Come now" is, curiously enough, the modern equivalent.

201. *sue and groan*] Some "restoration" seems necessary here, and the best we can do now is to accept the "and" supplied by the second Folio; but the missing word may equally well be another verb.

202. *lady . . . Joan*] Remembering the proverbial saying "Joan's as good as my lady." Compare Munday's *Downfall of Robert Earl of Huntington* (Hazlitt's *Dodsley*, viii. 157): "He is our lady's chaplain, but serves Joan. *Don.* Then from the Friar's fault perchance it may be The proverb grew, Joan's taken for a lady." Joan was a common name in all royal families at a much earlier period, but in Shakespeare's time it had (as Praed says) descended to the cottage and kitchen. See the last line of the closing song in this play (v. ii. 919): "While greasy Joan doth keel the pot."

ACT IV

SCENE I

Enter the Princess, Maria, Katharine, Rosaline, Boyet, *Lords, Attendants, and a Forester.*

Prin. Was that the king, that spurr'd his horse so hard
Against the steep-up rising of the hill?
For. I know not; but I think it was not he.
Prin. Whoe'er a' was, a' show'd a mounting mind.
Well, lords, to-day we shall have our despatch;
On Saturday we will return to France.
Then, forester, my friend, where is the bush
That we must stand and play the murderer in?

ACT IV

Scene I

Enter . . .] *Enter the Princesse, a Forrester, her Ladyes, and her Lordes* Qq, Ff. 1. *Prin.*] Ff, Q 2. *Quee.* Q 1 throughout the scene. 2. *steep-up rising*] *steep up rising* Qq; *steep uprising* F 1; *steep unrising* Ff 2, 3, 4. 3. *For.*] *Forr.* Q 1; *Boy.* Ff, Q 2.

Scene I

2. *steep-up*] Compare Sonnet vii. 5: "having climbed the steep-up heavenly hill"; and *The Passionate Pilgrim*: "Her stand she takes upon a steep-up hill." "Steep-down" occurs in *Othello*, v. ii. 280.

rising of the hill] Compare *The Two Gentlemen of Verona*, v. ii. 46: "meet with me Upon the rising of the mountain-foot." Sidney has "embushed his footmen in the falling of a hill, which was over-shadowed with a wood" (*Arcadia*, iii. [Feuillerat, i. 386]). But the best parallel is in Golding's Ovid's *Metamorphoses* (vii. 873, 4): "They lagged slowly after with theyr staves, and labored sore Ageinst the rysing of the hill."

4. *mounting mind*] Compare Peele, *Edward I.* I. i. (Dramatic Works, ed. Bullen, i. 93), *ante* 1593: "Sweet Nell, thou shouldst not be thyself, did not, with thy mounting mind, thy gift surmount the rest." This parallel was observed by Dyce. See earlier in Whetstone's *Remembraunce of Gascoigne* (Arber, p. 18), 1577: "and begging sutes from dunghill thoughts proceed: the mounting minde had rather sterve in need." It is found also in *The Troublesome Raigne of King John*, 1591.

8. *stand and play the murderer in*] The shooting of driven deer, with crossbows, from a specially erected "stand" was a popular amusement for formal occasions. See the

For. Hereby, upon the edge of yonder coppice;
A stand where you may make the fairest shoot.
Prin. I thank my beauty, I am fair that shoot,
And thereupon thou speak'st the fairest shoot.
For. Pardon me, madam, for I meant not so.
Prin. What, what? first praise me, and again say no?
O short-liv'd pride! Not fair? alack for woe!
For. Yes, madam, fair.
Prin. Nay, never paint me now:
Where fair is not, praise cannot mend the brow.
Here, good my glass, take this for telling true:
Fair payment for foul words is more than due.
For. Nothing but fair is that which you inherit.
Prin. See, see! my beauty will be saved by merit.
O heresy in fair, fit for these days!

11-40. *I thank . . . lord*] Consigned to the margin by Pope. 14. *and again*] Q 1; *and then again* F 1, Q 2; *then again* Ff 2, 3, 4. 18. [*giving him money*] Johnson. 22. *fair*] *faith* Collier MS.

account of the *Queen's Entertainment at Cowdray* (1591), and the German narrative (1602) of the visit of Frederick, Duke of Wirtemberg to Windsor in 1592. A common practice was to set on greyhounds to pull down the deer that were wounded but not killed—clearly a large proportion of the bag. Compare Holofernes at IV. ii. 59 below, from which it appears that hounds were being used on the present occasion.

18. *good my glass*] The forester is the mirror that shows the Princess her face at its true value. For the order, compare I. ii. 65 and III. i. 149.

20. *inherit*] own, possess; as in I. i. 73. A common use.

21. *saved by merit*] saved by that for which a person deserves recompense (as in *1 Henry IV.* I. ii. 121); but there is also a quibble upon the meaning of "merit," reward, recompense. See *Richard II.* I. iii. 156 for another example of the substantive. The Princess is referring to her "tip" to the forester, and likening it to the good works which the Catholics held would alone procure salvation, whereas the Protestants believed faith only was necessary. "Justification by faith" became one of the standard tests by which Protestant orthodoxy was tried—hence "heresy" of l. 22. "Merits" may also have a more concrete sense. Hart quotes Barnabe Googe's translation of Naogeorgus, *The Popish Kingdome*, 1570 (Chiswick, 1880): "They go and buy of other men, that commonly have more. But specially of Monkes that have the merites chiefe to sell, Sufficient both to keepe themselves and other men from hell" (Folio 40, The Third Booke). And on the following page, "All such as are not Monkes or saved by their merites heare, . . . and this makes fooles to buy their merites deare." "Merits" appears to mean certificates bought from the monks.

22. *fit for these days*] The passage may allude to what Elizabeth called the "abominable act," whereby

A giving hand, though foul, shall have fair praise.
But come, the bow: now mercy goes to kill,
And shooting well is then accounted ill.
Thus will I save my credit in the shoot:
Not wounding, pity would not let me do't;
If wounding, then it was to show my skill,
That more for praise than purpose meant to kill.
And out of question so it is sometimes,
Glory grows guilty of detested crimes,
When, for fame's sake, for praise, an outward part,
We bend to that the working of the heart;
As I for praise alone now seek to spill
The poor deer's blood, that my heart means no ill.

Boyet. Do not curst wives hold that self-sovereignty
Only for praise' sake, when they strive to be
Lords o'er their lords?

Prin. Only for praise; and praise we may afford
To any lady that subdues a lord.

Enter COSTARD.

Boyet. Here comes a member of the commonwealth.

Cost. God dig-you-den all! Pray you, which is the head lady?

32. *for praise*] Q 1, F 1; *to praise* Ff 2, 3, 4. 35. *that*] *tho'* Warburton conj. 42-54. Put in the margin by Pope.

Henri of Navarre, a champion of protestantism and her ally, bought the Catholic powers' recognition of his right to the throne of France by conversion to Rome. He was formally absolved and attended public mass on 25 July, 1593. The Princess' moralizings (ll. 30-33 below) must, on this assumption, be also aimed at Henri.

30. *out of question*] beyond question, certainly.

31. *glory*] vainglory, or the desire for glory.

36. *curst*] shrewish, cross-grained. Usually applied to women, but compare Ascham, *The Scholemaster* (Arber, p. 18), 1570: "the shrewde touches of many curste boyes."

41. *a member of the commonwealth*] Hart takes this (applied to Holofernes also at IV. ii. 76) as equivalent to a member of the *academe*, i.e. one of the study-group founded by the King. Costard can hardly be said to have been more than an affiliated member (see I. i. 178); and the phrase was common jargon—compare *Merchant of Venice*, III. v. 37. Here presumably jocular, meaning "one of the lower orders."

42. *God dig-you-den*] A mutilated form of "God give you good even." "God deven" occurs in *Gammer*

Prin. Thou shalt know her, fellow, by the rest that have no heads.
Cost. Which is the greatest lady, the highest?
Prin. The thickest and the tallest.
Cost. The thickest and the tallest! it is so; truth is truth.
An your waist, mistress, were as slender as my wit,
One o' these maids' girdles for your waist should be fit.
Are not you the chief woman? you are the thickest here.
Prin. What's your will, sir? What's your will?
Cost. I have a letter from Monsieur Berowne to one Lady Rosaline.
Prin. O! thy letter, thy letter; he's a good friend of mine.
Stand aside, good bearer. Boyet, you can carve;
Break up this capon.

50. *my wit*] *your wit* Johnson conj.

Gurton's Needle, 1575. The Folio has "*Godgigoden*" in *Romeo and Juliet*, I. ii. 59. See the *New Eng. Dict.* for other varieties. Ben Jonson has "God you good morrow" in *Bartholomew Fair*, I. i.

48, 49. *truth is truth*] proverbial. Compare Nashe, *Have With You to Saffron Walden*, 1596 (McKerrow, iii. 64): "Yet in truth (as truth is truth, and will out at one time or other, and shame the divell)"; and Gascoigne, *The Steel Glas* (Arber, p. 103), 1576: "I speake against my sex, So have I done before, But truth is truth, and muste be tolde, Though daunger kepe the dore."

50. *slender . . . wit*] Compare Lyly, *Sapho and Phao*, I. iii.: "*Molus.* You are grosse witted, master courtier. *Cryti.* And you master scholler slender witted."

54. *What's your will, sir?*] Obviously the Princess is snubbing Costard for his impertinence. Furness makes a doubt of it.

57, 58. *carve; Break up*] A technical term, originally for carving a deer, but subsequently of extended use. Compare Florio's Montaigne's *Essays*, i. 51. Montaigne quotes from Juvenal, *Sat.*, v. 127: "*Nec minimo sane discrimine refert, Quo gestu lepores, et quo gallina secetur.* What grace we use, it makes small difference, when We carve a Hare, or else breake up a Hen" ("decouper un lievre ou un poulet"). In *The Winter's Tale*, III. ii. 132, the expression occurs of a letter: "Break up the seals and read." The words "you can carve" are addressed to Boyet with a quibble on the sense "court affectedly" (used also of Boyet at v. ii. 323). Compare Gascoigne, *Glasse of Government*, 1575: "Oh how this comforteth my hart; thys letter commeth from my younger sonne: I will break it up." See also *The Merchant of Venice*, II. iv. 10.

58. *capon*] Theobald pointed out that "capon is here used like

Boyet. I am bound to serve.
This letter is mistook; it importeth none here;
It is writ to Jaquenetta.
Prin. We will read it, I swear.
Break the neck of the wax, and every one give ear.

Boyet. [*Reads.*] By heaven, that thou art fair, is most infallible; true, that thou art beauteous; truth itself, that thou art lovely. More fairer than fair, beautiful than beauteous, truer than truth itself, have commiseration on thy heroical vassal! The magnanimous and most illustrate king Cophetua

66. *illustrate*] *illustrious* Q 2.

the French *poulet*." Cotgrave has: "*Poulet:* a chicken, also a love-letter or love-message." Thackeray uses the term: "sate down to pen a poulet . . . to Mademoiselle" (*Vanity Fair*, chap. xxiv.). French was so commonly spoken, I suppose the joke did not seem far-fetched, especially as we are supposed to be in France. Furness refers to Laneham's *Letter* (1575) for a similar expression, "colld pigeon" (Feuillerat, *Cox*, 59), but it is a bad parallel. The expression there is equivalent to "cold pie," a rebuke or reprimand, and there is no mention of a letter.

59. *mistook*] Compare *Speeches to the Queen at Rycot*, 1592 (Nichols, iii. 170): "a French Page came with three other letters: the one written to the Lady Squemish, which being mistaken by a wrong superscription, was read before her Majestie."

61. *Break the neck*] Still alluding to the capon (Johnson).

64, 65. *More fairer than fair . . . truer than truth*, etc.] See note at I. ii. 157-59. Compare Sidney's *Arcadia*, bk. i. (ed. Fueillerat, i. 32), *ante* 1586: "That which made her fairenesse much the fayrer, was, that it was but a faire embassadour of a most faire minde," and often elsewhere.

66. *illustrate*] illustrious. See again V. i. 117. The word also had the sense resplendent, illuminated, as in Chapman's *Phyllis and Flora* (*Minor Poems*, etc., 1875, p. 48), 1595: "bright in blee As stars illustrate bodies be." The *New Eng. Dict.* has examples as early as 1526 in good English writers.

66, 67. *king Cophetua . . . beggar Zenelophon*] We have already had a reference to the ballad of the King and the Beggar (without names) "which the world was very guilty of some three ages since; but I think 'tis not now to be found; or, if it were, it would neither serve for the writing nor the tune." It is only reasonable to identify Armado's first ballad with the reference he makes to the King and the Beggar here. Shakespeare refers to the story again in *Romeo and Juliet*, II. i. 54: "Young Adam Cupid, he that shot so trim When *King Cophetua* loved the beggar maid"; and the name "King Cophetua" is mentioned (apparently a quotation) in a ranting passage in *2 Henry IV.* v. iii. 106; and again the title is recalled in *Richard II.* v. iii. 80. Ben Jonson also has "as rich as King Cophetua" in *Every Man in his Humour*, III. iv. There is a ballad on "King Cophetua and the Beggar-maid" in Percy's *Reliques*, 1st series, bk. ii. 6, from Johnson's *Crown Garland of Goulden Roses*, 1612, where its title is "A Song of a Beggar and a King." But the language of this ballad, as Capell says, "most certainly has not set eye upon the pernicious and indubitate beggar Zenelophon, and he it was that might rightly say, *veni, vidi, vici;* which to annothanize in the vulgar (O base and obscure vulgar!) *videlicet*, he came, saw, and overcame: he came,

67. *Zenelophon*] *Penelophon* Collier. 69. *annothanize*] Qq, F 1; *anatomize* Ff 2, 3, 4. 70. *saw*] Ff 2, 3, 4; *see* Qq, F 1.

the age that Moth speaks of." One line in it seems to me more likely to be a quotation from *Romeo and Juliet* than *vice versa*. In this ballad the name of the beggar is corrupted to "Penelophon." But, on Moth's authority, the early ballad was very different from the dainty and decorously-worded song in Percy. There is a passage in Marston's *Scourge of Villainy* (Bullen's *Marston*, iii. 302), 1598, which alludes to something more in keeping with Moth's reminiscences: "Go buy some ballad of the Fairy King, And of the Beggar-wench, some roguy thing. Which thou mayst chant unto the chamber-maid To some vile tune." Moth finds fault also with the tune. There seems to have been also a drama on the subject, which is referred to probably in *2 Henry IV.* and in D'Avenant's *Wits*, II. i. (1636): "spoke like the bold Cophetua's son!"

67. *indubitate*] certain. Not elsewhere in Shakespeare, but a long-used (Caxton, 1480) sound word. Schmidt suggests that Armado blunders, but he does not. An unmistakable beggar is set antithetically against a most illustrious king. In a letter to *The Times Literary Supplement* of 26 April 1947, Alan Keen pointed out that "indubitate" again appears with "illustrate" (actually "illustre") on the title (1548) of Edward Hall's *The Union of the two noble and illustre famelies of Lancastre and Yorke,—proceading to the reigne of the High and prudent Prince King Henry the eighth, the indubitate and very heire of the said linages.* Shakespeare clearly studied Hall deeply in preparing *Henry IV* and *Henry V.* If this letter is part of the "revision" of the play (see note on line 86 below) it might have been written in 1597, at the very time when Shakespeare was steeped in Hall.

68-70. *say, veni, vidi, vici . . . came, saw, and overcame*] The original source of this famous quotation is North's *Plutarch* (*Julius Caesar*), 1570: "Caesar . . . fought a great battell with King Pharnaces. . . . And because he would advertise one of his friends of the suddenness of this victory, he only wrote three words unto Anicius at Rome: *Veni, Vidi, Vici:* to wit, I came, saw, and overcame. These three words ending all with like sound and letters in the Latin, have a certain short grace, more pleasant to the ear, than can be well expressed in any other tongue" (Temple Classics, vii. 187). This passage, in North's words (from "three words" to "overcame"), is quoted earlier than by Shakespeare in T. Bowes' translation of De la Primaudaye's *French Academy* (1586), in chap. xii., "Of Speech and Speaking"; and from thence into Greene's prose-tracts (Grosart, v. 206, 276), in *Penelope's Web* (1587), and *The Spanish Masquerado* (1589), but without "came, saw, and overcame."

69. *annothanize*] usually taken as an old spelling of *anatomize*. But Alan Keen, in the letter quoted at line 67 above, suggests it is a mock-latin coinage meaning "annotate," "gloss."

69, 70. *vulgar* (*O base . . . vulgar*)] This is another Arcadianism. Compare bk. ii. (Feuillerat, i. 238): "Which when this good old woman

one; saw, two; overcame, three. Who came? the king: why did he come? to see: why did he see? to overcome. To whom came he? to the beggar: what saw he? the beggar: who overcame he? the beggar. The conclusion is victory: on whose side? the king's. The captive is enriched: on whose side? the beggar's. The catastrophe is a nuptial: on whose side? the king's; no, on both in one, or one in both. I am the king, for so stands the comparison; thou the beggar, for so witnesseth thy lowliness. Shall I command thy love? I may. Shall I enforce thy love? I could. Shall I entreat thy love? I will. What shalt thou exchange for rags? robes: for tittles? titles: for thyself?

71. *saw*] Rowe; *see* Qq, Ff. *overcame*] Q 2, Ff 3, 4; *covercame* Q 1, Ff 1, 2. 75. *the king's*] Q 2, Ff 3, 4; *the king* Q 1, F 1.

perceived—O the good wold woman!" and again: "her body (O sweet body!) covered," etc.; and again: "One day (O day that shined to make them dark!"). Lyly has the same trick (later than *Arcadia*) in *Endymion*, I. i.: "his person (ah sweet person) . . . his sharpe wit (ah wit too sharpe)," etc.

vulgar (O base and obscure vulgar!)] "Vulgar," meaning vernacular tongue, occurs again in *As You Like It*, v. i. 33, in a similar strain: "abandon, which is in the vulgar, leave." In I. ii. 46 above, we have had "the vulgar" used absolutely for the common people. Compare Puttenham, *Arte of English Poesie*, 1589 (but written earlier): "Offices of service and love towards the dead . . . called Obsequies in our vulgar" (p. 63); "such maner of Poesie is called in our vulgar ryme dogrell" (p. 89). "In theyr vulgar tongue," the full expression, is in "Publike Baptisme," in *The First Prayer Book of King Edward VI.*, 1549.

73-76. *To whom came he? to the beggar . . . on whose side? the beggar's*] This is Gabriel Harvey's favourite style. Compare *Pierce's Supererogation* (Grosart, ii. 176): "What the saluation of David Gorge? a nullitie: what the deification of N. H.? a nullitie: what the sanctification of Browne? a nullitie; what the communitie of Barrow? a nullitie: what the plausibilitie of Marten? a nullitie." In scene iii. of *Pedantius* (levelled at G. Harvey), *circa* 1581, there is a parallel noticed by Moore Smith (*Materialien zur kunde des älteren Englischen Dramas*, Band viii. p. xlvii.): "Quis in Grammatica Congruus? Nonne Pedantius? Quis in Poetarum hortis floridus? Nonne Pedantius? Quis in Rhetorum pompa potens? Nonne Pedantius?" For Harvey see Introduction, 5.22.

79, 80. *Shall I command . . . Shall I enforce thy love*] From Lyly: "I will not enforce marriage where I cannot compell love" (*Campaspe*, v. 4 [1581]); and "Well Semele, I will not command love, for it cannot be enforced: let me entreat it" (*Endymion*, v. 3 [?1586]); and *Sapho and Phao*, iv. 1 (1581): "Yeeld to me, Phao; I intreat where I may command; command thou, where thou shouldst intreat."

82. *exchange for*] obtain in exchange for. The *New Eng. Dict.* refers this "obsolete" sense to Spenser, *Faerie Queene*, VII. vi. 6.

for rags? robes:] "Cupid is blinde and shooteth at random, as soone hitting a ragge as a robe, and piercing as soone the bosome of a Captive as me. Thus, expecting thy reply, I profane my lips on thy foot, my eyes on thy picture, and my heart on thy every part.

Thine in the dearest design of industry,

DON ADRIANO DE ARMADO.

86. *Adriano*] Q 2 ; *Adriana* Q 1, Ff. *Armado*] Ff 2, 3, 4 ; *Armatho* Qq, F 1.

the brest of a Libertine" (Lodge, *Euphues Golden Legacie* [*Shakes. Lib.*, Hazlitt's edition, p. 33], 1590) ; and again : "Cupid shootes at a ragge as soone as at a roabe" (p. 68) : and again : "Venus jettes in Roabes not ragges" (p. 100) ; and "Will Venus joyne roabes and ragges together ?" (p. 117). Thackeray perhaps remembered this : "Lady Bareacres . . . a toothless bald old woman now—a mere rag of a former robe of state" (*Vanity Fair*, chap. xlix.).

tittles] jots, particles, points or small lines. Commonly used in the "criss-cross row." An early example occurs in *The Two Italian Gentlemen* (a translation of L. Pasqualigo's *Il Fedele*, Malone Soc., ed. P. Simpson, l. 1704), 1584 : "I ipse tipse tittle tittle este amen." A standard ending, quoted by Nashe in *Have With You*, etc. (McKerrow, iii. 46) : "a per se, con per se, tittle, est, Amen ! . . . he comes uppon thee with a whole Hornbooke" ; and in *How a Man may Chuse a Good Wife* (Hazlitt's *Dodsley*, ix. 42), *circa* 1600 : "I was five years learning to crish-cross from great A . . . so in process of time I came to e per se e and com per se, and tittle," etc., etc. This was probably the most familiar meaning.

for tittles ? titles] A quibble of Harvey's : "I am alwayes marvellously beholding unto you, for your bountifull Titles. . . . But to let Titles and Tittles passe, and come to the very point in deede" (*Letter to Spenser* [Grosart, i. 25], 1579). This is pre-euphuist, but it is a favourite mode of Lyly's and copied by many writers : for example, Drayton in his dedications to *The Harmonie of the Church* (1591) : "not as poems of poets, but praiers of prophets ; and vouchsafe to be their gracious patronesse against any graceless parasite" ; and "I speak . . . not of toyes in Mount Ida, but of triumphes in Mount Sion : not of vanitie, but of veritie ; not of tales, but of truethes."

83. *profane my lips*] "I kiss thy hand" was a common, respectful ending to a letter, especially from a lover or suitor. Compare *The Shepherdess Felismena* (Hazlitt's *Shakes. Lib.*, p. 284) : "all is mine doth wholly consist in your hands, the which, with all reverence and dutifull affection, a thousand times I kisse" ; and Nashe (mockingly), Ded. to *Lenten Stuffe* (McKerrow, iii. 150) : "and so I kisse the shadow of your feetes shadow."

85. *industry*] assiduity in ladies' service. In *The Queen's Entertainment at Cowdray*, 1591 (Nichols, iii. 109), industry is described as "careful and kind diligence." This word was used widely and affectedly. Gabriel Harvey has it several times while bestowing lavish praise on his friend Sidney and his "Countess of Pembroke's Arcadia" in *Pierce's Supererogation* (Grosart, ii. 99-102) : "Lord, what would himselfe have prooved in fine, that was the gentleman of Curtesy, the Esquier of Industry, and the Knight of Valour at those yeeres ? Live ever sweete Booke." Our "gallantry."

86. *Adriano de Armado*] Dover Wilson takes the unusual form of the name found here in the early texts and the setting of the letter in roman (as against the elaborate italic of that in I. i.) as evidences that the two belong to different drafts of Shakespeare's manuscript. See Introduction, 2.56.

Thus dost thou hear the Nemean lion roar
'Gainst thee, thou lamb, that standest as his prey ;
Submissive fall his princely feet before,
And he from forage will incline to play.
But if thou strive, poor soul, what art thou then ?
Food for his rage, repasture for his den.

Prin. What plume of feathers is he that indited this letter ?
What vane ? what weathercock ? did you ever hear better ?

Boyet. I am much deceiv'd but I remember the style.

Prin. Else your memory is bad, going o'er it erewhile.

Boyet. This Armado is a Spaniard, that keeps here in court ;
A phantasime, a Monarcho, and one that makes sport

98. *phantasime*] Qq, F 1 ; *phantasm* Ff 2, 3, 4 ; *phantasma* Capell conj. *Monarcho*] *monarcho* Q 2.

87. *Nemean lion*] So accented in *Hamlet*, I. iv. 83. The reference is to the first of Hercules' labours, which Shakespeare recalled from Golding's *Ovid*, ix. 242 : " The Nemean Lyon by theis armes lyes dead uppon the ground " (1567). Here it was he found his pronunciation of Nemean, an alternative in both the Greek and the Latin. This is the sonnet Armado promises us at I. ii. 174, so we must be content. We have here too the Armado of " high-born words," foreshadowed and foregone, of I. i. 171.

90. *from forage will incline*] will turn from his first intentions, which are naturally to prey.

94. *vane*] " vane " naturally suggests weathercock, but it should more properly be written here " fane," an obsolete word signifying " flag, banner, pendant " (*New Eng. Dict.*), also written " fan " as in Chapman's *Two Wise Men*, etc., IV. iii. (1619) : " I could devise them a crest as fit as a fan for a forehorse." There is a good illustrative passage in *The Feast of St. George observed at Utrecht*, 1586 (Nichols' *Progresses*, ii. 457) : " Then began the trumpets to sound in the service, which was most prince-like and aboundant, served on the knee, carved and tasted to her Majesties trencher ; . . . sundry sortes of musickes continued the entring of the first course ; which done and avoyded, the trumpets sounded in for the second, which was all baked meats of beasts and fowles ; the beasts, as lions, dragons, leopards, and such like bearing phaines or arms ; and the fowles, as peacocks, swans, pheasants, turkie cocks, and others in their natural feathers, spread in their greatest pride, which sight was both rare and magnificent."

weathercock] Taken as a type of showiness, as in *The Merry Wives of Windsor*, III. ii. 18. So Sidney, *Arcadia*, bk. iii. (Feuillerat, i. 419) : " woulde . . . proclayme his blasphemies against womankinde ; that namely that sex was . . . the shops of vanities, the guilded wethercocks."

95, 96. *style . . . going o'er it*] The same pun as in I. i. 197.

98. *phantasime*] This word, on which Quarto and First Folio agree, is not found elsewhere, though

To the prince and his book-mates.
Prin. Thou, fellow, a word.
Who gave thee this letter?
Cost. I told you; my lord.
Prin. To whom should'st thou give it?
Cost. From my lord to my lady.
Prin. From which lord to which lady?
Cost. From my lord Berowne, a good master of mine,
To a lady of France that he call'd Rosaline.
Prin. Thou hast mistaken his letter. Come, lords, away.
Here, sweet, put up this: 'twill be thine another
day. [*Exeunt Princess and train.*

105. *lords*] *ladies* Johnson conj.

"phantasims" of v. i. 19 is presumably the same. The sense required is something distinct from "phantasm"; not a creature of the fancy, but one full of fancies.

Monarcho] A real fantastical character of the time. He appears to have been a crazy hanger-on to the Court, whose vain-gloriousness made him a butt. Thomas Churchyard wrote a tedious epitaph to *The Phantasticall Monarke*, printed in a collection called his *Chance* (1580) which is given at length by Steevens. Steevens also quotes from *A briefe Discourse of the Spanish State, with a Dialogue annexed, intituled Philobasilis* (1590), p. 39: "The actors were that Bergamasco (for his phantastick humours) named Monarcho, and two of the Spanish embassadours retinue, who being about foure and twentie yeares past, in Paules Church in London, contended who was soveraigne of the world: the Monarcho maintained himself to be he, and named their king to be but his viceroy for Spaine, the other two with great fury denying it," etc., etc. He is honoured by other references in writers of the time. Farmer quotes from Meres' *Wits Commonwealth* (p. 178): "Peter Shakerlye of Paules, and Monarcho that lived about the court." Steevens refers also to Nashe's *Have With You to Saffron Walden* (McKerrow, iii. 76), 1596: "an insulting monarch above Monarcha the Italian, that ware crownes in his shooes" while Douce cites from Scot's *Discoverie of Witchcraft*, 1584, to the effect that, like Thrasibulus, he was "sore oppressed with the like spirit or conceipt" (ed. B. Nicholson, 1886, p. 42).

105. *mistaken*] taken to the wrong person, miscarried. See above, l. 59.

106. *be thine another day*] In *Notes and Queries* for 26 Feb. 1910 (p. 164), and again for 4 Jan. 1914 (p. 7), "M. P. T." quoted a number of parallel passages to show, convincingly, that this phrase does not mean, as Daniel suggested, "it will be of use to you hereafter," but "Your turn will come one day." The best is perhaps from Dekker, *Gul's Horn Booke* (ed. O. Smeaton, p. 52): "Marry, when silver comes in, remember to pay treble their [the watermen's] fare, and it will make your Flounder-catchers to send more thanks after you, when you do not draw, then when you doe; for they know, *It will be their owne another daie*." Evidently proverbial, though it does not occur again in Shakespeare.

Boyet. Who is the suitor? who is the suitor?
Ros. Shall I teach you to know?
Boyet. Ay, my continent of beauty.
Ros. Why, she that bears the bow.
Finely put off!
Boyet. My lady goes to kill horns; but if thou marry,
Hang me by the neck if horns that year miscarry.
Finely put on!
Ros. Well then, I am the shooter.
Boyet. And who is your deer?
Ros. If we choose by the horns, yourself come not near.
Finely put on, indeed!
Mar. You still wrangle with her, Boyet, and she strikes at the brow.
Boyet. But she herself is hit lower: have I hit her now?
Ros. Shall I come upon thee with an old saying, that

107. *suitor . . . suitor*] Steevens (Farmer); *shooter* Qq, Ff. 107 to end of scene. Put in margin by Pope. 114. *horns, yourself come*] Qq, Ff, Cambridge, Furness; *horns, yourself: come* Rowe, Steevens *et seq.*

107. *suitor*] Formerly, and still provincially, pronounced "shooter." Hence the quibble. There are three closely written pages on this in Furness. He cites a good example from Lyly's *Euphues* (Arber, p. 293): "There was a Lady in Spaine . . . hadde three sutors (and yet never a good Archer)."

108. *continent*] that which contains; the sum. Compare Greene, *Never Too Late* (Grosart, viii. 50): "they be women and therefore the continents of all excellence" (1590); and his *Alcida* (ix. 208), 1588: "women, the painted continents of flattery, of deceit," etc., etc.

109-115. *put off . . . put on*] These terms occur in antithesis in Gascoigne's *Hermit's Tale* (Works, ed. Cunliffe, ii. 480), 1576: "charged . . . to weare this punyshment with paciens, which necessyty did putt on, and destyny wold putt off." Perhaps military or fencing terms, to hit or strike at, and to guard, ward off or parry. Lyly has similar ejaculations of encouragement to punsters in *Mother Bombie*: "well brought about," "excellently applied."

113. *who is your deer?*] So in Lyly's *Gallathea*, II. i. (1585): "Saw you not the deere come this way . . . whose dear was it. . . . I saw none but mine own dear."

114. *yourself come not near*] Boyet is warned to keep off for fear of being shot—he is such a temptingly good "head." Or perhaps Rowe's punctuation may be right, and the meaning that Rosaline gives Boyet "the horns," as common chaff, and then cries "come not near," as he threatens active reprisals.

118. *come upon thee with*] attack thee with (as in Genesis xxxiv. 25). Compare *The Taming of the Shrew*, I. ii. 42: "O heavens! Spake you not these words plain, 'Sirrah, Knock me here' . . .? And come you now with 'Knocking at the gate'?"

was a man when King Pepin of France was a little boy, as touching the hit it?

Boyet. So I may answer thee with one as old, that was a woman when Queen Guinever of Britain was a little wench, as touching the hit it.

Ros. Thou canst not hit it, hit it, hit it,
Thou canst not hit it, my good man.
[*Exit.*

Boyet. An I cannot, cannot, cannot,
An I cannot, another can.

Cost. By my troth, most pleasant: how both did fit it!

Mar. A mark marvellous well shot, for they both did hit it.

Boyet. A mark! O! mark but that mark; a mark, says my lady.
Let the mark have a prick in't, to mete at, if it may be.

126. *An*] *And* Q 1; omitted Ff, Q 2.

129. *hit it*] F 4; *hit* Qq, Ff 1, 2, 3.

119. *King Pepin*] The founder of the Carlovingian dynasty, died 768. As a representative of ancient times we meet him again in *All's Well that Ends Well*, II. i. 79.

122. *Queen Guinever*] The name was used in contempt. See Nashe, *Have With You to Saffron Walden* (McKerrow, iii. 102), 1596: "Since the raigne of Queen Gueniver was there never seene worse"; and Dekker, *A Strange Horse-Race* (Grosart, iii. 358), 1613: "the Divell . . . had no sooner touched his old Laplandian Guenevora, but shee as speedily quickened." See also Dekker's *Satiromastix* (Pearson, i. 219), and Beaumont and Fletcher, *The Scornful Lady*, v. i.

124. *Thou canst not hit it*] The tune of this song, or catch, is given in Chappell's *Popular Music of the Olden Time* (1859) i. 239, from an MS. at Oxford bearing date 1620. It was a dance-tune; and the dance is mentioned in *Wily Beguiled* (Malone Soc. l. 2451), 1606: "Thou art mine own sweetheart, From thee Ile ne'er depart; Thou art my Ciperlillie And I thy Trangdidownedilly, And sing hey ding a ding ding: And do the tother thing, And when tis done not misse, To give my wench a kisse: And then dance canst thou not hit it? Ho, brave William Cricket!" Gosson refers to it as a dance in his *Quips for Upstart Newfangled Gentlewomen*, 1595: "*Can you hit it* is oft their daunce." The song is referred to in Rowley's *Match at Midnight*, I. i. (Hazlitt's *Dodsley*, xiii. 23): "A widow witty—Is pastime pretty . . . an old man—*Sim.* Then will she answer, *If you cannot, a younger can.*"

131. *mark . . . prick . . . mete at*] Minshew's *Guide into the Tongues* (ed. 1627) has: "a *Marke*, white or pricke to shoote at . . . L(atin), *Meta, à metendo*, quod posita sit in dimenso spatio."

prick] This word had a variety of derivative senses in archery, which are dealt with by Furnivall at considerable length in a note prefixed to *The Babees Book*, pp. c.-ciii., where

Mar. Wide o' the bow-hand ! i' faith, your hand is out.
Cost. Indeed, a' must shoot nearer, or he'll ne'er hit the clout.
Boyet. An if my hand be out, then belike your hand is in.
Cost. Then will she get the upshoot by cleaving the pin.
Mar. Come, come, you talk greasily ; your lips grow foul.
Cost. She's too hard for you at pricks, sir : challenge her to bowl.

135. *pin*] Ff 2, 3, 4 ; *is in* Qq, F 1.

many references will be found, including, of course, Ascham's *Toxophilus*. We are only concerned here with the primary meaning of "mark." But it is quite possible that this sense arose from the use of peeled wands (compare butchers' *pricks*) as a mark. Compare *Guye of Gisborne*, one of the earliest Robin Hood ballads (Percy Folio, ii. 232) : "they cutt them downe the summer shroggs Which grew both under a Bryar, And sett them 3 score rood in twinn To shoote the prickes full neare." See line 137 below, note.

to mete at] to measure, to aim or level at.

132. *Wide o' the bow-hand*] far from the mark ; literally, on the left or bow-hand side. An instruction from the butts called out to the archer, by those who gave aim. This is the earliest example of the expression in *New Eng. Dict.* It became common later in the dramatists. Compare Sir J. Harington, *A Brief View*, etc. (*Nugae Antiquae*, ed. 1779, i. 28), 1608 : "wide of the right way, upon the sinister or bow-hand, many miles."

133. *hit the clout*] The target was fixed by a pin or clout (Fr. *clou*), the head of which was painted white and marked the centre. Compare Ben Jonson, Epilogue to *The Staple of News* : "our hope Is though the clout we do not always hit, It will not be imputed to his wit." See also Marlowe's *Tamburlaine* (pt. ii.), iv. 8 : "For kings are clouts that every man shoots at." The derivation here given (supported by "clout-nail") may be doubtful ; it comes from Gifford, but is not quoted in *New Eng. Dict.* A "white rag" is possibly the true origin.

135. *upshoot*] upshot. It is so written in Bullen's *Old Plays*, iv. 137 ; and in *Masques Performed before the Queen*, 1592 (Nichols, iii. 208). Compare Nashe, *Anatomie of Absurditie* (McKerrow, i. 7), 1589 : "every man shotte his bolte, but this was the upshot" ; *How a Man may Chuse a Good Wife* (Hazlitt's *Dodsley*, ix. 23) : "who could miss the clout Having so fair a white, such steady aim ; This is the upshot : now bid for the game" ; and Middleton's *Family of Love*, v. iii. : "an arrow that sticks for the upshot against all comers." Not necessarily the deciding shot, but the best shot in, till it is beaten.

cleaving the pin] This expression occurs in *Guye of Gisborne* quoted above : "he clove the good pricke wand" ; and in Middleton's *No Wit no Help like a Woman's*, ii. i. : "I'll cleave the black pin i' the midst of the white." See also *Romeo and Juliet* II. iv. 15 ; and G. Harvey's *Three Proper Letters* (Grosart, i. 65), 1580 : "The second more speciall, as it were, hitting the white indeede, and cleaving the Pinne in sunder."

Boyet. I fear too much rubbing. Good night, my good owl. *Exeunt Boyet, Maria, and Katharine.*
Cost. By my soul, a swain! a most simple clown!
Lord, Lord, how the ladies and I have put him down!
O' my troth, most sweet jests! most incony vulgar wit;
When it comes so smoothly off, so obscenely as it were, so fit.
Armado to th'one side, O! a most dainty man,
To see him walk before a lady, and to bear her fan!

138. *Exeunt*] Theobald; Qq, Ff omit. 143. *Armado to th'one*] New; *Armatho ath toothen* Q 1; *Armathor ath to the* F 1; *Armado ath to* Ff 2, 3, 4; *Armado a'th to* Rowe; *Armado o' the one* Dyce, Cambridge; *Armado a th' t'other* Keightley.

136. *greasily*] indecently, in a "smutty" way. Marston speaks of "greasie Aretine" (Bullen's edition, iii. 320); and Ben Jonson, *Bartholomew Fair*, II. i.: "her language grows greasier than her pigs."

137. *at pricks*] Compare *Gesta Grayorum*, 1594 (Malone Soc., ed. Greg, p. 17): "any forbidden manner of Shooting; as at Pricks in common Highways."

138. *rubbing*] "rub" was a technical term in the game of bowls. It was definitely used of the touches of the bowl against others on its passage to the jack or mistress. But it was employed generally of the course of the bowl. Sir J. Harington says Martin Marprelate took "this taunting scoffe that the Bishop would cry Rub, rub, rub, to his bowle, and when it was gone too farre say, The Divell goe with it" (*A Brief View*, etc., 1608 [*Nugae Antiquae*, i. 21, ed. 1779]). Shadwell, in *Epsom Wells*, Act iii., has "Rub, rub, narrow, short, gone a thousand yards, and such like words of Bowlers."

owl] rhymes with *bowl*, which was evidently pronounced as *owl* now is. See for the word in its other sense, v. ii. 915, rhyming again with *owl*. Ben Jonson makes a point of this rhyme in a passage about "Crambo! another of the devil's games" in *The Devil is an Ass*, v. v. (1616): "Yes, wis, knight, shite, Poul, joul, owl, foul, troul, boul." The word is still heard so "in the vulgar."

142. *obscenely*] Costard's word is apt, whether he intends it or not. Maria's rebuke (line 136) might well have come ten lines earlier.

143. *to th'one*] To explain the Quarto reading Dover Wilson supposes that the compositor expanded "Armath," carelessly written, with a break between syllables, into "Armath ath."

143-147. *Armado . . . his page*] What are they doing in this scene? We must suppose that they took some part in it in an earlier draft. See note on l. 86 above for possible evidence of revision. The vagueness of the directions, in the Quarto and Folio, for the characters leaving the stage, may also be due to careless redrafting.

144. *bear her fan*] A correct attention, presumably, from a gallant of the time. Henry Hutton, satirizing a gallant in *Folies Anatomie* (1616), says: "I durst not use my mistres' fan Or walk attended with a hackney-man." These gentlemen would

To see him kiss his hand! and how most sweetly
a' will swear!
And his page o' t' other side, that handful of wit!
Ah! heavens, it is a most pathetical nit.
Sola, sola! [*Shout within.*
[*Exit Costard*

SCENE II

Enter HOLOFERNES, *Sir* NATHANIEL, *and* DULL.

Nath. Very reverend sport, truly: and done in the testimony of a good conscience.

145. Collier inserted a line of his own here: "Looking babies in her eyes his passion to declare." 146. *o' t' other*] *atother* Q 1, F 1; *at other* Q 2, Ff 2, 3, 4. 147. *a*] omitted in Qq, F 1. 148. *Sola*] *Sowla* Qq, Ff. [*Shout within*] F 4; *Shoot within* Q 1; *Shoote within* F 1; *Showte within* F 2. [*Exit . . .*] Capell; *Exeunt* Qq, Ff.

Scene II

Holofernes] *Holofernos, the Pedant* Qq, Ff.

purloin a feather as a keepsake: "this feather grew in her sweet fan sometimes" (Ben Jonson, *Every Man out of his Humour*, II. i.); and "A third . . . Will spend his patrimony for a garter Or the least feather in her bounteous fan" (*Cynthia's Revels*, III. ii.). We come from the sublime to the ridiculous when the Nurse in *Romeo and Juliet*, II. iv. 232, says: "Peter take my fanne and goe before and apace" (Q 1, Cambridge ed.). Farmer quotes from *The Serving Man's Comfort*, 1598: "The mistress must have one to carry her cloake and hood, another her fanne."

145. *To see him kiss his hand*] See also V. ii. 324. Malone believed a line was lost after line 145. Hence Collier's amazing insertion which gave rise to some entertaining notes.

147. *pathetical*] See I. ii. 92.

nit] anything very small, as in *The Taming of the Shrew*, IV. iii. 110. A speck. Properly the word means the egg (lens) of any small insect, especially a louse. Florio has: "*Lendini*, nits before they be lice, chits." Also a gnat, a fly, a fairy.

148. *Sola*] Compare Lancelot's "Sola, sola: wo ha ho, sola, sola" (*The Merchant of Venice*, V. i. 49). This is given as a hunting halloo in *A Twelfe Night Merriment* (*Narcissus*), 1602.

Shout within] As this is a hunting scene (and "Sola" a hunting cry) the "Shot" or "Shoot" of early texts may conceivably be correct. But "shouting" is printed as "shooting" in *Coriolanus*, I. i. 218 (F 1); and it would be difficult to produce an effective "noise off" from the twang or thud of a cross-bow.

Scene II

Enter Holofernes] The name was probably borrowed from Rabelais' *Gargantua* (1535), whose hero was taught Latin by "un grand docteur sophiste, nommé Maistre Thubal Holoferne."

1, 2. *in the testimony of a good conscience*] with the approbation or warrant of a good conscience. Compare 2 Corinthians i. 12.

Hol. The deer was, as you know, *sanguis*, in blood ; ripe as the pomewater, who now hangeth like a jewel in the ear of *coelo*, the sky, the welkin, the heaven ; and anon falleth like a crab on the face of *terra*, the soil, the land, the earth.

Nath. Truly, Master Holofernes, the epithets are sweetly varied, like a scholar at the least : but, sir, I assure ye, it was a buck of the first head.

3. *Hol.*] *Ped.* Qq, Ff. 4. *the*] Qq 1, 2 ; *a* Ff. 5. *coelo*] *celo* Qq, Ff 1, 2.

3. *sanguis, in blood*] Dover Wilson quotes a suggestion of W. W. Greg that Shakespeare wrote "sanguĩe," a recognized abbreviation for "sanguine," but the S may as easily be Holofernes' blunder as the compositor's. See also note on *coelo*, l. 5. These Latin words are devoid of any special force excepting that they are the emblems of the pedant's (schoolmaster's) trade, for testimony of which they are dragged in. "In blood, a term of the chase, in a state of perfect health and vigour" (Schmidt). Compare *1 Henry VI.* IV. ii. 48 ; *Coriolanus*, I. i. 163, and IV. v. 225. No satisfactory parallel has been given outside Shakespeare. But compare Ben Jonson, *The Sad Shepherd*, I. ii. : "*Robin.* What head? *John.* Forked : a heart of ten. *Marian.* He is good venison, According to the season in the blood."

4. *pomewater*] Once a popular apple, but long forgotten. Parkinson (1627) figures it in his *Paradisus :* "The *Pomewater* is an excellent good and great whitish apple, full of sap or moisture, somewhat pleasant sharp, but a little bitter withal : it will not last long, the winter frosts soone causing it to rot and perish." It was evidently in much demand since it was cried by the Irish costermongers. See Ben Jonson's *Irish Masque at Court*, 1613 : "I sherve ti majesties owne cashtermonger, be me trote ; and cry peepsh [pippins] and pomwatersh in ti majesties shervice, tis five year now" ; and Dekker, *Old Fortunatus*, 1600 : "Enter *Andelocia* and *Shadowe*, like Irish costarmongers . . . peeps of Tamasco, feene peeps : I fat 'tis de sweetest apple in de world, 'tis better den Pome-water, or apple John."

5. *coelo*] "*Cielo.* The heaven, the skie, the firmament or welkin" (Florio, *New World of Words*, 1611) ; "*Terra.* The element called earth. . . . Also, any land . . . or soile" (*ibid.* 1598). These definitions are given here because they support Dr. Warburton's conjecture that Holofernes stood for Florio, in which he was supported by Farmer and others. But the date of Florio's *Italian Dictionary* upsets that slight argument. Marshall altered *sanguis* to an Italian form (*sanguino*), according to the same theory probably.

10. *buck of the first head*] a fully grown buck. Steevens quotes here from the *Return from Parnassus* (1602), where the names of the "speciall beasts for chase" are given as in the text (ed. W. D. Macray, pp. 107, 108), and see Harrison's *Description of England*, bk. iii., chap. iv., 1577 (New Shakes. Soc., p. 26) : "The yoong males which our fallow deere doo bring foorth, are commonlie named according to their severall ages : for the first yeere it is a fawne, the second a puckot [pricket], the third a serell, the fourth a soare, the fift a bucke of the first head ; not bearing the name of a bucke till he be

Hol. Sir Nathaniel, *haud credo.*

Dull. 'Twas not a *haud credo*, 'twas a pricket.

Hol. Most barbarous intimation ! yet a kind of insinuation, as it were *in via*, in way of explication ; *facere*, as it were replication, or, rather, *ostentare*, to show, as it were, his inclination,—after his undressed, unpolished, uneducated, unpruned, untrained, or rather unlettered, or ratherest, unconfirmed fashion—to insert again my *haud credo* for a deer.

five yeers old : and from hencefoorth his age is commonlie knowne by his head or horns." The form *prekette* dates back to 1503 (Eden's *Translation of Vertomannus*).

11. *Sir*] The normal title for a priest. Marprelate even gives it to Saint Peter, to show how Catholics would make an ecclesiastic of him.

haud credo] This occurs in *The Troublesome Raigne of King John* (Hazlitt's ed. of *Shakespeare's Library*, p. 264), *ante* 1591 : "*Haud credo* Laurentius, that thou shouldst be pend thus In the presse of a Nun we are all undone." A. L. Rowse, in a letter to the *T.L.S.* of 18 July 1952, suggested that Dull hears this as awd (old) grey doe. He insists it is not a doe of any sort, but a young buck.

12. *pricket*] a two-year-old red-deer. See Cotgrave in v. *Brocart.* Compare Greene, *Carde of Fancie* (Grosart, iv. 68), 1584 : "the Lion seldome lodgeth with the Mouse, the Hart seldome feedeth with the Pricket." See note at line 10, and *Gesta Grayorum*, 1594 (ed. Greg, p. 18): "young Deer, Prickets or any other game."

13. *intimation*] I owe the following note to Professor J. A. K. Thomson : "Holofernes, like pedants in all ages, loves to use words in their *original* sense, because it shows their learning. I think that 'intimation' probably means 'thrusting into the very inside'—*intima.* He says it is 'a kind of insinuation'—*insinuare*, 'to insert' ('insert my haud credo for a deer'). Then 'explication' means 'unfolding,' 'replication' is 'folding back,' so as to reveal. Thus the general sense of the whole sentence would be 'Most ignorant interruption by an uneducated person offering his foolish explanation."

insinuation] Compare T. Wilson, *Art of Rhetorique*, 1553 : "A privy begynnyng, or crepyng in, otherwyse called Insinuation, must then and not els be used, when the iudge is greaved with us, and our cause hated of the hearers" (ed. 1562, fol. 53). Probably Holofernes has Wilson's, or Cox's earlier treatise on the same subject in his mind. Sir Philip Sidney has a similar passage in *Arcadia*, bk. i. : "his insinuation being of blushinge, and his division of sighes, his whole oration stood upon a short narration."

14, 15. *explication . . . replication*] Nashe uses the verbs *explicate*, *replicate*, in *Lenten Stuffe.* "*Replication* . . . a confirmation of one's saying with new allegations" (Blount, *Glossographia*, 1670).

19. *unconfirmed*] Unless there be a reference to the religious rite, and the word have the sense of "irreligious," "heathen," it is difficult to find a climax in "unconfirmed." The word occurs again in *Much Ado About Nothing*, III. iii. 124. Schmidt interprets it "inexperienced, raw." The expression *bis coctus* below expressly forbids that meaning here.

Dull. I said the deer was not a *haud credo ;* 'twas a pricket.

Hol. Twice-sod simplicity, *bis coctus !*
O ! thou monster Ignorance, how deform'd dost thou look.

Nath. Sir, he hath never fed of the dainties that are bred in a book.
He hath not eat paper, as it were ; he hath not drunk ink : his intellect is not replenished ; he is only an animal, only sensible in the duller parts ;
And such barren plants are set before us, that we thankful should be,
Which we of taste and feeling are, for those parts that do fructify in us more than he ;
For as it would ill become me to be vain, indiscreet, or a fool,
So were there a patch set on learning, to see him in a school :

28, 29. Prose Qq, Ff ; verse Hanmer *et seq.* 29. *of*] Tyrwhitt ; omitted in Qq, Ff. *do*] Q 1, Ff ; omitted in Q 2.

" Unratified," " unconsolidated," " unavouched," might be suggested, but each seems feeble as a superlatively strong qualification.

22. *Twice-sod . . . bis coctus !*] Probably a reference to the old proverb or aphorism about twice-sodden coleworts, used of a tale twice told, or a sentence twice uttered, like Dull's. The Greek form, Δὶς κράμβη θάνατος, is of remote antiquity ; and Pliny (xx. 9) says : " Coleworts . . . twice sodden, it bindeth the bellie " (Holland's trans. 1601). The proverbial use occurs in Lyly's *Euphues* (Arber, p. 391) : " they fell to the whole discourse of Philautus love, who left out nothing that before I put in, which I must omitte, least I set before you Coleworts twise sodden." In Laurence Humphrey's *Oration to Queen Elizabeth at Woodstock,* 1575 (Nichols, i. 589), it occurs in Latin : " *Cramben qui bis coctam apponit minister, mortem apponit, et qui eadem oberrat chorda citharædus, ridetur, et . . . coccysmus seu cuculi cantilena audienti insuavis est,*" etc., etc. Perhaps it will be found in some of the school-books of the time, like several others of the pedant's tags. It is in Burton's *Anatomy of Melancholy* (Democritus to the Reader) : " an unnecessary work, *cramben bis coctam apponere,* the same again and again in other words."

31. *So were there a patch set on learning*] it would be setting a fool to learn. " Patch " was a common word for a fool. Or we may take it " a fool intent on learning." I prefer the more active construction.

patch] fool. There has been much written upon this signification of the word, which occurs again in *The Tempest,* III. ii. 71 ; *The Comedy of Errors,* III. i. 32 ; and *The Merchant of Venice,* II. v. 46 ; and see the *New Eng. Dict.* There is no occasion to seek for derivations such as Wolsey's fool named " Patch " and the Italian *pazzo* (Florio). The word was used as a synonym for " pied-coat," from the fool's dress. Compare Rider's

But, *omne bene*, say I; being of an old father's mind,
Many can brook the weather that love not the wind.

Dull. You two are book-men: can you tell me by your wit
What was a month old at Cain's birth, that's not five weeks old as yet?

Hol. Dictynna, goodman Dull; Dictynna, goodman Dull.

Dull. What is Dictynna?

Nath. A title to Phoebe, to Luna, to the moon.

Hol. The moon was a month old when Adam was no more;
And raught not to five weeks when he came to five-score.
The allusion holds in the exchange.

Dull. 'Tis true indeed: the collusion holds in the exchange.

Hol. God comfort thy capacity! I say the allusion holds in the exchange.

34. *me*] Q 1; omitted in Ff, Q 2, Q 1, Ff 1, 2, 3; *Dictissima* Q 2, F 4. 36. *Dictynna*] Rowe; *Dictisima* 37. *Dictynna*] *Dictima* Qq, F 1; *Dictinna* Ff 2, 3, 4. 41. *raught*] *rought* Q 1; *wrought* Ff, Q 2.

Bibliotheca Scholastica, 1589: "Pied coate or Patch, *Sticte*."

32. *old father's*] Lodge has the same expression: "For tragedies and comedies Donate the Grammarian sayth, they wer invented by lerned fathers of the old time to no other purpose, but to yeelde prayse unto God" (*Reply to Gosson*, 1579, 1580); and see Golding's *Ovid* (vii. 449): "Here men (so auncient fathers said that were as then alive) did breede of deawie Mushrommes." The precise author of this particular aphorism has not been traced.

36. *Dictynna*] Steevens says Shakespeare might have found this uncommon title for Diana in the second book of Golding's translation of Ovid's *Metamorphoses*: "Dictynna garded with her traine and proud of killing deere." It occurs earlier in one of N. Grimald's songs in *Tottel's Miscellany* (Arber, p. 97), *ante* 1557: "Acteon may teach thee Dictynnaes ire." The Quarto and Folio spelling is a corruption that might easily arise from a misreading of *manuscript* (y taken for i long s, and the nn minims wrongly divided). See Introduction 2.4. It is doubtful if it is really necessary to correct the "Dictima" of line 37; it may be just Dull's blunder. See notes on I. i. 276 and line 92 below.

41. *raught*] reached.

42. *The allusion holds in the exchange*] i.e. "the riddle is as good when I use the name of Adam, as when you use the name of Cain" (Warburton). "Allusion" meant more in Shakespeare's time than now. Compare Cotgrave: "*Allusion*: an allusion or likening; an alluding or applying of one thing unto another." Blount (1670) in *Glossographia* is more explicit: "*Allusion*: a likening or applying of one thing to another, and it is as it were a dalliance or playing with words like in sound," etc., etc.—in fact a pun.

Dull. And I say the pollution holds in the exchange, for the moon is never but a month old; and I say beside that, 'twas a pricket that the princess killed.

Hol. Sir Nathaniel, will you hear an extemporal epitaph on the death of the deer? and, to humour the ignorant, I have call'd the deer the princess killed, a pricket.

Nath. *Perge*, good Master Holofernes, *perge;* so it shall please you to abrogate scurrility.

51. [*I have*] *call'd*] Rowe; *cald* Q 1; *call'd* Ff; *I will call* Singer; *call't* Furness; *call I* Cambridge. 54. *scurrility*] *squirilitie* Q 1.

46. *pollution*] This modernizing of the Quarto spelling "polusion" is justified by a parallel example in *The Rape of Lucrece*, line 1157. The word remains an instance of Dull's "mistaking." See "reprehend," I. i. 182. In a note to this passage Furness quotes from "Courthope, iv. 86" (*History of English Poetry*, London, 1903), to the effect that we owe Shakespeare's stage-representation of Dull to Lyly's "Master Constable and the Watch" in *Endymion*, characters further developed in *Much Ado About Nothing* and elsewhere. *Endymion* bears the date of 1591, but the similarities do not go deep, except for the introduction of Latin tags which characterizes both plays. Moreover Lyly's watch, although they have rusty wits and no wise words, do not "mistake words." See note at v. ii. 488 and 499, 500.

49, 50, *epitaph on the death of*] Capell said this should be "epigram" (adopted into the text by Rann). Furness says "of course, right—there cannot be an epitaph on the death of anything." Why? Is it not a perfectly common use of the word? For Shakespearian times, see *New Eng. Dict.:* "An Epitaphe made upon the dethe of Frenche" (1532); "A Booke of Epitaphes made upon the Deathe of Sir William Buttes" (1583), etc.

50, 51. *to humour the ignorant*] to satisfy Dull. But Holofernes has already given his decided opinion that the Princess's bag was a two-year-old pricket, and not a buck of antler, in his *haud credo*. Evidently they are introduced arguing the point at the opening of the scene, just as Shallow, Sir Hugh and Slender open *The Merry Wives of Windsor*. They were bystanders.

51. *I have call'd*] Rowe's emendation is as good as any, since it preserves the one surviving word of the early texts. The Quarto has also a misprint "ignorault," which may indicate a clumsy attempt to reinsert letters that had come loose from the chase. See Introduction 2.2.

54. *abrogate scurrility*] abolish coarseness. Puttenham gives examples of "pleasant speeches favouring some skurrility" in this sense (pp. 274, 275). "Scurrility" had the sense of foulness of speech. Gabriel Harvey has "fie on grosse scurility and impudent calumny" (*Foure Letters* [Grosart, i. 204]); and compare Webster's *Westward Ho*, II. i.: "ha ha! I must talk merrily, sir. *Justiniano* [a Pedant]. Sir, so long as your mirth be void of all squirrilitie, 'tis not unfit for your calling." This spelling (as in Q 1) was not rare. "Scullery" was spelt "squillery" likewise.

Hol. I will something affect the letter; for it argues facility.

The preyful princess pierc'd and prick'd a pretty pleasing pricket;
Some say a sore; but not a sore, till now made sore with shooting.
The dogs did yell; put 'ell to sore, then sorel jumps from thicket;
Or pricket sore, or else sore'll the people fall a-hooting.
If sore be sore, then 'ell to sore makes fifty sores—O—sorel!
Of one sore I an hundred make, by adding but one more l.

Nath. A rare talent!

Dull. If a talent be a claw, look how he claws him with a talent.

Hol. This is a gift that I have, simple, simple; a foolish extravagant spirit, full of forms, figures, shapes,

57. *preyful*] *prayfull* Qq, F 1; *praysfull* F 2, Malone. 57-62. Printed as twelve lines in Qq, Ff. 59. *'ell*] *ell* Ff; *l* Q 1. 61. *O —sorel !*] *o sorell* Q 1; *O sorell* Ff; *O sore L !* Capell; *of sorel* Warburton; *o' sorel* New; *one sorel* Cambridge, Globe. 66. *Hol.*] *Nath.* Qq, Ff (see line 73).

55. *affect the letter*] resort to alliteration. Compare E. Kirke, Ep. Ded. (to G. Harvey) to Spenser's *Shepheard's Calendar*, 1579: "I scorne and spue out the rakehellye route of our ragged rymers (for so themselves use to hunt the letter)" (Oxford edition, p. 417). In a letter of Gabriel Harvey's, "To my verie friende, M. Immerito" (Spenser), dated October, 1579, this passage occurs (Grosart, i. 18): "your gentle Masterships long, large, lavish, Luxurious, laxative letters withall (now a God's name, when did I ever in my life, hunt the Letter before? but belike there's no remedie, I must needes be even with you once in my dayes)."

58, 59. *sore . . . sorel*] See note, line 10. The term *Sorell*, for "a young buck," is in Palsgrave's *Lesclaircissement*, 1530. To explain the logical connection of Holofernes' lines may be a piece of pedantry worthy the man himself; but they are not pure nonsense, and lines 59 and 60 follow the actual course of the shoot, the baying of the hounds that starts the game moving, and the jeers of the bystanders when an archer misses, and fails even to wound. I am not sure whether in the next line a second yell greets a successful shot, or whether Holofernes has by this time fallen to quibbles merely of mathematical typography. "O—Sorel!" I take to be complacent mock-surprise at the new position to which his punning has carried him. The Warburton reading and its derivatives lack just that logic so unrelentingly pursued by Holofernes; he is making not fifty sores out of sorel, but sorel out of fifty sores.

59. *dogs did yell*] See *Venus and Adonis*, 688, for "yell" applied to the cry of hounds. The dogs here do not apparently agree with the "sport" at Cowdray or Windsor, 1591-2. But they may have been used to wake up the unfortunate animals in the paddock. See note at "stand," IV. i. 8.

64. *talent*] "talon" was commonly written "talent." "The greedie talents of the Eagles" (Grosart's *Harvey*, iii. 20). The pun is unavoidable.

claw] Quibbling on the word's two meanings, to scratch, and to flatter.

67. *figures*, etc.] Puttenham dwells upon this style: "a stile to be lift up

objects, ideas, apprehensions, motions, revolutions: these are begot in the ventricle of memory, nourished in the womb of *pia mater*, and delivered upon the mellowing of occasion. But the gift is good in those in whom it is acute, and I am thankful for it.

Nath. Sir, I praise the Lord for you, and so may my parishioners; for their sons are well tutored by you, and their daughters profit very greatly under you: you are a good member of the commonwealth.

Hol. Mehercle! if their sons be ingenious, they shall want no instruction; if their daughters be capable,

70. *pia mater*] Rowe; *primater* Qq, Ff. 72. *in whom*] *whom* Q 1. 73. *Nath.*] *Hol.* Qq, Ff (see line 66). 77. *Hol.*] *Nath.* Qq, Ff. *ingenious*] Capell; *ingenous* Q 1; *ingennous* F 1; *ingenuous* Q 2, Ff 3, 4.

and advaunced by choice of wordes, phrases, sentences, and figures, high, loftie, eloquent and magnifik in proportion" (Arber, p. 164). And again: "When so ever we multiply our speech by many words or clauses of one sence, the Greekes call it *Sinonimia*. . . . Ye see that all these words, face, looks, favour, features, visage, countenance, are in sence all but one. Which store, neverthelesse, doeth much beautifie and inlarge the matter" (p. 223). Armado and Holofernes share this affectation, which is very prevalent in Gabriel Harvey's letters; also in Lyly's plays, as: "How canst thou thus divine, divide, define, dispute, and all on the sodaine? *Manes*. Wit will have his swing; I am bewitcht, inspired, inflamed, infected" (*Campaspe*, iii. 2 [1581]); and in many writers of this period. See v. i. 61 for a different use of the word "figure." Here we may equate it with our idea, imagination.

68. *revolutions*] Applied to the gifts of the intellect, may mean any turning of the thoughts. Florio has "*Riuolgment:* a revolving, a revolution, a turning and tossing up and downe. Also a winding or crankling in and out. Also a cunning tricke or winding shift. Also a revolt . . . or rebellion."

69. *ventricle of memory*] Furness quotes here from Vicary, *The Anatomie of the Bodie of Man* (E. E. T. Soc. p. 31), 1548: "Next is the Brayne, of which it is marveylous to be considered and noted, how this Piamater devideth the substaunce . . . into three partes or ventrikles. . . . In the thirde Ventrikle, and last, there is founded and ordeyned the vertue Memorative: in this place is registred and kept those things that are done or spoken with the senses and keepeth them in his treasurie."

70. *pia mater*] "the fine membrane or pellicle called *Pia Mater*, which immediately lappeth and enfoldeth the braine" (Pliny's *Natural History* [trans. P. Holland, xxiv, 8], 1601). In the *Stanford Dictionary* (Cambridge, 1892) there is a quotation from *Jerome of Brunswick's Surgery*, 1525: "than the panne, than within be ij small fleces named dura mater and pia mater, than the substance of the braynes." And compare Nashe's *Christ's Teares*, Epistle to Reader (McKerrow, ii. 184), 1593: "having a huge heape of those worthlesse shreds of small English in my *Pia mater's* purse."

72. *acute*] See III. i. 64.

78. *capable*] The audience doubtless enjoyed the double meaning,

I will put it to them. But *vir sapit qui pauca loquitur*.
A soul ſeminine saluteth us.

Enter JAQUENETTA *and* COSTARD.

Jaq. God give you good morrow, master Person.

Hol. Master Person, *quasi* pierce-one. An if one should be pierced, which is the one?

Cost. Marry, master schoolmaster, he that is likest to a hogshead.

79. *sapit*] *sapis* Q 1, F 1. 82. *Hol.*] *Nath.* Qq, Ff. *pierce-one*] Hall; *Person* Q 1, F 1; *Persone* Ff 2, 3. 82-88. Put in the margin by Pope.

pointed by "under you" of l. 75, and Holofernes' unwitting admission of misconduct.

79. *vir . . . loquitur*] "with few words a wise man will compass much" (*Proverbs of Alfred* [Morris, *Specimens of Early Eng.* i. 329], *circa* 1250). The Latin form is in various collections.

82. *pierce-one*] Hall's emendation, which an Elizabethan might conceivably have spelt "Pers-on," is the simplest that will give Holofernes a clear meaning. The alternative is to read "Master *Parson*" in both lines and assume that Holofernes begins by deriving it correctly from "person" (persona); his imagination then takes wing, and he proceeds to suggest a more remote derivation from "pierce."

82-86. *pierce-one . . . piercing a hogshead*] "hogshead" was not uncommonly applied to a thick-witted person, especially in the old phrase "couch a hogshead," occurring as early as *Cock Lorel's Bote*. This explains Costard's impertinence. Compare Dekker's *Wonderfull Yeare* (Grosart, i. 142): "after they had laid their hogsheads togither, to draw out some holesome counsel." Hart was certain that this dialogue ("with its emphatic 'of'") was an echo of the passage in Gabriel Harvey's *Pierce's Supererogation* (1593) in which he quotes a certain gentlewoman's strictures on Nashe's *Pierce Penilesse*. "She knew what she said that intituled Pierce, the hoggeshead of witt: Penniles, the tosspot of eloquence: & Nashe the very inventor of Asses. She it is that must broach the barrell of thy frisking conceite, and canonise the[e] Patriarke of newe writers." This "parallel" is rendered less certain by a discovery of Mr. John Crow's, that "piercing a hogshead" was 16th–17th century slang for getting drunk. He draws my attention to an epigram in *Witt's Recreations*, 1640, (repr. J. C. Hotten, No. 239). It is entitled "On a Drawer Drunk," and runs: "Drawer with thee now even is thy wine, For thou hast pierc'd his hogs-head, and he thine." There would therefore be some point in the interchange without bringing in Harvey and Nashe. But see Introduction 5.22.

83. *pierced*] This word was pronounced as it is spelt in Qq, Ff. (*perst*). See the quibble in *1 Henry IV*. v. iii. 59: "If Percy be alive I'll pierce him." For the spelling compare Puttenham *Arte of English Poesie* (Arber, p. 176): "Her beautie perst mine eye, her speach mine wofull hart." Ellis (*Early English Pronunciation*) says "Pierce, the family name, is pronounced Perse in America." This is to be noted in connection with Nashe's tract, *Pierce Penilesse*.

Hol. Of piercing a hogshead ! a good lustre of conceit in a turf of earth ; fire enough for a flint, pearl enough for a swine : 'tis pretty ; it is well.

Jaq. Good master Person, be so good as read me this letter : it was given me by Costard, and sent me from Don Armado : I beseech you, read it.

Hol. *Facile precor gelida quando pecus omne sub umbra Ruminat*, and so forth. Ah ! good old Mantuan.

86. *Hol.*] *Nath.* Qq, Ff. 92. *Facile*] *Facile precor gellida quando pecas omnia* Q 1, F 1 ; *Fauste precor gelida quando pecus omne* Ff 2, 3, 4.

one] See Quarto reading at I. i. 165. Commonly pronounced *on* or *un* provincially. In Gabriel Harvey's early letters " one " is constantly written " on " (Grosart, i. 112, etc.). It seems to have been an affectation of Harvey's : " on of my standinge " (pp. 114-17), etc.

86. *Of piercing a hogshead*] Cambridge edd. suggest that " Of ", which commences this line in the old edition, was part of the stage-direction, " Holof.," which crept into the text. They make a similar guess at " O " (from " Bero.") at III. i. 144, etc. But it is odd that the form " Holof," which we should have to assume underlies the careless " Nath." of the Quarto, never occurs elsewhere. The " Of," a sort of savouring of the expression, is not impossible.

87. *turf of earth*] clod of earth. Compare Ben Jonson, *Every Man out of his Humour*, I. i. (1599) : " Who can endure to see blind fortune dote thus ? To be enamoured on this dusty turf, This clod, a whoreson puck-fist ! " And again in *Tale of a Tub*, I. iii. : " Whereas the father of her is a Turfe, A very superficies of the earth."

92, 93. *Facile . . . Ruminat*] The quotation is not given its strictly correct form in any text earlier than the second Folio. It is the beginning of the first eclogue of Mantuanus. Battista Spagnuoli, surnamed Mantuanus from the place of his birth, was a writer of pastora poems, who flourished towards the latter end of the fifteenth century. He died in 1516. A translation by George Turberville appeared in 1567. Mantuan's eclogues were in regular use as a school-book. The quotation had recently been a centre of skirmishing in the battles between Harvey and Nashe ; and it should be noted how the combatants treat the quotation. In Gabriel Harvey's *Foure Letters* (Grosart, i. 195), he attacks *M. Pierce Penilesse* (p. 194) in these words : " The summe of summes is, He lost his imagination a thousand waies, and I belieue searched every corner of Grammar-Schoole witte (for his margine is as deeplie learned, as *Fauste precor gelida*) to see if he could finde anie meanes to relieue his estate." Nashe, in his reply in *Foure Letters Confuted* (McKerrow's *Nashe*, i. 306), singles out this passage thus : " With the first and second leafe hee plaies verie pretilie, and in ordinarie termes of extenuating, verdits Pierce Penilesse for an Grammer Schoole wit : saies his Margine is as deepelie learnd as *Fauste præcor gelida*, that his Muse sobbeth and groneth verie piteouslie," etc. Here we have the words classified, by two of the chief writers before the public, as the one tag that even the worst of Grammar School dunces might be expected to

I may speak of thee as the traveller doth of Venice :

Venetia, Venetia,
Chi non ti vede, non ti pretia.

Old Mantuan ! old Mantuan ! who understandeth thee not, loves thee not. *Ut, re, sol, la, mi, fa.* Under pardon, sir, what are the contents ? or, rather, as Horace says in his—what, my soul ! verses ?

95, 96. *Venetia . . . ti . . . ti pretia*] Cambridge ; *Vemchie vencha, que non te unde, que non te perreche* Q 1, F 1 (more corrupt in Q 2, Ff 2, 3, 4). 98. *loves thee not*] Q 1 ; omitted Ff, Q 2.

remember. A line so well known and so recently notorious could hardly be misquoted by Shakespeare. Surely the blunder is Holofernes' ; and this raises the question of how far the other quotations from foreign languages are intentionally corrupt. The " Sapis " of line 79 is most probably a misprint ; but how much of the chaos, to which e.g. Florio's proverb (see next note) is reduced in the Quarto, is genuine Holofernes ? Unfortunately, we cannot now distinguish, but must restore all or nothing.

95, 96. *Venetia . . . pretia*] This proverb is given by Malone from Florio's *Second Fruites* (1591) : " *Venetia*, etc., with a tag, *Ma chi ti vede, ben gli costa.*" Theobald was the first to correct the old text. Furness states it is in Florio's *First Fruites* (1578) with translation : " Venise who seeth thee not, praiseth thee not, but who seeth thee, it costeth hym well." It has also been discovered by Wolfgang Keller in *The Garden of Pleasure*, translated by James Sandford from the Italian, in 1573. The English version is in *The Book of Riddels*, mentioned by Captain Cox in 1575. See Furnivall's *Captain Cox* (Ballad Society, 1871), p. cxiii. Howell has a very different conclusion in his *Italian Proverbs*, 1659.

98. *Ut . . . fa*] He hums the notes of the gamut as Edmund does in *King Lear*, I. ii.—and gets them wrong. See Chappell's *Popular Music*, pp. 14, 15, where the Latin hymn (about 774) for St. John Baptist's Day, from which they are taken, will be found. SI for B was not settled till nearly the end of the seventeenth century, and DO replaced UT about the same time, but the French retained UT. See again *The Taming of the Shrew*, III. i. 70-80. Ben Jonson uses this in a transferred sense in *Cynthia's Revels*, II. i. : " your courtier elementary is one but newly entered, or as it were in the alphabet, or ut-re-mi-fa-sol-la of courtship." Nashe has it where we should say " ding dong " : " *Summer*. Will Sol come before us ? *Vertumnus*. Sol, sol ; ut, re, mi, fa, sol. Come to church while the bell toll " (for the sake of a quibble) in *Summer's Last Will*, 1592. Holofernes is airing one part of his acquirements ; the instruction of children in singing, whether for chapel or theatre, was of the first importance. A schoolmaster was a singing-master.

100. *What, my soul ! Verses ?*] This sounds like a quotation, but its source has not been discovered. Holofernes' excitement, as he at last gets a sight of the letter over Nathaniel's shoulder, is too much for him, and his pose, of being too deeply absorbed in high thoughts to have time for vulgar curiosity, is shattered on the instant.

Nath. Ay, sir, and very learned.

Hol. Let me hear a staff, a stanze, a verse : *lege, domine.*

Nath. If love make me forsworn, how shall I swear to love?
Ah ! never faith could hold, if not to beauty vow'd ;
Though to myself forsworn, to thee I'll faithful prove :
Those thoughts to me were oaks, to thee like osiers bow'd.
Study his bias leaves and makes his book thine eyes,
Where all those pleasures live that art would comprehend.
If knowledge be the mark, to know thee shall suffice ;
Well learned is that tongue that well can thee commend ;
All ignorant that soul that sees thee without wonder ;
Which is to me some praise that I thy parts admire.
Thy eye Jove's lightning bears, thy voice his dreadful thunder,
Which, not to anger bent, is music and sweet fire.
Celestial as thou art, O ! pardon love this wrong,
That sings heaven's praise with such an earthly tongue.

103. *stanze*] F 1, Q 2 ; *stauze* Q 1 ; *stanza* Ff 2, 3, 4. 105. *Ah !*] *O !* Passionate Pilgrim. 106. *faithful*] *constant* P. P. 107. *were*] *like* P. P. 109. *would*] *can* P. P. 114. *Thy*] *Thine* P. P. *bears*] *seems* P. P. 116. *pardon love this*] *do not love that* P. P. 117. *That sings*] *To sing* P. P. ; *That sings the* S. Walker conj.

103. *a staff, a stanze*] Equivalent terms. The form "stanze" occurs in Armin's *Two Maides of More-clacke* (Grosart, p. 110, 1609). Puttenham says : "the meetre Heroicall of *Troilus and Cresseid* is very grave and stately, keeping the staffe of seven [lines] and the verse of ten [feet]" (Arber, p. 76) ; and a little later : "*Staffe* in our vulgare Poesie I know not why it should be so called. . . . The Italian called it *stanza*, as if we should say a resting place . . . a certaine number of verses allowed to go altogether and joyne." Florio has : "*Stanza* . . . properly a stanzo or stance or stave of eight or six verses."

104. *If love,* etc.] This sonnet was appropriated by William Jaggard in the collection he published in 1599 : "*The Passionate Pilgrim*, by W. Shakespeare." It contains pieces by Barnfield, Bartholomew Griffin, Weelkes, Marlowe, and others besides Shakespeare.

108. *bias*] tendency, bent.

his book thine eyes] See below, IV. iii. 299-301 ; and *A Midsummer Night's Dream*, II. ii. 126. So in Nashe's *Tragedie of Dido* (McKerrow, ii. 363), 1594 : "His glistering eyes shall be my looking glasse ; . . . His lookes shall be my only Librarie." "And folly's all they taught me," adds Thomas Moore.

116. *pardon love this wrong*] Wrongly punctuated in several modern editions (Rowe, Steevens, etc.) *pardon, love, this wrong.*

117. *That sings heaven's praise*] The last line of the canzonet appears to be a foot short ; although the Quarto prints "singes," and it has been suggested that this and "heaven" must each be given two syllables. Critics have even taken this possibility of a catch for the unwary reader as the ground for an explanation of Holofernes' comment on the poem, which many have found puzzling. In his notes on the play

Hol. You find not the apostrophus, and so miss the accent: let me supervise the canzonet. Here are only numbers ratified; but, for the elegancy, facility, and golden cadence of poesy, *caret*.

118. *apostrophus*] *New Eng. Dict.* conjecture; *apostraphas* Q 1, Ff 1, 2 Globe; *apostrophas* Q 2, Cambridge; *apostrophes* Ff 3, 4. 119. *canzonet*] Theobald; *cangenet* Qq, Ff. 119-127. *Here are . . . to you?*] Spoken by Hol. Theobald; Qq, Ff give to Nath.

in the Temple edition Sir Israel Gollancz wrote: "Does not Holofernes' criticism bear directly on the last line of the canzonet? Nathaniel should have read:—That singës heaven's praise with such an earthly tongue. It was usual to mark e's with two dots when sounded. Holofernes may mean by 'apostrophas,' 'diaereses'." The editors of the New Cambridge Shakespeare agree: "Nathaniel should have said 'singës' and Holofernes should have said 'diaeresis' (*N.E.D.* quotes the word from Cotgrave, 1611) but Holofernes blunders as usual, and employs a term which implies contraction rather than expansion." But Shakespeare, whose mind was always fixed on stage effect, could hardly have planned such a joke, which no one in the audience would be likely to grasp without a printed text before him. It is surely all much simpler: Holofernes, who has a reputation for learning to keep up, is bound to find fault with Nathaniel's reading. Any term, provided it *sounds* learned, will do to confound the poor curate, but should not bluff us into the belief that the sonnet (or even Nathaniel's reading of it) is necessarily faulty. The editor of the *Passionate Pilgrim*, far from attempting to mend the line, presents it in a form which no diaeresis can eke out.

118. *apostrophus*] Furness calls Murray's suggestion in the *New Eng. Dict.* "an *emendatio certissima*," but the form "apostrophes" of the third Folio would sound just as technical at this date. There were but the two forms of the word, *apostrophe* or *apostrophus*, meaning the sign (') indicating the omission of one or more letters. Ben Jonson gives a careful definition (overlooked in the *New Eng. Dict.*) in *The Second Book of the English Grammar* (*ante* 1637): "*Apostrophus* is the rejecting of a vowel from the beginning or end of a word. The note whereof, though it many times through the negligence of writers and printers, is quite omitted, yet by right . . . hath his mark, which is such a semicircle (') placed in the top." It is this negligence the pedant complains of as misleading Nathaniel. Ben Jonson confirms the reading I give.

119. *supervise*] Again Holofernes uses a word in its root sense "look over." See note on line 13 above.

canzonet] T. Morley (1593) is the earliest use given in the *New Eng. Dict.* of this term, the present example, I suppose, being somewhat uncertain. Florio has: "Canzonetta, a canzonet or dittie." Ben Jonson uses the word early: "I will have a canzonet made with nothing in it but Sirrah" (*Cynthia's Revels*, IV. i. [1600]). "Cangenet" of the Quarto may be Holofernes' error.

120. *numbers ratified*] verses brought into proportion or rate. From the context this appears to be the speaker's meaning.

elegancy] A frequent form of "elegance." It occurs in Gabriel Harvey and Ben Jonson (*Every Man out*, etc.).

121. *facility*] fluency. Puttenham advises "makers" to use "this or that

Ovidius Naso was the man: and why, indeed, *Naso*, but for smelling out the odoriferous flowers of fancy, the jerks of invention? *Imitari* is nothing; so doth the hound his master, the ape his keeper, the tired horse his rider. But, damosella virgin, was this directed to you?

Jaq. Ay, sir, from one Monsieur Berowne, one of the strange queen's lords.

Hol. I will overglance the superscript. 'To the snow-white hand of the most beauteous Lady Rosaline.' I will look again on the intellect of the letter, for the

124. *invention? Imitari*] Theobald; *invention imitarie* Qq, Ff. 126. *tired*] *tyred* Qq, Ff; *try'd* Theobald; *'tired* Capell. 130-135. *I will . . . Berowne*] Given to Nath. Qq, Ff.

kind of figure, according to the facilitie of each man's utterance" (Arber, p. 304).

cadence] Not elsewhere in Shakespeare. In the sense of rhythmical measure the term is in Chaucer. Puttenham uses it: "there can not be in a maker a fowler fault, then to falsifie his accent to serve his cadence, or by untrue orthographie to wrench his words to helpe his rime . . . such a maker is not . . . his craft's master" (p. 94).

123. *Naso . . . for smelling*] Compare Harvey's *Letters* (Grosart, i. 85), 1580: "Eyed, like to Argus, Earde, like to Midas, Nosd, like to Naso."

124. *jerks of invention*] strokes or sallies of wit. A very proper figure for a schoolmaster's use, since "jerking" was equivalent to whipping. In Greene's *Never Too Late* (Grosart, viii. 193), 1590, there is a good example: "if they have childrens malladies, twere good to use childrens medicines, and that's a rod: for be they never so froward, a jerck or two will make them forward." Shakespeare has not "jerk" again, although he uses the verb "yerk" twice.

126. *the tired horse*] Furness explained this as dull-spirited, or with the independent spirit broken in him. This may be so, but the passage he quoted in support from Gervase Markham's *Masterpeece*—the chapter "Of Tyred Horses" (the first of two numbered LXII in the 1703 revised edition)—suggests no such meaning. Markham expressly says that as a technical term "tired horse" implies one that "*refuseth* reasonable Labour" and will not obey his rider.

128. 129. *Berowne . . . queen's lords*] It is odd that Jaquenetta, who at line 91 thought her letter came from Armado, now knows it is Berowne's; odder that she takes him for one of the *Princess'* suite. Dover Wilson reads "Boyet" and assumes an original intrigue lost in revision; the blunder may be more simply put down to "pure ignorance" on the part of the author.

130. *superscript*] superscription, address. See Greene's *Third Parte of Conney-catching* (Grosart, x. 150): "and sewed an old card upon it, whereupon he wrote a superscription unto the Maister of the Maide, and at what signe it was to be delivered." See note at IV. i. 59.

132. *intellect*] intelligence conveyed or meaning. Furness quotes from Baynes (*Shakespeare Studies*) a reference to Wilson's *Arte of Rhetorique*

nomination of the party writing to the person written unto: 'Your ladyship's in all desired employment, Berowne.' Sir Nathaniel, this Berowne is one of the votaries with the king; and here he hath framed a letter to a sequent of the stranger queen's, which, accidentally, or by the way of progression, hath miscarried. Trip and go, my sweet; deliver this paper into the royal hand of the king; it may concern much. Stay not thy compliment; I forgive thy duty: adieu.

Jaq. Good Costard, go with me. Sir, God save your life!

Cost. Have with thee, my girl.

[*Exeunt Costard and Jaquenetta.*

Nath. Sir, you have done this in the fear of God, very religiously; and, as a certain father saith,—

Hol. Sir, tell not me of the father; I do fear colourable

133. *writing* Rowe; *written* Qq, Ff. 135. *Berowne.' Sir Nathaniel*] See collation at IV. ii. 130-135; *Berowne.* Ped. *Sir Holofernes* Qq; *Berowne.* Per. *Sir Holofernes* Ff; *Biron. Sir Nathaniel* Capell. 140. *royal*] Q 1; omitted in Ff, Q 2. 142. *compliment*] *complement* Qq, Ff.

where the figure *Synecdoche* (Puttenham's "Figure of quick conceite") is rendered by "intellection." The writer parallels Holofernes' use of "superscript" above for "superscription," and suggests this as the source of his far-fetched term.

133. *party*] person. Several times in Shakespeare. Compare Lodge, *Euphues Golden Legacie* (*Shakes. Lib.* 1875, p. 52): "the party beloved is froward, and having curtsie in her lookes, holdeth disdaine in her tongues ende."

137. *sequent*] follower.

139. *Trip and go*] Chappell says this was "one of the favourite Morris-dances of the sixteenth and seventeenth centuries." The expression became proverbial and is often made use of. "O how she scudded! O sweet scud how she tripped! O delicate trip and go!" (Ben Jonson, *The Case is Altered*, IV. iv. [1598]); and in Nashe's *Summer's Last Will* (McKerrow, iii. 240), 1592, a morris-dance is introduced, with "three clowns and three maids singing this song, dancing": "Trip and goe, heave and hoe, Up and downe, to and fro. . . . A Maying, a playing; Love hath no gainsaying, So merrily trip and goe." Chappell gives the music. Nashe refers to it again in *Foure Letters Confuted* (McKerrow, i. 276), in the same manner as Holofernes does: "Thou shalt not breath a whit, trip and goe." See also Gosson, *Schoole of Abuse* (Arber, p. 25), 1579: "Trip and goe, for I dare not tarry."

142. *duty*] She is excused a curtsy. For "compliment" see note on I. i. 167.

148, 149. *colourable colours*] plausible pretexts. The substantive is common, but the adjective not elsewhere in Shakespeare. It is used in the same sense in Sidney's *Arcadia*, bk. ii.: "If my soul could have been

colours. But to return to the verses: did they please you, Sir Nathaniel?

Nath. Marvellous well for the pen.

Hol. I do dine to-day at the father's of a certain pupil of mine; where, if (before repast) it shall please you to gratify the table with a grace, I will, on my privilege I have with the parents of the foresaid child or pupil, undertake your *ben venuto;* where I will prove those verses to be very unlearned, neither savouring of poetry, wit, nor invention. I beseech your society.

Nath. And thank you too; for society, saith the text, is the happiness of life.

Hol. And, certes, the text most infallibly concludes it. [*To Dull*] Sir, I do invite you too: you shall not say me nay: *pauca verba.* Away! the gentles are at their game, and we will to our recreation.

[*Exeunt.*

153. *before*] Q 1; *being* Ff, Q 2, Hart. 156. *ben venuto*] Rowe; *bien venuto* Q 1, Ff 2, 3, 4; *bien vonuto* F 1, Q 2.

polluted with treachery, it would likewise have provided for itself colourable answers." Holofernes is quibbling on the stock phrase "I fear no colours." On its occurrence in *Twelfth Night*, I. v. 6 this is said by Maria to be a saying "born in the wars." Presumably it means "I do not fear the enemy's standards," and so "I fear no foe."

151. *Marvellous well for the pen*] See below, v. ii. 39, 40. Lodge has the same retort in *Euphues Golden Legacie* (*Shakes. Lib.* 1875, p. 80), 1590: "How like you this sonnet? quoth Rosader. Marry, quoth Ganimede, for the pen well, for the passion ill."

153. (*before repast*)] As Dover Wilson points out, Holofernes takes care to emphasize that he is offering a free dinner, not merely the honour of saying grace and hearing the conversation after it.

156. *undertake your* ben venuto] act as your sponsor, introduce you to the host, and ensure your welcome. Hortensio makes the same promise to Petruchio at the end of the first act of *The Taming of a Shrew.* The French form *bien venue* was anglicized much earlier, and occurs in Peele and Nashe.

160. *saith the text*] The text has not yet been identified. A similar passage occurs in *Damon and Pithias* (Hazlitt's *Dodsley*, iv. 8): "*Amicitia inter bonos*," saith a learned man.

164. *pauca verba*] Nym has "pauca, pauca," in *The Merry Wives of Windsor*, I. i. 123. No use earlier than the present is known, the next being Jonson's *Every Man in his Humour*, 1598, where it is labelled "the bencher's phrase" (IV. i. 40).

SCENE III

Enter BEROWNE, *with a paper.*

Ber. The king he is hunting the deer; I am coursing myself: they have pitched a toil; I am toiling in a pitch,—pitch that defiles: defile! a foul word. Well, set thee down, sorrow! for so they say the fool said, and so say I, and I the fool: well proved, wit! By the Lord, this love is as mad as Ajax: it kills sheep, it kills me, I a sheep: well proved again o' my side! I will not love; if I do, hang me; i' faith, I will not. O! but her eye,—by this light, but for her eye, I would not love her; yes, for her two eyes. Well, I do nothing in the world but lie, and lie in my throat. By heaven, I do love, and it

Scene III

4. *set*] Qq, Ff; *sit* Hanmer.

Scene III

2. *pitched a toil*] set a snare. "The hay's a pitching" [hay=rabbit-net] (Ben Jonson, *Alchemist*, II. i.). Ben Jonson in his translation of Horace ("*Beatus ille*," etc. [Odes, v. ii.]) has: "Or hence, or thence, he drives with many a hound Wild boars into his toils pitched round" (*ante* 1619). And Beaumont and Fletcher's *Woman's Prize*, IV. iv.: "How daintily and cunningly you drive me up like a deer to the toil." "The Master of the Toyles and Tents" is an office at Court mentioned in Powell's *Plaine Pathway to Preferment* (New Shakes. Soc. p. 168). And in an *Account of the Queen's Purse from 1559 to 1569* (Nichol's *Progresses* [1823], i. 269), "The Toyle" appears amongst necessary charges for the queen's horses and deer: "maiking and fynishing 75 clothes for the Toyle."

2, 3. *toiling in a pitch*] Is not Berowne recalling the deep black of Rosaline's eyes to which he refers as "two pitchballs"? (III. i. 194) (Furness). Jonson said "alluding to lady Rosaline's complexion, who is through the whole play represented as a black beauty," although we are distinctly told (III. i. 193) she was a "whitely wanton" (with snow-white hands). Berowne shows at once (lines 9, 10) it is her eyes he means. He is careful to correct "her eye" (a pitch) to "her two eyes."

4. *set thee down, sorrow!*] Costard's remark at I. i. 298.

6, 7. *love is as mad as Ajax: it kills sheep*] "so it kills me" is added by Thomas Fuller, M.D., in his *Gnomologia*, 1732 (No. 3287). See again note at "He's a god," v. ii. 634; and at line 88 of this scene.

mad as Ajax: it kills sheep] This occurs again in 2 *Henry VI.* v. i. 26: "like Ajax Telamonius, On sheep or oxen could I spend my fury." There were at least two plays concerning Ajax acted, one at Court and one at Cambridge, before this time.

12. *lie in my throat*] occurs several times in Shakespeare, e.g. 2 *Henry IV.* I. ii. 93, *Othello*, IV. iv. 13. A very

hath taught me to rhyme, and to be melancholy; and here is part of my rhyme, and here my melancholy. Well, she hath one o' my sonnets already: the clown bore it, the fool sent it, and the lady hath it: sweet clown, sweeter fool, sweetest lady! By the world, I would not care a pin if the other three were in. Here comes one with a paper: God give him grace to groan! [*Stands aside.*

Enter the KING, *with a paper.*

King. Ay me!

Ber. Shot, by heaven! Proceed, sweet Cupid: thou hast thumped him with thy bird-bolt under the left pap. In faith, secrets!

13. *melancholy*] *mallichollie* Qq, Ff.

20. [*Stands aside*] *Gets up into a tree* Capell.

deep lie. Berowne refers here to the perjury of his loving. A lie, not of the tongue or lips, but coming from the heart. Sidney has it: "Thou lyest in thy throate (said Zelmane)" (Feuillerat, i. 506), *ante* 1586, and Gabriel Harvey, *Three Proper Letters* (Grosart, ii. 73) *ante* 1580: "Out lyar out, thou lyest abhominably in thy throat."

17. *sweet . . . sweeter . . . sweetest*] See note at I. ii. 157-159.

17, 18. *By the world*] Used twice by Armado, v. i. 97 and 100; and in *The Taming of the Shrew*, II. i. 161.

23. *thumped*] Greene has "fro mine eyes I gave her such a thump on the brest that she would scarce say no" (*Never Too Late* [Grosart, viii. 198]).

bird-bolt] a kind of blunt-headed arrow used for shooting birds with. Steevens says in a note to *Much Ado About Nothing*, I. i.: "Such are to this day in use to kill rooks with, shot from a cross-bow." Marston has "gross-knobbed birdbolt" in *What You Will.* Playfully applied to Cupid's arrows, which are presumably of the sharpest and most piercing description, probably because used by a boy. Nares refers to Cooke's *Greene's Tu Quoque*, and Steevens to Shirley's *Love in a Maze.* Often spelt "burbolt."

23, 24. *left pap*] Compare *A Midsummer Night's Dream*, v. i. 305: "left pap Where heart doth hop." And see *The Shepherdess Felismena* (from B. Yonge's translation of Montemayor's *Diana*) (*Shaks. Lib.* 1875, p. 306), *ante* 1598: "But Felismena helped him out of that trouble, by putting another arrow into her bow, the which transpiercing his armour, she left under his left pap, and so iustly smote his heart that this knight also followed his two companions." The expression is also in Speed's *History of Great Britain* (ed. 1632), at the year 1585: "Henry Percy, Earle of Northumberland . . . being upon suspicion of treason committed to the Tower of London, he laid violent hands upon his owne life, by discharging a Dag, charged with three bullets, under his left pappe, wherewith he pierced his heart."

King [*Reads.*]

So sweet a kiss the golden sun gives not
  To those fresh morning drops upon the rose,
As thy eye-beams when their fresh rays have smote
  The night of dew that on my cheeks down flows :
Nor shines the silver moon one half so bright
  Through the transparent bosom of the deep,
As doth thy face through tears of mine give light ;
  Thou shin'st in every tear that I do weep :
No drop but as a coach doth carry thee ;
  So ridest thou triumphing in my woe.
Do but behold the tears that swell in me,
  And they thy glory through my grief will show :
But do not love thyself ; then thou will keep
My tears for glasses, and still make me weep.
O queen of queens ! how far dost thou excel,
No thought can think, nor tongue of mortal tell.

How shall she know my griefs ? I'll drop the paper :
Sweet leaves, shade folly. Who is he comes here ?
[*Steps aside.*
What, Longaville ! and reading ! listen, ear.

Enter LONGAVILLE, *with several papers.*

Ber. Now, in thy likeness, one more fool appear !
Long. Ay me ! I am forsworn.
Ber. Why, he comes in like a perjure, wearing papers.

27. *smote*] *smot* Qq, Ff. 28. *night of dew*] Qq, Ff ; *dew of night* Singer. 37. *will*] Q 1 ; *wilt* Ff. 46. *perjure*] *perjured* F 2.

25. *kiss the golden sun*] Compare Sonnet xxxiii. : "a glorious morning . . . kissing with golden face," etc. For the connection between this play and the Sonnets see Introduction, 3.21.

27. *night of dew*] night's allowance of tears ; or tears as many as there are drops of dew produced in a night.

33. *coach*] See below, line 153.

44. *in thy likeness . . . appear*] in thy shape, thyself. Compare *Romeo and Juliet*, II. i. 21, and *The Tempest*, III. ii. 138. Dekker uses this expression very violently to our ears, meaning in person, in the flesh : "At last the wise Gentleman appeared in his likenesse : Are you the Constable saies the player ; yes that I am for fault of a better, quoth he" (*Iests to to make you Merrie* [Grosart, ii. 279], 1607) ; "No sooner were their backes turned, but I that all this while had stood in a corner (like a watching candle) appeared in my likeness" (*Belman of London* [Grosart, iii. 91], 1608). See also *Martins Months Minde* (Grosart's Nashe, i. 173), 1589 : "Martin dares not land in his likenes at Lambeth staiers."

46. *perjure*] perjurer. "But now black-spotted Perjure as he is, He takes a truce with Elnor's damned brat" (*Troublesome Raigne of King John*, part i. [*Shakes. Lib.* ed. 1875, p. 351], 1591).

King. In love, I hope: sweet fellowship in shame!
Ber. One drunkard loves another of the name.
Long. Am I the first that have been perjur'd so?
Ber. I could put thee in comfort: not by two that I know.
Thou mak'st the triumviry, the corner-cap of society,
The shape of love's Tyburn, that hangs up simplicity.
Long. I fear these stubborn lines lack power to move.
O sweet Maria, empress of my love!
These numbers will I tear, and write in prose.
Ber. O! rhymes are guards on wanton Cupid's hose:
Disfigure not his shop.

47 *King*. Rowe; *Long* Q 1. 51. *triumviry*] Rowe (ed. 2); *triumphery* Qq, Ff 1, 2; *triumphry* Ff 3, 4; *triumvirate* Rowe (ed. 1). 57. *shop*] Qq, Ff; *slop* Theobald; *shape* Collier MS.

wearing papers] "To sette openly with a paper on his hed to be mocked in perjury for forging of evidences, or such like. *Catamidio*" (J. Rider, *Bibliotheca Scholastica*, 1589). And compare Chettle, *Kind-Hartes Dreame* (Bodley Head Quarto, p. 54), 1592: "an odd Atturney, was not long since disgraded of his place by pitching over the Barre, yet promoted to looke out of a wodden window, cut after the Dove hole fashion, with a paper on his suttle pate, containing the iugling before shewed." Steevens gives references to Holinshed (p. 838 [1587]), which ascribes the penance to Cardinal Wolsey's invention, and to *Leicester's Commonwealth*. In Harrison's *England* the punishment was the pillory and the letter P branded in the forehead. Longaville has presumably a spare sonnet tucked into his hatband.

51. *corner-cap*] Was the college-cap or mortar-board ever three-cornered? In the *Queen's Entertainment*, 1591, Nereus is described as "having a cornerd cappe on his curled heade," and the picture shows it to be square (Nichol's *Progresses*, iii. 101, 110). The corner-cap is mentioned in *New Custom* (Hazlitt's *Dodsley*, iii. 11). *ante* 1573, cited in *New Eng. Dict*, Furness quotes from Stubbes' *Anatomie of Abuses* (New Shakes. Soc. p. 69), 1583: "Cappes with three hornes, three corners I should saie, like the forked cappes of Popishe Priestes." As the emblem of the Bishops, it was more commonly referred to, by both Marprelate and his opponents, as "cater-cap" which, with its derivation from "quatre," plainly implies *four* corners.

52. *The shape of . . . Tyburn*] References to the triangular shape of the gallows are abundant, and cuts of this form of gibbet are frequent, as in Holinshed's *Chronicle* (Halliwell). The "tripple tree" is a name for the gallows in Harman's *Caveat*. Others were—three trees, tripple trestle, ride the three-legged mare, the three foote crosse (Chettle); three-cornered tree (N. Breton). Dekker has a parallel allusion: "Well, suppose the sessions past, our dreamer awake, and caried in a cart to have a corner of Doctor Stories cap" (*Iests to make you Merrie* [Grosart, ii. 309], 1607). Doctor Story was a "Romish canonical Doctor" who was hanged at Tyburn for high treason (1st June 1571). His cap became proverbial.

56. *guards*] embroideries.

57. *shop*] I follow Dover Wilson in retaining the Quarto reading, which

Long. This same shall go. [*Reads the Sonnet.*

Did not the heavenly rhetoric of thine eye,
'Gainst whom the world cannot hold argument,
Persuade my heart to this false perjury?
Vows for thee broke deserve not punishment.
A woman I forswore; but I will prove,
Thou being a goddess, I forswore not thee:
My vow was earthly, thou a heavenly love;
Thy grace being gain'd cures all disgrace in me.
Vows are but breath, and breath a vapour is:
Then thou, fair sun, which on my earth dost shine,
Exhal'st this vapour-vow; in thee it is:
If broken then, it is no fault of mine:
If by me broke, what fool is not so wise
To lose an oath to win a paradise?

Ber. This is the liver vein, which makes flesh a deity;
A green goose a goddess; pure, pure idolatry.
God amend us, God amend! we are much out o' th' way.
Long. By whom shall I send this?—Company! stay.
[*Steps aside.*
Ber. All hid, all hid; an old infant play.
Like a demi-god here sit I in the sky,

59. *cannot*] *could not* Passionate Pilgrim. 61. *deserve*] *deserves* Q 2. 64. *earthly*] *earthy* Ff 3, 4. 66. *Vows are but breath*] *My vow was breath* P. P. 67. *which on my earth dost*] *that on this earth doth* P. P. 68. *Exhal'st*] *Exhale* P. P. 71. *lose*] *break* P. P. 73. *idolatry*] *ydotarie* Q 1.

makes sense (the organ of generation, and hence codpiece). See note on iii. i. 181).

58. *Did not*, etc.] This sonnet is in *The Passionate Pilgrim.* See note above, iv. ii. 104.

65. *grace*] favour.

68. *Exhalst*] Exhale, "of the sun drawing up vapours and thus causing meteors" (Schmidt), is used several times by Shakespeare, as in *Lucrece*, 779; *1 Henry IV.* v. i. 19; *Romeo and Juliet*, iii. v. 13. To absorb. So in *The Troublesome Raigne of King John* (Hazlitt's *Shakes. Lib.* p. 301): "And when their vertue is exhaled drie, I'll hang them."

71. *lose*] The Quarto spelling *loose* was used for either meaning.

72. *liver vein*] vein or style of love. The liver was held to be the seat of passionate love. "In Aprile and May, the liuer veine must be lette bloudde" (Paynel, *Salarnes Regim.*, 1538 [*New Eng. Dict.*]). See *The Merry Wives of Windsor*, ii. i. 121; *Much Ado*, iv. i. 233; *As You Like It*, iii. ii. 449. Dowden noted the following: "But when the whole body aboundeth with melancholike bloud, it is best to begin the cure with letting of bloud, and you must cut the liver vaine on the arme" (Philip Barrough, *The Method of Physick*, lib. i. ch. xxviii. p. 46 [1590]).

73. *green goose*] see note i. i. 97.

74. *out o' the way*] gone wrong. Compare *Othello*, i. iii. 365.

76. *All hid*] "*Cline-mucette:* The game called Hodman-blind; Harry-racket; or are you all-hid" (Cotgrave, 1611). It is mentioned in

And wretched fools' secrets heedfully o'er-eye.
More sacks to the mill ! O heavens ! I have my wish :

Enter DUMAIN, *with a paper.*

Dumain transform'd : four woodcocks in a dish !
Dum. O most divine Kate !
Ber. O most profane coxcomb !
Dum. By heaven, the wonder in a mortal eye !
Ber. By earth, she is not, corporal ; there you lie.
Dum. Her amber hairs for foul have amber quoted.
Ber. An amber-coloured raven was well noted.
Dum. As upright as the cedar.
Ber. Stoop, I say ;
Her shoulder is with child.

Enter . . . paper] Dyce. 83. *in*] Q 1 ; *Of* Ff, Q 2. 84. *not, corporal*] *but corporal* Theobald. 87. *Stoop*] Qq, Ff ; *—stoup* New.

Jonson's *Epicene*, IV. ii. : " *Truewit* [*binds his eyes*]. Come, sir [*leads him forward*]. All hid, Sir John ! " Truewit is here master of the ceremonies and arranging a sport for others to play at. Berowne is in the same position of supervisor.

79. *More sacks to the mill*] plenty of drudgery to do ; lots more to come. A proverbial expression. Compare Skelton, *Why Come Ye not to Courte ?* (Dyce, ii. 30) : " Good reason and good skyll, They may garlycke pyll, Cary sackes to the myll, Or pescoddes they may shyll, Or elles go rost a stone : Ther is no man but one That hathe the strokes alone " ; and *Pasquil's Apologie* (McKerrow's *Nashe* i. 123), 1590 : " To the next, to the next, more sacks to the Myll."

80. *woodcocks*] simpletons. The word was in common use for a fool from Stephen Gosson (1579) down to Motteux's *Rabelais* (1708) ; it is a favourite of both Jonson and Shakespeare. The bird had not the wit to keep its neck out of the noose. " Snipe " was often used in the same sense. Compare especially Heywood's parallel, " two snights to a dish " (*Fair Maid of the Exchange* [Pearson, p. 69]).

84. *she is not, corporal*] A much-disputed passage. Many editors follow Theobald, " she is but corporal," using " corporal " in the sense of corporeal as elsewhere in Shakespeare. Berowne, however, has already applied the name (" corporal of his field," III. i. 184) to himself when he discovered he was in love. And why not now to Dumain ? Berowne means to contradict Dumain emphatically ; it is Rosaline, not Kate, who is the wonder.

86. *raven*] as a type of foul (fowl), in opposition to fair or amber.

87. *Stoop*] Berowne merely contradicts Dumain's " upright," concisely and ungrammatically. "Stoop" signified a bow or to bow. Compare *Henry V.* v. ii. 168 : " a straight back will stoop " ; and Nashe, *The Unfortunate Traveller* (McKerrow, ii. 222) : " all feare you, love you, stoup to you. Therefore, good sir, be ruld by mee, stoup your fortune so low, as to," etc. Berowne's word implies an injunction to Dumain to come down from his stately images.

88. *shoulder . . . child*] The worthy Thomas Fuller, M.D. (not Thomas Fuller, D.D., of *The Worthies*), has

Dum. As fair as day.
Ber. Ay, as some days ; but then no sun must shine.
Dum. O ! that I had my wish.
Long. And I had mine !
King. And I mine too, good Lord !
Ber. Amen, so I had mine. Is not that a good word ?
Dum. I would forget her ; but a fever she
Reigns in my blood, and will remember'd be.
Ber. A fever in your blood ! why, then incision
Would let her out in saucers : sweet misprision !
Dum. Once more I'll read the ode that I have writ.
Ber. Once more I'll mark how love can vary wit.
Dum. [*reads his sonnet*]

On a day, alack the day !
Love, whose month is ever May,
Spied a blossom passing fair
Playing in the wanton air :

91. *I*] Johnson ; omitted in Qq, Ff. [*reads his sonnet*] Qq, Ff. 97. *ode*] *Odo* Q 1 (Devon copy). 100. *month is ever May*] Q 1 ; *month was ever May* England's Helicon ; *month is every May* Ff, Q 2.

this vulgarism in his *Gnomologia*, No. 2493. He had evidently the good sense to study Shakespeare when making his collection. See note above at "Ajax," line 6.

92. *Is not that a good word*] is not that kind of me ? "Good word" is commonly used meaning an expression of kindness in Shakespeare.

95. *incision*] blood-letting. A favourite word with Shakespeare in this sense. Nashe speaks of a doctor's "incision-knife" (lancet) in *The Unfortunate Traveller* (McKerrow, ii. 306) ; and see *Captain Smith* (Arber, p. 74), 1607-9 : "to scarifie or make incision, their best instruments are some splinted stone."

96. *saucers*] Furness quotes here from Halliwell : "The practise of bleeding in fevers was very common in Shakespeare's time, and it was not unusual for the barber-chirurgions to exhibit their saucers with blood in them as signs of their profession. . . ." Amongst the MSS. of the Company of Barbers in London is the following order under the date 1606 : "Item, it is ordeyned that no person usinge flebothomy or bloudlettinge within London . . . shall at any tyme hereafter set to open shewe any (of) his or their porrengers, saucers, or measures with bloud, upon peyne to forfeyt," etc. These saucers seem to be of the rarest mention ; perhaps the custom of exhibiting them was short-lived. "Bleeding basin" was the accepted name a little later for the vessel used to receive the blood.

99. *On a day*, etc.] This poem is in *The Passionate Pilgrim*. See note above, IV. ii. 104. It is also in *England's Helicon*, 1600. There is a pretty little pastoral poem of twenty-six lines, by Nicholas Breton, in *The Queen's Entertainment at the Earl of Hertford's*, 1591 (Nichols' *Progresses*, iii. 117), which bears a family likeness to this piece. It begins : "In the merrie moneth of May, In a

Through the velvet leaves the wind,
All unseen can passage find ;
That the lover, sick to death,
Wish'd himself the heaven's breath.
Air, quoth he, thy cheeks may blow ;
Air, would I might triumph so !
But alack ! my hand is sworn
Ne'er to pluck thee from thy thorn :
Vow, alack ! for youth unmeet,
Youth so apt to pluck a sweet.
Do not call it sin in me,
That I am forsworn for thee ;
Thou for whom Jove would swear
Juno but an Ethiop were ;
And deny himself for Jove,
Turning mortal for thy love.

This will I send, and something else more plain,
That shall express my true love's fasting pain.
O! would the king, Berowne, and Longaville,
Were lovers too. Ill, to example ill,
Would from my forehead wipe a perjur'd note ;
For none offend where all alike do dote.

Long. [*advancing*]. Dumain, thy love is far from charity,
That in love's grief desir'st society :

103. *velvet leaves the*] *Velvet , leaves the* Qq, Ff 1, 2, 3 ; *velvet leaves, the* F 4. 104. *can*] *'gan* Theobald ; *gan* Passionate Pilgrim and England's Helicon. 105. *lover*] *shepheard* E. H. 106. *Wish'd*] Ff 2, 3, 4, P. P. ; *Wish* Qq, F 1. 108. *alack*] *alas* P. P. and E. H. *is*] *hath* ibid. 110. *thorn*] E. H., Rowe (ed. 2) ; *throne* Qq, Ff, P. P. 113, 114. *Do . . . thee*] omitted in P. P. and E. H. 115. *whom Jove*] *whom ev'n Jove* Rowe (ed. 2) *et seq.* 120. *fasting*] *fest'ring* Theobald conjecture ; *lasting* Capell.

morne by breake of day, Forth I walked," etc. And compare with these two the song in *The Passionate Pilgrim*, by Richard Barnfield (1595), beginning "As it fell upon a day, In the merrie month of May, Sitting in a pleasant shade," etc. (Oxford Book of English Verse, no. 203).

116. *Ethiop*] blackamoor ; as a type of ugliness. See *Much Ado About Nothing*, v. iv. 38. Ben Jonson uses this form as a noun, Nashe as an adjective. "It is a dowry, Me thinkes should make that sun-burnt proverbe false, *And wash the Ethiop white*" (Webster, *White Devil* [Lucas, i. 179]).

120. *fasting*] hungry, "hunger-starved," pain of abstinence.

123. *perjur'd note*] See notes at "perjure" and "wearing papers," line 46 above.

126. *grief desir'st society*] Referring to the commonly used proverb "Solamen miseris socios habuisse dolores" ; or as Chaucer writes : "Men seyn, to wrecche is consolacioun, To have another felawe in his peyne."

You may look pale, but I should blush, I know,
To be o'erheard and taken napping so.

King [*advancing*]. Come, sir, you blush; as his your case
is such;
You chide at him, offending twice as much:
You do not love Maria! Longaville
Did never sonnet for her sake compile,
Nor never lay his wreathed arms athwart
His loving bosom to keep down his heart.
I have been closely shrouded in this bush,
And mark'd you both, and for you both did blush.
I heard your guilty rhymes, observed your fashion,
Saw sighs reek from you, noted well your passion:
Ay me! says one; O Jove! the other cries;
One, her hairs were gold, crystal the other's eyes:
You would for paradise break faith and troth;
[*To Long.*]
And Jove, for your love would infringe an oath.
[*To Dum.*]
What will Berowne say when that he shall hear
A faith infringed, which such zeal did swear?

128. *o'er-heard*] *ore-hard* Q 1. 129. *you blush*] *do, blush* Capell conjecture; *blush you* Collier MS.; *your blush* S. Walker conjecture. 131. *Maria!*] *Maria?* Qq, Ff 1, 2; *Maria*, Ff 3, 4; *Maria;* Cambridge. 140. *One, her*] Q 1; *On her* F 1, Q 2; *Her* Ff 2, 3, 4; *One's* S. Walker conjecture. 141, 142. [*To Long.*] [*To Dum.*] Johnson. 144. *A faith*] Ff 2, 3, 4; *Faith* Qq, F 1; *Of faith, Faith so, Such faith, Faiths* various conjectures. 144. *zeal*] *a zeal* F 2.

128. *taken napping*] Oliphant (*New English*) says this occurs in Bishop Pilkington's *Sermons* (Parker Society) about 1560. Harington (*Orlando Furioso*, xxxix. 58) has "At last he said, as erst Sileno said, To those that took him napping in the cave." "Taken napping as Moss caught his mare" was a common version, arising out of the title of a ballad (1569, 1570), according to Hazlitt. See Cotgrave in v. *Desprouven*. In Ebbsworth's notes to *Westminster Drollery* it appears that the mare was caught up a tree. How unlucky it is that the words are not addressed to Berowne, where Capell placed him (line 20).

133. *wreathed arms*] See III. i. 178 "folded arms," and again, "arms crossed," III. i. 16.

138. *sighs reek from you*] "love is a smoke made with the fume of sighs" (*Romeo and Juliet*, I. i. 196).

141. *faith and troth*] So in Lodge's *Euphues Golden Legacie* (*Shakes. Lib.* 1875, p. 113), 1590: "we know fewe subtilties, and litle eloquence for that we lightly account of flattery: onely faith and troth thats shepheards wooing." And in Nicholas Breton's *In the Merrie Moneth of May* (Nichols'

How will he scorn ! how will he spend his wit !
How will he triumph, leap, and laugh at it !
For all the wealth that ever I did see,
I would not have him know so much by me.

Ber. Now step I forth to whip hypocrisy. [*Advancing.*
Ah ! good my liege, I pray thee, pardon me :
Good heart ! what grace hast thou, thus to reprove
These worms for loving, that art most in love ?
Your eyes do make no coaches ; in your tears
There is no certain princess that appears :
You'll not be perjur'd, 'tis a hateful thing :
Tush ! none but minstrels like of sonneting.
But are you not asham'd ? nay, are you not,
All three of you, to be thus much o'ershot ?

146. *leap*] *geap* Warburton. 147. *I*] *eye* Capell conjecture. 149. [*Advancing*] *Coming from his tree* Capell. 153. *coaches ; in*] Hanmer ; *couches in* Qq, Ff, *coaches in* Rowe (ed. 2).

Progresses of Queen Elizabeth [1823], iii. 117) : " Thus with many a pretie Oath, Yea and nay and faith and troth Such as silly shepheards use, When they will not love abuse " (1591).

146. *leap, and laugh at it*] " That heavy Saturn laugh'd and leap'd with him " (Sonnet xcviii.). " We should certainly read *geap*, i.e. jeer, ridicule " (Warburton). Warburton, who " wrote for Warburton and not for Shakespeare," meant " jape." Ben Jonson has " To sit and clap my hands, and laugh and leap, knocking my head against my roof with joy " (*Every Man out of his Humour*, i. 1). Compare below, v. ii. 291.

148. *by me*] concerning me. Compare *Merchant of Venice*, I. ii. 60 : " How say you by the French lord ? "; and 1 Corinthians, 4.

152. *worms*] Here applied to lovers, as in *The Tempest*, III. i. 31. Compare Lyly, *Campaspe*, v. 4 : " Two loving wormes " ; and *Mother Bombie*, ii. 2 : " the loving worme my daughter."

153. *coaches*] Referring to the King's sonnet above, line 33. Rowe (ed. 2, 1714) first corrected the misreading " couches," according to Furness, and was followed by Pope, etc. The same misprint occurs in *Euphues Golden Legacie* (by Lodge), 1590 (*Shakes. Lib.* 1875, p. 131), where the text reads : " No sooner did Phoebus Henchman appeare in the skie, to give warning that his maisters horses should be trapt in his glorious couch."

156. *sonneting*] For this contemptuous reference to " sonneting " see *Two Gentlemen of Verona*, III. ii. 68, and *Romeo and Juliet*, II. iv. 41-44. The word " sonnet " had originally a musical connotation—hence " minstrels." Byrd published more than one set of " Psalms, Songs and *Sonnets*."

158. *o'ershot*] astray in your aim ; gone wrong, as in " out of the way " above, line 74. Compare *Julius Caesar*, III. ii. 155 ; and Ben Jonson, *Silent Woman*, IV. ii. : " You shall not overshoot yourself to send him that word by me." See *New Eng. Dict.* (*overshoot*) for a minute analysis of the general sense, " fall into error."

You found his mote ; the king your mote did see ;
But I a beam do find in each of three.
O ! what a scene of foolery have I seen,
Of sighs, of groans, of sorrow, and of teen ;
O ! me with what strict patience have I sat,
To see a king transformed to a gnat ;
To see great Hercules whipping a gig,

159. *mote . . . mote*] Rowe ; *moth . . . moth* Qq, Ff. 164. *gnat*] *knot* Theobald ; *sot* Johnson conjecture.

159. *mote*] There is constant confusion between the words *moth* and *mote*. See *Othello*, I. iii. 257 and *Pericles*, IV. iv. 21. Apparently they were often used synonymously and spelt at haphazard. Compare *King John*, IV. i. 92. "Mote," in our sense, was spelt "moth," as it is twice in this line in the old editions ; and "moth" seems to have been pronounced "mote." R. G. White and Ellis agree that "Moth" (the name) was pronounced "Mote" ; but the probability is it was unfixed. There is here an undoubted allusion to the figure of the mote and the beam (Matthew vii. 3-5 ; Luke vi. 41, 42) ; *cf.* "festu (straw) or a litil mote" and "festu other a mot" (Wyclif). But where is the line to be drawn in the quibbling between moth and mote, beam of the sun and chip or fescue of wood ? It may not have been in Wyclif, but it is in the A.V. ; and as "Rabbi Zeal-of-the-Land Busy, a Banbury man," says in his confusion : "that remains, as I may say, a beam, a very beam, not a beam of the sun, not a beam of the moon, nor a beam of the balance, neither a house-beam, nor a weaver's beam, but a beam in the eye, in the eye of the brethren, a very great beam, an exceeding great beam" (Ben Jonson, *Bartholomew Fair*, v. iii.).

162. *teen*] grief. A common word from Chaucer downwards, especially with rhymers. See *The Tempest*, I. ii. 64. In *Romeo and Juliet*, I. iii. 13, it is used non-rhymingly for the sake of a "vile pun."

164. *gnat*] an insignificant insect ; a "worm." The editors have searched for a further meaning here, and to assist them have imagined that the text needed alteration ; "knot," "sot," and "quat," having been proposed or adopted. Hart thought "gnat" was suggested by the moth above, and (like "coaches") by the eye-beams that smote the King's cheek in his sonnet. The King is a gnat playing, like the other moths or motes, in the beams of love. Ben Jonson has the same expression : "They that before, like gnats, played in his beams, And thronged to circumscribe him, now not seen" (*Sejanus*, v. 10 [1603]). There is no commoner simile from Chaucer downwards than "as thick as motes in the sun-beam." But it is the later emblem or proverb of the moth or gnat singeing in the flames that illuminates this passage. Whitney's emblem, *In amore tormentum* (edited H. Green, p. 219), 1586, gives the King's position : "Even as the gnattes, that flie into the blaze, Doe burne their wings and fall into the fire ; So, those too muche on gallant showes that gaze, Are captives caught and burne in their desire."

165, 166, 167, 168. *Hercules, Solomon, Nestor, Timon*] Compare Webster, *White Devil* (ed. F. L. Lucas, i. 187) : "*Flamineo.* Whither shall I go now ? O Lucian thy ridiculous purgatory—

And profound Solomon to tune a jig,
And Nestor play at push-pin with the boys,
And critic Timon laugh at idle toys!

166. *to tune*] Q 1; *tuning* Ff, Q 2. 168. *toys*] *toyles* Q 2.

to finde Alexander the great cobling shooes, Pompey tagging points, and Julius Caesar making haire buttons, Haniball selling blacking, and Augustus crying garlike," etc., etc. And see Rabelais, ii. 30.

165. *whipping a gig*] whipping a top. See v. i. 63. Gabriel Harvey uses the word: "I may chance rattle him like a baby of parchment, or kneade him like a cake of dowe, or chearne him like a dish of butter, or girke him like a hobling gig" (*New Letter*, [Grosart, i. 283]). "Whirligig" preserves this word. According to Halliwell, a gig was a special kind of top. He says: "It is described by an aged person as having been generally made of the tip of a horn, hollow, but with a small ballast at the bottom of the inside." Its connection with a horn is referred to at v. i. 63 below.

166. *jig*] A dance, or the music to it. See Greene, *James the Fourth* (*ante* 1592) (Grosart, xiii. 209, 210): "I have two sonnes, that with one Scottish gigge shall breake the necke of thy Antiques . . . gather uppe your legges and daunce me forthwith a gigge worth the sight."

167. *play at push-pin*] more commonly "put-pin." Halliwell quotes from the MS. play of *Misogonus* (*ante* 1577) (Hazlitt): "That can play at put-pin, Blow-poynte and near [ne'er] lin." In Nashe's *Foure Letters Confuted* (McKerrow, i. 303) it is again "put-pin": "I will play at put-pinne with thee for all that thou art woorth." And also in Marston's *Scourge of Villainy*, Satire viii.: "Playing at put-pin, doting on some glass. . . . Toying with babies." Later, in Beaumont and Fletcher, in Massinger and in Herrick, it is "push-pin." The earliest definition appears to be that in John Ash's *New and Complete Dictionary of the English Language* (1775): "*Push-pin*, a child's play in which pins are pushed with an endeavour to cross them." From a reference in *New Eng Dict.*, it seems that the game was familiar at least as late as 1825.

168. *critic*] critical, censorious. "Sitting like a looker-on Of this worldes stage, doest note, with critique pen, The sharpe dislikes of each condition" (*Edmund Spenser to Gabriel Harvey:* "Dublin: this xviii. of July: 1586" [Oxford Spenser, p. 603].

critic Timon laugh at idle toys] Greene refers to Timon earlier: "Now hote now could, first as courteous as Traian, and then as currish as Tymon, one while a defender of lust, and an other time a contemner of love" (*Tritameron* [Grosart, iii. 79], 1584); and "Tymonlike to condemne those heavenlie creatures whose onlie sight is a sufficient salve against all hellish sorrowes" (*Carde of Fancie* [iv. 40], 1587). See Plutarch's *Life of Mark Anthony*. Timon the misanthropist was a snarler at everything, and the force of this line would seem to be that he became as good-humoured and cheerful as a sportive kid. But "idle toys," or "toys of an idle head," had a definite sense of foolish mental or literary efforts; and it is possible that the meaning of the line is that the academics, professedly as severe on human follies as Timon, have now been caught taking a delight in mere idle sonneteering. At line 199 below Berowne shows what he means by "a toy"; his own sonnet to Rosaline is "a toy, my liege, a toy."

Where lies thy grief? O! tell me, good Dumain,
And, gentle Longaville, where lies thy pain?
And where my liege's? all about the breast:
A caudle, ho!

King. Too bitter is thy jest.
Are we betray'd thus to thy over-view?

Ber. Not you by me, but I betray'd to you:
I, that am honest; I, that hold it sin
To break the vow I am engaged in;
I am betray'd, by keeping company
With moon-like men, men of inconstancy.
When shall you see me write a thing in rhyme?
Or groan for Joan? or spend a minute's time
In pruning me? When shall you hear that I

172. *caudle*] Q 1, Rowe, Theobald, Johnson; *candle* Ff, Q 2. 174. *by me . . . to you*] Qq, Ff; *by me . . . by you* Theobald; *to me . . . by you* Capell. 178. *moon-like men, men of inconstancy*] Steevens; *men like men of inconstancy* Qq, F 1; *men like men of strange inconstancy* Ff 2, 3, 4. 180. *Joan*] *Ione* Q 1; *Loue* Q 1 (Duke of Devonshire copy). 181-184. Q 1 prints as prose.

172. *caudle*] occurs (as noun) only once again in Shakespeare (in *2 Henry VI.*), and there as well as here the Folios read *candle*. A warm, thin drink of gruel and ale or wine, with sugar, etc., given to women, children, and especially invalids.

178. *men of inconstancy*] The line is clearly corrupt, and the insertion of "strange" in the later Folios an attempt at a cure that is earlier, but no more worthy of acceptance, than any other. Of many ingenious suggestions Steevens' is perhaps the happiest; of all words that might have been dropped from the middle of the line a repeated "men" is likeliest, and "moon" in English script might easily be misread as "men," especially if, as Dover Wilson suggests, Shakespeare spelt it "mon." And the moon is a standard symbol of inconstancy in Shakespeare; compare "the inconstant moon" of *Romeo and Juliet*, II. ii. 109, and the quibbles on the moon's changes in the present play, V. ii. 212 ff.

180. *Joan*] The reading "Loue" is a fine illustration of the additional corruptions to be found in the copy of the Quarto that formerly belonged to the Duke of Devonshire and is now in the Huntington Library. Dover Wilson took them as evidence that this copy was one of the last copies printed, when the compositor's original blunders had been extended by disturbance of the type in the course of printing and the "machine-minder's" attempts to repair the damage. See introduction 2.2. Mr. John Crow has, however, shown me that the state at least of the present sheet (sig. E) is better explained if the Devonshire Quarto is regarded rather as an *early* copy, lacking the corrections that were later to be made while the book was printing (a common Elizabethan practice).

181. *pruning*] preening, or pryning, as birds do their feathers; trimming. Ben Jonson has "prunes his mustaccio," and "pruning his clothes," in *Cynthia's Revels* (Induction, and III. ii.), 1600.

Will praise a hand, a foot, a face, an eye,
A gait, a state, a brow, a breast, a waist,
A leg, a limb—?

King. Soft! whither away so fast?
A true man or a thief that gallops so?

Ber. I post from love; good lover, let me go.

Enter JAQUENETTA *and* COSTARD.

Jaq. God bless the king!

King. What present hast thou there?

Cost. Some certain treason.

King. What makes treason here?

Cost. Nay, it makes nothing, sir.

King. If it mar nothing neither,
The treason and you go in peace away together.

Jaq. I beseech your grace, let this letter be read:
Our Person misdoubts it; 'twas treason, he said.

King. Berowne, read it over. [*Berowne reads the letter.*
Where hadst thou it?

Jaq. Of Costard.

190. *away*] omitted Ff 2, 3, 4.

192. *'twas*] *it was* Ff, Q 2.

183. *state*] an "act of standing" as opposed to gait (Steevens). A pose.

brow] the countenance; as above at IV. i. 17, and often in Shakespeare.

184. *whither away so fast*] This expression occurs four times in Shakespeare. Compare *King Leir* (Malone Soc., ed. Greg, 991) 1593: "My honest friend, whither away so fast?"

185. *true man*] honest man. Very commonly set in opposition to a thief, as in *1 Henry IV.* II. ii. 105, and Chaucer's *Squire's Tale*: "A true wight and a thief thinkest not one." Nashe has "One true man is stronger than two theeves" (*Foure Letters Confuted* [McKerrow, i. 298]); and Heywood (ed. Sharman, p. 158), 1546: "When thieves fall out true men come to their good." In *The Famous Victories of Henry V.* (*Shakes. Lib.* 1875, p. 329) occurs: "*Theafe.* It is not too late for true men to walke. [*Dericke.*] We know thee not to be a true man."

186. *post*] ride with urgency.

187. *present*] writing, presentment. Compare *As You Like It*, I. ii. 132; and Ben Jonson, *Cynthia's Revels*, V. ii.: "Be it known to all that profess courtship, by these presents, that we" (*per has literas presentes*, legal). Very unusual in the singular.

189. *makes . . . mar*] "To make or mar" is a proverbial expression traced back in N.E.D. to Lydgate's *Assembly of Gods* (c. 1420). This and its parallel, "mend or mar," were very common in Shakespeare's time. See *Macbeth*, II. iii. 26; *King Lear*, I. i. 97, etc., etc. Tusser has it in *Verses* (1573): "to disagree Is ventring all to make or mar" (Eng. Dial. Soc. p. 204).

192. *misdoubts*] suspects, mistrusts.

King. Where hadst thou it?
Cost. Of Dun Adramadio, Dun Adramadio.
King. How now! what is in you? why dost thou tear it?
Ber. A toy, my liege, a toy: your grace needs not fear it.
Long. It did move him to passion, and therefore let's hear it.
Dum. [*gathers up the pieces*]. It is Berowne's writing, and here is his name.
Ber. [*To Costard.*] Ah! you whoreson loggerhead, you were born to do me shame.
Guilty, my lord, guilty! I confess, I confess.
King. What?
Ber. That you three fools lack'd me, fool, to make up the mess;
He, he, and you, and you, my liege, and I,
Are pick-purses in love, and we deserve to die.
O! dismiss this audience, and I shall tell you more.
Dum. Now the number is even.
Ber. True, true; we are four.
Will these turtles be gone?
King. Hence, Sirs; away!
Cost. Walk aside the true folk, and let the traitors stay.
[*Exeunt Costard and Jaquenetta.*

198. *is in*] Qq, Ff 1, 2; *mean* Ff 3, 4. 201. [*gathers up the pieces*] Capell.

199. *toy*] For the "toy" see IV. ii. 104-17; and see note at "idle toys," line 168 above.

202. *loggerhead*] blockhead. The earliest example in *New Eng. Dict.* It is used again in *1 Henry IV.* II. iv. 4. Nashe makes an adjective of it: "This loggerhead Legend of lyes" (*Have With You to Saffron Walden* [McKerrow, iii. 71], 1596).

204. *make up the mess*] make up the party of four. "At great dinners and feasts the company was usually arranged into fours, which were called messes" (Nares), who gives plenty of examples of the common expression, as: "Foure makes a messe, and we have a messe of masters that must be coozened" (Lyly, *Mother Bombie*, II. i.). See below, V. ii. 361, and *3 Henry VI.* I. iv. 73. A good example occurs in Lodge's *Euphues Golden Legacie* (*Shakes. Lib.* 1875, p. 118), 1590: "which Ganimede espying thinking hee [Saladyne] had had his Mistresse long inough at shrift, sayd: what, a match or no? A match (quoth Aliena) or els it were an ill market. I am glad (quoth Ganimede), I would Rosader were wel here to make up a messe."

205. *and you, and you*] Both referring to "my liege." Reed omitted one "and you."

Ber. Sweet lords, sweet lovers, O! let us embrace.
As true we are as flesh and blood can be:
The sea will ebb and flow, heaven show his face;
Young blood doth not obey an old decree:
We cannot cross the cause why we were born;
Therefore, of all hands must we be forsworn.
King. What! did these rent lines show some love of thine?
Ber. Did they? quoth you. Who sees the heavenly Rosaline,
That, like a rude and savage man of Inde,
At the first opening of the gorgeous east,
Bows not his vassal head, and strooken blind,
Kisses the base ground with obedient breast?
What peremptory eagle-sighted eye
Dares look upon the heaven of her brow,
That is not blinded by her majesty?
King. What zeal, what fury hath inspir'd thee now?
My love, her mistress, is a gracious moon;
She an attending star, scarce seen a light.

213. *show*] *shew* Q 1; *will shew* Ff, Q 2. 215. *were*] Q 1, Ff 3, 4; *are* Ff 1, 2, Q 2. 218. *quoth you*] omitted Capell. 221. *strooken*] Qq, Ff 1, 2, 3; *strucken* F 4, Cambridge.

216. *of all hands*] on every side.

219. *man of Inde*] Craig quotes from Ascham's *Toxophilus* (Arber, p. 212): "The men of Inde had theyr bowes made of a rede." Inde was a common early name for India, abundantly illustrated in *New Eng. Dict.*

223. *peremptory*] originally a law term meaning "decisive," "final"; hence "determined," "obstinately resolute." See *King John*, II. i. 454: "Not death himself In mortal fury half so peremptory As we to keep this city."

eagle-sighted] A reference to the eagle's supposed power, alone of all birds, of looking at the sun. It is mentioned in Chaucer's *Assembly of Foules*. See Pliny, I. xxvii. (Holland's translation, p. 160); and Greene, *Menaphon* (Grosart, vi. 105), 1589: "Pardon me, faire sheepheardesse, . . . for I cannot chuse, being Eagle-sighted, but gaze on the Sunne the first time I see it"; and in his *Mourning Garment* (ix. 157): "I am not Eagle-sighted, and therefore feare to flie too nigh the Sunne."

227, 228. *moon . . . scarce seen a light*] Compare *Gesta Grayorum*, 1594 (ed. Greg, p. 68): "at the Royal Presence of Her Majesty, it appeared as an obscured Shadow: in this, not unlike unto the Morning-star, which looketh very chearfully on the World, so long as the Sun looketh not on it." Perhaps from Horace, *Odes* I, 12. Compare *Entertainment of Ambassador to Landgrave of Hesse*, 1596: "There was the Lady Anna . . . and many that waited on the Princess. And she herselfe, as Horace says of Julium Sidus, stood by her bedside, *velut inter ignes luna minores*" (Nichols' *Progresses*, iii. 388-9).

Ber. My eyes are then no eyes, nor I Berowne :
O ! but for my love, day would turn to night.
Of all complexions the cull'd sovereignty
Do meet, as at a fair, in her fair cheek ;
Where several worthies make one dignity,
Where nothing wants that want itself doth seek.
Lend me the flourish of all gentle tongues,—
Fie, painted rhetoric ! O ! she needs it not :
To things of sale a seller's praise belongs ;
She passes praise ; then praise too short doth blot.
A wither'd hermit, five-score winters worn,
Might shake off fifty, looking in her eye :
Beauty doth varnish age, as if new-born,
And gives the crutch the cradle's infancy.
O ! 'tis the sun that maketh all things shine.
King. By heaven, thy love is black as ebony.
Ber. Is ebony like her ? O wood divine !
A wife of such wood were felicity.
O ! who can give an oath ? where is a book ?
That I may swear beauty doth beauty lack,
If that she learn not of her eye to look :
No face is fair that is not full so black.

246. *wood*] Rowe (ed. 1) ; *word* Qq, Ff.

228. *attending star*] Staunton says : " It was a prevailing notion formerly that the moon had an attending star. . . . Sir Richard Hawkins, in his *Observations on a Voyage to the South Seas in 1593*, remarks : " Some I have heard say, and others write, that there is a starre which never separateth itself from the moon, but a small distance." Lodge mentions Hawkins' star in *Euphues Golden Legacie* (*Shakes. Lib.* 1875, p. 79), 1590 : " for as the Moone never goes without the starre Lunisequa, so a lover never goeth without the unrest of his thoughts." I doubt if Shakespeare refers to it here.

230, 236, 243, 247, 280, 284, 286, etc. *O*] For Berowne's ejaculation " O ! " see above, III. i. 144, note.

233. *worthies*] excellencies, things of worth.

236. *painted rhetoric*] Compare Lodge, *Euphues Golden Legacie* (*Shakes. Lib.*, 1875, p. 18) : " A painted tongue may shroud a subtle heart " ; and R. Edwards, *Damon and Pithias* (Hazlitt's *Dodsley*, iv. 88), *ante* 1566 : " these need no subtle sleight, No painted speech the matter to convey."

237. *a seller's praise*] Compare above, II. i. 16, Sonnet 21, and (for the whole passage) Sonnet 82.

242. *crutch . . . cradle*] " From cradle to crutch, from infancy to old age," was a symbolical expression used several times by Greene, e.g. " from the cradle to the crouch, and from the crouch had one legge in the grave " (*Penelope's Web* [Grosart, v. 224], 1587).

250. *No face . . . black*] See Sidney's *Astrophel and Stella*, vii : " whereas

King. O paradox ! Black is the badge of hell,
The hue of dungeons and the school of night ;
And beauty's crest becomes the heavens well.
Ber. Devils soonest tempt, resembling spirits of light.
O ! if in black my lady's brows be deck'd,
It mourns that painting and usurping hair
Should ravish doters with a false aspect ;
And therefore is she born to make black fair.

252. *school*] *schoole* Qq, Ff ; *scowl* Theobald ; *stole* Hanmer ; *soul*, *soil*, *shade*, *scroll*, *shroud*, *seal*, and *suit* various conjectures and lections. 253. *crest*] *dress*, *crete*, *craye*, *cresset*, and *best* various conjectures and lections. 256. *and*] F 4 ; omitted Qq, F 1 ; *an* Ff 2, 3.

blacke seemes Beauties contrarie, Shee even in blacke doth make all Beauties flowe." Stella, however, combined black eyes with a pink-and-white complexion and golden hair. See Introduction 5.24.

252. *school of night*] Almost all the editors were agreed on the need for emending this phrase (but not on the emendation) until Arthur Acheson suggested, in his *Shakespeare and the Rival Poet* (1903), that there was a real "Schoole of Night" existing at this time, and that it was synonymous with the "Schoole of Atheism" of which Sir Walter Ralegh was reputed by contemporaries to be the chief patron. See Introduction 5.23. E. A. Strathmann, in *The Textual Evidence for "The School of Night"* (Modern Language Notes, LVI, March 1941), insists that this is historically unproven and textually impossible. I find the second part of his argument unconvincing, since it rests on two false assumptions—that the chaotic punctuation of the Quarto, including the comma after "dungeons," is as likely to be Shakespeare's as its oddities of spelling ; and that Shakespeare habitually took care to balance his clauses. Strathmann would substitute for "schoole" some word more closely corresponding to the "badge" and "hue" of the other comparisons, and suggests "suit," which Shakespeare (who used "shue" for "sue" at III. i. 201) may well have spelt "shoote." (Indeed, the man who wrote "scilens" for "silence" may easily have written "schoote" for "suit"). To drop the comma seems to me the simpler solution.

253. *beauty's crest*] There have been many explanations and emendations of this passage, but none of them very convincing. The explainers can be broadly divided into two schools. One takes the last line as ironical, and construes the King's speech : "black is the badge of *hell ;* you make it the badge of beauty—a fine emblem for what is usually regarded as a *heavenly* quality !" The other sees the line as a straight rejoinder to Berowne's claim (line 243) that his black beauty is a sun. It would mean "true (i.e. fair) beauty, not that which Berowne admires, is the proper subject for such heavenly comparisons," and it aptly provokes the reply that this conventional beauty is often a screen for evil deeds. The first interpretation better suits the drift of the King's speech, the second that of the dialogue as a whole.

254. *Devils . . . spirits of light*] Compare 2 Corinthians xi. 14.

258, 259. *black . . . turns the fashion*] Lyly has the same thought : "such a common thing it is amongst

Her favour turns the fashion of the days,
For native blood is counted painting now :
And therefore red, that would avoid dispraise,
Paints itself black, to imitate her brow.
Dum. To look like her are chimney-sweepers black.
Long. And since her time are colliers counted bright.
King. And Ethiops of their sweet complexion crack.
Dum. Dark needs no candles now, for dark is light.
Ber. Your mistresses dare never come in rain,
For fear their colours should be wash'd away.
King. 'Twere good, yours did ; for, sir, to tell you plain,
I'll find a fairer face not wash'd to-day.
Ber. I'll prove her fair, or talk till doomsday here.
King. No devil will fright thee then so much as she.
Dum. I never knew man hold vile stuff so dear.
Long. Look, here's thy love : my foot and her face see.
[*Showing his shoe.*
Ber. O ! if the streets were paved with thine eyes,
Her feet were much too dainty for such tread.
Dum. O vile ! then, as she goes, what upward lies
The street should see as she walk'd overhead.
King. But what of this ? Are we not all in love ?
Ber. O ! nothing so sure ; and thereby all forsworn.
King. Then leave this chat ; and, good Berowne, now
prove
Our loving lawful, and our faith not torn.
Dum. Ay, marry, there ; some flattery for this evil.
Long. O ! some authority how to proceed ;
Some tricks, some quillets, how to cheat the devil.

263. *black*] *blake* Q 1. 265. *sweet*] *swart* anonymous conjecture. *crack*] Q 2, Ff 3, 4 ; *crake* Q 1, Ff 1, 2. 268. *their*] *her* Q 2. 274. [*Showing his shoe*] Johnson, Steevens, Craig, etc. 280. *O ! nothing*] Qq, F 1 ; *Nothing* Ff 2, 3, 4 Cambridge.

you to commend, that oftentimes for fashion's sake you call them beautiful whom you know blacke " (*Campaspe*, iv. 2 [1581]).

265. *crack*] boast.

274. [*Showing his shoe*] Furness writes : " It is almost humiliating to have to record that a large majority of editors, following Johnson, have deemed it necessary to add a stage-direction here." I like it. Even so the point is generally missed when the play is staged, for designers do not choose that Longaville should be shod, as he must be, in black.

285. *quillets*] subtleties. Compare *2 Henry VI.* III. i, 261 : " do not stand on quillets how to slay him :

Dum. Some salve for perjury.
Ber. O! 'tis more than need.
Have at you then, affection's men-at-arms:
Consider what you first did swear unto,
To fast, to study, and to see no woman;
Flat treason 'gainst the kingly state of youth.
Say, can you fast? your stomachs are too young,
And abstinence engenders maladies.
[And where that you have vow'd to study, lords,
In that each of you have forsworn his book,
Can you still dream and pore and thereon look?
For when would you, my lord, or you, or you,
Have found the ground of study's excellence
Without the beauty of a woman's face?
From women's eyes this doctrine I derive:
They are the ground, the books, the academes,
From whence doth spring the true Promethean fire.
Why, universal plodding poisons up

286. *O! 'tis*] *O tis* Qq, Ff 2; *'Tis* Cambridge. 302. *poisons*] *poysons* Qq, Ff; *prisons* Theobald *et seq.*

Be it by gins, by snares, by subtlety, sleeping or waking, 'tis no matter how." The use in the text is the earliest in *New Eng. Dict.* Origin obscure, but perhaps a variant of "quiddit." Gabriel Harvey has "quillity" earlier. Compare also Holland's *Plinie*, xi. 3 (1601): "to judge and determine of these doubtful quillets and their causes." Shakespeare uses the word several times later.

289. *To fast . . . no woman*] So Lucio says in *Measure for Measure*, I. iv. 60, 61: "Blunt his natural edge with profits of the mind, study and fast."

296-301. *For when would you . . . true Promethean fire*] Dyce omits these lines, also lines 309-316, on account of their repetition either verbally or in substance elsewhere in the speech. Capell notices this, and attributed it to the intermingling of two different drafts of MSS. Dover Wilson defines the early draft more probably than Dyce, as running from line 293 to line 314. The new draft begins at line 315; its first six lines are a close rendering of lines 293-298, the next three a much freer one of 302-305. At 324 begins a rhapsody of twenty-four lines that is entirely new; but lines 347-351 return to take up lines 299-301, hitherto passed over, and the final eleven lines are an expansion of 306-314. See Introduction 2.51.

297. *ground*] base, foundation.

300. *academes*] see note, I. i. 13.

301. *Promethean fire*] Chapman has this expression about the same date: "Therefore Promethean poets with the coals Of their most genial, more than human souls, In living verse created men like these" (*The Shadow of Night*, 1594). See Introduction 5.23.

302. *poisons up*] Dyce pointed out that the Folio misprints *poison'd* for *prison'd* in *1 Henry VI.* v. iv. 120. Halliwell and Furnivall retain "poisons." Furnivall says: "You

The nimble spirits in the arteries,
As motion and long-during action tires
The sinewy vigour of the traveller.
Now, for not looking on a woman's face,
You have in that forsworn the use of eyes,
And study too, the causer of your vow ;
For where is any author in the world
Teaches such beauty as a woman's eye ?
Learning is but an adjunct to ourself,
And where we are our learning likewise is :
Then when ourselves we see in ladies' eyes,
Do we not likewise see our learning there ?]
O ! we have made a vow to study, lords,
And in that vow we have forsworn our books :
For when would you, my liege, or you, or you,
In leaden contemplation have found out
Such fiery numbers as the prompting eyes
Of beauty's tutors have enrich'd you with ?
Other slow arts entirely keep the brain,
And therefore, finding barren practisers,
Scarce show a harvest of their heavy toil ;
But love, first learned in a lady's eyes,
Lives not alone immured in the brain,
But, with the motion of all elements,
Courses as swift as thought in every power,
And gives to every power a double power,
Above their functions and their offices.

305. *sinewy*] *sinnowy* Qq, Ff. 310. *beauty*] *duty* Warburton ; *leaving* Collier MS. 313, 314. *eyes, Do*] Ff 2, 3, 4 ; *eyes, With our selves. Do* Qq, F 1 (insertion of half line).

don't want the metaphor of nimble spirits struggling to burst their prison : you want them dulled and numbed by poison." But if these lines were redrafted as 321-323 below, only "prisons" can have suggested "keep the brain," and "immured" (line 325). Much may be said on both sides, but it is better to adhere to the originals.

305. *sinewy*] The old spelling "sinnowy" is of interest here, since it has led to the quaint misprint in Marlowe's *Tamburlaine* (part I., act II. i.) : "His arms and fingers long and snowy."

313. *eyes*] The additional fragment preserved in the early texts is again evidence that two drafts overlap here.

319. *fiery numbers*] Referring to the sonnets and "toys" of the lovers.

321. *keep*] inhabit, remain in.

It adds a precious seeing to the eye ;
A lover's eyes will gaze an eagle blind ;
A lover's ear will hear the lowest sound,
When the suspicious head of theft is stopp'd :
Love's feeling is more soft and sensible
Than are the tender horns of cockled snails :
Love's tongue proves dainty Bacchus gross in taste.
For valour, is not Love a Hercules,
Still climbing trees in the Hesperides ?
Subtle as Sphinx ; as sweet and musical
As bright Apollo's lute, strung with his hair ;

336. *dainty Bacchus*] Ff 2, 3, 4 ; *dainty, Bacchus* Qq, F 1.

333. *suspicious head of theft*] Farmer says " the head suspicious of theft," supporting this by " to watch like one that fears robbing," in *Two Gentlemen of Verona*, II. i. 26. From which slight and accidental assistance Furness declares that this interpretation carries conviction. The obvious meaning is surely the correct one. Compare *3 Henry VI.* V. vi. 11-12 : " Suspicion always haunts the guilty mind : the thief doth fear each bush an officer." Nashe implies that the thought was proverbial : " Wee, carelesse of these mischances, helde on our flight, and saw no man come after us but we thought had pursued us. A theefe, they saie, mistakes everie bush for a true man ; the winde ratled not in any bush by the way as I rode, but I straight drew my rapier " (*The Unfortunate Traveller* [McKerrow, ii. 319], 1594). It occurs again in *Time's Whistle*, Satire 7, 3485 (1615). Sir E. Maunde Thompson suggested " th' eft," which pairs, in my opinion too well, with the cockled snail two lines later.

335. *cockled*] " inshell'd like the fish called a cockle " (Steevens). I incline rather to the meaning puckered, folded, wrinkled. See the figure of " The Snail Mount " in Nichols, iii. 101, of date 1591, where the shell is forgotten when the horns are prominent.

338. *Hesperides*] Frequently used as the name of the garden in which the golden apples grew, watched by the daughters of Hesperus, the Hesperides of Grecian mythology. The final " labour " that Hercules was called upon to perform was to enter the garden, overcome a guardian dragon, and pick the applies from the tree. Peter Martyr's *Decades of the Ocean* (1516) (translated by M. Lok, Hakluyt [1587], ed. 1812, vol. v. p. 206) identifies the islands with the Fortunate Isles : " the Islands of Hesparides, now called Caboverde."

339. *Subtle as Sphinx*] " and if I coulde have found a Sphinx to have expounded ther ridel " (*Letters of Elizabeth to James* (Camden Soc. p. 173), *ante* 1586. The Sphinx of Greek mythology *posed* the riddle ; it was Oedipus who expounded it. The passage in the text is the earliest cited in this sense in the *Stanford Dictionary*.

340. *Apollo's . . . hair*] Apollo's hair is often mentioned by Greene, not as lute-strings, but as a type of sunshiny loveliness. In *Menaphon* (Grosart, vi. 126), 1587, he writes : " Apollo, when my Mistres first was borne, Cut off his lockes and left them on her head, And said : I plant these wires in Naturis scorne, Whose beauties shall appeare when

And when Love speaks, the voice of all the gods
Make heaven drowsy with the harmony.
Never durst poet touch a pen to write
Until his ink were temper'd with Love's sighs ;
O ! then his lines would ravish savage ears,
And plant in tyrants mild humility.
From women's eyes this doctrine I derive :
They sparkle still the right Promethean fire ;
They are the books, the arts, the academes,
That show, contain, and nourish all the world ;

341, 342. *the voice . . . heaven*] *the voice makes all the gods of heaven* Farmer conjecture. 346. *humility*] *humanity* Mrs. Griffith, Walker, Dyce.

Time is dead." And in *Tullies Love*, 1589 (Grosart, vii. 105) : " His haire was like the shine of Apollo, when shaking his glorious tresses, he makes the world beauteous." Steevens quotes from *How a Man may Chuse a Good Wife from a Bad* (Hazlitt's *Dodsley*, ix. 77), 1602 : " Hath he not torn those gold wires from your head, Wherewith Apollo would have strung his harp, And kept them to play music to the gods ? " This seems to be a somewhat incoherent echo of the passage in the text. Lyly makes Pan say to Apollo : " Tell mee, Apollo, is there any instrument so sweete to play on as one's mistresse ? Had thy lute beene of laurell and the strings of Daphne's haire thy tunes might have been compared to my notes " (*Mydas*, iv. 1 [?1589]).

341, 342. *Love speaks . . . Make heaven drowsy*] Tyrwhitt remarked about a century and a half ago, that " Few passages have been more canvassed than this " ; and a long list of subsequent comments is given by Furness. Tyrwhitt alters the pointing ; Farmer transposes words ; Warburton changes them (*Mark !* for *Make*), which Heath reprints, saying Warburton's note is " one of the completest pieces of nonsense extant." Furness finishes with Knight's words as the most satisfactory. He says : " The meaning appears to us so clear amidst the blaze of poetic beauty, that an explanation is hardly wanted. When love speaks, the responsive harmony of the voice of all the gods makes heaven drowsy." Compare Shirley's *Love Tricks*, iv. 2 (about 1625) : " The tongue that's able to rock Heaven asleep And make the music of the spheres stand still." The power of harmony to make the hearers drowsy is commonly referred to by Shakespeare. All the gods are mouthpieces of the musical eloquence of Love.

346. *humility*] Halliwell quotes Huloet's *Abecedarium*, 1552 : " *Humilitie* is a gentlenes of the mynde, or a gentle patience withoute all angre or wrathe," as a protest against the necessity of adopting " humanity," as several editors took upon themselves to do. Schmidt gives the sense of " benevolence, kindness, humanity," to humility ; an interpretation not recognized by *New Eng. Dict.* though supported by the use of " humble " in v. ii. 621 and 727 below. Humility in the sense of meekness is very reasonably placed in opposition to the pride that characterizes a tyrant.

347-349. *From women's eyes . . . academes*] See notes above, lines 296-301.

Else none at all in aught proves excellent.
Then fools you were these women to forswear,
Or, keeping what is sworn, you will prove fools.
For wisdom's sake, a word that all men love,
Or for love's sake, a word that loves all men,
Or for men's sake, the authors of these women,
Or women's sake, by whom we men are men,
Let us once lose our oaths to find ourselves,
Or else we lose ourselves to keep our oaths.
It is religion to be thus forsworn;
For charity itself fulfils the law;
And who can sever love from charity?

King. Saint Cupid, then! and, soldiers, to the field!

Ber. Advance your standards, and upon them, lords!
Pell-mell, down with them! but be first advis'd,
In conflict that you get the sun of them.

Long. Now to plain-dealing; lay these glozes by:
Shall we resolve to woo these girls of France?

King. And win them too: therefore let us devise
Some entertainment for them in their tents.

Ber. First, from the park let us conduct them thither;
Then homeward every man attach the hand

355. *loves*] *moves* Hanmer; *leads* Mason; *joyes* Heath; *learns* Bailey.
356. *authors*] Capell; *author* Qq, Ff.

357. *love . . . a word that loves all men*] love that impresses itself, or inspires its being into all men—makes them lovers. The verb seems to be given an unique sense. Compare the old "to meat," to supply with meat; and Ralegh's use of the verb "scorn" in his earliest known verses, prefixed to Gascoigne's *Steel Glas* (1576): "this medicine may suffyse To scorne the rest and seke to please the wise." "Scorn" seems perforce to mean here "to make subject to scorn." Capell explained *loves* "is a friend to," or, as Malone put it, "is pleasing to," used as the verb "like"; but that seems too mild a sense for the antithesis.

361. *charity . . . law*] The "Bishops'" Bible, 1568, has (Romans xii. 8): "(For he that loveth another, hath fulfylled the lawe)."

365. *Pell-mell*] confusedly, with violence. Greene has "least love entering pell mell with war" (*Tullies Love* [Grosart, vii. 135]).

367. *Now to plain-dealing . . . glozes by*] This may be interpreted in two ways: "Now to business, mere verbal flourishes achieve nothing" and "Now for honest plain sense; enough of bawdy double-meanings, such as those with which Berowne has just crammed his speech."

glozes] marginal comment, or superficial word-play. Shakespeare does not have the noun elsewhere but the sense "empty verbal dexterity" is reflected in his use of the verb in *Richard II*, II. i. 10.

Of his fair mistress : in the afternoon
We will with some strange pastime solace them,
Such as the shortness of the time can shape ;
For revels, dances, masks, and merry hours,
Forerun fair Love, strewing her way with flowers.

King. Away, away ! no time shall be omitted
That will be time, and may by us be fitted.

Ber. *Allons ! allons !* Sow'd cockle reap'd no corn ;
And justice always whirls in equal measure :
Light wenches may prove plagues to men forsworn ;
If so, our copper buys no better treasure.

[*Exeunt*.

377. *her*] *his* Capell conjecture. 379. *be time*] Qq, Ff; *betime* Rowe (ed. 2) Cambridge. 380. *Allons ! allons !*] Theobald (Warburton) ; *Alone, alone* Qq, Ff.

376. *revels, dances, masks, and merry hours*] This line is found in *England's Parnassus*, 1600.

380. *Allons ! allons !*] At the last words of Act ii. of *The Merry Wives of Windsor*, the Quarto of 1602 reads : "Alon, alon, alon." Nashe has the expression in *Have With You to Saffron Walden* (McKerrow, iii. 110). It occurs also in Marston's *What You Will*, III. I ("aloun, aloun") ; and in Day's *Parliament of Bees*, chap. iv. ("all oone"). "Alone" for "*allons*" occurs again in the present play, v. i. 146.

cockle . . . corn] The name "cockle" was often used by early writers—incorrectly, and much to the annoyance of such botanical precisians as William Turner (*The Names of herbes*, 1548)—for "darnel," a grass whose seed might be mistaken for corn. In Wyclif's Bible, and in some other editions later, in Matt. xiii. 25, cockel is used instead of tares or darnel. See also Skeat's Chaucer's *Canterbury Tales* (T. 14403) : "or springen [sprinkle] cokkel in our clene corn." Abundant references are to be found in *New Eng. Dict.* Berowne's note of warning here comes in rather inharmoniously after his magnificent address of loyalty to Love. What he says amounts to : "we are forsworn, we must look out for squalls, these girls may bring us the punishment we deserve."

ACT V

SCENE I

Enter HOLOFERNES, *Sir* NATHANIEL, *and* DULL.

Hol. Satis quid sufficit.

Nath. I praise God for you, sir : your reasons at dinner have been sharp and sententious ; pleasant without

ACT V

Scene I

1. *quid*] Qq, Ff ; *quod* Rowe *et seq.*

Scene I

1. *Satis quid sufficit*] Correctly " *satis est quod sufficit*," according to some lists. Compare Lodge, *Euphues Golden Legacie* (*Shakes. Lib.*, 1875, p. 51), 1590 : " Mistresse I have so much Latin, *Satis est quod sufficit*." It occurs also in *A Twelfe Night Merriment* (*Narcissus*), 1602 (ed. M. L. Lee) : " It is a most condolent tragedye wee shall move. *Porter. Dictum puta ; satis est quod suffocat. Sec.* In faith, I tickle them for a good voice. *Porter. Sufficiente quantitate*, a woord is enough to the wise " (p. 5). The English extension " enough is as good as a feast " is in Heywood's *Proverbs*, 1546.

2, 4, 5. *reasons . . . audacious . . . opinion*] " It may be proper just to note, that reason here, and in many other places, signifies discourse ; and that audacious is used in a good sense for spirited, animated, confident. Opinion is the same with obstinacy or opiniâtreté " (Johnson). Johnson says further : " I know not well what degree of respect Shakespeare intends to obtain for this vicar, but he has here put into his mouth a finished representation of colloquial excellence."

3. *sententious*] pithy. Puttenham has a chapter (xix.) " Of Figures sententious, otherwise called Rhetoricall." On page 207 he speaks of words " pithie or sententious."

3-6. *pleasant . . . heresy*] Furness quotes from Chalmers, *Supplemental Apologie*, 1799 (p. 281), to the effect that " the original of these lines " is in Sidney's *Arcadia* (p. 17, ed. 1598). The words that are somewhat parallel to those in the text are : " her speach being as rare as pretious, her silence without sullennesse ; her modestie without affectation ; her shamefastnesse without ignorance " (Works, ed. A. Feuillerat, i. 32). There is a structural resemblance. Gabriel Harvey delighted in this method of apposition when he waxed eloquent. See his " Earthquake Letter " (Grosart, pp. 69-72) ; and again in his *Letters*, p. 72 (1580). Later, as in his *Foure Letters* (1592), he cannot proceed without it.

scurrility, witty without affection, audacious without impudency, learned without opinion, and strange without heresy. I did converse this quondam day with a companion of the king's, who is intituled, nominated, or called, Don Adriano de Armado.

Hol. *Novi hominem tanquam te:* his humour is lofty, his discourse peremptory, his tongue filed, his eye ambitious, his gait majestical, and his general behaviour vain, ridiculous, and thrasonical. He is too

4. *affection*] Qq, F 1; *affectation* Ff 2, 3, 4. 10. *hominem*] Ff 3, 4; *hominum* Qq, Ff 1, 2.

4. *affection*] the act of affecting; affectation. See again v. ii. 407, and *Hamlet*, II. ii. 473 (Quarto reading).

audacious] See note at line 2 above. Steevens quotes from Jonson's *Epicene*, II. iii.: "She that shall be my wife must be accomplished, with courtly and audacious ornaments."

5. *opinion*] self-conceit (*New Eng. Dict.*), over-confidence in the rightness of one's own opinion. *New Eng. Dict.* parallels *1 Henry IV.* III. i. 185, and *Troilus and Cressida*, I. iii. 353.

8. *intituled*] Dover Wilson declares that this is merely "entitled" in a common Elizabethan spelling.

10. *Novi . . . te*] I know the man as well as I know you. This phrase is given in "Lyly's Grammar" (*Brevissima Institutio*, 1549, etc.) as an example of the use of *tamquam* (Syntaxis: Adverbii constructio, under *Quasi*). It may have become a catchword. Harvey has similar expressions in his *Letters to Spenser* (Grosart, i. 74), 1580: "With as many gentle goodnights as be Letters in this tedious Letter. *Nosti manum tanquam tuam*"; and p. 84: "*nosti homines, tanquam tuam ipsius cutem.*" See Introduction 5.22.

11. *peremptory*] See note on IV. iii. 223.

his tongue filed] polished. "Filed tongue" was an old and common expression. The first example of the verb "to file," in the figurative sense of "to smooth, to polish" in *New Eng. Dict.*, is from *Romaunt of the Rose*, *circa* 1400 (381/2): "His tunge was fyled sharpe & square." The phrase is in Spenser's *Colin Cloutes Come Home Again*, 701-2 ("a filed toung furnisht with tearmes of art"), several times in Lyly's plays, and in Beaumont and Fletcher's *Loyal Subject*, III. ii.

12. *majestical*] grand, stately, as in *Henry V.* IV. i. 284. Compare Lyly's *Endymion*, v. ii.: "O sir your chinne is but a quyller yet, you will be most majesticall when it is full fledge." An earlier form than "majestic," and apparently introduced by Lyly.

13. *thrasonical*] boastful, from Thraso, the braggart soldier in Terence's play *Eunuchus*. Though Furness gives a 1578 reference from Richard Tarlton, the adjective was probably the invention of Stanyhurst who had begun to write in 1570 the *Conceits* printed in 1582. This volume contains the famous epigram (in English hexameter) on a "loftye Thrasonical huf snuffe" so scoffed at by Nashe in the Epistle Dedicatory prefixed to Greene's *Menaphon*, 1589 (McKerrow, iii. 320). Greene uses the word elsewhere, as does also G. Harvey a couple of times.

picked, too spruce, too affected, too odd, as it were, too peregrinate, as I may call it.

Nath. A most singular and choice epithet.

[*Draws out his table-book.*

Hol. He draweth out the thread of his verbosity finer than the staple of his argument. I abhor such fanatical phantasimes, such insociable and point-

16. [*Draws*] Ff 3, 4; *Draw* . . . Qq, Ff 1, 2. 19. *phantasimes*] Cambridge, Globe; *phantasims* Qq, Ff 1, 2, 3; *phantasms* F 4.

14. *picked*] neat, elaborate, over-refined. Compare Nashe, *Foure Letters Confuted* (McKerrow, i. 286): "Shrouded a picked effeminate Carpet Knight under the fictionate person of Hermaphroditus." Furness refers to Grosart's Green's *Works* (xi. 72), where the passage "certayne quaint, pickt and neate companions" occurs in the *Defence of Conny-catching* 1592 (author unknown; an attack on Greene). See also Rider's *Bibliotheca Scholastica*, 1589: "Picked or curious. *Argutus, elegans, accuratus, eximius, exquisitus.*" Ainsworth's seventh sense of *argutus* is "short, neat, picked."

spruce] here means *over*-elegant, affected. Compare v. ii. 407, and Nashe, *Terrors of the Night* (McKerrow, i. 366), 1594: "Whose names if you aske, hee claps you in the mouth with halfe a dozen spruce titles, never til he invented them heard of by any Christian."

15. *peregrinate*] having the air of a traveller or foreigner—like "Italianate." No other example in *New Eng. Dict.*, excepting in Lytton's *My Novel*, taken from here.

16. *singular*] unparalleled, excellent. Ascham uses the word frequently in this sense: "So singular in wisedome (in their owne opinion) as scarse they count the best Counsellor the Prince hath comparable with them" (*The Scholemaster* [Arber, p. 85], 1568.

[*Draws out his table-book*] The direction is given as an imperative in early texts, a sign that they derive from an original that had at least been used as a prompt-book. "Tables," a book in which to jot down anything noteworthy either read or overheard, were standard equipment for any Elizabethan with pretensions to learning or fashion. Compare *Hamlet*, I. v. 107: "My tables! meet it is I set it down."

18. *staple*] thread, pile or texture of wool or flax. An early use of this technical word, which is perhaps implied in the following passage: "flockes Yeelding forth fleeces stapled with such woole, As Lecester cannot yeelde more finer stuffe" (Greene [Grosart, xiii. 71], *Friar Bacon and Friar Bungay*).

19. *fanatical*] frantic, extravagant. applied to persons this use has escaped the *New Eng. Dict.* being considerably earlier than their first example. The meaning of the word was hardly fixed. Nashe speaks of "phanatical strange hierogliphicks" where he means puns and ciphers (McKerrow, ii. 182); and in another place (*Foure Letters Confuted* [i. 321]) he calls Harvey "the foresaid fanatical Phobetor, geremumble, tirleriwhisco, or what you will." For "phantasime" see note on IV. i. 98 above.

insociable] impossible to associate with, intolerable. In the sense of "incompatible" the *New Eng. Dict.* has one earlier example from Savile's *Tacitus*, 1581; the passage here is not dealt with. "Insociable" occurs

devise companions; such rackers of orthography, as to speak dout, fine, when he should say doubt; det, when he should pronounce debt,—d, e, b, t, not d, e, t; he clepeth a calf, cauf; half, hauf; neighbour *vocatur* nebour; neigh abbreviated ne. This is abhominable, which he would call abomin-

20. *orthography*] *ortagriphie, ortographie, ortagriphy, ortagraphy* early edd. 21. *fine*] Qq, Ff.; sine *b* New Temple. 25. *he*] *we* Ff 3, 4. *abominable*] Ff 3, 4; *abbominable* Q 1; *abhominable* Ff 1, 2.

again in this play (v. ii. 789) with the meaning unsociable, and is the earliest example in the *New Eng. Dict.* None of these three words occur elsewhere in Shakespeare.

19, 20. *point-devise*] precise, affectedly exact. See *As You Like It*, III. ii. 401. Generally used adverbally with a preposition: "Uprist this jolly lover Absolon, and him arayeth gay at point devise."

20. *orthography*] The spelling "ortographie" occurs several times in Puttenham (p. 127), but the omission of the *h* would be abominable here. Furness gives several extracts from commentators, and notes, upon the principles of pronunciation dealt with in the text. But Holofernes gives much more information than any of them, and they are mainly conjectural. Furness refers to a communication which appeared in the *New York Times Literary Review* (July, 1899) by Mr. Noyes, "our highest living authority on the subject of Elizabethan pronunciation." He quotes from Baret's *Alvearie* (1573?), where it is expressly stated that the *h* was not sounded in "abhominable," and that "negh" was pronounced "nay." Apparently, therefore, Holofernes would confute the Baret school? Puttenham says: "I would as neare as I could observe and keepe the lawes of the Greeke and Latin versifiers, that is to prolong the sillable which is written with double consonants or by dipthong . . . and to shorten all sillables that stand upon vowels if there were no cause of *elision*, and single consonants, and such of them as are most flowing and slipper upon the tongue as n. r. t. d. l. and for this purpose to take away all aspirations." Evidently Holofernes is railing against such innovations as a pedant should; but the trend of the times was against him, and for simplification of pronunciation, as of spelling. In one of his *Letters to Spenser* (Grosart, iii. 103-105), 1580, Gabriel Harvey has a tirade against the pedantries of "Orthography or rather Pseudography." Harvey's patron, Sir Thomas Smith, was another eminent "racker of orthography." See Introduction, 5.22.

22. *debt*] I owe to Mr. John Crow an example of the adoption of Holofernes' recommended pronunciation as late as 1625, when Hugh Holland, in his *A Cypres Garland* (C^3), could write: "Then you great Lord, that were to me so gracious, In twenty weekes (a time not very spacious) To cause me thrice to kisse (me thrice your depter) That hand which bore the Lillybearing Scepter."

23. *calf, cauf*; *half, hauf*] Holofernes would sound the Ls.

25. *abhominable*] A common spelling of the time, and earlier, arising from a mistaken etymology, *ab homine* instead of *ab omine*. It is found in early dictionaries: *Promptorium*, 1450, and Levin's *Manipulus*, 1570. Minshew (ed. 1627) has it "Abominable, *vide Abhominable*." Cotgrave has it right in 1611, but Sherwood (1672) sets Cotgrave straight with

able, it insinuateth me of insanie : *ne intelligis domine ?* to make frantic, lunatic.

Nath. Laus Deo, bone intelligo.

Hol. Bone ? Bon, fort bon ; Priscian a little scratched : 'twill serve.

26. *insanie*] Theobald (Warburton conj.) ; *infamie* Qq, Ff. *ne*] *nonne* Johnson conj. ; *anne* Porson conj. MS. 28. *bone*] Theobald ; *bene* Qq, Ff. 29. *Bone ? Bon fort bon ; Priscian*] New ; *Bome boon for boon prescian*, Qq, Ff ; *Bone ?—bone for bene ; Priscian* Theobald ; *Bon, bon, fort bon Priscian !* Cambridge.

the insertion of the *h* he omitted. Nashe, Harvey, Greene and all writers of the time, as well as every use in the Shakespeare Folio (1st and 2nd) have the *h*, I believe. Indeed, if we accept the Q 1 " abbominable," it is apparently the earliest example of the omission of the aspirate intentionally. The two *b*'s in the Quarto conform with the Italian of John Florio's dictionary, *New World of Words*.

26. *insinuateth me of insanie*] Most commentators construe " suggests insanity to me." Professor J. A. K. Thomson, however, has suggested (privately) that Holofernes is giving an English version of the Latin " insinuat in me insaniam " and means " it introduces frenzy into me," i.e. " drives me frantic," as he explains in the next line. Renaissance schoolmasters were always " inculcating " or " insinuating " knowledge into their pupils. See note on IV. ii. 13.

insanie] No other example of this word is known than that adduced by Steevens, and given in the *New Eng. Dict.*, although Furness says : " Unfortunately I cannot verify this quotation." The dictionary dates it 1572. Steevens quotes from " a book entitled, *The Fall and evil Successe of Rebellion from Time to Time*, by Wilfride Holme : " In the days of sixth Henry Jack Cade made a brag, With a multitude of people ; but in the consequence, After a little insanie they fled tag and rag, For Alexander Iden he did his diligence."

29. *Bone ? . . . bon !*] " Priscian a little scratched " points to a fault in Nathaniel's Latin and " Bome " shows clearly where it lies ; but " boon " must represent a distinct word from " bome." " Forboon " stands for " fort bon " in Heywood's *If You Know not me you Know Nobody* and may well do so here. A similar corruption occurs in *Romeo and Juliet*, II. iv. 37 (" bones " for " bons ") and note " alone " of IV. iii. 380 above.

Priscian a little scratched] Priscian, the grammarian, who wrote about A.D. 525, and several of whose works have come down to us, gave rise to the proverb in English, " to break Priscian's head," used to such as speak false Latin (" *diminuis Prisciani caput* "). Holofernes means " your Latin is a little mutilated " (or wounded). The earliest example I have of the proverb is from Skelton's *Speke Parrot*, line 176 (1515) : " Prisian's hed broken now handy dandy, And *Inter didascolos* is rekened for a fole." Puttenham has it (Arber, p. 258). Sir John Harington has an interesting passage in *The Metamorphosis of Ajax*, 1596 (Chiswick repr. p. 84) : " Yet least old Priscian should say I brake his head when I never came near him, I will keep me in this," with a marginal note : " There is a Comedy called *Priscianus vapulans ;* where if one should

Enter ARMADO, MOTH, *and* COSTARD.

Nath. Videsne quis venit?

Hol. Video, et gaudeo.

Arm. Chirrah!

Hol. Quare chirrah, not sirrah?

Arm. Men of peace, well encountered.

Hol. Most military sir, salutation.

Moth. They have been at a great feast of languages, and stolen the scraps.

Cost. O, they have lived long on the alms-basket of words. I marvel thy master hath not eaten thee

say *ignem hanc,* Priscian would cry, his head were broken."

31. *Videsne quis venit*] Classical Latin would require "veniat," but "venit" is good enough colloquial usage and it is not necessary to assume a blunder on the part of either Holofernes or the compositor. Furness quotes from T. S. Baynes, *Shakespeare Studies* (1896, p. 181): "These scraps of Latin dialogue exemplify the technical Latin intercourse between master and pupils in their work, as well as the formal colloquies the latter were required to prepare as exercises." Baynes quotes *Familiares Colloquendi Formulae:* "Who comes to meet us? *Quis obviam venit?* He speaks improperly, *Hic incongrue loquitur;* He speaks false Latin, *Diminuit Prisciani caput;* 'Tis barbarous Latin, *Olet barbariem.*" This particular book is a seventeenth-century work, but no doubt borrows from those contemporary with the play. As this was a standard method of teaching Latin, there were many manuals, the chief being the *Colloquies* of Erasmus and of Cordier, the *Sententiae Pueriles* of Leonhard Cullmann, and Vives' *Exercitatio.* In view of lines 51-5 below (see note) the model here may be the last.

32. *Video et gaudeo*] *Video & taceo* was "Her Maiesties poesie at the great Lotterie in London 1568: and ende 1569" (Whitney's *Emblems* [ed. H. Greene, p. 61], 1586).

33. *Chirrah*] "Sirrah" was the correct title from a master to his page. See *Merry Wives of Windsor,* I. iii. 88. The odd form, to which Holofernes calls attention, must have a special point, and M. C. Bradbrook (*The School of Night,* 1936) has suggested that it is a take-off of Sir Walter Ralegh's west-country accent. See Introduction 5.25. An alternative solution has been put forward by Professor J. A. K. Thomson—that the word is Armado's attempt at "chaere" (χαῖρε), one of the forms of salutation listed by Erasmus in the first and most elementary section of his *Familiaria Colloquia,* on which Elizabethan schoolboys cut their teeth. This chimes well with the pedantry and bungled learning on which much of the fun of this scene depends.

39. *alms-basket*] "The refuse of the table was collected by the attendants, who used wooden knives for the purpose, and put into a large basket [or tub], which was called the alms-basket, the contents of which were reserved for the poor" (Halliwell). It is mentioned in Greene's *Quip for an Upstart Courtier:* "I sit and dine with the Nobility, when thou art faine to waite for the reversion of the almes basket" (Grosart, xi. 224).

for a word ; for thou art not so long by the head as *honorificabilitudinitatibus* : thou art easier swallowed than a flapdragon.

Moth. Peace ! the peal begins.

Arm. [*To Hol.*] Monsieur, are you not lettered ?

The term is, it may be noted, only relevant to feasts and banquets. Ben Jonson has a similar metaphor in his "Ode to Himself" (*New Inn*) : "For who the relish of these guests will fit Needs set them but the alms-basket of wit." And see Day, *Isle of Gulls*, I. i., where "alm's basket scraps" reminds one of the present passage.

42. *honorificabilitudinitatibus*] "often mentioned as the longest word known" (Johnson). Steevens refers to Marston's *Dutch Courtesan* and Nashe's *Lenten Stuffe ;* Grey gives Taylor's example, who adds a syllable in the middle. See, too, Fletcher's *Mad Lover* (Glover and Waller, ii. 10), I. i. These are later than Shakespeare. Dyce quoted Hunter, who found it scribbled somewhere in a MS. of the reign of Henry VI. Furness gives an exhaustive and learned note from Hermann, *Euphorion*, 1894, who traces the word back, in the Latin schoolmaster vein, to Dante's treatise, *De vulgari eloquentia* (*circa* 1300) ; and to *Excerpts* from Petrus of Pisa, Charlemagne's teacher. Hermann finds it in two old German comedies of about 1580, both of which place their action in the schoolroom. He finds it derived from *Honorifica* in a *Liber derivationum* of the twelfth century, and he gives several references to its appearance in dictionaries from 1200 to 1500. Murray (*New Eng. Dict.*) gives a reference to *The Complaynt of Scotland*, 1548-9. The extract was quoted in *Notes and Queries* (June, 1902) by G. Stronach ; it concludes : "There vas ane uthir that writ in his verkis, [thir langtailit vordis,] *gaudet honorificabilitudinitatibus.*" Hermann says this term enfolds the names of Dante and Shakespeare ; and reveals how a purely literary word can survive, by means of the schools (as he believes), for nine hundred years—a span of life to which neither by origin nor by form it had any title. It finds its way into *New Eng. Dict.*, as an English word, *honorificabilitudinity* (a mere mouthful), given in Blount's *Glossographia*, and Philips' *New World of Words*.

42, 43. *easier swallowed than a flapdragon*] Said to be the thing, usually a burning plum or raisin, floating and snapped at in our Christmas game of Snapdragon. "Flapdragon," as a swaggering humour, is mentioned in Ben Jonson's *Cynthia's Revels*, V. iii. (1600). Like many other drinking expressions, it seems to have been of Dutch extraction. Compare the following quotations : "In the time a Fleming drinks a flap-dragon" (Dekker, *The Wonder of a Kingdom*, Act i. [1636]). "My brother Swallows it with more ease than a Dutchman Does flapdragons" (Barry, *Ram Alley*, 1611 ; Hazlitt's *Dodsley*, vol. x., p. 298). "swallow it like flapdragons, as if you had lived With chewing the cud after" (Webster, *Devil's Law Case*, II. i. [1623]). It seems to have been a lover's exploit, from the passage at the end of *Cynthia's Revels :* "From stabbing of arms, flapdragons, healths, whiffs, and all such swaggering humours, [*Chorus*] Good Mercury, defend us."

44. *the peal begins*] as of bells, not as Schmidt says, "a mighty sound." To ring one a peal was a common expression for a torrent of words. "I will go and ring a peale through both his ears for this dishonest behaviour" (*Menechmus* [by W. W.], v. i. [1595]).

Moth. Yes, yes, he teaches boys the horn-book. What is a, b, spelt backward with the horn on his head?

Hol. Ba, *pueritia*, with a horn added.

Moth. Ba! most silly sheep with a horn. You hear his learning.

Hol. *Quis*, *quis*, thou consonant?

Moth. The last of the five vowels, if you repeat them; or the fifth, if I.

Hol. I will repeat them; a, e, i,—

Moth. The sheep: the other two concludes it; o, u.

Arm. Now, by the salt wave of the Mediterraneum, a

52. *last*] Qq, Ff; *third* Theobald *et seq.* 56. *wave*] *wane* Q 1.

46. *horn-book*] "A leaf of paper containing the alphabet (often with the addition of the ten digits, some elements of spelling, and the Lord's Prayer), protected by a thin plate of translucent horn, and mounted on a tablet of wood with a projecting piece for a handle" (*New Eng. Dict.*). "The horn-book gradually gave way to the 'battledore' and 'primer'" (Chambers, *Book of Days*). In A. W. Tuer's *History of the Horn-book* it is recorded that the last order for them, as school-requisites, came from the country about 1799. From that time the demand wholly ceased. Specimens are now unobtainable of the early black-letter type. There is no earlier example than the one in the text of the use of the word in the *New Eng. Dict.* The quotation therein from (Lyly's) *Pappe with a Hatchett* preceded *Love's Labour's Lost*, since Harvey wrote his answer to it in 1589. The earlier name for the primer, or alphabet-book, was the Christ's cross-row, or Cross-row.

51. *consonant*] Compare with this a quotation in *New Eng. Dict.* from Walkington's *Optic Glasse*, 1607: "Like the foole, a consonant when hee should bee a Mute." Apparently used derisively in the sense of that which has no existence alone; a nonentity, since it requires the vowel sound.

52. *last*] Furness "suggests that Moth purposely framed his answer ambiguously so as to lure the Pedant, to a repetition of the vowels." To Moth, Holfernes remains "you" (and so the sheep) no matter who repeats the vowels.

55. *concludes it*] both "proves the proposition" and "completes the list of vowels." F. A. Yates (*A Study of Love's Labour's Lost*, 1936) draws attention to a passage in Vives' *Exercitatio Linguae Latinae* in which the pupil is exhorted to remember the Spanish word "oueia" (sheep) as a mnemonic for the vowels. Their mere repetition would therefore suggest "sheep" to any Elizabethan schoolboy.

56. *salt*] Suggested perhaps by the sense of acutely witted, as in Gascoigne: "unlesse the invention have in it also *aliquid salis* . . . some good and fine devise, shewing the quicke capacitie of a writer" (Arber, p. 31) (1575). Jonson uses it.

Mediterraneum] Greene has this form: "resting himself on a hill that over-peered the great Mediterraneum noting how Phœbus fetched his Lavaltos on the purple Plaines of Neptunus . . . the Dolphines (the sweete conceipters of Musicke) fetcht their carreers on the calmed waves" (*Menaphon* [Grosart, vi. 36], 1587).

sweet touch, a quick venue of wit! snip, snap, quick and home! it rejoiceth my intellect;. true wit!

Moth. Offered by a child to an old man; which is wit-old.

Hol. What is the figure? what is the figure?

Moth. Horns.

Hol. Thou disputes like an infant: go, whip thy gig.

Moth. Lend me your horn to make one, and I will whip about your infamy *manu cita*. A gig of a cuckold's horn!

Cost. An I had but one penny in the world, thou should'st have it to buy gingerbread. Hold, there is the very remuneration I had of thy master, thou

57. *venue*] Dyce, Cambridge, Globe; *vene we* Q 1, F 1; *venewe* F 2; *venew* Ff 3, 4. 63. *disputes*] Qq, F 1; *disputes't* Ff 2, 3; *disputest* F 4. 65. *manu cita*] Anon. conjecture, Cambridge; *unū cita* Q1; *unum cita* Ff; *circum circa*, Theobald *et seq.*; *unum cito!* Furnivall.

57. *touch*] stroke, trick, taste of one's "quality." Compare Ascham, *The Scholemaster* (Arber, p. 18), 1570: "Playing both with the shrewde touches of many courste boyes, and with the small discretion of many leude Scholemasters."

venue of wit] assault of wit. See *Merry Wives of Windsor*, I. i. 295. In fencing, the attack leading to a hit. See Lodge, *Euphues Golden Legacie* (*Shakes. Lib.* p. 98), 1590: "Love . . . seeing the parties at the gaze, encountered them both with such a veny, that the stroke . . . could never after be raced out."

snip, snap] See *Merry Wives of Windsor*, IV. v. 3. Gabriel Harvey, in *Pierce's Supererogation* (Grosart, ii. 313) has: "if any whosoever will needes be offering abuse in fact or snip-snapping in termes"; and Nashe in his Epistle Dedicatorie to *Have With You* (McKerrow, iii. 10) has "torment him, & deal as snip snap snappishly with him as ever he was delt withall." See above, III. i. 19.

59, 60. *wit-old*] The word on which Moth quibbles only occurs once in Shakespeare, in *Merry Wives of Windsor*, II. ii. 314 (and "wittolly" line 284). It is a synonym of "cuckold," also in Greene's *Philomela* (Grosart, xi. 166), of about this date.

61. *figure*] Our "figure of speech."

63. *disputes*] Shakespeare often has this form of the second person singular. There is another example at V. ii. 208.

gig] See IV. iii. 165, (note). The "infamy" at which Moth gibes in return must be a topical hit; there is some buried quibbling here I cannot reach. Why should Holofernes be a cuckold?

65. *manu cita*] with ready, or energetic hand. Theobald's emendation is right in principle—the phrase must be a schoolboy or benchers' tag—but it is a pity to reject the one part of the Quarto reading that sounds right. *Manu* is not unquestionable, but "'twill serve"; a persevering reader of the Elizabethans' Latin phrase-books and legal documents might well find something better.

halfpenny purse of wit, thou pigeon-egg of discretion. O, an the heavens were so pleased that thou wert but my bastard, what a joyful father wouldst thou make me. Go to ; thou hast it *ad dunghill*, at the fingers' ends, as they say.

Hol. O, I smell false Latin ; dunghill for *unguem.*

Arm. Arts-man, preambulate : we will be singled from the barbarous. Do you not educate youth at the charge-house on the top of the mountain ?

76. *preambulate*] Cambridge ; *preambulat* Qq, Ff ; *praeambula* Theobald. *singled*] Ff, Q 2 ; *singuled* Q 1, Cambridge. 78. *charge-house*] *church-house* Theobald conjecture ; *large house* Collier MS.

70. *halfpenny purse*] These small purses, probably for holding the little silver halfpence of the time, are mentioned again in *Merry Wives of Windsor*, III. v. 149 ; and Lyly, *Mother Bombie*, III. iv. (1589).

70, 71. *discretion*] This recalls Harvey's jibe at Nashe. See Note on III. i. 26.

73-75. *ad . . . unguem*] to the nail. A common proverbial phrase, said to be borrowed from sculpture (Horace, *Satires*, I. v. 31-33). Compare Ben Jonson's translation of Horace, *De Arte Poetica* (" Perfectum decies non castigavit ad unguem ") : " Not ten times o'er corrected to the nail." It was used of a lesson learnt perfectly : " But, Sirra, see you learne your lesson perfectlie, and have it without booke *ad unguem* " (*Martins Months Minde* [Grosart's *Nashe*, i. 203], 1589). And Webster, *Westward Ho*, ii. 1 : " She has her letters *ad unguem*." Jonson has it several times. They are the last words in Harvey's much laughed at *Judgement on Earthquakes* (Grosart, i. 74), 1580.

75. *false Latin*] See note, line 31.

76. *Arts-man*] scholar, learned person. *New Eng. Dict.* gives an example from Bacon's *Advancement of Learning*. The word was commoner in the sense of workman, as in Chapman's *Homer*. We have elsewhere in this play " man of peace " and " warman."

singled] separated, Similarly in Greene, *Alcida* (Grosart, ix. 73), 1588 : " When wee were in the greene meades, Meribates and my daughter had singled themselves."

78. *charge-house*] school. Not known elsewhere. Probably one where children were taught at the charge of the parish, or else merely a house for their charge or care. The commentators have worked hard to find topical explanations of this passage, some of which are discussed in the Introduction 5.21 and 5.23. The point may, however, be much simpler. Professor J. A. K. Thomson draws my attention to the conversation that follows the *salutandi formulae* at the outset of Erasmus' *Familiaria Colloquia*. It is between Georgius and Livinus, who has just arrived from Paris. Georgius asks *unde prodis*, " where do you come from ? " and Livinus replies *e collegio Montis acuti*," from the college of the Mountain with the sharp crest." G. *ergo ades nobis onustus literis*, " so you have come to us laden with learning ? " L. *immo pediculis*, " no, with lice." It is easy to believe that Elizabethan schoolboys would have loved this passage, and that the " charge-house on the Mountain " would be a byword with them as a sort of Dotheboys Hall. Erasmus was in fact having his revenge on the Collège de Mont

Hol. Or *mons*, the hill.

Arm. At your sweet pleasure, for the mountain.

Hol. I do, sans question.

Arm. Sir, it is the king's most sweet pleasure and affection to congratulate the princess at her pavilion in the posteriors of this day, which the rude multitude call the afternoon.

Hol. The posterior of the day, most generous sir, is liable, congruent, and measurable for the afternoon : the word is well culled, chose ; sweet and apt, I do assure you, sir ; I do assure.

Arm. Sir, the king is a noble gentleman, and my familiar, I do assure ye, very good friend. For what is inward between us, let it pass ; (I do beseech thee, remember thy courtesy—I beseech thee, apparel thy

82. *most*] omitted Q 2. 88. *chose*] Qq, F 1 ; *choise* F 2 ; *choice* Ff 3, 4. 89. *you*] omitted Q 2. 93. *remember*] *refrain* Capell ; *remember not* Malone.

Aigu in Paris, where he had been unhappy in his own youth.

84. *posteriors*] The word occurs in the Prologue to Harington's *Metamorphosis of Ajax*, 1596.

86. *liable*] suitable, apt. See *King John*, IV. ii. 226. In *New Eng. Dict.* there is a quotation from a letter dated 1570 : "To chewse persons lyable to give good information." This quotation is not satisfactory *per se*. It may mean "likely," which is nearer Sense 3.

87. *congruent*] Armado has already used this word (I. ii. 13), which is not elsewhere in Shakespeare. *New Eng. Dict.* has an early reference to Higden, *Rolls* (*ante* 1453). Craig quotes from Udall's *Erasmus* (Roberts' repr. p. 93), 1542 : "He thought not the name of a manne to bee a congruente or a right name for such persones as lived not according to reason." A stilted and neglected word. Sir Owen ap Meredith, the Welsh knight in *Patient Grissel* (by Dekker and Chettle) ridicules it in 1600 (Collier's edition, pp. 21, 22).

measurable] meet, competent. Compare *Coriolanus*, II. ii. 127 : "He cannot but with measure fit the honours which we devise him." Cotgrave has "*Moyen :* mean, indifferent, moderate, measurable, competent, reasonable."

88. *chose*] for "chosen." Holofernes' synonyms may seem better balanced if we accept the reading "choice." The corruption is easy if Shakespeare used the spelling "choise," as in the Second Folio ; it was common at this time—compare Nashe's MS. poem *The Choise of Valentines*.

90. *familiar*] particular friend ; as in *2 Henry IV*. II. i. 144. Compare Lodge, *Euphues Golden Legacie* (*Shakes. Lib.*, 1875, p. 30) : "Rosader . . . accompanyed with a troupe of yoong gentlemen that were desirous to be his familiars."

91, 92. *inward*] confidential, private.

93. *remember thy courtesy*] the usual explanation ("don't forget your head is uncovered") assumes Holofernes to have been bareheaded since "salutation," at line 36. Armado notices it and tells him to apparel his head. Dyce quoted as parallel the following from Ben Jonson's

head) and among other importunate and most serious designs, and of great import indeed, too, but let that pass; for I must tell thee, it will please his grace, by the world, sometime to lean upon my poor shoulder, and with his royal finger, thus, dally

94. *importunate*] Ff, Q 2; *importunt* Q 1; *important* Cambridge.

Every Man in his Humour, I. ii.: "*Servant*. . . . I was required . . . to deliver you this letter, sir. *Knowell*. To me, sir! What do you mean? Pray you remember your courtesy. [*Reads*.] . . . Nay, pray you be covered"; but the meaning may well be the reverse. Knowell is insulted when he says: "What do you mean?" He bids the servant remove his hat by the expression, he keeps him bareheaded while he reads the letter, and not till he speaks to him again does he bid him be covered. We shall have then to take opposite meanings from the two passages. Armado reminds Holofernes to conclude his courtesy or salutation; Knowell reminds his servant to begin it. Parallels to the signification given here have been adduced from *Lusty Juventus* (Hazlitt's *Dodsley*, ii. 74), and from Marlowe's *Doctor Faustus* (Case ed., p. 156). The latter has nothing to do with the text, excepting that the words "remember your courtesy" (make a leg or bow) occur: the former ("be remembered and cover your head") carries no weight one way or the other. Hart provided an alternative explanation that is most attractive. His note runs: "It was the custom to uncover at the name of the king, or during a conversation about the king. This is the *courtesy* Armado claims for his friend the King. In *Lusty Juventus* there is so far a parallelism that Juventus may have uncovered at Hypocrisy's introduction of the Deity into the conversation. As a mark of deference to the King's mention, a passage in Beaumont and Fletcher's *Noble Gentlemen* (Act III.) drew my attention, and be it remembered the scene is laid also in France: '*Shatillion*. Can you give me reason From whence this great duke sprang that walks abroad? *Lady*. E'en from the king himself. *Shat*. As you're a woman, I think you may be cover'd: Yet your prayer would do no harm good woman. *Lady*. God preserve him! *Shat*. I say Amen, and so say all good subjects.' If the mode was French, no doubt other parallels will be found, but this one is so exact as to be conclusive. The hat was removed as evidence that the wearer prays for the king upon specific reference to him; as we do at 'God save the King!' Holofernes may have been bare since Armado began to talk of the King, and be now released from his courtesy; or he may be reminded of it by these words."

95, 96. *but let that pass*] never mind about that. A common colloquialism. Dekker's Shoemaker's wife can hardly open her lips without using the catch-phrase. Sidney puts it into the mouth of Miso, in that much abused but highly entertaining part of *Arcadia* (Feuillerat, i. 237) where he depicts the dialogue of the people: "I might have had an other-gaines husband, then Dametas. But let that passe, God amend him! And yet I speake it not without good cause" (Book ii.). Ben Jonson has it in his *Staple of News*, I. vi. (Herford and Simpson, vi. 300); and see *Gesta Grayorum*, 1594 (ed. Greg, p. 59): "Well, let that pass, and to the purpose now."

97. *by the world*] See IV. iii. 17.

with my excrement, with my mustachio: but, sweet heart, let that pass. By the world, I recount no fable: some certain special honours it pleaseth his greatness to impart to Armado, a soldier, a man of travel, that hath seen the world: but let that pass. The very all of all is, but, sweet heart, I do implore secrecy, that the king would have me present the princess, sweet chuck, with some delightful ostentation, or show, or pageant, or antic, or firework. Now, understanding that the curate and your sweet self are good at such eruptions and sudden breaking out of mirth, as it were, I have acquainted you withal, to the end to crave your assistance.

Hol. Sir, you shall present before her the Nine Worthies.

105. *secrecy*] *secretie* Q 1.

99. *excrement*] "that which grows out or forth" (*New Eng. Dict.*). See *Merchant of Venice*, III. ii. 87, and *Winter's Tale*, IV. iv. 733. The earliest known use of the word in this sense (hair, nails, feathers) is probably that in *Solyman and Perseda*, I. iii. 136: "whose chin bears no impression of manhood. Not an hayre, not an excrement." The play is attributed to Kyd, and dated approximately 1592.

104. *all of all*] sum of everything.

106. *chuck*] chick, or chicken. A term of endearment, used familiarly, occurring several times in Shakespeare. It is in Jonson and Chapman's *Eastward Ho*, V. 1.

107. *ostentation*] No other example of this use of the word (spectacular show) is given in *New Eng. Dict.* The following comes near it: "The lockes of haire with their skinnes he hanged on a line unto two trees. And thus he made ostentation as of a great triumph at Werowocomoes" (*Captain Smith* [Arber, p. 82], 1612).

antic] a grotesque pageant. Compare *Captain Smith* (Arber, p. 123), 1608: "Being presently presented with this anticke, 30 young women came naked out of the woods (only covered behind and before with a few greene leaves), their bodies all painted . . . every one different. . . . The leader had a faire paire of stagges hornes on her head . . . every one with their severall devises . . . with most hellish cries and shouts." Fernando in Ford's *Love's Sacrifice*, III. ii., speaks of "an antic, a rare conceit he saw in Brussels" performed by knights and ladies of the Court. Ben Jonson seems to have foreseen the strictures of Nares, Gifford and others upon this word in *The Fox*, III. vi.: "And my dwarf shall dance, My eunuch sing, my fool make up the antic, Whilst we, in changed shapes, act Ovid's parts."

113. *Nine Worthies*] They were, according to Gerard Legh, *Accedens of Armorye* (who gives all their blazons), Duke Josua, Hector, David, Alexander, Judas Machabeus, Julius Cesar, King Arthure, Charlemayne, Sir Guy (of Warwicke). But the latter was sometimes replaced amongst "the learned and authentic fellows" (see Dyce's *Beaumont and*

Sir Nathaniel, as concerning some entertainment of time, some show in the posterior of this day, to be rendered by our assistance, the king's command, and this most gallant, illustrate, and learned gentleman, before the princess; I say, none so fit as to present the Nine Worthies.

Nath. Where will you find men worthy enough to present them?

Hol. Joshua, yourself; [myself and] this gallant gentleman, Judas Maccabæus; this swain, because of his great limb or joint, shall pass Pompey the Great; the page, Hercules—

114. *Sir Nathaniel*] Capell, Steevens, Craig; *Sir Holofernes* Qq, Ff; *Sir* Rowe. 116. *rendered*] *rended* Q 1. *assistance*] Hanmer; *assistants* Qq, Ff, Hart. *the*] *at the* F 2. 122. [*myself and*] Cambridge; *myself, and* Qq, Ff; *myself* ——, *and* New; *myself or* Steevens (1793); omitted Rowe. 124. *pass*] *pass for* Capell.

Fletcher, i. 143) by Godfrey of Bouillon. Douce says it has not been accounted for why Shakespeare includes Hercules and Pompey. In the second part of Whetstone's *Promos and Cassandra* (the source of *Measure for Measure*), 1578, the "nyne worthyes" are to "Be so instauld, as best may please the eye" (I. iv.), amongst the shows and pageants welcoming the king upon his return. Two men "apparalled like greene men at the Mayor feast, with clubbes of fyre-worke" keep a passage clear. The only name given of those represented is Hercules conquering monsters, though it is not stated he was one of the Worthies. This may account for his inclusion here. The recognized Worthies were often trifled with. Nashe says: "To Charles the fifte then Emperour, they reported how he shewed the nine worthies, David, Salomon, Gedeon, and the rest, in that similitude and likenes that they lived upon earth" (*The Unfortunate Traveller* [McKerrow, ii. 253], 1594). And Greene: "Which if I should obtaine, I would count it a more rich prize then ever Scipio or any of the nine Worthies wonne by conquest" (*Alcida* [Grosart, ix. 49], 1588). Ritson (*Remarks*, 38) gave a specimen of a "Pageant of the Nine Worthies" from an original MS. of Edward IV.'s time, which is reprinted in Furness' Variorum edition. See Introduction 5.1 (*h*).

116. *assistance*] Hanmer's emendation (first suggested by Theobald) is supported by Armado's use of the word a few lines earlier. The "assistants" of the Quarto may be explained either as a misreading of manuscript or, possibly, as archaic spelling, though Hart's parallel from Nashe's *Christ's Teares* rests on a misinterpretation.

117. *illustrate*] See IV. i. 66 (note).

122. [*myself and*] By the time the pageant appears, it has been largely recast, and we may take this passage to be an unrevised draft, with no part as yet assigned to Holofernes.

124. *pass*] represent, perform. An easy sense to give a verb of such wide powers. The sense of execute, or complete, in Ben Jonson's *Fox*, III. vi.: "I told his son, brought,

Arm. Pardon, sir; error: he is not quantity enough for that Worthy's thumb: he is not so big as the end of his club.

Hol. Shall I have audience? he shall present Hercules in minority: his enter and exit shall be strangling a snake; and I will have an apology for that purpose.

Moth. An excellent device! so if any of the audience hiss, you may cry "Well done, Hercules! now thou crushest the snake!" That is the way to make an offence gracious, though few have the grace to do it.

Arm. For the rest of the Worthies?

Hol. I will play three myself.

Moth. Thrice-worthy gentleman!

Arm. Shall I tell you a thing?

Hol. We attend.

Arm. We will have, if this fadge not, an antic. I beseech you, follow.

Hol. *Via*, goodman Dull! thou hast spoken no word all this while.

hid him here, Where he might see his father pass the deed," comes near to it. It seems to me absurd to suppose *pass* can mean surpass (a common sense) here; as if Costard was a real giant. He is not intended to excel Pompey, only to reproduce him. Malone (followed by Furness) is positive *pass* means surpass.

125, 128. *Hercules . . . club*] See note at line 113. For the hero's exploit "in minority" compare "It is my Cradle game To vanquish Snakes" (Golding's Ovid's *Metamorphoses*, ix. 79-80 [1567]).

129. *have audience*] be heard. See *As You Like It*, v. iv. 157, etc.

130. *enter*] *New Eng. Dict.* has two other examples, both earlier, of the substantive "enter"; the act of entering.

141. *fadge*] suit, succeed, turn out well. See *Twelfth Night*, II. ii. 34. The earliest example of this verb in *New Eng. Dict.* is from Whetstone's *Promos and Cassandra*, part i. (1578). The passage in the text would probably be the next historically, but it occurs again in the second part of the same old play. The sixth scene of Act i.—to which the words ending "clubbes of fyre worke" (note above, line 113) are a stage instruction—begins "*Phallax.* This geare fadgeth now, that these fellowes peare." Coupled with the remaining allusions, and with the exactly parallel use of *fadge* as referring to a pageant, it amounts to a certainty that Shakespeare recalled Whetstone's play while writing this scene. For *antic* see above, line 107.

143. *Via*] "An adverbe of encouraging much used by commanders, as also by riders to their horses, Goe on, forward, on, away, goe to, on quickly" (Florio, *New World of Words*, 1611). It seems here to mean rather "buck up," "what cheer." It occurs several times in Shakespeare, and his contemporaries, Jonson, Fletcher and Chapman. The example in the text is the earliest yet quoted.

Dull. Nor understand none neither, sir.

Hol. Allons ! we will employ thee.

Dull. I'll make one in a dance, or so ; or I will play on the tabor to the Worthies, and let them dance the hay.

Hol. Most dull, honest Dull. To our sport, away !

[*Exeunt.*

146. *Allons !*] *Alone* Qq, Ff. 146-149. Given as two lines verse ending *play, hay,* Halliwell, Dyce, Cambridge, Globe ; as prose Steevens and old texts.

146. *Allons*] See IV. iii. 380.

147. *make one*] be of the party. See *Merry Wives of Windsor,* II. iii. 48 and *1 Henry IV.,* I. ii. 113. *N.E.D.* gives a reference to Udall's *Erasmus,* 1542. The expression occurs several times in Shakespeare.

or so] See II. i. 212.

148. *tabor*] A small drum played with one hand ; with the other the musician held his pipe, playing the two instruments simultaneously. See *Winter's Tale,* IV. iv. 183. When Kemp started on his *Nine Daies Wonder Performed in a Morrice from London to Norwich* on "The first Mondaye in Lent" (1600), he was "attended by Thomas Slye, hys Taberer." On the title of his tract is a figure of the pair, the tabor being held apparently by a single band round the left wrist, which hand also holds the pipe to the mouth, the right using the short stick. The tabor is about twice the length of its diameter, covered at each end alike. No doubt it was also attached by a string round the neck.

148, 149. *dance the hay*] "A country dance, having a winding or serpentine nature, or being of the nature of a reel" (*New Eng. Dict.*). "To dance the hay became a proverbial expression signifying to twist about or wind in and out without making any advance" (Chappell's *Popular Music* [1859], ii. 629). There were several varieties of hay. Furness quotes from *Orchesographie,* 1588, already referred to in a note to "brawl" (III. i. 6). The French writer gives a description of the *Braule de la Haye,* which Furness quotes, and points out its resemblance to the grand chain in a quadrille. This may not be the English hay, which is mentioned by Skelton in 1529. *New Eng. Dict.* says "*haye d'allemaigne* is used in 15 c. French by C. Marot." Marlowe has "dance an antic hay" in his *Edward II.* I. i. (Chase ed., p. 73). Hart took pleasure in pointing out that there was a special variant called the Irish hay which was unusually boisterous. Guilpin mentions it in *Skialetheia,* Satire iv. (repr. p. 43), 1598 : "His head is like a windmils trunke so bigge Wherein ten thousand thoughts run whirlegigge, Play at barleybreake, and daunce Irish hay, Civill and peacefull like the Centaurs fray" ; and Day, *Law Tricks,* 1608 : "A company of bottlenos'd devils dauncing the Irish hay" ; and Dekker, *Strange Horse-Race* (Grosart, iii. 365), 1613 : "The Daunce was an infernall Irish hay."

SCENE II

Enter the PRINCESS, MARIA, KATHARINE, *and* ROSALINE.

Prin. Sweet hearts, we shall be rich ere we depart,
If fairings come thus plentifully in :
A lady wall'd about with diamonds !
Look you what I have from the loving king.
Ros. Madam, came nothing else along with that ?
Prin. Nothing but this ! yes ; as much love in rhyme
As would be cramm'd up in a sheet of paper,
Writ o' both sides the leaf, margent and all,
That he was fain to seal on Cupid's name.
Ros. That was the way to make his godhead wax ;
For he hath been five thousand year a boy.

Scene II

Enter . . . Rosaline] *Enter the Ladyes* Q 1. 1. *Prin.*] *Quee.* Q 1 throughout. 3, 4. Transposed Hudson (S. Walker conjecture), New. 8. *o'*] Cambridge ; *a* Q 1 ; *on* Ff, Q 2. 11. *year*] *yeare* Q 1, *yeeres* F 1.

Scene II

2. *fairings*] Compare Greene's *Never Too Late* (Grosart, viii. 195), 1590 : "Oenone chose Paris . . . thinking the sweetest face the best fayring for a gentlewoman's eye." In these days almost anything, or everything, was purchased at fairs.

3. *A lady . . . diamonds*] A favourite design of Elizabethan jewellers. For parallels see *Queen Elizabeth's New Year's Gifts* (reproduced in Nichol's *Progresses*, 1823). Here is an example dating from 1581-2 : "Item, a juell of golde, being the personage of a woman . . . garnished, with smale rubyes and dymondes, and a smale perle pendent geven by Thomas Howarde." Plenty more occur. At ii. 72 (1577-8) there is "a man of golde ennamuled grene, hanging at a small cheyne" ; at ii. 79 "a woman ennamuled . . . the bodye garneshed with sparks of diamunds and rubyes" ; and at ii. 419 (1583-4) "a juell of golde, being a personage of a woman of mother-of-perle, garnished on the one side with smale diamondes." In view of such evidence, it is hard to maintain, with Hart, that "The Princess points to herself bedecked with the gems, probably she had others as well, and calls herself a lady enclosed in diamonds." To make the passage quite clear Walker (followed by Hudson and Dover Wilson) would transpose this line to follow line 4 ; and Dover Wilson supports the change by claiming that the Quarto printing of the lines as prose indicates corrected copy, of which the compositor could not make out either the order or the metrical form. I cannot, however, see that there is any real difficulty in the passage as it stands in the Quarto.

10. *wax*] increase (with quibble).

11. *thousand year a boy*] Halliwell compares Sidney, *Arcadia* (p. 174, ed. 1590) : "This is thy worke, thou God for ever blinde ; Though thousands old, a Boy entitled still."

Kath. Ay, and a shrewd unhappy gallows too.
Ros. You'll ne'er be friends with him: a' kill'd your sister.
Kath. He made her melancholy, sad, and heavy;
And so she died: had she been light, like you,
Of such a merry, nimble, stirring spirit,
She might ha' been a grandam ere she died;
And so may you, for a light heart lives long.
Ros. What's your dark meaning, mouse, of this light word?
Kath. A light condition in a beauty dark.
Ros. We need more light to find your meaning out.
Kath. You'll mar the light by taking it in snuff;
Therefore I'll darkly end the argument.

12. *shrewd*] *shrowd* Q 1. 13. *ne'er*] *neare* Q 1. 17. *ha'*] *a* Qq Ff 1, 2; *have* Ff 3, 4. *a grandam*] *Grandam* Q 1.

12. *shrewd*] curst, unlucky, evil. From Middle English *schrewe*, malicious.

gallows] gallows bird, one fit for the hangman. Compare *The Tempest*, I. i. 32: "his complexion is perfect gallows"; and *Measure for Measure*, IV. ii. 35: "hanging look." Beaumont and Fletcher's *Knight of the Burning Pestle* gives an example: "he be a notable gallows." Shakespeare applies the equally uncomplimentary epithet of "hangman" to Cupid in *Much Ado About Nothing*, III. ii. 11, as an executioner of human hearts. This would have supported Furness in his incorrect conjecture that "*gallows*" here means "hangman," based on an extract from *Arcadia*.

13-17. Abel Lefranc's discoveries suggest that this story was developed later by Shakespeare, and its heroine christened Ophelia. See Introduction 4.2.

18. *a light heart lives long*] Udall's *Ralph Roister Doister* (1550) opens with "*Matthew Merrygreek.* [*He entereth singing.*] As long lyveth the mery man (they say), As doth the sory man, and longer by a day." A frequent saying.

18, 19, 20, 21, 22, 25, 26. *light*] cheery or merry, casual or unimportant, frivolous or wanton, information, a candle, irresponsible, light in weight.

19. *mouse*] An endearing term. See *Hamlet*, III. iv. 183. Craig gives a quotation from *The Triall of Treasure*, 1567 (Hazlitt's *Dodsley*, iii. 293). In *Speeches to the Queen at Bisham* (1592), Pan says to two virgins: "be not agaste, sweet mice. . . . Can you love?" (Nichols, iii. 133); and Lyly (*Mother Bombie*, IV. ii.): "God save you, pretty mouse."

22. *taking it in snuff*] A very common expression representing the expression of disgust at the smell of a snuffed candle. See *1 Henry IV.* I. iii. 41 for another example; and Greene, *Penelope's Web* (Grosart, v. 211), 1587: "Calamus hearing this rough replye of his Tenant was driven into a marvellous choler, so that scarce affoording her a farewell, hee flung out of doores. . . . The goodwife glad that he took the matter so in snuffe, commanded," etc. The verb "to snuff," to resent, be angry with, is older, and influenced this saying. Palsgrave (*Lesclaircissement*, 1530) has "I snoffe, as a man doth or a horse, *Je reniffle.* This boye wyll be of a stubborn herte and he lyve, herke howe he snoffeth."

Ros. Look what you do, you do it still i' the dark.
Kath. So do not you, for you are a light wench.
Ros. Indeed I weigh not you, and therefore light.
Kath. You weigh me not? O! that's you care not for me.
Ros. Great reason; for past care is still past cure.
Prin. Well bandied both; a set of wit well play'd.
But, Rosaline, you have a favour too:
Who sent it? and what is it?
Ros. I would you knew:
An if my face were but as fair as yours,
My favour were as great; be witness this.
Nay, I have verses too, I thank Berowne:
The numbers true; and, were the numbering too,
I were the fairest goddess on the ground:
I am compar'd to twenty thousand fairs.
O! he hath drawn my picture in his letter.
Prin. Any thing like?
Ros. Much in the letters, nothing in the praise.
Prin. Beauteous as ink; a good conclusion.
Kath. Fair as a text B in a copy-book.
Ros. Ware pencils, ho! let me not die your debtor,

28. *care . . . cure*] Qq, Ff; *cure . . . care* Theobald (Thirlby conjecture). 43. *pencils*] Rowe; *pensalls* Q 1; *pensals* F 1; *pensils* (the rest). *ho!*] Hanmer; *How?* Qq, Ff.

24. *Look what you do*] whatever you do. An idiom; again in *Merchant of Venice*, III. iv. 51: "look what notes and garments he doth give thee, Bring them."

28. *past care . . . past cure*] Greene has: "rather remember the olde proverbe, not so common as true: past cure, past care, without remedie, without remembrance" (*Mamillia* [Grosart, ii. 154], 1583). Theobald's reading gives the proverb its usual form and makes the neatest sense; but it is strange that the compositor should blunder over something so well known, and Shakespeare has it again in this odd inverted form, with almost a pun on "care," in Sonnet 147: "Past cure I am, now reason is past care,"—"without medical attention, without remedy."

30, 33. *favour*] token of love, personal appearance.

37. *fairs*] beautiful women. The senses, a beautiful person or beauty itself, occur several times in this play, as they both do in Lodge's *Euphues Golden Legacie*.

39, 40. *Any thing like? Much in the letters*] Compare IV. ii. 151.

41, 42. Both lines taunt Rosaline on her dark colouring, compared to ink. 'Text' hand was a formal script.

43. *Ware*] take heed of, beware. Still in sporting use. Compare "Ware horns, ho!" (*Troilus and Cressida*, V. vii. 12); and Greene's *Mamillia* (Grosart, ii. 91): "if thou waver, ware dost not as the dogge, loose both bones."

pencils] small, finely-pointed brushes for the insertion of spots or lines

My red dominical, my golden letter :
O ! that your face were not so full of O's.
Prin. A pox of that jest ! and I beshrew all shrows !
But, Katharine, what was sent to you from fair
Dumain ?
Kath. Madam, this glove.
Prin. Did he not send you twain ?
Kath. Yes, madam ; and moreover,
Some thousand verses of a faithful lover ;
A huge translation of hypocrisy,
Vilely compil'd, profound simplicity.
Mar. This, and these pearls to me sent Longaville :
The letter is too long by half a mile.
Prin. I think no less. Dost thou not wish in heart
The chain were longer and the letter short ?
Mar. Ay, or I would these hands might never part.
Prin. We are wise girls to mock our lovers so.

45. *not so*] Q 1 ; omitted Ff, Q 2. 46. *Prin.*] Qq, Ff ; *Kath.* Theobald ; Kath. *A pox . . . jest !* Prin. *And I . . .*] New. 47. *But*] Qq, Ff ; Prin. *But* Theobald, Steevens, Cambridge. 53. *pearls*] Ff ; *pearle* Q 1.

(not here for " laying on colours," as Schmidt explains). Rosaline, with a transition from the writing-master's art to that of the painter, retaliates upon Katharine by calling her spotty-faced and flame-coloured. Compare Greene, *Planetomachia* (Grosart, v. 75), 1585 : " Diana is painted kissing Vertue, and spotting beauties face with a Pensel." Dover Wilson suggests that there is a quibble on " pencel " (pennoncel), the pennon or streamer on a knight's lance, and that Rosaline's phrase is a battle-cry " Look out for cavalry ! "

44. *My red dominical*] So in Sharpham's *Cupid's Whirligig*, Act ii. (1607) : " he lookes for all the world like the Dominicall Letter in his red Coate." The red S for Sunday in the old almanacs.

golden letter] The excellent, or Sunday letter, with a reference to Katharine's " amber locks."

45. *O's*] spots, pimples ; pock-marks are implied perhaps by the next line. " O " was used as a substantive of anything round, especially of spangles.

46, 47. *A pox . . . Dumain ?* Dover Wilson divides line 46 between Katharine and the Princess, supposing that the unmetrical " Katharine " is a scribbled speech-heading which the compositor bundled into the speech.

46. *I beshrew all shrows*] I condemn all shrews : my curse on them. Compare Dodsley's *Old Plays*, iv. 69 : " I beshrew . . . that great knave's heart." A common imprecation. The Princess desires to put an end to their wrangling and uses strong language. Her first expression in this speech was, it is said, often in Queen Elizabeth's mouth. Ben Jonson says it was " most courtly " (*Poetaster*, ii. 1 [1600]).

Ros. They are worse fools to purchase mocking so.
That same Berowne I'll torture ere I go.
O ! that I knew he were but in by the week.
How I would make him fawn, and beg, and seek,
And wait the season, and observe the times,
And spend his prodigal wits in bootless rimes,
And shape his service wholly to my hests
And make him proud to make me proud that jests !
So Pair-Taunt like would I o'ersway his state
That he should be my fool, and I his fate.

65. *wholly to my hests*] Dyce (Knight conjecture), Cambridge, New ; *wholly to my device* Qq, F 1 ; *all to my behests* Ff 2, 3, 4. 66. *that*] Qq, F 1 ; *with* Ff 2, 3, 4. 67. *Pair-Taunt like*] *perttaunt like* Q 1 ; *pertaunt-like* Ff, Q 2 ; *pedant-like* Theobald ; *portent-like* Hanmer ; *pageant-like* Capell.

61. *in by the week*] caught, trapped. Compare *Ralph Roister Doister*, I. ii. (Malone Soc., ed. Greg, line 72) : " I tolde you I, we should wowe an other wife. [*Aside*] *R. Roister*. Why did God make me suche a goodly person ? *M. Merry*. He is in by the weke." A passage in Webster's *White Devil* (ed. F. L. Lucas, i. 135) suggests imprisonment : " [*Enter* Flamineo *and* Marcello *guarded*, *and a lawyer*.] *Lawyer*. What, are you in by the weeke ? So—I will try now whether thy wit be close prisoner." These examples and two or three others have been quoted, but the phrase is not common, nor satisfactorily explained. Taken in connection with the Princess's words, " mockery merriment " (line 139), it is evident Rosaline means caught in earnest.

65. *wholly to my hests*] It is rash to emend a Quarto reading merely on the grounds that it does not fit what an editor believes is Shakespeare's rhyme-scheme (collation, I. i. 106) ; but here the pattern is particularly rigid and metre as well as rhyme is broken. Knight's conjecture does the least violence to the original.

66. *make me proud*] There is no need to equate this with the " flesh being proud " of *Lucrece* 712. The line may be paraphrased : " And deck himself out in order to make me proud of him—when all the time I am not taking the affair seriously." The phrase " proud array," and " pride " in the sense of finery, are common in the literature of the period ; and " make him proud " is surely parallel to " shape his device " rather than to " make him fawn."

67. *Pair-Taunt like*] The Quarto reading baffled every editor until 1945, when Dr. Percy Simpson (in a letter to the *Times Literary Supplement* of 24 February) explained its meaning. " Paire-Taunt " is the winning hand in the obsolete card-game of Post and Pair. Simpson quoted the description on p. 74 of Randle Holme's *The Academy of Armory*, left in manuscript and only printed in 1905 (for the Roxburgh Club) : " A Paire is two cards of a sort, as 2 Kings, 2 Aces, 2 tens &c. A Paire Royall is three cards of a sort. A double Paire Royall, or a Paire-Taunt is foure cards of a sort ; " and the last lines of an epigram (" Mortal Life compared to Post and Pare ") from *Wittes Pilgrimage* (1605) in which John Davies of Hereford uses the term in much the same image as Shakespeare's : " *PUR Ceit* deceives the expectation Of him, perhaps, that took the stakes away ;

Prin. None are so surely caught, when they are catch'd,
As wit turn'd fool: folly, in wisdom hatch'd,
Hath wisdom's warrant and the help of school
And wit's own grace to grace a learned fool.
Ros. The blood of youth burns not with such excess
As gravity's revolt to wantonness.
Mar. Folly in fools bears not so strong a note
As foolery in the wise, when wit doth dote;
Since all the power thereof it doth apply
To prove, by wit, worth in simplicity.

Enter BOYET.

Prin. Here comes Boyet, and mirth is in his face.
Boyet. O! I am stabb'd with laughter. Where's her grace?

74. *wantonness*] Ff 3, 4; *wantonesse* F 2; *wantons be* Qq, F 1. 79. *is*] Q 1; omitted Ff, Q 2. 80. *stabb'd*] F 1; *stable* Q 1; *stuff'd* Keightley conjecture.

Then to *PUR Tant* he's in subjection, For Winners on the Losers oft do play." Rosaline means that, whenever Berowne thinks he holds the winning cards, she will always produce a hand to beat them.

74. *wantonness*] See notes to I. i. 106 and line 65 above. Here it is sense and metre that the Quarto outrages, though the use of "be" for "is" and "are" is Shakespearean ("Lord what fools these mortals be.") Dover Wilson thinks Shakespeare wrote "wantones," taken as "wantons" by the compositor, who filled up an apparently defective line as best he could.

75. *bears not so strong a note*] *Note* has here the sense of "stigma"—as we say "a black mark." Elyot, *The Governor* (1531), 80, has: "Augustus . . . only for playing at dice, . . . sustaineth in hystories a note of reproche." Derived from the mark of censure made by the Roman censors.

78. *simplicity*] foolishness. The wise man turned to folly will devote all his cleverness to proving that folly is more valuable than wisdom.

80. *stabb'd with laughter*] The Folio is clearly right, in spite of Collier, who pronounced this "an awkward and unusual expression." Furness says dogmatically: "Barron Field (*Shakes. Soc. Papers*, ii. 56) rightly interpreted the word '*stabb'd*' by 'the *stitch* in the side, which is sometimes brought on by laughter.'" But "that idiot, laughter," is not half the thing it used to be, at least in "good society." In lines 115-16 these characters, royal and noble, are said to "tumble on the ground with zealous laughter." And compare Nashe, *The Unfortunate Traveller* (McKerrow, ii. 219), 1594: "If (I say) you had seene but halfe the actions that he used . . . you wold have laught your face and your knees together." See line 465 below (note). In T. B.'s translation of Primaudaye's *French Academy*, 1586, occurs: "Felt such a motion in them of the spleene, that they were stifled with laughter" (chap. iii).

Prin. Thy news, Boyet?

Boyet. Prepare, madam, prepare!
Arm, wenches, arm! encounters mounted are
Against your peace: Love doth approach disguis'd,
Armed in arguments; you'll be surpris'd:
Muster your wits; stand in your own defence;
Or hide your heads like cowards, and fly hence.

Prin. Saint Denis to Saint Cupid! What are they
That charge their breath against us? say, scout, say.

Boyet. Under the cool shade of a sycamore
I thought to close mine eyes some half an hour,
When, lo! to interrupt my purpos'd rest,
Towards that shade I might behold addrest
The king and his companions: warily
I stole into a neighbour thicket by,
And overheard what you shall overhear:
That, by and by, disguis'd they will be here.
Their herald is a pretty knavish page,
That well by heart hath conn'd his embassage:
Action and accent did they teach him there;
"Thus must thou speak, and thus thy body bear":
And ever and anon they made a doubt
Presence majestical would put him out;
"For," quoth the king, "an angel shalt thou see;
Yet fear not thou, but speak audaciously."
The boy replied, "An angel is not evil;
I should have fear'd her had she been a devil."
With that all laugh'd and clapp'd him on the shoulder,
Making the bold wag by their praises bolder.

89. *sycamore*] *siccamone* Q 1. 93. *companions: warily*] *companions warely* Q 1. 96. *they*] *thy* Q 1.

82-88. *mounted . . . charge*] raised in readiness, as of cannon. Compare *King John*, II. i. 381: "Mounted their battering cannon charged to the mouths."

85. *Muster your wits*] So Dekker, *News from Hell* (Grosart, ii. 95): "I mustred all my wits about me."

102. *majestical*] See v. i. 12. Here means "princely."

107. *clapp'd him on the shoulder*] patted him on the back in approval. Compare Lyly, *Campaspe*, i. 2 (1581): "He commendeth one that is an excellent musition, then stand I by and clap another on the shoulder and say, this is a passing good cooke." Similarly used in *Much Ado About Nothing*. It also had the sense of "take into custody."

One rubb'd his elbow thus, and fleer'd, and swore
A better speech was never spoke before;
Another, with his finger and his thumb,
Cry'd " *Via!* we will do't, come what will come";
The third he caper'd, and cried, "All goes well";
The fourth turn'd on the toe, and down he fell.
With that, they all did tumble on the ground,
With such a zealous laughter, so profound,
That in this spleen ridiculous appears,
To check their folly, passion's solemn tears.

Prin. But what, but what, come they to visit us?

Boyet. They do, they do; and are apparell'd thus,
Like Muscovites, or Russians, as I guess.

118. *folly, passion's solemn*] Theobald; *follie pashions solembe* Q 1; *folly passions solemne* F 1, Q 2; *folly passions, solemn* Ff 2, 3, 4; *folly's passion, solemn* Staunton conjecture. 120. S. Walker thinks a following line may be lost. 121. *as*] Qq, F 1; *or* F 2; *and* Ff 3, 4.

109. *One rubb'd his elbow*] When the elbows itched it was a sign of satisfaction. "Their elbows itch for joy" (Nashe, *Lenten Stuffe* [McKerrow, iii. 192]). Compare *1 Henry IV.* v. i. 77: "Gape and rub the elbow at the news of hurly burly innovation"; and Guilpin's *Skialetheia* (repr. p. 22), 1598: "He'll cry oh rare! and scratch the elbow too To see two butchers curres fight."

fleer'd] grinned. Gascoigne speaks of "Flearing Flattery" (*The Steel Glas* [Arber, p. 51], 1576). The verb occurs several times in Shakespeare. See *Othello*, iv. i. 83 for his one use of the noun "fleer."

111. *his finger and his thumb*] snaps his fingers in exuberance of spirits.

112. *Via*] See note to line 143 in the previous scene.

114. *turn'd on the toe*] A light and airy gesture of departing. Compare Chettle's *Kind-Hartes Dreame*, 1592, Bodley Head Quarto, p. 44: "So wishing the cheareful, pleasaunce endlesse; and the wilful sullen, sorrow till they surfet; with a turn on the toe I take my leave. *Richard Tarleton*." Here presumably a pirouette.

117. *spleen*] See iii. i. 74, and note.

118. *passion's solemn tears*] Theobald compares *A Midsummer Night's Dream*, v. i. 69, 70: "more merry tears The passion of loud laughter never shed."

120. Furness says "Tiessen (*Eng. Studien*, ii. 189 [1878]) kindly supplies the [supposed] missing line: 'Hats furr'd, bootes piked, in long and motley dress.'" How grateful we should feel! Tiessen drew his archaisms from Ritson's extract (see next note).

121. *Muscovites, or Russians*] Ritson quotes from Hall (*Henry VIII.* p. 6) to prove that a mask of Muscovites had been previously shown. In the first year of Henry VIII., at a banquet for the foreign ambassadors at Westminster, "came the lorde Henry, Earle of Wiltshire, and the lorde Fitzwater, in twoo long gounes of yellowe . . . after the fashion of *Russia* or *Ruslande*, with furred hattes of grey . . . and bootes with pykes turned up." This is very ancient history. Lodge, in his *Reply to Gosson*, must be alluding to a more recent stage-show when he says: "If I may speak my mind I think we shall

Their purpose is to parle, to court and dance ;
And every one his love-feat will advance
Unto his several mistress, which they'll know
By favours several which they did bestow.

Prin. And will they so ? the gallants shall be task'd ;
For, ladies, we will every one be mask'd,
And not a man of them shall have the grace,
Despite of suit, to see a lady's face.
Hold, Rosaline, this favour thou shalt wear,
And then the king will court thee for his dear :
Hold, take thou this, my sweet, and give me thine,
So shall Berowne take me for Rosaline.
And change you favours too ; so shall your loves
Woo contrary, deceiv'd by these removes.

122. *parle, to*] Capell ; *parlee, to* Qq, Ff 1, 2 ; *parlee* Ff 3, 4. 123. *love-feat*] Q 1, Ff ; *love-seat* Q 2 ; *love-suit* Dyce (S. Walker conjecture). 134. *you*] Q 1 ; *your* Ff, Q 2. *too*] Ff ; *two* Q 1.

find but few poets if it were exactly wayd what they oughte to be : your Muscovian straungers, your Scithian monsters wonderful, by one Eurus brought upon one stage in ships made of Sheepeskins wyll not prove you a poet" (1579-80). A very close parallel, in the Gray's Inn Revels for 1594-5, was noted by Sir E. K. Chambers in his *William Shakespeare* and elaborated independently by R. Taylor (*The Date of Love's Labour's Lost*, 1932). These Revels, at which had already occurred a notorious performance of the *Comedy of Errors*, concluded with a pageant whose theme was the return of Knights from a campaign in Russia against "Negro-Tartars." They brought prisoners who were "attired like Monsters and Miscreants" and may conceivably have been blackamoors. There followed a "Russian ambassador," at whose request the "Prince of Purpoole" (the benchers' master of ceremonies) made a state visit to Russia. His "return" was made the occasion of a further pageant, when the Prince declared that he was only prevented from paying his respects to Elizabeth by the fact that his body "by length of my Journey, and my sickness at Sea, is so weakened." This has been taken as proof that the present scene at least could not have been written before 1595. But Muscovy was much in the news throughout the eighties and nineties. See Introduction 3.228.

122. *parle*] hold conference, discuss matters. Compare Greene, *Carde of Fancie* (Grosart, iv. 57) : "But Castania altogether unwilling to parle with her new patient, kept herself out of his sight." The noun is common.

123. *love-feat*] exploit, deed or effort prompted by love, or in connection with love ; love-affair. The sense is strained, but not impossible, and is perhaps well in keeping with that of "advance," which in Shakespeare almost invariably implies aggression rather than suggestion (but "suit" of line 129 supports Walker's guess). We may give the expression a sarcastic touch, since the purport of Boyet's speech, as well as the Princess's, is to belittle the "mockery merriments" of the King and his party.

Ros. Come on, then; wear the favours most in sight.
Kath. But in this changing what is your intent?
Prin. The effect of my intent is to cross theirs:
They do it but in mockery merriment;
And mock for mock is only my intent.
Their several counsels they unbosom shall
To loves mistook, and so be mock'd withal
Upon the next occasion that we meet,
With visages display'd, to talk and greet.
Ros. But shall we dance, if they desire us to't?
Prin. No; to the death we will not move a foot:
Nor to their penn'd speech render we no grace;
But while 'tis spoke each turn away her face.
Boyet. Why, that contempt will kill the speaker's heart,
And quite divorce his memory from his part.
Prin. Therefore I do it; and I make no doubt
The rest will ne'er come in, if he be out.
There's no such sport as sport by sport o'erthrown,
To make theirs ours and ours none but our own:
So shall we stay, mocking intended game,
And they, well mock'd, depart away with shame.
[*Sound trumpet.*
Boyet. The trumpet sounds: be mask'd; the maskers come.

139. *mockery merriment*] Q 1; *mocking merriment* Ff, Q 2. 148. *her*] Ff 2, 3, 4; *his* Qq, F 1. 149. *speaker's*] Q 1; *keepers* Ff, Q 2. 152. *ne'er*] Ff 2, 3, 4; *ere* Qq, F 1. 156. *Sound trumpet*] Q 1; *Sound* Ff, Q 2.

136. *most in sight*] conspicuously.

139. *mockery merriment*] These words are to be noted; they rob the Princess's plans of any ill-nature at once. See "in by the week," above, line 61.

146. *No; to the death*] not as long as we live; never. Equivalent here to our "to death," with no suggestion of conflict. Compare *Richard III*, III. ii. 55: "I will not do it, to the death" (I will never do it). Schmidt wrongly equates this with the sense mortally, fatally.

147. *penn'd*] specially composed and written out for the occasion.

149. *kill the speaker's heart*] utterly dishearten him. Compare *Winter's Tale*, IV. iii. 88: "offer me no money, I pray you; that kills my heart." It is an old expression, as in Malory's *Morte d'Arthur* (Book x., ch. lviii): "Fie upon treason, said Sir Tristram, for it killeth my heart to hear this tale." "Speaker" here refers expressly to Moth.

151, 152. *no doubt . . . will ne'er come in*] The use of the negative after expressions of doubt is notoriously tricky, so perhaps Shakespeare did write the ungrammatical "e'er."

157. *Blackamoors*] African negroes. They seem to have become very popular on the stage. Ben Jonson

Enter Blackamoors with music; MOTH *with a speech; the* KING *and the rest of the lords disguised like Russians, and visored.*

Moth. All hail, the richest beauties on the earth!
Boyet. Beauties no richer than rich taffeta.
Moth. A holy parcel of the fairest dames,
[*The Ladies turn their backs to him.*
That ever turn'd their—backs—to mortal views!
Ber. "Their eyes," villain, "their eyes."
Moth. That ever turn'd their eyes to mortal views!
Out—
Boyet. True; "out" indeed.
Moth. Out of your favours, heavenly spirits, vouchsafe
Not to behold—
Ber. "Once to behold," rogue.
Moth. Once to behold with your sun-beamed eyes,
—with your sun-beamed eyes—
Boyet. They will not answer to that epithet;
You were best call it "daughter-beamed eyes."

Enter . . .] *Enter Blackmores with musicke, the Boy with a speech, and the rest of the Lords disguised* Qq, Ff; *Enter Blackamoors with Music; Moth; the King, Berowne, Longaville, and Dumain, in Russian habits and masked*, Dyce, Cambridge; *Enter Blackamoors with music* omitted Craig. 159. *Boyet.*] Theobald; *Berow.* Q 1; *Ber.* F 1, Q 2; *Bir.* Ff 2, 3, 4. 160. *The Ladies* . . .] after *views* (line 161) Qq, Ff. 161. *ever*] Ff; *even* Q 1. 165. and 171. *Boyet.*] Qq, F 1; *Ber.* Ff 2, 3, 4. 166. *spirits*] Qq, F 1; *spirit* Ff 2, 3, 4.

tells all about them in his *Masque of Blackness* (1605), saying it was "her majesty's will to have them (the masquers) blackmoors." We cannot tell when this stage-direction was inserted, or by whom, but it is at least as old as 1597. Taylor (see note on line 121 above), thinks that these blackamoors are a reflection of the Negro-Tartars in the Gray's Inn Revel; but the prisoners of the Gray's Inn Knights are not clearly stated to have been captured in their Negro-Tartar campaign, nor is there much connection between prisoners and attendants with music. The visors, mentioned often in this scene, were necessary to a masque. Speaking of the *Mountebank's Masque* (16 February 1618), Chamberlain says: "their show, for I cannot call it a masque, seeing they were not disguised, nor had vizards" (*Court and Times of James I.* ii. 66).

159. *Beauties . . . rich taffeta*] all their visible beauty is that of their taffeta masks. It is just possible that the play on "rich" has topical significance. See Introduction 5.25.

169-172. *sun . . . daughter*] This grievous pun occurs about a dozen times in Shakespeare, collected by Schmidt in v. *Son.* There is one painful example (not mentioned by Schmidt) in that most beautiful of sonnets (xxxiii.).

Moth. They do not mark me, and that brings me out.
Ber. Is this your perfectness? be gone, you rogue!
[*Exit Moth.*
Ros. What would these strangers? know their minds, Boyet.
If they do speak our language, 'tis our will
That some plain man recount their purposes:
Know what they would.
Boyet. What would you with the princess?
Ber. Nothing but peace and gentle visitation.
Ros. What would they, say they?
Boyet. Nothing but peace and gentle visitation.
Ros. Why, that they have; and bid them so be gone.
Boyet. She says, you have it, and you may be gone.
King. Say to her, we have measur'd many miles
To tread a measure with her on this grass.
Boyet. They say, that they have measur'd many a mile
To tread a measure with you on this grass.
Ros. It is not so. Ask them how many inches
Is in one mile: if they have measur'd many,
The measure then of one is easily told.
Boyet. If, to come hither, you have measur'd miles,
And many miles, the princess bids you tell
How many inches doth fill up one mile.

174. [*Exit Moth*] Cambridge; [*Moth withdraws*] Capell; omitted Qq, Ff. 175. *strangers*] *stranges* Q 1. 178. *princess*] *Princes* Q 1. 185. *her on this*] Q 1; *you on the* Ff, Q 2.

173. *brings*] puts; as in the expression "bring one on his way."

out] Compare "out of countenance," below, line 272. Here the meaning is, "out of my part," as proved by line 336 below. Compare *Cynthia's Revels*, Induction (1600): "some satisfaction in your prologue, or, I'll be sworne, we have marred all. *2 Child.* Tut, fear not, child, this will never distaste a true sense: be not out, and good enough."

179. *visitation*] visit. See *Measure for Measure*, III. ii. 255. "Visit" (substantive) does not occur in this sense in Shakespeare. It is in Jonson, *Underwoods*, xxxii.

185. *tread a measure*] The proper expression to apply to this stately dance. It is in Lyly's *Campaspe*, IV. iii. (1581): "But let us draw in, to see how well it becomes them to tread the measures in a daunce, that were wont to set the order for a march." An earlier use occurs in Gosson's *Schoole of Abuse* (Arber, p. 26), 1579: "Terpandrus when he ended the brabbles at Lacedoemon, neyther pyped Rogero nor Turkelony, but . . . taught them too treade a better measure."

Ber. Tell her we measure them by weary steps.
Boyet. She hears herself.
Ros. How many weary steps,
Of many weary miles you have o'ergone,
Are numbered in the travel of one mile?
Ber. We number nothing that we spend for you:
Our duty is so rich, so infinite,
That we may do it still without account.
Vouchsafe to show the sunshine of your face,
That we, like savages, may worship it.
Ros. My face is but a moon, and clouded too.
King. Blessed are clouds, to do as such clouds do!
Vouchsafe, bright moon, and these thy stars, to shine,
Those clouds remov'd, upon our watery eyne.
Ros. O vain petitioner! beg a greater matter;
Thou now requests but moonshine in the water.

208. *requests*] Qq, Ff; *request'st* Theobald.

200. *account*] The archaic "accompt" is retained here, and in one or two other passages where it deals with a money reckoning, by several modern editors. In the first Folio "accompt" occurs thirteen times, and "account" seventeen times in the sense of reckoning.

202. *like savages, may worship*] See above, IV. iii. 219-22; and *Cymbeline*, III. iii.

203. *face . . . moon . . . clouded*] Rosaline refers here to her "whitely" and dark colouring—perhaps; she may mean that she is in reality only a lesser light; or that her light is borrowed (Dover Wilson). Her clue is missed. The King thinks she is the Princess.

204. *Blessed are clouds*] blessed is the cloud, veil or mask that does as yours does, kisses your face. "These happy masks that kiss fair lady's brows" (*Romeo and Juliet*, I. i. 236). The quibbling upon the cloud and mask here, and again at line 297, was first noted by Hart, who wrote: "It is perfectly necessary for the sense. A cloud in this material sense would be familiar to dramatists. Compare Cunningham's *Extracts from Revels Accounts* (Shakes. Soc. p. 147), 1579: 'For a hoop and blew lynnen to mend the clowde that was Borrowed and cut,' etc."

205. *bright moon, and these thy stars*] The King makes a similar remark at IV. iii. 227-228: "gracious moon; She an attending star," which tends to show that Shakespeare was not referring to the supposed star Lunisequa but to any of the stars. Furness quotes Staunton: "Lilly calls it Lunisequa" (no reference). It is mentioned by Lodge, *Euphues Golden Legacie* (*Shakes. Lib.* 1875, p. 79), quoted already (IV. iii. 228).

208. *moonshine in the water*] A thing of naught, waste of time. An old proverbial expression. It is in *The Proverbs of John Heywood* (Sharman's edition, p. 77), 1546: "Farewell he (quoth I), I will as soon be hilt [held?] As waite againe for the mooneshine in the watter. But is not this a pretie piked matter?" And in North's *Doni's Moral Philosophie* (Jacob's repr. p. 182), 1570: "How

King. Then, in our measure do but vouchsafe one change.
Thou bidd'st me beg; this begging is not strange.
Ros. Play, music, then! nay, you must do it soon.
Not yet?—no dance:—thus change I like the moon.
King. Will you not dance? How come you thus estranged?
Ros. You took the moon at full, but now she's changed.
King. Yet still she is the moon, and I the man.
The music plays; vouchsafe some motion to it.
Ros. Our ears vouchsafe it.
King. But your legs should do it.
Ros. Since you are strangers, and come here by chance,
We'll not be nice: take hands:—we will not dance.
King. Why take we hands then?
Ros. Only to part friends.
Court'sy, sweet hearts; and so the measure ends.
King. More measure of this measure: be not nice.
Ros. We can afford no more at such a price.

209. *do but vouchsafe*] Q 1; *vouchsafe but* Ff, Q 2. 212. *Not yet?—no dance*] New; *Not yet no dance;* Qq, Ff; *Not yet? no dance?* Pope, Theobald; *Not yet; no dance:* Capell; *Not yet! no dance! Cambridge.* 216. Given to Rosaline in Qq, Ff; corrected by Theobald. 220. *we*] Q 1; *you* Ff, Q 2.

they laboured and toyled for life about moone shine in the water." It appears in Lyly's *Endymion*, II. ii. (?1585) and is very common later, as in Burton's *Anatomy of Melancholy* (Democritus to the Reader); Harington, *Epigrams*, ii. 56; Ben Jonson, *Staple of News*, III. i. And see Cotgrave in v. *Debatre*. Hence our "it's all moonshine." Ellis notes that "water" rhymes with "matter" in *King Lear*, III. ii. 81, 82; Heywood (*ut supra*) gives an early instance.

209. *change*] The King puns on changes of the moon and "changes" (distinct figures or rounds) in the dance.

210. *this begging is not strange*] The King means, although we are strangers (foreigners), you understand what begging means.

211. *do it soon*] Nonplussed by Rosaline's sudden consent the King is not quick enough to take advantage of it before she changes her mind and revokes it.

215. *Yet . . . man*] Theobald believed this verse about the man in the moon to be spurious, because it breaks in on the rhyme, and because "the conceit of it is not pursued." Capell omitted it. But the conceit *is* pursued. I am a partner for you, will you dance? Perhaps an alteration in punctuation would make this plainer.

221. *Court'sy*] Compare *The Tempest*, I. ii. 443: "Curtsied when you have, and kist." The curtsy and the kiss began the dance. The King alludes to the kiss, perhaps (line 222).

King. Price you yourselves : what buys your company?
Ros. Your absence only.
King. That can never be.
Ros. Then cannot we be bought : and so adieu ;
Twice to your visor, and half once to you !
King. If you deny to dance, lets hold more chat.
Ros. In private then.
King. I am best pleased with that.
[*They converse apart*.
Ber. White-handed mistress, one sweet word with thee.
Prin. Honey, and milk, and sugar ; there is three.
Ber. Nay then, two treys, an if you grow so nice,
Metheglin, wort, and malmsey : well run, dice !
There's half-a-dozen sweets.

224. *Price*] Rowe (ed. 1) ; *Prise* Qq, Ff 1, 2, 3 ; *Prize* F 4. *you yourselves*] Q 1 ; *yourselves* F 1, Q 2 ; *yourselves then* Ff 2, 3, 4. 229, 237, 241, 255 [*They converse apart*] Capell ; [*They walk away chatting*] Furnivall. 232. *an*] Q 1, F 1 ; *and* Q 2, Ff 2, 3, 4.

224. *Price you*] seems to be preferable to *Prize* in continuation of Rosaline's remark. "Price" was very commonly written *prise*. So, however, was "prize."

227. *Twice . . . you*] Hart explains this as "two kisses for your mask (identical with Berowne's), little for the man behind it"—another doubtful speech hinting at the speaker's not being the Princess ; but his interpretation is forced. Dover Wilson is probably right in deducing from this and the "Fair befall your mask" of II. i. 124, a contemporary joke about masks which is now lost to us.

228. *deny*] refuse. Compare *Winter's Tale*, V. ii. 139 : "You denied to fight with me the other day because I was no gentleman born." This construction occurs several times in Shakespeare ("deny to wed," *Taming of the Shrew*, II. i. 180, etc.), but I have not noted it elsewhere.

232. *treys*] threes, at dice. Not again in Shakespeare, but frequently used. Craig gives a quotation from Chaucer's *The Pardoner's Tale*, line 19 : "Seuen is my chaunce and thyn is cink and treye." Although the word does not stand alone in Shakespeare again, it probably forms the first part of "tray-trip," a game at dice, mentioned in *Twelfth Night*, II. v. 207.

nice] subtle, sophistical (Schmidt). Compare *1 Henry VI*. II. iv. 7 : "These nice sharp quillets of the law" ; and *3 Henry VI*. IV. vii. 58. Our "nice point."

233. *Metheglin*] A Welsh drink of honey and water, herbs and other ingredients. See *Merry Wives of Windsor*, V. v. 167, where Sir Hugh Evans classes it with sack and wine.

wort] unfermented beer ; "the sweet infusion of malt" (Schmidt). It is mentioned in Chaucer's *Canterbury Tales*, and in Holland's *Plinie* (xviii. 7, p. 560 [1601]) : "The skum or frothe that gathereth aloft by the working of the woort."

malmsey] "A strong sweet wine, originally the product of the neighbourhood of Monemvasia (Napoli di Malvasia), in the Morea, but now obtained from Spain, etc. . . . as well

Prin. Seventh sweet, adieu.
Since you can cog, I'll play no more with you.
Ber. One word in secret.
Prin. Let it not be sweet.
Ber. Thou griev'st my gall.
Prin. Gall! bitter.
Ber. Therefore meet.
[*They converse apart.*
Dum. Will you vouchsafe with me to change a word?
Mar. Name it.
Dum. Fair lady,—
Mar. Say you so? Fair lord,—
Take that for your fair lady.
Dum. Please it you,
As much in private, and I'll bid adieu.
[*They converse apart.*
Kath. What! was your visor made without a tongue?
Long. I know the reason, lady, why you ask.
Kath. O! for your reason; quickly, sir; I long.
Long. You have a double tongue within your mask,
And would afford my speechless visor half.

240. *Take that*] Q 1; *Take you that* Ff, Q 2. 242, 244, 247, 248, 249, 253, 255. *Kath.*] Rowe; *Mar.* Qq, Ff.

as from Greece" (*New Eng. Dict.*). It is called *malvesie* in Chaucer. Greene speaks of a cheater in a tavern at some market-town who there "tipled so much malmesie that he had never a ready woord in his mouth" (*Notable Discovery of Coosnage*, 1591 [Grosart, x. 11]); so that it appears to be rather a vulgar drink at this time. Speaking of the ale provided for Queen Elizabeth on her way to Kenilworth in 1575, Lord Leicester writes: "We were fain to send to London with bottels, to Kenelworth, to divers other places where ale was. Her own bere was such as there was no man able to drink it; yt had been as good to have drank malmsey" (Nichols, i. 526).

235. *cog*] cheat. Expressly applied to cheating with dice. Compare Gabriel Harvey, *An Advertisement for Papp-hatchett* (Grosart, ii. 214), 1589: "He'll cogg with the dye of deceit." This is the oldest sense of the verb, and is abundantly illustrated from 1532 downward in *New Eng. Dict.* It was transferred to every sort of deceit. See Lyly's *Sapho and Phao*, i. 3 (1581): "We fall from cogging at dice to cogge with states."

238. *change a word*] Compare *Much Ado About Nothing*, IV. i. 185. Interchange a word. Compare *Romeo and Juliet*, III. v. 31: "Some say the lark and loathed toad changed eyes."

245. *double tongue . . . mask*] In a letter to *The Times Literary Supplement* (7 June 1923) W. J. Lawrence wrote: "This deft passage-at-arms . . . is really witty. The old vizard was what the youngster of today calls "a false face." Made of black

Kath. Veal, quoth the Dutchman. Is not veal a calf?
Long. A calf, fair lady!
Kath. No, a fair lord calf.
Long. Let's part the word.
Kath. No, I'll not be your half:
Take all, and wean it: it may prove an ox.
Long. Look, how you butt yourself in these sharp mocks.
Will you give horns, chaste lady? do not so.
Kath. Then die a calf, before your horns do grow.
Long. One word in private with you ere I die.
Kath. Bleat softly then; the butcher hears you cry.
[*They converse apart.*
Boyet. The tongues of mocking wenches are as keen
As is the razor's edge invisible,
Cutting a smaller hair than may be seen;
Above the sense of sense; so sensible
Seemeth their conference; their conceits have wings
Fleeter than arrows, bullets, wind, thought, swifter things.

251. *butt*] *but to* Ff 2, 3, 4. 257. *invisible*] *invincible* Theobald. 259. *sense; so sensible*] Pope; *sence so sensible*, Q 1; *sence so sensible;* Ff, Q 2. 261. *bullets*] omitted Capell.

velvet on a leather base, it covered the entire features and was kept in place by a tongue, or interior projection, held in the mouth. Of a surety all annotated editions of the play should have a note to this effect appended to the passage." I concur and comply. Longaville's "double" surely has a hint of "ambiguous" or "quibbling"; there may even be a suggestion of the supposedly venomous "double tongue" of snakes.

247. *Veal, quoth the Dutchman*] Viel, plenty, answers Longaville's plea for half. The Dutch skipper in Dekker's *Shoemaker* (II. ii. 127) says "Yaw, yaw, ic heb veale ge drunck."

Is not veal a calf? It is, and more: "*Veau:* A calf or Veal; also a lozel, hoiden, dunce, jobbernol, doddipole" (Cotgrave). Boswell cites *Doctor Dodypoll* (1600): "me be right glad for see veale. *Hans.* What, do you make a Calfe of me, M. Doctor? *Doct.* O no pardona moy; I say vell, be glad for see you vell, in good health." In the present passage, however, the puns are four deep. Besides anticipating Doctor Dodypoll's ambiguity Katharine glances at Longaville's disguise, his visor or *veil* (often spelt "veal" at this time; compare Spenser's *Letter to Harvey* [Oxford *Spenser*, p. 611] "his Moother with a Veale hath coovered his face"); and she also reveals by a quibble that she knows who is behind it. The last word of her previous speech was "long"; with the first word of this she completes his name. She has indeed afforded him halves.

249. *your half*] your better-half, your wife. See *J. Cæsar*, II. i. 274.

261. *bullets*] Capell conjectures that

Ros. Not one word more, my maids: break off, break off.
Ber. By heaven, all dry-beaten with pure scoff!
King. Farewell, mad wenches: you have simple wits.
Prin. Twenty adieus, my frozen Muscovites.
[*Exeunt Lords and Blackamoors.*
Are these the breed of wits so wonder'd at?
Boyet. Tapers they are, with your sweet breaths puff'd out.
Ros. Well-liking wits they have; gross, gross; fat, fat.
Prin. O poverty in wit, kingly-poor flout!
Will they not, think you, hang themselves to-night?
Or ever, but in visors, show their faces?
This pert Berowne was out of countenance quite.

265. *Exeunt . . .*] *Exeunt* F 1 (after line 264); omitted Q 1. 269. *wit, kingly-poor*] *wit, kingly poor* Qq, Ff; *wit, kill'd by pure* Collier MS.; *wit, poor-liking* Staunton conjecture.

"bullets" was a prior word, changed for "arrows," and left in the text through an oversight.

263. *dry-beaten*] literally, bruised without blood drawn. Occurs in the transferred sense, as here, in *Martins Months Minde* (Grosart's *Nashe*, i. 175), 1589: "old Martin first drie beaten, & therby his bones broken . . . made a Maygame upon the Stage, and so bang'd both with prose and rime on everie side." Greene has "dry blows" similarly several times: "these dry blowes could draw no blood" (*Mamillia* [Grosart, ii. 150]).

264. *mad wenches*] See II. i. 257.

268. *Well-liking*] in good condition. See *Merry Wives of Windsor*, II. i. 54 (for the noun); and *1 Henry IV.* III. iii. 6. Steevens refers to Job xxxix. 4: "Their young ones are in good liking."

Well-liking . . . fat] Rosaline's "flout" is equivalent to "Fat paunches have lean pates" (I. i. 26: see note). Fatness and wit were held to disagree with one another. Compare Udall's *Erasmus* (Roberts' repr. p. 128), 1542: "For that sort of men are fedde up with the grosse kindes of meates, which in deed conferres to the body hard braune, and clene strength, but as for the witte, it maketh as grosse and dulle as can be thought."

269. The Princess retorts upon Rosaline's poverty in wit, in making such a grievous pun on "king" in her "well-li*king*." She proves that is her thought by continuing it in "*king*ly-poor." I do not believe there is any further profundity in her remark, which has been worked into many shapes from the supposition her words refer to the King's last speech. Her "kingly-poor" is merely "well-liking" with an inserted quibble, mocking Rosaline.

272. *out of countenance*] disconcerted. Hardly distinguishable from Moth's "out" at line 173 above. Compare Puttenham, *Arte of English Poesie* (Arber, p. 149), 1582: "These great Madames of honoure . . . if they want their courtly habillements . . . would be halfe ashamed or greatly out of countenaunce." *N.E.D.* has an example from a ballad (early 16th century).

Ros. O, they were all in lamentable cases!
The king was weeping-ripe for a good word.
Prin. Berowne did swear himself out of all suit.
Mar. Dumain was at my service, and his sword:
No point, quoth I: my servant straight was mute.
Kath. Lord Longaville said, I came o'er his heart;
And trow you what he call'd me?
Prin. Qualm, perhaps.
Kath. Yes, in good faith.
Prin. Go, sickness as thou art!
Ros. Well, better wits have worn plain statute-caps.
But will you hear? the king is my love sworn.

273. *O*] Ff 2, 3, 4; omitted Qq, F 1.

274. *weeping-ripe*] See *3 Henry VI.* I. iv. 172. The expression occurs in Sidney's *Arcadia*, bk. i. (Feuillerat, i. 107), *ante* 1586: "But Lalus (even weeping ripe) went among the rest, longing to see some bodie that would avenge Uranias wronge." It occurs also in Heywood's *Rape of Lucrece* (Pearson, p. 193), 1608, and in Armin's *Italian Taylor* (Grosart, p. 180), 1609. Elsewhere Shakespeare has *reeling-ripe* and *sinking-ripe*. Beaumont and Fletcher give us *dropping-ripe*, *tumbling-ripe* and *crying-ripe*. All seem to be built on the expression *rope-ripe* (fit for hanging, crack-halter), which occurs in Adlington's *Apuleius' Golden Asse*, chap. 30 (1566); and in Wilson's *Arte of Rhetorique* (according to Malone), 1553. *Dropping-ripe* is in Marlowe's *First Book of Lucan*.

275. *out of all suit*] out of fitness, agreement, or suitability. Compare "out of suits with fortune" (*As You Like It*, I. ii. 258), where the plural is equivalent to the collective "all." Cotgrave, Florio and Miege distinguish *suit* in this sense (*Quadrer*) with the spelling "sute." The Princess may allude to the love-suit Berowne was engaged in. "All" was similarly inserted for emphasis in several old expressions, as: "*out of all* ho," "*out of all* cry," "*out of all* nick," "*out of all* count," "*out of all* scotch and notch." These are all about the date of *Love's Labour's Lost*, excepting the first two, which are earlier.

276. *service*] Again connected with "suit" in lines 829-30 below. Perhaps through the law term "suit and service" (Feudal).

277. *No point*] See II. i. 190. Not at all.

279. *Qualm*] There must have been more similarity in the pronunciations of "qualm" and "came" than at present if this quibbling is to be recognized. Compare Gabriel Harvey (Grosart, ii. 279), *Pierce's Supererogation:* "to ravish the affections, and even to mealt the bowels of bravest mindes: see, see what a woundrous quaime."

281. *better wits have worn plain statute-caps*] Johnson said this line was "not universally understood because every reader does not know that a statute-cap is part of the academical habit." Grey quoted from Strype's *Annals of Queen Elizabeth* (ii. 74) an Act of Parliament of 1571 "for continuance of making and wearing woollen caps in behalf of the trade of cappers; providing that all above the age of six years (except the nobility and some others) should on sabbath days and holy

Prin. And quick Berowne hath plighted faith to me.
Kath. And Longaville was for my service born.
Mar. Dumain is mine, as sure as bark on tree.
Boyet. Madam, and pretty mistresses, give ear.
Immediately they will again be here
In their own shapes ; for it can never be
They will digest this harsh indignity.
Prin. Will they return ?
Boyet. They will, they will, God knows ;
And leap for joy, though they are lame with blows :
Therefore change favours ; and when they repair,
Blow like sweet roses in this summer air.

days, wear caps of wool, knit, thicked and dressed in England, upon penalty of ten groats." Johnson, however, still stuck to his explanation. Grey's is clearly nearer the truth, though it does not explain the meaning of "plain," and it is too universal, applying as it did to the whole community almost. Steevens quotes passages from Marston, *Dutch Courtesan* (Bullen, ii. 60), 1605 : "though my husband be a citizen, and his cap's made of wool, yet I have wit" ; and from Middleton's *The Family of Love* (Bullen, iii. 102), 1608 : "'Tis a law enacted by the common-council of statute-caps." It is obvious that whatever explains these passages is also the explanation of the line in the text. But there is nothing of citizens in the 1571 Act, nor is it an enactment of the Common Council. The best solution is that of Hart, who showed that in 1582 there were "Regulations recommended for the Apparel of London Apprentices," and "'Twas by the Lord Mayor and Common Council enacted. That from henceforth no Apprentice should presume—1. To wear any apparel but what he receives from his Master. 2. To wear no hat within the City and liberty thereof, nor any thing instead thereof, but a woollen cap, without any silk in or about the same . . . [there are eight more clauses, concluding with :] every Apprentice offending . . . for the first offence to be punished at the discretion of his Master ; for the second to be publicly whipped at the Hall of his Company," etc. (Nichols' *Progresses*, ii. 393, 394). The passage in the play appears to refer directly to the prentice caps of London. There were so many statutes of apparel that Nashe says : "Why they [Harvey's *Letters*] are longer than the Statutes of Clothing or the Charter of London" (*Have With You*, 1596 [McKerrow, III. 34]).

285. *bark on tree*] inseparable, closely united, hand and glove. Compare J. Heywood *Proverbs* (Sharman, p. 98), 1562 : "It were a folly for me, To put my hand betweene the barke and the tree. . . . Between you" (*New Eng. Dict.*) ; and Marmion, *A Fine Companion* (near the end), 1633 : "Master Dotario and my daughter *Æmilia*, hand in hand, and married together . . . there they are, bark and tree."

291. *leap for joy*] See IV. iii. 146.

292. *favours*] Some part of the presents (ribbons or gloves), or the presents themselves, given by the different suitors to their mistresses, and worn, as we are told, to confuse the

Prin. How blow? how blow? speak to be understood.
Boyet. Fair ladies, mask'd, are roses in their bud:
Dismask'd, their damask sweet commixture shown,
Are angels vailing clouds, or roses blown.
Prin. Avaunt, perplexity! What shall we do
If they return in their own shapes to woo?
Ros. Good madam, if by me you'll be advis'd,
Let's mock them still, as well known as disguis'd.
Let us complain to them what fools were here,
Disguis'd like Muscovites, in shapeless gear;
And wonder what they were, and to what end
Their shallow shows and prologue vilely penn'd,
And their rough carriage so ridiculous,
Should be presented at our tent to us.
Boyet. Ladies, withdraw; the gallants are at hand.

296, 297. *Dismask'd . . . blown*] *Or angel-vailing clouds: are roses blown, Dismaskt . . . shewn* Theobald (Warburton conjecture). 297. *Are . . . blown*] *Are angels (val'd the clouds) . . . blown* Becket conjecture; *Are angels veil'd in clouds of roses blown* Peck conjecture. *vailing*] Ff, Q 2; *varling* Q 1.

donors. See lines 30, 130, 134. The masks are now removed. See above, "be masked" (line 157), where the editors usually insert a stage-direction, "The ladies mask." Perhaps another, "The ladies dismask," might be inserted at line 296 for uniformity's sake. They are "known" now (line 301) and no longer disguised. Boyet expresses his approbation at line 297. For *favours*, see, again, line 455 below.

296. *damask*] red and white, like the Damascus rose. Compare *As You Like It*, III. v. 125 (quoted in *New Eng. Dict.* as the earliest use in this sense); and Holland's *Plinie*, xii. 11 (1601): "another tree . . . bearing a blossom like to a damaske or incarnate rose," where "incarnate" means flesh-coloured. More punning.

commixture] "Commistura, a commixture, a blending" (Florio's *World of Words*, 1611). Complexion. Shakespeare has the word in *3 Henry VI.* II. vi. 6, in the sense of "compound."

297. *vailing*] lowering, letting fall. Commonly used in the nautical expression "vail bonnet" which Greene has twice (metaphorically) in *Arbasto*, 1584. Compare *Venus and Adonis*, 956: "She vailed her eyelids," etc.

angels vailing clouds] angels letting down (or lowering) clouds or veils (or masks) that hid their fairness. "Vailing" has the actual sense of unveiling. Johnson put it quite clearly: "Ladies unmasked are like angels vailing clouds, or letting those clouds which obscured their brightness sink from before them." This is obvious when we give clouds the meaning of masks or disguises, which the word seems to bear at line 204 above.

298. *Avaunt, perplexity*] "Enough, you riddler!" (to Boyet). Compare *Romeo and Juliet*, III. v. 171, "hold your tongue, Good prudence."

303. *shapeless gear*] uncouth dress.

305. *vilely penn'd*] See line 147.

Prin. Whip to our tents, as roes run o'er the land.
[*Exeunt Princess, Rosaline, Katharine, and Maria.*

Re-enter the KING, BEROWNE, LONGAVILLE, *and* DUMAIN, *in their proper habits.*

King. Fair sir, God save you! Where's the princess?
Boyet. Gone to her tent. Please it your majesty,
Command me any service to her thither?
King. That she vouchsafe me audience for one word.
Boyet. I will; and so will she, I know, my lord. [*Exit.*
Ber. This fellow pecks up wit, as pigeons pease,
And utters it again when God doth please.
He is wit's pedlar, and retails his wares
At wakes, and wassails, meetings, markets, fairs;

309. *roes run o'er the*] F 4 (*runs ore the* F 3); *roes runnes ore* Qq, Ff 1, 2, Cambridge; *roes run over* Steevens, Craig. *Re-enter . . .*] *Enter the King and the rest* Qq, Ff. 310. *Where's*] Qq, Ff; *Where is* Steevens. 312. *thither*] Q 1; omitted Ff, Q 2. 315. *pecks*] Q 1; *picks* Ff, Q 2. 316. *God*] Q 1; *Jove* Ff, Q 2.

309. *Whip*] move quickly (to or from a place). Compare Greene's *Disputation betweene a Hee and a Shee Conney-Catcher* (Grosart, x. 219), *ante* 1592: "Why then, quoth shee, steppe into this closet: hee whipt in hastily and never remembered his cloathes"; and Fenton's *Bandello*, 1567 (Henley, ii. 146): "She whipped into the house and shoot the doare upon the nose of her amarus clyent."

roes . . . land] "fleeter than the roe" occurs in *Taming of the Shrew*, Induction, II. 50; and it is an odd coincidence that in the old *Taming of a Shrew* (*Shakes. Lib.* 1875, p. 496) there is the same defect in the metre as here, from *over* and *o'er*, and the same obsolete form (a northern dialect plural) of the verb: "Your hounds stands readie cuppeld at the doore. Who in running will oretake the Row," etc. Greene has the same simile: "Never went roe bucke swifter on the downes Than I will trip it till I see my George" (Grosart, xiv. 151).

the land] i.e. the "laund" (lawn) as in *3 Henry VI.* III. i. 2: "Through this laund anon the deer will come." "Laund" is properly an open space in a wood, or surrounded by trees. Compare Lodge, *Euphues Golden Legacie* (*Shakes. Lib.* 1875, p. 130): "She tript alongst the Lawnes full of joy."

310. *Where's the princess*] Steevens sought to restore verse-form to a line which, together with the next two, is printed in early texts as prose.

315. *This fellow pecks up wit*] The whole simile later became proverbial as can be seen from Thomas Coriate, *Traveller for the English Wits*, 1616: "He pickes up wit as pigeons pease, And utters it when God doth please." It is in this debased form that it appears in the Folio.

316. *utters*] issues, distributes, offers for sale. This, the original sense of the word as given in *New Eng. Dict.*, is preserved in the legal phrase "to forge and utter" bad coin.

318. *wakes*] Compare Stubbes, *Anatomie of Abuses*, 1583: "The

And we that sell by gross, the Lord doth know,
Have not the grace to grace it with such show.
This gallant pins the wenches on his sleeve;
Had he been Adam, he had tempted Eve.
A' can carve too, and lisp: why, this is he
That kiss'd his hand away in courtesy;

323. *A' can*] Q 1; *He can* Ff, Q 2. 324. *his hand away*] Q 1; *away his hand* Ff, Q 2.

manner of keeping wakesses and feasts in England . . . manie spend more at one of their wakesses than in all the whole year besides." Every village had its annual "wake-day."

wassails] health-drinkings, revels. "The jolly wassal walks the often round" (Ben Jonson, *Forest*, iii.). Usually applied to a special drink, or act of drinking. See *Hamlet*, I. iv. 9.

319. *by gross*] by wholesale. Opposed to "retail" in Gabriel Harvey, *Pierce's Supererogation* (Grosart, ii. 34), 1592: "Some have called them knaves in grose: I have found them fooles in retayle." And in William Covell [Dowden], *Polimanteia* (Grosart, p. 54), 1595: "Compelled to retaile that which they had bought by grosse."

321. *pins the wenches on his sleeve*] The idea is probably from the wearing of favours on the sleeve, with a pun on the wenches' *penchant* for themselves hanging on their lovers' arm. Compare *The Comedy of Errors*, II. ii. 177: "Come, I will fasten on this sleeve of thine: Thou art an elm, my husband, I a vine." The expression is found in Greene's *Mourning Garment* (Grosart, ix. 173), 1590: "What it is for mee to pinne a fayre meacocke and a witty milksop on my sleeve, who dare not answere with their swords in the face of the enemy?" And again, in *Farewell to Follie* (ix. 327), 1591: "to avoide iealousie, you may ever wear her pinde on your sleeve." And earlier, in Lyly's *Sapho and Phao*, ii. 4 (1581): "But bee not pinned alwayes on her sleeves, strangers have green rushes, when daily guests are not worth a rush."

323. *carve*] See *Merry Wives of Windsor*, I. iii. 49: "she carves, she gives the leer of invitation." "Carve" was a fashionable word of the day, difficult of explanation, with some such sense as "show great courtesy and affability" (Schmidt), but especially applying to courtship. An early example of the noun was found by Hart in Greene's *Philomela* (Grosart, xii. 117), printed in 1592 but stated in the Epistle Dedicatory to be one of "the first frutes of my witts": "Feeding upon this passion that knaweth like envy upon hir owne flesh, he called to minde to which of his friends she shewed the most gratious lookes, uppon whom she glaunst the most smiling favours, whose carver she would be at the table, to whom she would drink, and who had most curteus intertainment at hir hands."

324. *kiss'd his hand away in courtesy*] Compare Ben Jonson, *Cynthia's Revels*, iii. 11 (1600): "Another swears His scene of courtship over . . . anon, doth seem . . . As he would kiss away his hand in kindness." Jonson's line is taken by Hart as establishing the Folio against the Quarto reading. For other references to the kissing hands, or fingers, in courtesy, see *As You Like It*, III. ii. 50, *Othello*, II. i. 173. The "*fore-finger kiss*" is in G. Harvey's "Speculum Tuscanismi" (1580). The courtesy was

This is the ape of form, monsieur the nice,
That, when he plays at tables, chides the dice
In honourable terms: nay, he can sing
A mean most meanly, and, in ushering,
Mend him who can: the ladies call him sweet;
The stairs, as he treads on them, kiss his feet.
This is the flower that smiles on every one,
To show his teeth as white as whale his bone;
And consciences, that will not die in debt,
Pay him the due of honey-tongu'd Boyet.

332. *whale his*] Ff 2, 3, 4, Rowe; *whales* Qq, F 1, Steevens; *whale's* Cambridge; *whales'* Halliwell. 334. *due*] Q 1; *duty* Ff, Q 2.

of French origin appropriate to Monsieur Boyet. Compare Florio's *Montaigne*, bk. ii. chap. 12: "to see them ignorant of the French tongue, of our kissing the hands, of our low-lowting courtesies."

325. *form*] observance of etiquette; as in *Hamlet*, III. i. 161: "The glass of fashion and the mould of form." Our "good form."

326. *tables*] backgammon. The oldest name for one of the oldest games which is said to have been discovered in the tenth century as a rival to chess in order to combine chance and skill to bring together players of unequal talents. See Strutt's *Sports and Pastimes* for a figure of players at tables of the thirteenth century. It was always played with dice on the folding boards or tables used also for draughts. The word is still used in the game, but not usually of the game.

328. *A mean*] a middle or "fill up" part between treble and bass. The quibble is common. See Greene's *Farewell to Follie* (Grosart, ix. 279), 1591: "The meane that grees with countrie musicke best." Lyly has it in *Gallathea* (acted 1585?), v. 3: "Can you sing? . . . Basely. . . . And you? . . . Meanly. . . . And what can you doe? . . . If they double it I will treble it."

328-330. *ushering . . . he treads*] Similarly Jonson speaks of "fine-paced huishers" (*Devil is an Ass*, II. iii.). The gentleman-usher was specially selected with "little legs of purpose" (Jonson, *Every Man out of his Humour*, iii. 1 [1599]) for the sake of his fine or delicate pacing.

332. *as white as whale his bone*] An old simile. It occurs in the romance *Eglamore* (Percy Folio, ed. Furnivall and Hales, ii. 342), *ante* 1400: "The Erle had noe child but one a maiden as white as whalles bone." And the Earl of Surrey in *Tottel's Miscellany* (Arber, p. 218), 1557: "I might perceive a wolfe as white as whale bone." And Greene, *Never Too Late* (Grosart, viii. 213): "Legges as white as whales bone: so white and chaste was never none." The division into two words representing the old pronunciation seems a necessary modernization. Whalebone here probably meant the ivory of the walrus.

333, 334. *die in debt, Pay*] Compare *Romeo and Juliet*, I. i. 244: "I'll pay that doctrine or else die in debt." See also line 43 above.

334. *honey-tongu'd*] It is interesting to note here that Meres, who gives us the earliest reference to *Love's Labour's Lost* by name, and also the earliest tribute of praise to Shakespeare by name, applies this term to Shakespeare himself. The quotation is

King. A blister on his sweet tongue, with my heart,
That put Armado's page out of his part!

Re-enter the PRINCESS, *ushered by* BOYET; ROSALINE, MARIA, KATHARINE, *and Attendants*.

Ber. See where it comes! Behaviour, what wert thou
Till this madman show'd thee? and what art thou now?
King. All hail, sweet madam, and fair time of day!
Prin. Fair in all hail is foul, as I conceive.
King. Construe my speeches better, if you may.
Prin. Then wish me better: I will give you leave.
King. We came to visit you, and purpose now
To lead you to our court: vouchsafe it then.
Prin. This field shall hold me, and so hold your vow:
Nor God, nor I, delights in perjur'd men.
King. Rebuke me not for that which you provoke:
The virtue of your eye must break my oath.
Prin. You nickname virtue; vice you should have spoke;
For virtue's office never breaks men's troth.
Now, by my maiden honour, yet as pure

338. *madman*] Qq, Ff, Cambridge, Globe; *man* Theobald, New
350. *men's* Ff 3, 4; *mens* Q 1; *men* Ff 1, 2, Q 2.

classical: "As the soule of Euphorbus was thought to live in Pythagoras: so the sweete wittie soule of Ovid lives in mellifluous & honey-tongued Shakespeare, witnes his *Venus and Adonis*, his *Lucreece*, his sugred Sonnets among his private friends, &c." (*Wits Treasurie*, 1598). These two are the only early examples in *New Eng. Dict.*

336. *out of his part*] See line 173.

338. *Till this madman*] Dover Wilson would drop the "mad," as disturbing to the metre, and plausibly suggests that the compositor caught it from the "madam" of the next line. But a mere roughness of metre should not damn the livelier reading.

madman] jester. See notes at "madcap," II. i. 215; and at "mad wenches," II. i. 257.

339. *All hail*] The quibble here occurs in *The Two Noble Kinsmen*, III. v.; and in *The Faithful Friend*, III. ii.; both have been ascribed to Beaumont and Fletcher, the second doubtfully, but Shakespeare himself may well have helped Fletcher with the first. So too, in Dekker's *Old Fortunatus* (Pearson, p. 113): "Brother all haile. *Shadow*. There's a rattling salutation."

348, 349. *virtue . . . virtue*] power . . . goodness.

349. *nickname*] "To name by mistake: to assert wrongly to be something" (*New Eng. Dict.*) Simply, to miscall.

As the unsullied lily, I protest,
A world of torments though I should endure,
I would not yield to be your house's guest;
So much I hate a breaking cause to be
Of heavenly oaths, vow'd with integrity.

King. O! you have liv'd in desolation here,
Unseen, unvisited, much to our shame.

Prin. Not so, my lord; it is not so, I swear:
We have had pastimes here and pleasant game.
A mess of Russians left us but of late.

King. How, madam! Russians!

Prin. Ay, in truth, my lord;
Trim gallants, full of courtship and of state.

Ros. Madam, speak true. It is not so, my lord:
My lady, to the manner of the days,
In courtesy gives undeserving praise.
We four, indeed, confronted were with four
In Russian habit: here they stay'd an hour,
And talk'd apace; and in that hour, my lord,
They did not bless us with one happy word.
I dare not call them fools; but this I think,
When they are thirsty, fools would fain have drink.

Ber. This jest is dry to me. My gentle sweet,
Your wit makes wise things foolish: when we greet,

352. *unsullied*] Ff 2, 3, 4; *unsallied* Qq, F 1. 356. *oaths*] *oath* Q 2. 368. *Russian*] *Russia* F 1, Q 2. 373. *My*] Malone; om. Qq, F 1; *Fair* Ff 2, 3, 4. 374. *wit makes*] Ff 2, 3, 4; *wits makes* Qq, F 1.

352. *unsullied*] Some editors like to retain the obsolete alternative spelling *unsallied* of the first editions. This spelling (*sally* for *sully*) occurs again in the Quarto *Hamlet*, II. i. 39, and possibly (*sallied* for *sullied*) at I. ii. 129 as well. The Princess may have the lily of France in her thoughts. At the beginning of Dekker and Chettle's *Patient Grissel*, "sully not this morning" is spelt "*sally*." See Collier's edition.

361. *mess*] See IV. iii. 204 (note). A mess was a set of four.

365. *to the manner of the days*] according to the fashion of the times.

369. *talk'd apace*] chattered. Tibet Talkapace is the name of a chatterbox in *Ralph Roister Doister*. See *Measure for Measure*, III. ii. 116, where the form used is "speak apace."

372. *When . . . drink*] One of the numerous paraphrases for "you're a fool." Compare *The Penniless Parliament of Threadbare Poets*, 1608 (*Harl. Misc.* iii. 73): "Some shall be so humorous in their walks as they cannot step one foot from a fool." And the Scotch "When you're served, a' the geese are watered."

373. *My gentle sweet*] Malone's "my" is the most likely word to

With eyes best seeing, heaven's fiery eye,
By light we lose light: your capacity
Is of that nature that to your huge store
Wise things seem foolish and rich things but poor.

Ros. This proves you wise and rich, for in my eye,—

Ber. I am a fool, and full of poverty.

Ros. But that you take what doth to you belong,
It were a fault to snatch words from my tongue.

Ber. O! I am yours, and all that I possess.

Ros. All the fool mine?

Ber. I cannot give you less.

Ros. Which of the visors was it that you wore?

Ber. Where? when? what visor? why demand you this?

Ros. There, then, that visor; that superfluous case
That hid the worse and show'd the better face.

King. We were descried: they'll mock us now downright.

Dum. Let us confess, and turn it to a jest.

Prin. Amaz'd, my lord? Why looks your highness sad?

Ros. Help! hold his brows! he'll swoon. Why look you pale?
Sea-sick, I think, coming from Muscovy.

Ber. Thus pour the stars down plagues for perjury.
Can any face of brass hold longer out?

385. *was it*] *what it* F 1. 389. *were*] Q 1; *are* Ff, Q 2. 390. *Dum.*] *Duman.* Q 1; *Du.* F 1, Q 2; *Duke* Ff 2, 3, 4. 392. *swoon*] Pope Steevens; *sound* Qq, F 1; *swound* Ff 2, 3, 4.

have been dropped by the compositor after "me." But it is perhaps unnecessary to fill out the line at all.

375. *heaven's fiery eye*] Craig quotes Spenser, *Faerie Queene*, I. iii. 4: "The great eye of heaven" (referring to the sun), and Marlowe's *Tamburlaine* (part ii.), IV. iv. 7 (1586): "The horse that guides the golden eye of Heaven." It is also in *Venus and Adonis*, 178; Sonnet xlix. 6; Sonnet xviii.; *King John*, III. i. 79, etc., etc.

392. *hold his brows*] Compare *King John*, IV. i. 41-5: "When your head did but ache, I knit my handkercher about your brows. . . . And with my hand at midnight held your head".

393. *sea-sick . . . coming from Muscovy*] May be an echo of the Gray's Inn Revels, 1594-5. See line 121, note.

395. *face of brass*] assurance, confident manner. This passage is given in *New Eng. Dict.* as the first example of the expression. The next use is from Fuller, half a century later. Shakespeare may have found it in Whetstone's *Promos and Cassandra* (part ii.), III. i. (1578): "My troubled hart with guiltynesse agrev'd Lyke fyre doth make my eares and cheekes to glow: . . . Well, I wyll set a face of brasse on it." "Brazen-face" is in *Merry Wives of Windsor*, IV. ii. 145.

Here stand I, lady ; dart thy skill at me ;
Bruise me with scorn, confound me with a flout ;
Thrust thy sharp wit quite through my ignorance ;
Cut me to pieces with thy keen conceit ;
And I will wish thee never more to dance,
Nor never more in Russian habit wait.
O ! never will I trust to speeches penn'd,
Nor to the motion of a school-boy's tongue,
Nor never come in visor to my friend,
Nor woo in rhyme, like a blind harper's song,
Taffeta phrases, silken terms precise,
Three-pil'd hyperboles, spruce affection,

396. *I, lady ;*] *I, Ladie* Qq, Ff ; *I ; lady,* Cambridge. 407. *affection*] Qq, Ff, Malone, Halliwell ; *affectation* Rowe, Cambridge.

397. *flout*] a mocking speech. "Knowest thou not that a deniall at the first is a graunt, and a gentle answere a flattering floute ?" (Greene *Arbasto* [Grosart, iii. 214], 1584).

400. *wish thee*] entreat thee.

401. *wait*] attend upon, do service.

404. *friend*] sweetheart. Compare *Measure for Measure,* I. iv. 29 ; *Merry Wives of Windsor,* III. iii. 124, etc.

405. *like a blind harper's song*] Compare Lyly, *Sapho and Phao,* IV. iii. : "Harping alwaies upon love, till you be as blind as a harper." Blind harpers were proverbial as early as John Heywood's *Proverbs* (Sharman's edition, p. 137), 1542 : "Proface. Have among you, blind harpers (say'd I) ; the mo the merrier." Hart noted that the race of blind harpers and fiddlers is hardly yet extinct in Ireland : they were the survivors of those (incapacitated by blindness from smallpox) who were unfitted for any profession save that of music. Puttenham, *Arte of English Poesie* (Arber, p. 97), 1589, has : "Blind harpers or such like taverne minstrels that give a fit of mirth for a groat."

406. *Taffeta phrases*] Similarly used by Nashe in his Epistle to the Gentleman Students prefixed to Greene's *Menaphon* McKerrow, iii. 323) 1589 : "Sundry other sweete Gentlemen I doe know, that have vaunted their pennes in private devices, and tricked up a companie of taffaty fooles with their feathers." He refers to actors, whose stage-clothes are as little natural to them as the lines they speak. Berowne means that fine speech, like actors' dress, is put on for the occasion.

407. *Three-pil'd*] The best quality as of the richest velvet. See *Measure for Measure,* I. ii. 33, and *Winter's Tale,* IV. iii. 14. Dekker has "three-pil'd oaths" in *A Strange Horse-Race* (Grosart, iii. 354).

hyperboles] Shakespeare uses this expression elsewhere only in *Troilus and Cressida,* I. iii. 161 : "Which from the tongue of roaring Typhon dropp'd, Would seem hyperboles ; at this fusty stuff The large Achilles," etc. There, as here, the word is trisyllabic. Puttenham has a page or two (Arber, pp. 202, 203) on the "*Hyperbole,* Or the Over-reacher, otherwise called the loud lyer" (*Arte of English Poesie,* 1589). The word occurs in *Gesta Grayorum,* 1594 : "Such like hyperbolies" (Malone Soc., p. 29).

spruce] See note on V. i. 14.

407. *affection*] affectation. See above, V. i. 4. "Affection" is

Figures pedantical ; these summer flies
Have blown me full of maggot ostentation :
I do forswear them ; and I here protest,
By this white glove (how white the hand, God knows),
Henceforth my wooing mind shall be express'd
In russet yeas and honest kersey noes :
And, to begin : Wench,—so God help me, law !—
My love to thee is sound, sans crack or flaw.

Ros. Sans " sans," I pray you.

Ber. Yet I have a trick
Of the old rage : bear with me, I am sick ;

414. *to begin : Wench —so*] *to begin Wench, so* Qq, Ff ; *to begin, wench, so* Theobald *et seq.*

quadrisyllabic here, as above, in I. i. 9. Malone said : " The modern editors read *affectation*. There is no need of change." There is every reason against it, except a rigid adherence to rhyme, which is absolutely no argument. Shakespeare uses the shorter form again in *Hamlet*, II. ii. 473.

408. *Figures*] turns of rhetoric (Schmidt). See I. ii. 52 and v. i. 61 (note).

pedantical] Compare G. Harvey, *An Advertisement for Papp-hatchett* (Grosart, ii. 129), 1589 : " He is no boddy, but a few pilfred Similes ; a little Pedanticall Latin ; and the highest pitch of his witt, Bulles motion, alias the hangman's apron." Harvey's tract was written before *Love's Labour's Lost.*

408, 409. *flies . . . blown . . . maggot*] *New Eng. Dict.* has this in v. *blow* (28) (" To fill with eggs ") as the earliest example. Compare " fly-blown," which occurs in Gabriel Harvey, 1573.

409, *ostentation*] vanity, affectation, " pretentious parade " (*New Eng. Dict.*). The word occurs above (v. i. 107) in a different use.

411. *By this white glove*] Slender burlesques this in *Merry Wives of Windsor* (" by these gloves," I. i. 156, 161, 168) : Jonson has it in *Every Man Out of his Humour.*

413. *russet*] Fr. *rousset*, reddish-brown (Cotgrave) ; the colour of the peasants' cloth. Compare *Hamlet*, I. i. 166. " Russet coat " was a term for a rustic, as in Porter's *Two Angry Women of Abingdon* (Malone Soc., ed. Greg, line 1369) ; and Ben Jonson's *Tale of a Tub*, III. v. Sometimes it was " russeting " ; " Vile russetings Are matcht with monarchs and with mighty kings " (Hall, *Satires*, I. iii. [1598]).

kersey] coarse woollen cloth, a staple English export of the period. Plain, homely, unsophisticated.

414. *Wench*] This—to a lady-in-waiting—must mark the beginning of Berowne's new bluntness.

law] perhaps a corruption of *La*, an exclamation to call attention, occurring several times in *Merry Wives of Windsor*. " Law," generally used as an asseveration, is now confounded with *Lor'* for *Lord*. See also *New Eng. Dict.* (*La*, *Lo*). " Law " occurs in Marston several times, as in *Eastward Ho*, v. i. " La " is in Jonson's *Every Man out of his Humour*, III. i.

416. *Sans " sans," I pray you*] " Sans " is a spruce " affection " ; " give it up," Rosaline says. We have had it before (v. i. 81). Common in Lyly : " The boy hath wit sance measure, more than needs " (*Mother Bombie*, II. i.).

I'll leave it by degrees. Soft! let us see:
Write "Lord have mercy on us" on those three;
They are infected, in their hearts it lies;
They have the plague, and caught it of your eyes:
These lords are visited; you are not free,
For the Lord's tokens on you do I see.

419. "*Lord have mercy on us*"] At first a name for an intestinal affliction known as the "iliac passion." See Higgins, *Nomenclator*, 1585: "Ileus . . . the Iliake passion . . . which the homelier sort of Physicians doe call, *Lord have mercy upon me*." Thence transferred to the plague. Halliwell says: "This touching inscription was frequently a printed placard which was generally surmounted by a red cross. . . . In Shakespeare's time the inhabitants of every infected house were compelled to place some conspicuous mark upon it to denote the fact," etc. Steevens gives several quotations, one of which is from *More Fools Yet*, by R(oger) S(harpe), 1610: "A doore belonging to a house infected, Whereon was plac'd (as 'tis the custom still) *The Lord have mercy on us*: this sad bill The sot perus'd." It is used by Nashe in *The Unfortunate Traveller* (McKerrow, ii. 286), 1594: "[Whilest I was in Rome] So it fel out that it being a vehement hot summer . . . there entred such a hotspurd plague . . . it was but a word and a blowe, *Lord have mercie upon us* and he was gone." And by Dekker, *The Dead Tearme* (Grosart, iv. 81), 1608: "Two such Ravens (who preied uppon a dead body) flew that way, cryed presently out, *Lord have mercy uppon us*, clapping their hard handes on their country-breastes, and looking more pale than the sheete in which the man was buryed." This suggests that the prayer was fixed upon the winding-sheet of the dead body passing to burial. F. P. Wilson (*The Plague in Shakespeare's London*, 1927, p. 61) has shown that the inscription was in use in 1568, if not earlier, and is therefore worthless for the dating of the play.

420. *infected*] Nashe refers to the great plague of 1592 as "this last infection" (*Foure Letters Confuted* [McKerrow, i. 301], 1593).

422. *visited*] The technical term for attacked by plague. Compare Dekker, *The Wonderfull Yeare* (Grosart, i. 115), 1603: "let us therefore with bag and baggage march away from this sore Citie, and visit those that are fled into the country. But alas! *Decidis in Scyllam*, you are peppered if you visit them, for they are visited alreadie: the broad Arrow of Death flies there up & downe as swiftly as it doth here." The plague was known as the "*visitation*" distinctively. See Nashe, in McKerrow's edition, ii. 166, ii. 287, etc. The year 1592-3 was one of the worst visitations: "This yeare was no Bartholomew faire kept at London for the avoiding of concourse of people whereby the infection of the pestilence might have increased" (Stowe's *Chronicles*, Abridgment, p. 395, 1618). This plague passage is taken by Dover Wilson as evidence that the play was written in 1593. Charlton says such jesting would be impossible with the plague at its worst. He underrates the Elizabethans.

423. *tokens*] plague-spots. Compare "death-tokens" (*Troilus and Cressida*, II. iii. 187), and "token'd pestilence" (*Antony and Cleopatra*, III. x. 9). Cotgrave has "*Tac*: A kind of rot among sheep; also, a plague-spot or God's token on one that hath the Plague" (1611). In her reply

Prin. No, they are free that gave these tokens to us.
Ber. Our states are forfeit : seek not to undo us.
Ros. It is not so. For how can this be true,
That you stand forfeit, being those that sue ?
Ber. Peace ! for I will not have to do with you.
Ros. Nor shall not, if I do as I intend.
Ber. Speak for yourselves : my wit is at an end.
King. Teach us, sweet madam, for our rude transgression
Some fair excuse.
Prin. The fairest is confession.
Were not you here, but even now, disguis'd ?
King. Madam, I was.
Prin. And were you well advis'd ?
King. I was, fair madam.
Prin. When you then were here,
What did you whisper in your lady's ear ?
King. That more than all the world I did respect her.
Prin. When she shall challenge this, you will reject her.
King. Upon mine honour, no.
Prin. Peace ! peace ! forbear :
Your oath once broke, you force not to forswear.
King. Despise me, when I break this oath of mine.
Prin. I will ; and therefore keep it. Rosaline,
What did the Russian whisper in your ear ?

433. *not you*] Q 1 ; *you not* Ff, Q 2.

the Princess takes up the implied pun on the love-tokens given by the lords, and twists " free " (i.e. not infected) to mean fancy-free. This form of cross-talk, in which each speaker by catching up one word in his partner's sally and giving it a new turn produces as it were a surprising modulation, is characteristic of the play. The " set of wit " between Katharine and Rosaline at lines 20-8 above is another good example.

425. *seek not to undo us*] we are hopeless, it is useless trying to relieve us of our forfeiture.

426, 427. *how can . . . sue*] The point lies in the two senses of " sue " —to beg, and to bring a suit at law. " You are suing," says Rosaline, " therefore plaintiffs ; how can you also be the condemned ? "

434. *were you well advis'd ?*] was it a rational proceeding ? Compare *Comedy of Errors*, II. ii. 215. In your sober senses.

440. *force not*] value not. You set no value on your oath. " I force not," " it forceth not," " no fors of," are common early expressions. " No force of two straws " (*The Four Elements* [Hazlitt's *Dodsley*, i. 8], 1519) ; " No force for that " (Whetstone, *Promos and Cassandra*, II. iv. and v. iv. [1578]) ; " If . . . blood be spilt in every place they force it not a mite " (B. Googe, *The Popish Kingdome* [repr. p. 8], 1570).

Ros. Madam, he swore that he did hold me dear
As precious eyesight, and did value me
Above this world ; adding thereto, moreover,
That he would wed me, or else die my lover.
Prin. God give thee joy of him ! the noble lord
Most honourably doth uphold his word.
King. What mean you, madam ? by my life, my troth,
I never swore this lady such an oath.
Ros. By heaven, you did ; and to confirm it plain,
You gave me this : but take it, sir, again.
King. My faith and this the princess I did give :
I knew her by this jewel on her sleeve.
Prin. Pardon me, sir, this jewel did she wear ;
And Lord Berowne, I thank him, is my dear.
What, will you have me, or your pearl again ?
Ber. Neither of either ; I remit both twain.
I see the trick on 't : here was a consent,
Knowing aforehand of our merriment,
To dash it like a Christmas comedy.
Some carry-tale, some please-man, some slight zany,

446. *thereto*] Qq, F 1 ; *there* Ff 2, 3, 4. 454. *the*] *to th'* Ff 3, 4. 463. *slight zany*] *sleight saine* Q 1.

455. *jewel . . . sleeve*] See line 292 (note) above.

459. *Neither of either*] Compare *A Yorkshire Tragedy*, Scene i. (1608) : "But sirrah is neither our young master return'd, nor our fellow Sam come from London ? *Ralph.* Neither of either, as the Puritan bawd says." Tyrrell says, in a note to this passage (the play was attributed to Shakespeare) : "This quiet, good-humoured, little sarcasm is in the manner of Shakespeare." It was more in his manner than the editor had noticed.

remit] resign, give up.

460. *a consent*] an understanding or compact, an agreement. Compare *The Tempest*, II. i. 203.

462. *dash*] frustrate, spoil. If the Muscovites (line 121) derive from Gray's Inn, this may be a reference to the ragging of *The Comedy of Errors* there on 28 December 1594. But the custom was general. See Introduction 4.33.

463. *carry-tale*] tale-bearer, spy. *New Eng. Dict.* gives an earlier example from Holinshed's *Chronicle of Ireland* (iii. 1062), 1577. Compare Nashe, *Pierce Penilesse* (McKerrow, i. 232), 1592 : "there are spirits called spies & tale-carriers, obedient to Ascaroth, whom the Greeks call *Daimona*, and *S. John*, the accuser of the brethren." Shakespeare has the compound again in *Venus and Adonis*, 657 ; and compare "one Mistress Tale-porter," in *Winter's Tale*, IV. iv. 273.

please-man] sycophant or toady.

zany] The rustic servant of the pantaloon in the Commedia dell' Arte. Florio has "*Záne*, the name of Iohn in some parts of Lombardy, but commonly used for a silly John, a simple fellow, a servile drudge or

Some mumble-news, some trencher-knight, some Dick,
That smiles his cheek in years, and knows the trick
To make my lady laugh when she's disposed,
Told our intents before ; which once disclos'd,
The ladies did change favours, and then we,
Following the signs, woo'd but the sign of she.
Now, to our perjury to add more terror,
We are again forsworn, in will and error.

465. *smiles his*] *smiles, his* Q 1 ; *smites his* Jackson conjecture. *years*] *jeers* Theobald ; *fleers* Hanmer ; *tears* Jackson conjecture.

foolish clowne in any commedy or interlude play" (*New World of Words*, 1611). And compare Nashe, *Pierce Penilesse* (McKerrow, i. 215), 1592 : "Our Sceane is more statelye furnisht than ever it was in the time of Roscius, our representations honourable, and full of gallant resolution, not consisting, like theirs, of a Pantaloun, a Whore, and a Zanie, but of Emperours, Kings, and Princes." See Introduction 4.32.

464. *mumble-news*] prattler. The verb was often used of repeating the paternoster. Compare Florio : "*Novellante*, A teller of newes and tidings, a teller of tales, fables and fond discourses. Also, a merry jester, a pleasant buffon."

trencher-knight] compare *carpet-knight*. One who is a valiant man at the trencher or plate. See "*trencher-friends*" (parasites), *Timon of Athens*, III. VI. 106 ; and "*trencher-man*," *Much Ado About Nothing*, I. i. 51. Compare Greene, *Never Too Late* (Grosart, viii. 165), 1590 : "Oh Francesco (quoth hee), how fond hast thou bene lead away with every looke, fed uppon with Trencher flies, eaten alive with flatterers." Here the word is synonymous with the rest, a parasite, table-friend.

Dick] fellow, companion, jack. A contemptuous term, first known in the combination "desperate *Dick*," which occurs in Wilson, *Arte of Rhetorique*, 1553 ; in *Triall of Treasure* (Hazlitt's *Dodsley*, iii. 280), 1567 ; and in Churchyard's *Queen's Reception at Bristol*, 1574, and often later. Nashe enumerates various Dicks in his attack on Richard Harvey (McKerrow, iii. 85). "Dapper Dick" was also common, as in Greene, *Quip for an Upstart Courtier* (Grosart, xi. 239) : "I might see comming downe the hill a brave dapper Dicke, quaintly attired in velvet and Sattin."

465. *smiles his cheek in years*] laughs his face into wrinkles. Compare *Twelfth Night*, III. ii. 79 ; *Merchant of Venice*, I. i. 80 ; *2 Henry IV*. v. i. 96-8 ; *Troilus and Cressida*, I. i. 40. Farmer quotes from Webster, *Duchess of Malfi*, where a lady cannot endure to be in merry company, for she says too much "laughing . . . fils her too full of the wrinkles."

466. *disposed*] disposed to be merry. See above, II. i. 250 (note).

469. *she*] mistress, woman. Compare *As You Like It*, III. ii. 10 : "Carve on every tree The fair, the chaste and unexpressive she." And Nashe, *Have With You*, etc. (McKerrow, iii. 110, 111), 1596 : "hee is as infinite in commending her as Saint Jerome in praise of Virginitie. . . . In one place he calls her *the one shee*, in another *the credible Gentlewoman*, in a third *the heavenly plant*, and the fourth a new starre in Cassiopeia," etc., etc.

Much upon this 'tis :—and might not you [*To Boyet.*
Forestall our sport, to make us thus untrue ?
Do not you know my lady's foot by the square
And laugh upon the apple of her eye ?
And stand between her back, sir, and the fire,
Holding a trencher, jesting merrily ?
You put our page out : go, you are allow'd ;

472. [*To Boyet*] Rowe. 474. *square*] F 4, Rowe ; *squier* Qq, Ff 1, 2, 3, Pope, Cambridge ; *squire* Capell, Malone. 475. *apple*] *appeal* Ulrici (Furness cit.). 478. *allow'd*] Ff 3, 4 ; *aloude* Q 1 ; *alow'd* F 1, Q 2.

472. *Much upon this 'tis*] it is very nearly this way. Compare *Measure for Measure*, III. ii. 242, and IV. i. 17 (" much upon this time ").

474. *know my lady's foot by the square*] Varied from the older " have the length of her foot." It occurs in Lyly's *Euphues and his England* (Arber, p. 290), 1580 : " you shall not know the length of my foot until by your cunning you get commendation." And in *Pasquils Jests and Mother Bunches Merriments* (Hazlitt repr. p. 31) : " The counterfeiting young mistris with kind words and knavish wiles, finding the length of his foote, gate many tokens of his love." And Dekker, *The Bachelars Banquet* (Grosart, i. 263), 1603 : " having now the full length of his foot, then shewes she herselfe what she is, unmasking her dissembling malice." In the earlier examples the expression has the meaning it has in the text—to know how to win one's love ; to win one's love. Later, as in Mrs. Behn's *Roundheads*, Act. i. (1682), and *The Bagford Ballads* (Wade's *Reformation*, p. 7), etc., etc., it had a somewhat baser sense—to know one's foibles, to take one's measure, for selfish ends.

square] carpenter's rule. Halliwell quotes from Palsgrave (*Lesclaircissement*, 1530) : " *Sqyar* for a carpentar, *esquierre* " ; and " *Squyer* a rule, *riglet*." See, again, *Winter's Tale*, IV. iv. 348, and *1 Henry IV*. II. ii. 13. The old form *squire* or *squier* is retained by most editors. By a curious orthography the word seems to have become " square " in the transferred usage earlier than this, in the expression " wisdom's square." Roger Ascham has " square, rule, and line of wisdom " (*The Scholemaster*, 1570). Higgins' *Nomenclator* has " *Norma*, *regula* . . . a squire or square." Florio and Cotgrave use both spellings indiscriminately.

475. *laugh upon the apple of her eye*] laugh upon in an intimately affectionate and endearing way. Shakespeare only once elsewhere has the expression " apple of the eye," in *A Midsummer Night's Dream*, III. ii. 104, where it is used literally, as here, of the pupil ; not in the more familiar sense, of the object of one's tenderest solicitude. It comes close to the expression " looking babies " in one's mistress's eye. Compare T. Bowes' trans. of Primaudaye's *French Academy*, p. 145 (1586) : " We see our owne eies shine within the apples of our neighbour's eies."

477. *Holding a trencher*] See above, line 464. The reference is not to a menial, but to an attentive sycophant.

478. *You put our page out*] See line 173.

you are allow'd] admitted (or permitted) as a fool, you have licence. See above, I. ii. 123. And compare " an allowed fool " (*Twelfth Night*, I. v. 101). See " beg us," below, line 490.

Die when you will, a smock shall be your shroud.
You leer upon me, do you? there's an eye
Wounds like a leaden sword.

Boyet. Full merrily
Hath this brave manage, this career, been run.

Ber. Lo! he is tilting straight. Peace! I have done.

Enter COSTARD.

Welcome, pure wit! thou part'st a fair fray.

Cost. O Lord, sir, they would know,
Whether the three Worthies shall come in or no.

481. *merrily*] *merely* Q 1. 482. *Hath this brave manage*] Theobald; *hath this brave nuage* Q 1; *hath this brave manager* Ff, Q 2. 484. *part'st*] *prat'st* Ff 3, 4.

479. *smock . . . shroud*] wholly effeminate. Perhaps there is a reference to an expression occurring a couple of times in Greene, of one sentenced by a verdict of women, "the verdict of the smock"; "tried by the verdict of the smock. Upon this they panneld a jurie" (*The Art of Conny-catching* [Grosart, x. 60]). Women will be the death of you.

481. *leaden sword*] Swords and daggers of lead or lath are commonly mentioned figuratively as mock-weapons in Shakespeare; familiar as stage-properties.

482. *manage*] A term from the riding-school, an evolution to which a horse is trained, "specially a short gallop at full speed" (*New Eng. Dict.*). The term occurs in Laneham's *Letter* (*Captain Cox*, ed. Furnivall, Ballad Soc. 1871, p. 24), 1575: "The Brydegroom for preeminens had the fyrst coors at the Quintyne, brake hiz spear *tres hardiments;* but his marc in his manage did a littl so titubate, that mooch a doo had hiz manhood to sit in his sadl."

career] A term in horsemanship, practically identical with the last in meaning. *New Eng. Dict.* quotes from Holinshed's *Chronicle*, iii. 1033/2, 1577-87: "They were better practised to fetch in booties than to make their manage or careire." Both terms belonged specially to the tilting-yard. Gabriel Harvey uses the term as it is here of any course or action: "Extra jocum, and to leave thessame stale karreeres you knowe full well it woulde suerly quite mare all" (*Letters to Spenser* [Grosart, i. 133], 1573-80), and again (of the Countess of Pembroke): "Her hoattest fury may fitly be resembled to the passing of a brave career by Pegasus" (Grosart, ii. 322).

483. *Lo! he is tilting straight*] Look at him, sparring for a wit-combat at once. He is at it again. *Straight* is for "straightway," immediately.

484. *part'st . . . fray*] occurs again in *Much Ado About Nothing*, v. i. 114. Compare G. Whetstone, *Promos and Cassandra* (pt. ii.) III. ii. (*Shakes. Lib.* vi. 277), 1578: "To parte this fraye it is hye time, I can tell, My Promoters else of the roste wyll smell." See, too, Sir P. Sidney's *Masque before the Queen at Wanstead* (*The May-Lady*), 1578 (Works, ed. Feuillerat, vol. ii. 330): "Maister Rombus . . . came thither, with his authority to part their fray."

485, 494, 497. *O Lord, sir*] See also I. ii. 6 above. The retort seems

Ber. What, are there but three ?
Cost. No, sir ; but it is vara fine,
For every one pursents three.
Ber. And three times thrice is nine.
Cost. Not so, sir ; under correction, sir, I hope it is not so.
You cannot beg us, sir, I can assure you, sir ; we know what we know :
I hope, sir, three times thrice, sir,—
Ber. Is not nine.
Cost. Under correction, sir, we know whereuntil it doth amount.
Ber. By Jove, I always took three threes for nine.

491. *hope, sir*] *hope* Ff 3, 4.

to have been seized upon by fools and fops, who found in it a means to make stylish conversation without having to commit themselves to an opinion. Jonson makes much fun of it : Asotus (*Cynthia's Revels*, I. i.) uses it to fend off compliments he finds overwhelming ; Orange (*Every Man out of his Humour*, III. i.) to keep his end up in a learned discussion. And Orange's character is thus described : " as dry an orange as ever grew : nothing but salutation, and ' O Lord, sir ! ' and ' It pleases you to say so, sir ! ' " The phrase is ridiculed again by Shakespeare in *All's Well that Ends Well*, II. ii.

486. *Worthies*] See note, v. i. 113.

488. *pursents*] presents, i.e. represents. See note, lines 499, 500.

489, 492. *under correction*] Not elsewhere in Shakespeare in this form. Probably a usual rustic apology in addressing a superior. Compare Ben Jonson, *For the Honour of Wales* (Herford and Simpson, vii. 500) : " I am a subject by my place, and two heads is better than one, I imagine, under correction." See *New Eng. Dict.* for examples, earlier, of " I speak under correction," and " under your correction " in serious language, as in *Measure for Measure*, II. ii. 10, and *Henry V.* III. ii. 130, and v. ii. 144.

490. *You cannot beg us*] Periphrastic for " we are not fools," " you cannot beg us for fools." The word " fool " is omitted here, as at line 478. The allusion is to the begging of wardship or guardianship of idiots by favourites. See Nares (*Beg*), who refers to Blackstone (i. 8, 18) for the writ *de idiota inquirendo.* Johnson says : " One of the legal tests of a natural is to try whether he can number." Compare Harington, *Metamorphosis of Ajax* (Chiswick, p. 62), 1596 : " *Stultorum plena sunt omnia :* the world is full of fools, but take heed how you beg him for a fool : for I have heard of one that was begged in the Court of Wards for a fool, and when it came to trial he proved a wiser man by much than he that begged him." And Ben Jonson, *Every Man out of his Humour*, III. i. (1599) : " He were a sweet ass : I'd beg him i' faith." The Court of Wards was established by Henry VIII., and suppressed under Charles I.

492, 498. *whereuntil*] " whereunto " occurs in *Cymbeline* twice. Such compounds were often used. Greene has " whetherto " in *Euphues his Censure* (Grosart, vi. 228) ; " whereout " occurs in Sidney's *Arcadia*, bk. iii. ; " whereunder " is in Petty's *Narration of Drake's Famous Voyage*

Cost. O Lord, sir! it were pity you should get your living by reckoning, sir.

Ber. How much is it?

Cost. O Lord, sir! the parties themselves, the actors, sir, will show whereuntil it doth amount: for mine own part, I am, as they say, but to parfect one man in one poor man, Pompion the Great, sir.

Ber. Art thou one of the Worthies?

Cost. It pleased them to think me worthy of Pompey the Great: for mine own part, I know not the degree of the Worthy, but I am to stand for him.

Ber. Go, bid them prepare.

Cost. We will turn it finely off, sir; we will take some care. [*Exit.*

King. Berowne, they will shame us; let them not approach.
Ber. We are shame-proof, my lord; and 'tis some policy
To have one show worse than the king's and his company.
King. I say they shall not come.
Prin. Nay, my good lord, let me o'er-rule you now.
That sport best pleases that doth least know how.
Where zeal strives to content, and the contents

499. *they*] *thy* Q 1. *parfect*] Q 1; *perfect* Ff, Q 2; *pursent* Grant White (Walker conjecture); *present* Collier. *in*] *e'en* Malone. 502. *Pompey*] Qq, Ff, Capell, Malone; *Pompion* Rowe (ed. 2), Cambridge, etc. 509. *king's*] *king* Ff 3, 4. 512. *least*] Ff, Q 2; *best* Q 1. 513, 514. *contents Dies . . . presents*] Qq, Ff, Cambridge, Globe (with corrupt-passage mark); *content Dies . . . presents* Rowe (ed. 1); *content Dies in the zeal of*

(Hayluyt), 1579; and in *Histrio-mastix*, Act ii.; and compare "where against" in *Coriolanus*, IV. v. 113.

495. *reckoning*] See I. ii. 39.

499. *parfect*] Probably Costard would say "perform," or "present." "Perform" for "play" (a part) occurs several times in Shakespeare.

500. *Pompion*] pumpkin (for Pompey). "The earliest example of the humour of using wrong words by ignorant people on the stage that I have noticed" (wrote Hart) "is in *Promos and Cassandra*, 1578." In Sidney's masque, *The Lady of May*, 1578 (Feuillerat, ii. 329 ff.), he attributes this foible to Rombus, a schoolmaster; and also "to Lalus, the old shepherd," who says "disnounce" for "announce," "bashless" for "bashful" (like "pursent" for "present"). There is no need to correct Costard any more than Dull or Holofernes. See above I. i. 183 and IV. ii. 92.

502. *Pompey*] Costard's indecision about his words is rather enhanced by the legitimate reading, which I see no reason to alter unless we also read "Pompion" below after he reappears in his part. Rowe (ed. 2) made the change.

513, 514. *contents . . . presents*] For a summary of the explanations, with or without alteration of the text, the reader may refer to Furness'

Dies in the zeal of that which it presents;
Their form confounded makes most form in mirth,
When great things labouring perish in their birth.
Ber. A right description of our sport, my lord.

Enter ARMADO.

Arm. Anointed, I implore so much expense of thy royal sweet breath as will utter a brace of words.

[*Converses with the King, and delivers a paper to him.*

Prin. Doth this man serve God?
Ber. Why ask you?
Prin. A' speaks not like a man of God's making.
Arm. That is all one, my fair, sweet, honey monarch; for

that it doth present Hanmer; *content Die in the zeal of them which it presents* Steevens; *content Lies in the zeal of those which it present* Mason conjecture; *contents Die in the zeal of them which it presents* Malone, Craig.
519. [*Converses* . . .] Capell; [*Talks apart with the King*] Furness. 522. *A'*] Q 1; *He* Ff, Q 2. *God's*] *God his* Q 1. 523. *That is*] Q 1. *That's* Ff, Q 2.

Variorum edition. "Contents" means here the subject-matter of the entertainment, which "dies" (as we speak of a piece being "murdered") as a result of the over-eagerness to please of those who present it. "Dies" is a "northern plural (see line 309 above); and "that" (the company of performers) is the subject, "it" (the sport) is the object, of "presents." The next couplet is a repetition, in another form, of the same idea—it is the collapse of an ambitious project that provides the best entertainment. It is the whole speech that Berowne finds applicable to the masque of Muscovites. Compare *Midsummer Night's Dream,* v. i. 81-105.

519. [*delivers a paper*] Capell inserted this in order to explain the King's speech after Armado's exit.

522. *a man of God's making*] A proverbial expression. Compare Peele, *Edward I.*, II. ii. (Bullen, i. p. 102), 1593: "My masters and friends, I am a poor friar, a man of God's making, and a good fellow as you are, legs, feet, face . . . right shape and christendom." And *The Return from Parnassus,* pt. i. (ed. W. D. Macray, p. 43), ii. 1 (1599): "Luxurio, as they say, a man of God's makinge, as they saye, came to my house, as they saye." Day has it in *The Ile of Guls* (1606), with variations: "a woman of God's making and a ladie of his own, and wearing their own haire."

523. *That is all one*] That does not matter, it is *all the same* to me. Compare Feste's refrain at the end of *Twelfth Night:* "But that's all one, Our play is done."

honey monarch] A common term of endearment still. Compare *Promos and Cassandra* (pt. i.), IV. vii. (1578): "Sweete honny Grimball . . . hony sweete Grimball"; and Sidney's *Arcadia* (Feuillerat, ii. 20): "honny Dorus tell them me." And in *Timon* (*Shakes. Lib.* 1875, p. 443), III. v.: "Art thou well pleas'd with this, my hony?" Shakespeare makes a verb of it in *Hamlet,* III. iv. 93: "honeying and making love."

I protest, the schoolmaster is exceeding fantastical; too, too vain; too, too vain: but we will put it, as they say, to *fortuna de la guerra*. I wish you the peace of mind, most royal couplement! [*Exit.*

King. Here is like to be a good presence of Worthies. He presents Hector of Troy; the swain, Pompey the Great; the parish curate, Alexander; Armado's page, Hercules; the pedant, Judas Maccabæus.
And if these four Worthies in their first show thrive,
These four will change habits, and present the other five.

Ber. There is five in the first show.

King. You are deceived, 'tis not so.

Ber. The pedant, the braggart, the hedge-priest, the fool, and the boy:—

526. *de la guerra*] Theobald, Camb., New; *delaguar* Qq, Ff; *della guerra* Hanmer, Hart. 527. [*Exit*] Capell.

525. *too, too*] The intensive reduplication occurs several times in Shakespeare, and was very common. Formerly the two words were hyphened or written as one. See *Lucrece*, 174, *Two Gentlemen of Verona*, II. iv. 205, and *Merry Wives of Windsor*, II. ii. 261.

526. *fortuna de la guerra*] Compare Ben Jonson, *Case is Altered*, I. i. (1598): "*Juniper.* Valentine, I prithee ruminate thyself welcome. What, *fortuna de la guerra!*" Juniper's business is to ridicule "forced words." The expression occurs in Middleton's *More Dissemblers besides Women*, V. i. (1623); and in a letter dated 1624 in *Court and Times of James I*, ii. 461, but on both occasions is given its Italian form. Sometimes it is rendered in English: "Once again to prove the fortune of warre" (M. Lok, 1612 [Hakluyt (ed. 1812), v. 391]).

527. *couplement*] couple. *New Eng. Dict.* cites Spenser, *Faerie Queene*, VI. v. 24: "And forth together rode, a comely couplement."

528. *Worthies*] see above, V. i. 113.

535. *You are deceived*] The inability to count of the comic characters in this play was first pointed out by the two editors of the *New Cambridge Shakespeare*. Armado, in I. ii. admits he is "ill at reckoning," and Costard, in lines 489-495 above, unwittingly betrays the same weakness. Here the malady seems to have spread to the King. See Introduction, 5.23.

536. *The pedant, the braggart*] These are generic names of stock characters in Italian comedy. They appear often elsewhere in this play as headings to the speeches of Holofernes and of Armado. Both characters clearly owe something to Italian models. See Introduction 4.32. The heading "Boy" is similarly used in several places to designate Moth, while Nathaniel and Costard appear as "Curate" and "Clown."

hedge-priest] Ascham uses this term in *The Scholemaster* (Arber, p. 136): "and therefore did som of them at Cambridge (whom I will not name openlie) cause hedge-priestes sette out of the contrie, to be made fellowes in the universitie" (1568). A contemptuous term for those plying their business under hedges or by the roadside. Compare

Abate throw at novum, and the whole world again
Cannot pick out five such, take each one in his vein.
King. The ship is under sail, and here she comes amain.

Enter COSTARD *for Pompey.*

Cost. I Pompey am,—
Ber. You lie, you are not he.
Cost. I Pompey am,—
Boyet. With libbard's head on knee.

538. *Abate*] Qq, F 1; *A bare* Ff 2, 3, 4; *Abate a* Malone. 539. *pick*] Q 1; *prick* Ff, Q 2. *in his*] Q 1; *in 's* Ff, Q 2. 541. *Ber.*] *Bero.* Q 1; *Ber.* F 1, Q 2; *Boyet* Ff 2, 3, 4.

hedge-school, *hedge-schoolmaster*, etc. Nashe has the expression "hedge rakt up termes" (McKerrow, iii. 27) to express illiterateness.

538. *Abate throw at novum*] Except for the throw at "novum"—as we might say, "bar a throw."

novum] "A game at dice properly called *novem quinque*, from the two principal throws being nine and five" (*Schmidt*). It looks as if a throw of five might in some circumstances stand for nine, just as Armado's five players were to stand for the nine Worthies—hence Berowne's joke.

541. *Berowne*] The majority of editors have unreasonably followed the second Folio in giving this retort to Boyet. Berowne and Boyet here join forces in mocking the Worthies, and it is this alliance that reconciles them.

You lie] Staunton suggested that the point of this must rest in a piece of stage-business: that "Pompey," on entering, trips over his accoutrements and falls prostrate. The pun is certainly a favourite with Shakespeare; compare *Hamlet*, v. i. 131, and *Othello*, III. iv. 1.

542. *libbard's head*] leopard's head. "In old French, the language alike of heraldry and of our early statutes, the term *leopart* means a lion passant guardant. . . . The *leopard's head*, therefore, is properly the head of a lion passant guardant, which in fact is a lion's front face" (Cripps, *Old English Plate*, p. 46 [1891]). J. Bossewell, however, *Workes of Armorie*, 1572, says a leopard is a cross between lion and pard (a kind of panther). Presumably Boyet is referring to "arms" traditionally borne by Pompey, as were the lion and axe by Alexander (see note on lines 570-1). Pompey's arms are given by S. Daniel in a preface to his translation (1585) of Paolo Giovio's *Dialogo dell' Imprese Militari et Amorose* (B ii^{v}) as "a Lyon with a sword clasped in his claw"; and Daniel is not alone in taking Pompey's signet-ring, as described by Plutarch, for an *impresa*, or badge, "Ensifer Leo." John Ferne, *The Blazon of Gentrie* (1586), p. 197, describes Pompey's "insigne, and banner of Armes" as "in a field Gewles, a Lyon erected Or, holding a swoord, point in chefe argent, poigne de purpre." Though I cannot find Pompey's lion anywhere described as "passant guardant," I suspect that Costard bore some such figure on his shield, and that the text covers more stage-business (see preceding note). As he struggles to his feet again, Costard may hold his shield either clutched to his knee, or outstretched, as if offering the Princess a platter

Ber. Well said, old mocker: I must needs be friends with thee.
Cost. I Pompey am, Pompey surnam'd the Big,—
Dum. The Great.
Cost. It is "Great," sir; Pompey surnam'd the Great;
That oft in field, with targe and shield, did make my foe to sweat:
And travelling along this coast, I here am come by chance
And lay my arms before the legs of this sweet lass of France.
If your ladyship would say, "Thanks, Pompey,"
I had done.
Prin. Great thanks, great Pompey.
Cost. 'Tis not so much worth; but I hope I was perfect.
I made a little fault in "Great."
Ber. My hat to a halfpenny, Pompey proves the best Worthy.

Enter Sir NATHANIEL *for Alexander.*

Nath. When in the world I liv'd, I was the world's commander;
By east, west, north, and south, I spread my conquering might:
My scutcheon plain declares that I am Alisander,—
Boyet. Your nose says, no, you are not; for it stands too right.

"on the knee." Theobald quoted Cotgrave: "*Masquine.* The representation of a lion's head, &c., upon the elbow, or knee of some old-fashioned garments." In Sherwood's *English-French Dictionary* (1672) this is given "A libbard's head (on the knees or elbows . . .), *Masquine.*" See note at "vane," IV. i. 94 for an illustration of the second suggestion.

548. *targe*] shield. Common in earlier writers.

556. *My hat to a halfpenny*] Halliwell quotes from Lodge, *Wits Miserie* (p. 63), 1596: "Hee is the only man living to bring you where the best licour is, and it is his hat to a halfe penny but hee will be drunke for companie." See note at "I'll lay my head to any good man's hat" (I. i. 291). Berowne seems to be fond of betting in hats. Caps were commoner in this connection; perhaps earlier.

560. *nose . . . stands too right*] refers to a well-known physical peculiarity of Alexander. Compare North's *Plutarch*, 1579: "Lysippus . . . hath perfectly drawn and resembled Alexander's manner of holding his neck, somewhat hanging down towards the left side" (Temple edition, vii. 5). And in De la Primaudaye's *French Academy*, 1577 (trans. T. B., chap. xiii. [1586]): "Wee reade that Alexander the Great and Alphonsus, King of Arragon, having each of them somewhat a wry necke, this by

Ber. Your nose smells " no," in this, most tender-smelling knight.

Prin. The conqueror is dismay'd. Proceed, good Alexander.

Nath. When in the world I liv'd, I was the world's commander,—

Boyet. Most true ; 'tis right : you were so, Alisander.

Ber. Pompey the Great,—

Cost. Your servant, and Costard.

Ber. Take away the conqueror, take away Alisander.

Cost. [*To Nathaniel.*] O ! sir, you have overthrown Alisander the conqueror. You will be scraped out of the painted cloth for this : your lion, that holds his poll-axe sitting on a close-stool, will be given to Ajax : he

561. *this*] ; Ff, Q 2 *his* Q 1.

nature, the other through custome, the flatterers and courtiers held their necks on the one side, to counterfeit that imperfection." This part of the *French Academy* has been utilized by Robert Greene, and the above passage will be found in his *Tritameron*, part ii. (1587) (Grosart, iii. 148). Puttenham refers to the feature in *The Arte of English Poesie* (Arber, p. 302), 1589 : " It was misliked in the Emperor Nero, and thought uncomely for him to counterfet Alexander the Great, by holding his head a little awrie, and neerer toward the tone shoulder, because it was not his owne naturall." Steevens first drew attention to this point.

561. *Your nose smells " no "*] Compare again North's *Plutarch, ut supra :* " I remember I read also in the commentaries of Aristoxenus, that his skin had a marvellous good savour, and that his breath was very sweet, insomuch that his body had so sweet a smell of it self, that all the apparel he wore next unto his body, took thereof a passing delightful savour." Berowne suggests it is *Boyet's* nose, and delicate sense of smell, that detects the impostor.

570. *painted cloth*] cloth or canvas, variously painted in oil, and used as hangings, or for decoration, or in forming partitions in interiors. This may be taken as the exact sense here, on account of the words " scraped out," but the term was also used of the arras or tapestry (in spite of Dyce's *Glossary*) which formed the hangings in many cases. " The Nine Worthies " was a favourite subject : " Thou woven worthy in a piece of Arras, Fit only to enjoy a wall " (*The Double Marriage*, IV. iii. [Waller, *Beaumont and Fletcher*, vi. 384]). Alexander was the chiefest worthy. Compare Whitlock, *Zootomia* (p. 171), 1654, quoted by Nares : " That Alexander was a souldier, painted cloths will confesse ; the painter dareth not leave him out of the nine worthies."

570, 571. *lion . . . close-stool*] In Gerard Legh's *Accedens of Armourye*, 1563, the arms of the worthies are given : " The fourth was Alexander, the which did beare Geules, a lion or, seiante in a chayer, holding a battle-ax argent." Legh's treatise had been republished in 1591. See also Introduction 5.21.

571. *Ajax*] punning on a *jakes*, an old name for a privy. The word occurs again in *King Lear*, II. ii. 72. The quibble became very common from the title of a work by Sir John Harington, *The Metamorphosis*

will be the ninth Worthy. A conqueror, and afeard to speak! run away for shame, Alisander. [*Nathaniel retires.*] There, an't shall please you: a foolish mild man; an honest man, look you, and soon dashed! He is a marvellous good neighbour, faith, and a very good bowler; but, for Alisander,—alas! you see how 'tis,—a little o'erparted. But there are Worthies a-coming will speak their mind in some other sort.

Prin. Stand aside, good Pompey.

Enter HOLOFERNES *for Judas, and* MOTH *for Hercules.*

Hol. Great Hercules is presented by this imp,
Whose club kill'd Cerberus, that three-headed *canus*;
And, when he was a babe, a child, a shrimp,

572. *afeard*] Q 1; *afraid* Ff, Q 2. 573. [*Nath. retires*] Capell. 576. *faith*] Q 1; *in sooth*] Ff, Q 2.
577. *'tis*] Johnson, Cambridge; *tis* Q 1, Ff; *it's* Q 2; *'tis;* Capell, Steevens. 582. *canus*] Qq, Ff.; *canis* Rowe, Cambridge.

of Ajax, 1596. See Nashe's *Works* (McKerrow, iii. 38). "The pithie tractate of *Ajax*," as Henry Hutton calls it, is constantly referred to by contemporary writers. Sir John was forbidden the Court for it, but in 1598 his friend Robert Markham wrote to him, saying, "Your book is almost forgiven and I may say forgotten, but not for its lacke of wit or satyr . . . and tho' her Highness signified displeasure in outward sort, yet did she like 'the marrow of your book'" (*Nugæ Antiquæ*, ii. 287) (1779). Sir John Harington may have borrowed his quibble from this passage, but likely enough it was common property earlier.

575-7. *an honest man . . . and a very good bowler*] "*An honest man and a good bowler*" occurs in Clarke's *Parœmiologia*, 1639 (*Centurie of Prayse*). Probably in general use before Shakespeare. "Good bowler" may mean no more than "a good sport."

575. *dashed*] dispirited, disheartened. See above, line 462, for a slightly different use. Compare *Othello*, III. iii. 214.

578. *o'erparted*] given too difficult a part. Compare Ben Jonson, *Bartholomew Fair*, III. i. (1614) (Herford and Simpson, vi. 69): "*Quarlous*. How now, Numps! almost tir'd i' your Protectorship? overparted? overparted?" *New Eng. Dict.* quotes this.

581, 582. *Hercules . . . club*] See note at V. i. 113. Hercules with his club was another favourite in the painted cloth, or "worm-eaten tapestry" (*Much Ado About Nothing*, III. iii. 145, 146).

581. *imp*] See I. ii. 5 (note).

583. *shrimp*] Compare *1 Henry VI*. II. iii. 23: "Alas, this is a child, a silly dwarf! It cannot be this weak and writhled shrimp Should strike such terror to his enemies." Gabriel Harvey uses it in *Pierce's Supererogation* (Grosart, ii. 46), 1592: "Agrippa was an urcheon, Copernicus a shrimpe, Cardan a puppy, Scaliger a baby, Paracelsus a scab, Erastus a patch, Sigonius a toy, Cuiacius a patch to this Termagant." And in *How a Man may Chuse a Good Wife* (Hazlitt's *Dodsley*, ix. 40),

Thus did he strangle serpents in his *manus*.
Quoniam he seemeth in minority,
Ergo I come with this apology.
Keep some state in thy exit, and vanish. [*Moth retires.*
Judas I am,—
Dum. A Judas!
Hol. Not Iscariot, sir.
Judas I am, ycleped Maccabæus.
Dum. Judas Maccabæus clipt is plain Judas.
Ber. A kissing traitor. How, art thou prov'd Judas?
Hol. Judas I am,—
Dum. The more shame for you, Judas.
Hol. What mean you, sir?
Boyet. To make Judas hang himself.
Hol. Begin, sir; you are my elder.
Ber. Well follow'd: Judas was hang'd on an elder.
Hol. I will not be put out of countenance.

593. *prov'd*] F 2; *proud* Q 1; *prou'd* F 1, Q 2.

1602: "That shrimp, that spindle-shank, that wren, that sheep biter, that lean chitty-face."

590. *Not Iscariot*] From John xiv. 22, as Furnivall notes.

592. *clipt*] The two senses, to shear and to embrace, are quibbled with, as well as the word-play with "cleped."

593. *A kissing traitor*] A "Judas kiss" became proverbial at an early date. Compare *The Booke in Meeter of Robin Conscience* (Hazlitt, *Early Popular Poetry*, iii. 245), *circa* 1550: "And that you have given him many a Judas kisse Your act will declare how you have done amisse."

How, art thou proved] Now then, haven't I proved you are Judas? "Judas clipt" is kissing Judas, the traitor.

598. *you are my elder*] a proverbial bit of chaff. Compare Lyly's *Endymion*, II. ii.: "You will be mine elder, because you stand upon a stoole." And see *Comedy of Errors*, V. i. 420. Still in use?

599. *Judas . . . elder*] An old legend. Dyce quoted *Sir John Mandevill* (E.E. Text Soc., p. 61), 1364: "And faste by is zit the Tree of Eldre, that Judas henge him self upon, for despeyr that he hadde whan he solde and betrayed oure lord." See also *The Vision of Piers the Plowman* (edited Skeat, i. 26): "Judas he japede with the Iewes seluer, And on an ellerne treo hongede him after." And in Shakespeare's time in Marlowe, *Jew of Malta*, IV. vi. 68 (Case ed., p. 145): "The hat he wears, Judas left under the elder when he hanged himself"; and Ben Jonson, *Every Man out of his Humour*, IV. iv.: "He shall be your Judas, and you shall be his elder-tree to hang on." Brand quotes from Gerard's *Herbal*, ed. Johnson, p. 1428: "The *Arbor Judæ* [*Cercis siliquastrum*] is thought to be that whereon Judas hanged himself, and not upon the elder-tree, as it is vulgarly said." It is doubtful, to say the least of it, if our elder grew within reach of Judas. It is not native in Palestine.

Ber. Because thou hast no face.
Hol. What is this?
Boyet. A cittern-head.
Dum. The head of a bodkin.
Ber. A death's face in a ring.
Long. The face of an old Roman coin, scarce seen.
Boyet. The pommel of Cæsar's falchion.

607. *falchion*] *fauchion* Q 1 ; *faulchion* Ff, Q 2.

603-11. This personal description of Holofernes recalls that of Gabriel Harvey by Nashe in *Have With You to Saffron Walden* (McKerrow, iii. 73, etc.). But there is much to be said against the identification. See Introduction 5.22.

603. *cittern-head*] "The cittern had usually a head grotesquely carved at the extremity of the neck and finger-board" (Nares). Nares cites several parallels and compares Gargantua's lamentation for "Badebec, who had a face like a rebec" (Motteux's *Rabelais*, ii. 24). See Marston's *Scourge of Villainy* (Bullen's *Marston*, iii. 301): "Shall brainless cittern-heads, each jobbernoul, Pocket the very genius of thy soul?" And Dekker, *Match mee in London*, Act i. (Pearson, iv. 137): "Fidling at least half an hour on a citterne with a man's broken head at it, so that I think 'twas a barber surgeon"; and see Fletcher's *Love's Cure:* "You cittern-head, you ill-countenanced cur." For a description of this musical instrument, somewhat like the guitar, see Chappell's *Popular Music* [1859], i. 101.

604. *head of a bodkin*] Bodkins, long jewelled pins for ladies' hair, appear abundantly as New Year's gifts to Queen Elizabeth from 1580 to 1590. See Nichols' *Progresses of Queen Elizabeth*, ii. 289-499. The heads or tops were various in form, often flowers in gold or small precious stones. In 1586-7 two occur: "Item twoe bodkins of golde, th' one a flye, th' other a spider," and "a bodkinne of silver with a little ostridge of gold." They seem to have been very fashionable at this especial period. Compare here Florio's *New World of Words:* "*Puntarvolo*, a bodkin, a head-needle, a goldsmith's pouncer. Also a nice, a coy, or selfe-conceited fellow, a man that stands upon nice faultes, a finde-faulte, a carper, a scrupulous, over-weening man."

605. *death's face in a ring*] Death's head rings, with the motto *memento mori*, were in early popularity. See *1 Henry IV.* III. iii. 34, 35; *Merchant of Venice*, I. ii. 55; and *2 Henry IV.* II. iv. 255. An early example found by Hart is in Greene's *Farewell to Follie* (Grosart, ix. 239), 1591: "The olde Countesse spying on the finger of Seignior Cosimo a ring with a death's head ingraven, circled with this poesie, *Gressus ad vitam.*" And see Greene's *Never Too Late* (Grosart, viii. 30) for the real thing: "I have in my cell A dead man's scull which calls this straight to mind That as this is so must my ending be."

607. *Cæsar's falchion*] I presume this is also from a painted cloth representation of Cæsar. Cæsar's sword is, however, famous in legend. Bayle says (*Dictionary of History*, ed. 1735, ii. 419, note): "I forgot an Act of Religion which is very curious. The Arverni boasted to have Julius Cæsar's sword, and showed it still in Plutarch's time, hung up in one of their Temples. Cæsar saw it and laughed but would not suffer his Men to take it away. He considered

Dum. The carved bone face on a flask.
Ber. Saint George's half-cheek in a brooch.
Dum. Ay, and in a brooch of lead.
Ber. Ay, and worn in the cap of a toothdrawer.
And now, forward; for we have put thee in countenance.
Hol. You have put me out of countenance.
Ber. False: we have given thee faces.
Hol. But you have outfaced them all.
Ber. An thou wert a lion, we would do so.
Boyet. Therefore, as he is, an ass, let him go.

608. *carved bone*] *carv'd-bone* Qq, Ff. 617. *as he is, an ass*] Q 1, Ff 1, 2; *as he is an ass* Q 2, Ff 3, 4.

it as consecrated Thing" (Plutarch, in *Apoph.* p. 720 E). It is a long jump from this to the days of Smollett. In *Peregrine Pickle*, chap. xxxiv. (1750), this sword is in our own country: "The company walked up hill to visit [Dover] castle, where they saw the sword of Julius Cæsar, and Queen Elizabeth's pocket pistol." Cæsar was much more in evidence in Elizabethan times than now; existing popularly perhaps, only in "as dead as Julius Cæsar." But in those days Cæsar's wine was at Dover (H. Peacham, in *Coryat*). Cæsar's bread (gone sour) is in Beaumont and Fletcher and in Ben Jonson. Deloney saw salt and wine in the Tower of London which had been there ever since Cæsar left it: "the wine was grown so thick it might have been cut like a jelly." Nashe mentions the wine also. Cæsar's salt beef is in Beaumont and Fletcher's *Love Pilgrimage*. His money is in *The Jests of George Peele.* These imaginings did not arise from any pictorial Cæsar.

608. *carved bone on a flask*] See *Romeo and Juliet*, III. iii. 132. Cotgrave has "*Flasque*, as *Flascon;* also, a flask, or box, for powder." There are several prints of early flasks in Demmin's *Arms and Armour* (pp. 535, 536, Bell's ed. 1877). Some are of horn of the end of the sixteenth century, of German origin, all ornamented with carved work. One is a "German primer" of this period inlaid with ivory, circular, with a grotesque central face.

609. *half-cheek*] profile, side-face. The same as "half-face" in *King John*, I. i. 94.

brooch] an ornament or jewel often worn in the hat; or a badge of leather or pewter to indicate the wearer's business. Compare Dekker's *If this be not a good Play* (Pearson, iii. 289): "The cittie water-bearers (trimly dight) With yellow oaken tankards (pind upright) Like brooches in their hats." See next note.

610, 611. *brooch of lead . . . in the cap of a toothdrawer*] Compare Taylor, *Wit and Mirth* (Hazlitt's repr. p. 62), 1630: "In Queen Elizabeth's dayes, there was a fellow that wore a brooch in his hat like a toothdrawer, with a Rose and Crown and two letters: this fellow had a warrant from the Lord Chamberlaine at that time to travell with an exceeding brave ape which hee had; whereby hee gat his living from time to time at markets and fayres." Evidently the common badge of the trade.

613. *out of countenance*] See above, line 272.

616, 617. *lion . . . ass*] Suggested by Æsop's fable of the ass in the lion's skin. Compare Nashe, *Foure*

And so adieu, sweet Jude! nay, why dost thou stay?
Dum. For the latter end of his name.
Ber. For the ass to the Jude? give it him:—Jud-as, away!
Hol. This is not generous, not gentle, not humble.
Boyet. A light for Monsieur Judas! it grows dark, he may stumble. [*Holofernes retires.*
Prin. Alas! poor Maccabæus, how hath he been baited.

Enter ARMADO *for Hector.*

Ber. Hide thy head, Achilles: here comes Hector in arms.
Dum. Though my mocks come home by me, I will now be merry.
King. Hector was but a Troyan in respect of this.
Boyet. But is this Hector?
King. I think Hector was not so clean-timbered.
Long. His leg is too big for Hector's.
Dum. More calf, certain.
Boyet. No; he is best indued in the small.

627. 665. *Troyan*] Qq, Ff; *Trojan* Rowe, etc. 630. *Hector's*] Capell, Cambridge; *Hectors* Q 1; *Hector* Ff, Q 2. 632. *in*] *with* Ff 3, 4.

Letters Confuted (McKerrow, i. 290), 1593: "steale Tully, steale Tully, away with the Asse in the Lions skinne." And Ben Jonson, *Case is Altered*: "put off this lion's head, your ears have discovered you." The application of the fable is generally as here, when the lion is found to be an ass he is told to clear out. Another quibble is suggested here by Furnivall, from Heywood's *Proverbs and Epigrams*, 1562 (Spenser Soc. p. 92): "An ass was given to a rapacious governor named Jude," etc. A standing joke. Lyly has the same quibble on the name Mydas (iv. 1).

621. *humble*] "courteous, benevolent, kind" (Schmidt). The context suggests this meaning, but no such sense is admitted in *New Eng. Dict.* See line 727 below.

622. *Monsieur Judas*] The frequent use of "Monsieur" reminds us we are in France.

dark . . . stumble] perhaps refers to St. John II, *v.* 10: "If a man walk in the night, he stumbleth"; and 13, *v.* 30: "Judas having received the sop went immediately out, and it was night."

625. *Come home by me*] come back on my own head, like a boomerang.

627. *Troyan*] merely an ordinary kind of good fellow. See line 665 below.

629. *clean-timbered*] well-built. Compare Ben Jonson, *Every Man out of his Humour*, Induction: "O, good words, good words; a well-timbered fellow, he would have made a good column"; and Greene, *A Quip for an Upstart Courtier* (Grosart, xi. 290): "His Comrade that bare him company was a iolly light timber'd Iack a Napes."

631. *calf*] fool; as well as part of leg.

632. *small*] the part of the leg below the calf (Schmidt). The

Ber. This cannot be Hector.
Dum. He's a god or a painter ; for he makes faces.
Arm. The armipotent Mars, of lances the almighty,
Gave Hector a gift,—
Dum. A gilt nutmeg.
Ber. A lemon.

637. *A gilt nutmeg*] Ff, Q 2 ; *A gift nutmeg* Q 1.

expression occurs twice in Sidney's *Arcadia*, bk. i. (*ante* 1586) : " in her going one might sometimes discerne the smal of her leg, which with the foot was dressed in a short paire of crimson velvet buskins " (Feuillerat, i. 75) ; and in bk. v. : " Pyrocles came out led by Sympathus, cloathed after the Greeke manner, in a long coate of white velvet, reaching to the small of his legge " (ii. 169). Craig noted another instance in Hakluyt (Maclehose ed., vi. 4) : " about their armes and smalles of their legs they have hoops of golde " (*Voyage of John Eldred*, 1583).

634. *He's . . . faces*] Proverbial, in Fuller's *Gnomologia*. See *Mery Tales, Wittie Questions and Quicke Answeres, Very Pleasant to be Readde*, 1567 (*circa* 1540), edited W. C. Hazlitt, 1864, pp. 106-7 ; and Taylor, *The Sculler*, 1612 (iii. 22 [1630]).

635. *armipotent*] a title of Mars. It occurs in Chaucer's *Knight's Tale*, ii. 24 : " Ther stood the tempul of Marz armypotent."

637. *gilt*] Hart wrote : " A sense of *gild*, equivalent to the old cookery term ' endore,' which seems to have escaped the dictionaries and commentators. The term is used by Hugh Plat (*Delights for Ladies*), 1600 ; *The Art of Preserving* (ed. 1611) : ' a, 13. The making of sugar-plate, and casting thereof in carved moldes. . . . Set it (the paste) against the fire till it bee dry on the inside, then with a knife get it out as they used to doe a dish of butter, and drie the backside, then gilde it on the edges with the white of an egge laide round about the brim of the dish with a pensile, and presse the golde downe with some cotton, & when it is drie skew or brush off the golde with the foote of an Hare or Conie.' Probably, though not so stated, saffron was used. No gold was used in this gilding. Was there ever any in the '*gilded pill*' ? Yolk of egg, quicksilver and salt armoniak are the ingredients. Hence the gilded rosemary, gilt wheat, gilded bride-branches, etc., of Ben Jonson and others. And in Nichols' *Progresses*, ii. 78 : ' a greate pye of quynses and wardyns guilt ' (1577-8)."

gilt nutmeg] Compare Ben Jonson, *The Gipsies Metamorphosed*, 1621 : " I have lost an inchanted nutmeg, all gilded over, was inchanted at Oxford for me, to put in my sweetheart's ale a mornings." In an *Account of Receipts* (*Harleian Miscellany*, vii. 159) " A dozen of gilt nutmegs " occurs in 1660. See last note. No doubt the nutmeg lasted a long time, a slight sprinkle of the strong flavour being sufficient in ale, port-wine, etc. The gilding may have been a preservative from the effects of atmosphere, from dust, and also ornamental.

638, 639. *lemon. Stuck with cloves*] Oranges were more commonly used in this manner, but oranges and lemons seem to have been used indiscriminately for the same purposes. In the little volume of Hugh Plat, quoted from at line 637, we are told what the use of the orange stuck with cloves was. It was, like the nutmeg, for the ale. See (a, 32) : " *Divers excellent kindes of bottle Ale*. . . . Some commende the hanging

Long. Stuck with cloves.
Dum. No, cloven.
Arm. Peace!
The armipotent Mars, of lances the almighty,
Gave Hector a gift, the heir of Ilion;
A man so breath'd that certain he would fight; yea
From morn till night, out of his pavilion.
I am that flower,—
Dum. That mint.
Long. That columbine.
Arm. Sweet Lord Longaville, rein thy tongue.
Long. I must rather give it the rein, for it runs against Hector.
Dum. Ay, and Hector's a greyhound.
Arm. The sweet war-man is dead and rotten; sweet

641. *Peace!*] omitted Ff, Q 2. 644. *fight; yea*] Qq, Ff, Steevens, Cambridge, Globe; *fight ye* Rowe (ed. 2), Dyce, etc.

of roasted Oranges prickt full of cloves in the vessel of ale, till you finde the taste thereof sufficientlie graced to your owne liking." Halliwell quotes from Bradwell, 1636, that a lemon stuck with cloves was a good thing to smell occasionally against pestilence; and Dr. Rawlinson states that the executioner of Charles I. found an orange full of cloves in the king's pocket. More to the purpose is Steevens' extract from Lupton's *Notable Things:* "Wine wyll be pleasant in taste and flavour if an orenge or a lymon (stickt round about with cloaves) be hanged within the vessell that it touch not the wyne. And so the wyne wyll be preserved from foystines and evyll savor" (ii. 36 [1595]). H. B. Charlton suggested (M.L.R., xii. [1917]) that in offering *drinkers'* aids the jokers pun on the hint of potations in "armi*potent*." See *Othello,* II. iii. 80, "potent in potting."

644. *breath'd*] in such good wind and condition that he would fight, yea from morn to night. The alteration to "ye" enfeebles the sense. For "breathed" see *Taming of the Shrew,* Induction, ii. 50: *Venus and Adonis,* 678, etc. Compare the old play of *The Taming of a Shrew,* 1594 (*Shakes. Lib.* 1875, p. 165), I. i.: "Make the long breathde Tygre broken winded."

645. *pavilion*] the ceremonial tent from which the champion issued to the lists. This Hector is the hero of the medieval romances, not of the *Iliad.*

646. *columbine*] Compare *A Twelfe Night Merriment* (*Narcissus*), 1602 (ed. M. Lee, 1893): "Looke, O thou flower of favour, thou marigold of mercye and columbine of compassion, looke, O loke on the dolourous dewe dropps distilld from the limbeckes of loopeholes of their eyes." A very popular flower at this time.

650. *Hector . . . greyhound*] This name is given in a "Catalogue of some general Names of Hounds and Beagles" in *The Gentleman's Recreation,* by Nicholas Cox, p. 14, ed. 1721.

651. *war-man*] See *The Troublesome Raigne of King John,* 1591 (*Shakes. Lib.* 1875, p. 294): "Here comes the warmen all." And again at pp. 306, 308.

chucks, beat not the bones of the buried; when he breathed, he was a man. But I will forward with my device. Sweet royalty, bestow on me the sense of hearing. [*Berowne steps forth*

Prin. Speak, brave Hector; we are much delighted.

Arm. I do adore thy sweet grace's slipper.

Boyet. Loves her by the foot.

Dum. He may not by the yard.

Arm. This Hector far surmounted Hannibal,
The party is gone—

Cost. Fellow Hector, she is gone; she is two months on her way.

Arm. What meanest thou?

Cost. Faith, unless you play the honest Troyan, the

652, 653. *when he . . . man*] Q 1, Capell *et seq.*; omitted Ff, Q 2. 655. [*Berowne steps forth*] Q 1; [*Berowne steps to Costard and whispers him*] Capell; [*Berowne whispers Costard*] Steevens, Craig; omitted Cambridge, Globe.

dead and rotten] Not again in Shakespeare. See Harrison's *Description of England*, bk. ii. chap. iii. (New Shakes. Soc. p. 88), 1577-87: "I tell you, sirs, that I judge no land in England better bestowed than that which is given to our universities; for by their maintenance our realme shall be well governed when we be dead and rotten." A speech of King Henry the Eighth.

652. *chucks*] See v. i. 106.

655. [*Berowne steps forth*] See note on line 661.

659. *by the yard*] More "talking greasily." "Yard," like "prick" (IV. i. 131-7), is the organ of generation.

661. *The party is gone*] Granville Barker's explanation of this (*Prefaces to Shakespeare*, I. p. 46) is dramatically the most convincing. The Quarto prints the words in italics, and centred. They are generally taken to be a stage direction; but were it not for the centring (which may be a blunder) they would clearly be a continuation of Hector's speech (also in italics), here interrupted by Costard. He hears "Hector" claim to have "surmounted" somebody, a word that he interprets as meaning the same as the "mounted" of *Cymbeline*, II. v. 17. When Armado proceeds to say that "the party is gone" in consequence, Costard cannot resist breaking in with "Indeed she is—two months gone." His outburst would then be directly prompted by Armado's speech, and there is no need of the elaborate preparation provided by Capell at line 655 except as a gloss on the enigmatic direction in the Quarto at that point.

665. *Troyan*] "Trojan" generally stood for a "good fellow" amongst Shakespeare's contemporaries, and see *I Henry IV*. II. i. 77. This is the sense here also, but hardly in *Henry V*. v. i. 20, 32, unless Pistol means by "base Trojan," thou disgrace to good fellows. See line 627, above, for another slang example. References may be given to Ben Jonson, *Every Man in his Humour*, IV. ii; Dekker. *Gentle Craft* (Pearson p. 42); Heywood, *Woman Killed with Kindness*;

poor wench is cast away: she's quick; the child brags in her belly already: 'tis yours.

Arm. Dost thou infamonize me among potentates? Thou shalt die.

Cost. Then shall Hector be whipped for Jaquenetta that is quick by him, and hanged for Pompey that is dead by him.

Dum. Most rare Pompey!

Boyet. Renowned Pompey!

Ber. Greater than great, great, great, great Pompey! Pompey the Huge!

Dum. Hector trembles.

Ber. Pompey is moved. More Ates, more Ates! stir them on! stir them on!

Dum. Hector will challenge him.

Ber. Ay, if a' have no more man's blood in his belly than will sup a flea.

Arm. By the north pole, I do challenge thee.

Cost. I will not fight with a pole, like a northern man:

679. *on! stir*] Rowe; *or stir* Qq, Ff. 681. *in his*] Q 1; *in's* Ff, Q 2.

Marston, *Pasquil and Katherine*; Kemp, *Nine Daies Morrice*, etc. In all these the name is friendly, or gives the idea of some liking.

668. *infamonize*] Armado's perversion of "infamize," to defame. Nashe, who was great at verbs in *ize* (see III. i. 49), seems to have coined "infamize": "There is no other unlascivious use or end of poetry, but to infamize vice, and magnifie vertue" (*Foure Letters Confuted* [McKerrow, i. 285], 1592-3). He has it again later in *Have With You to Saffron Walden* (McKerrow, iii. 31), 1596: "Baffull and infamize my name when I am in heaven." Gabriel Harvey, Nashe's antagonist, seized on it in his list of expressions from Nashe held up to ridicule in *Pierce's Supererogation* (Grosart, ii. 276), 1593: "infamizers of vice." This is a reply to Nashe's *Foure Letters Confuted*.

676. *Pompey the Huge*] See above, line 545. Marston recalls this in *The Malcontent* I. i. (1604): "And run the wildgoose-chase even with Pompey the Huge." For a similar mock-heroic use see Jonson's *Sejanus*, V. viii. 3: "To tender your All Hail in the wide hall Of huge Sejanus."

678. *Ates*] the spirits of discord and strife.

682. *sup a flea*] Compare *Twelfth Night*, III. ii. 61. For "sup" used transitively, see *Taming of the Shrew*, Induction, i. 28.

684. *fight with a pole, like a northern man*] Hart's note ran: "I am not satisfied there is any reference here to the quarter-staff, as Halliwell suggested, which was expressly a Devonshire and western game. See *New Eng. Dict.* for quotation from *Dicke of Devonshire*, 1626, who calls it "my own country weapon"; and see Strutt's *Sports and Pastimes* for further proof. The reference is rather to outlaws and

I'll slash; I'll do it by the sword. I bepray you, let me borrow my arms again.

Dum. Room for the incensed Worthies!

Cost. I'll do it in my shirt.

Dum. Most resolute Pompey!

Moth. Master, let me take you a button-hole lower. Do you not see Pompey is uncasing for the combat? What mean you? you will lose your reputation.

Arm. Gentlemen and soldiers, pardon me; I will not combat in my shirt.

Dum. You may not deny it; Pompey hath made the challenge.

Arm. Sweet bloods, I both may and will.

Ber. What reason have you for't?

Arm. The naked truth of it is, I have no shirt. I go woolward for penance.

685. *bepray*] Q 1; *pray* Ff, Q 2, Cambridge.

thieves. Boorde says, speaking of "a Scotishe man" (*Boke of Knowledge*, chap. iv. [1542]): "In these partyes be many out lawes and strong theeves, for much of their lyving standeth by stelyng and robbyng." Add to this what Harrison says (*Description of England*, bk. ii. chap. xvi. [1577-87]): "I might here speake of the excessive staves which diverse that travell by the waie doo carrie upon their shoulders, whereof some are twelve or thirteen foote long, beside the pike of twelve inches: but as they are commonlie suspected of honest men to be theeves and robbers, or at the least scarse true men which beare them; so by reason of this . . . no man travelleth by the waie without his sword, or some such weapon." The quarter-staff was about half the length of these staves. The pole here is that of the border reavers.

690. *take you a button-hole lower*] help you off with your garment, with a reference to the proverbial phrase meaning to humiliate one. Moth means that he will expose his poverty of underwear. Compare Nashe, *Pierce Penilesse* (McKerrow, i. 204): "The haire shirt will chase whordome out of their boanes, and the hard lodging on the boards take their flesh downe a button hole lower." It meant "take one down a peg." See Cotgrave in v. "*Mettre de l'eau dedans le vin là.* To temper, cool, tame or take a hole lower." Compare also "*Serrer le bouton à*" in Cotgrave, an equestrian expression, which occurs in T. B.'s translation of Primaudaye's *French Academy*, chap. xlix. (1586). In Chapman's *Humerous Days Mirth* (Parrott, ii. 60), 1599, it occurs again: "Decline me, or take me a hole lower, as the prouerbe is."

691. *uncasing*] undressing.

697. *bloods*] gallant fellows. Occurs again in *Julius Cæsar* and *King John*. Greene has it in *The Carde of Fancie* (Grosart, iv. 179), 1587: "Three of the boldest blouds in Alexandria were not able to abide the force of Clerophontes."

699, 700. *no shirt . . . go woolward for penance*] "Woolwarde, without any

Boyet. True, and it was enjoined him in Rome for want of linen; since when I'll be sworn he wore none but a dishclout of Jaquenetta's, and that a' wears next his heart for a favour.

Enter Monsieur MARCADE, *a Messenger.*

Mar. God save you, madam!
Prin. Welcome, Marcade,
But that thou interrupt'st our merriment.
Mar. I am sorry, madam; for the news I bring
Is heavy in my tongue. The king your father—
Prin. Dead, for my life!
Mar. Even so: my tale is told.
Ber. Worthies, away! The scene begins to cloud.
Arm. For mine own part, I breathe free breath. I have

702. *a'*] Q 1; *he* Ff, Q 2. 706-709. Prose in Qq, Ff.

lynnen nexte ones body (*Sans chemyse*)" (Palsgrave, 1530). See Skeat's edition of *Piers the Plowman* (ii. 247) and Nares where the word is well explained: "Dressed in wool only, without linen, often enjoined by way of penance." See a quotation from Nashe at line 690 for the similar penance of a hair shirt. Nashe has the phrase in the text also, which was evidently a standard joke: "Such as have but one shirt shall go woolward till [while] that be a washing" (*A Wonderfull Prognostication* [McKerrow, *Nashe*, iii. 189], 1591). Farmer quotes from Lodge's *Wits Miserie*, 1596: "When his shirt is a washing then he goes woolward." And Steevens, from Rowland's *Letting of Humours Blood*, 1600: "His shirt's a washing: then hee must goe woollward." Nares has it from *Witts Recreations*, 1641.

705. *Marcade*] This gentleman may be, as well as Navarre and his friends, an historical person—Abel Lefranc has found the name Mercadé or Marcadé with that of Boyet in contemporary French records. If so, the Princess should probably give him his *e* acute and so preserve the blank verse line.

713-15. *I have seen . . . soldier*] Hart's note deserves reprinting if only for the satisfaction it gave him: "Armado's character receives in this speech a pathetic touch to his credit that has not been noticed. He has been publicly insulted, and his sinfulness has found him out; and he resolves to reform and do justice to himself and Jaquenetta as a soldier, a man of honour, should. See, for the result, his next speech, as evidence of his reformation (at line 872): 'I am a votary: I have vowed to Jaquenetta to hold the plough for her sweet love three years.' This is what Armado refers to; there is no renewal here of the preceding paltry quarrel; his thoughts were as much deeper as they were more creditable. 'The little hole of discretion' may be made clearer if we give Sense 2, *New Eng. Dict.*, 'judgment of others,' to the word 'discretion,' a not uncommon early use."

seen the day of wrong through the little hole of discretion, and I will right myself like a soldier.

[*Exeunt Worthies.*

King. How fares your majesty?
Prin. Boyet, prepare: I will away to-night.
King. Madam, not so; I do beseech you, stay.
Prin. Prepare, I say. I thank you, gracious lords,
For all your fair endeavours; and entreat,
Out of a new-sad soul, that you vouchsafe
In your rich wisdom to excuse or hide
The liberal opposition of our spirits,
If over-boldly we have borne ourselves
In the converse of breath; your gentleness
Was guilty of it. Farewell, worthy lord!
A heavy heart bears not a humble tongue.
Excuse me so, coming too short of thanks
For my great suit so easily obtain'd.
King. The extreme parts of time extremely forms

714. *day*] *days* Warburton's note. *wrong*] *right* Warburton. 720. *entreat,*] *entreat:* Q 1; *entreats:* Ff; *intreats:* Q 2.
727. *not*] *but* Collier MS. *a humble*] Qq, F 1; *an humble*, Ff 2, 3, 4; *a nimble* Theobald, Camb., New. 730. *parts*] *past* Theobald; *haste* Singer; *dart* Staunton conjecture.

714. *seen the day . . . little hole*] An "old saw," equivalent to "I am no fool." Armado's application is, as might be expected, somewhat stilted. Compare Heywood's *Proverbs* (ed. Sharman, p. 45), 1546: "I see day at this little hole. For this bood [bud] sheweth what fruite will follow"; and Gabriel Harvey, *Letters* (Grosart, i. 138), 1573-80: "being on that can as soone as an other spye lighte at a little hole"; and Lyly, *Euphues and his England* (Arber, p. 318), 1580: "I can see day at a little hole, thou must halt cunningly if thou beguile a Cripple"; and as late as Ravenscroft, *Canterbury Guests*, v. 5 (1695), and Tom Browne's *Works*, ed. 1708, iii. 27 (*Pleasant Letters*, 1700).

725. *converse of breath*] intercourse of breath, conversation. Compare *Othello*, IV. ii. 5.

your gentleness] your courtesy and kindness encouraged us to be over-bold.

727. *humble*] complimentary, civil. Compare *Lucrece*, 1093-8: "True grief is fond and testy as a child," etc.; and see above, line 621, note. The inexcusable reading "nimble" has nothing to recommend it except ingenuity. Furness says of the Princess: "out of her new-sad soul she has attempted to apologize for her conduct; but she breaks off abruptly . . . saying that sorrow is not *humble*, is too self-centred for apologies, which in themselves imply humility."

730-733. *The extreme . . . arbitrate*] The necessity of a sudden decision settles all questions and hesitations. That very instant or extremity of time's limit, shapes everything to the one purpose, speedy resolve.

All causes to the purpose of his speed,
And often, at his very loose, decides
That which long process could not arbitrate :
And though the mourning brow of progeny
Forbid the smiling courtesy of love
The holy suit which fain it would convince ;
Yet since love's argument was first on foot,
Let not the cloud of sorrow justle it
From what it purpos'd ; since, to wail friends lost
Is not by much so wholesome-profitable
As to rejoice at friends but newly found.

Prin. I understand you not : my griefs are double.

Ber. Honest plain words best pierce the ear of grief ;
And by these badges understand the king.
For your fair sakes have we neglected time,
Play'd foul play with our oaths. Your beauty, ladies,
Hath much deform'd us, fashioning our humours

733. *process*] *process of time* Ff 3, 4. 740. *wholesome*] *holdsome* Q 1. 742. *double*] Qq, Ff ; *deaf* Capell ; *dull* Collier MS., Dyce, Craig ; *hear dully* Staunton conjecture. 743. *ear*] Q 1 ; *ears* Ff 1, 2, Q 2 ; *cares* Ff 3, 4. 744. *badges*] Qq, Ff ; *bodges* New.

" Extremely " has the sense of " to the extremity." Compare the King's " latest minute of the hour," below, line 777. " Forms " may be a " northern " plural, but both this and the " his " of lines 731, 732 are easily explained on the assumption that as the sentence proceeds the simple idea " time " comes to stand for " time's parts."

732. *loose*] A technical term for the discharge of an arrow, hence " the critical moment " (Schmidt). The term is used figuratively by Jonson in *The Alchemist*, ii. 1. See Puttenham, *Arte of English Poesie*, 1586-9 (Arber, p. 289) : " His [Cupid's] bent is sweete, his loose is somewhat soure, In joy begunne ends oft in wofull houre." And, again, p. 185, quoted by Dyce : " The Archers terme who is not said to finish the feate of his shot before he give the loose and deliver his arrow from his bow." Earlier, in Lyly's *Sapho and Phao*, v. i. (1581) : " this arrow . . . must Phao be stricken withal ; and cry softly to thyself in the very loose, Venus ! "

736. *convince*] establish, prove.

742. *double*] can this possibly mean " bewildering " ? The sense " deceiving " or " ambiguous " (preserved in the modern " duplicity ") is common in Shakespeare's work. Berowne's " honest " may pun on this meaning. If we take " double " literally, which is inadvisable, the Princess's second grief would be either her coming departure from the King, whose intentions she hardly understands, or a mere courtesy.

744. *badges*] emblems, symbols, the formal words by which the King (and Berowne) try to convey their real feeling. Dover Wilson's " bodges " (i.e. patchwork, *bungled* speeches) is attractive.

Even to the opposed end of our intents;
And what in us hath seem'd ridiculous,—
As love is full of unbefitting strains;
All wanton as a child, skipping and vain;
Form'd by the eye, and therefore, like the eye,
Full of strange shapes, of habits, and of forms,
Varying in subjects, as the eye doth roll
To every varied object in his glance:
Which party-coated presence of loose love
Put on by us, if, in your heavenly eyes,
Have misbecom'd our oaths and gravities,
Those heavenly eyes, that look into these faults,
Suggested us to make. Therefore, ladies,
Our love being yours, the error that love makes
Is likewise yours: we to ourselves prove false,
By being once false for ever to be true
To those that make us both,—fair ladies, you:
And even that falsehood, in itself a sin,
Thus purifies itself and turns to grace.

Prin. We have receiv'd your letters full of love;

753. *strange*] Capell *et seq.*; *straying* Qq, Ff. 758. *misbecom'd*] *misbecombd* Q 1. 760. *make*] *make them* Pope.

750. *strains*] tendencies.

753. *strange*] Cappell's emendation is generally accepted. In support of it, the Cambridge editors write: "In the *Lover's Complaint* (ed. 1609), line 303, 'strange' is spelt 'straing'; and in Lyly's *Euphues* (Arber, p. 113), '*straying*' is a misprint for 'straunge.'" More probably an old spelling than a misprint for it occurs again in Hand D's part of *Sir Thomas More* (l. 8): "they bring in straing rootes, which is meerly to the vndoing of poor prentizes, for whatſ a sorry psnyp to a good hart." Cf. *Promos and Cassandra* (*Shakes. Lib.*, vi. 228) pt. i., iii. 1: "O straying effectes of blinde affected Love, From wisdomes pathes, which doth astraye our wittes," etc. Halliwell quoted the first line here, with the simple remark that "straying" was the same misprint for "strange." The pun again suggests it is no misprint but a recognised spelling. Shakespeare has expressions many times from *Promos and Cassandra*. The parallel in *Midsummer Night's Dream*, v. i. 12-17, would support either "strange" (as the equivalent of "things unknown") or "straying" (as the opposite of having a "local habitation").

754, 755. *subjects . . . object*] A kind of antithesis the Euphuists delighted in. "You shall not be as objects of warre, but as subjects to Alexander" (Lyly's *Campaspe*, I. i).

754. *eye doth roll*] Compare *A Midsummer Night's Dream*, v. i. 14.

756. *party-coated*] in motley, like a fool. See note at "patch," IV. ii. 31.

760. *Suggested*] tempted. See *Othello*, II. iii. 364, *Richard II.*, III. iv. 75, and *The Two Gentlemen of Verona*, III. i. 34; and compare I. i. 157.

Your favours, the ambassadors of love;
And in our maiden council, rated them
At courtship, pleasant jest, and courtesy,
As bombast and as lining to the time.
But more devout than this in our respects
Have we not been; and therefore met your loves
In their own fashion, like a merriment.
Dum. Our letters, madam, show'd much more than jest.
Long. So did our looks.
Ros. We did not quote them so.
King. Now, at the latest minute of the hour,
Grant us your loves.
Prin. A time, methinks, too short
To make a world-without-end bargain in.
No, no, my lord, your grace is perjur'd much,
Full of dear guiltiness; and therefore this:
If for my love, as there is no such cause,
You will do aught, this shall you do for me:
Your oath I will not trust; but go with speed
To some forlorn and naked hermitage,
Remote from all the pleasures of the world;
There stay, until the twelve celestial signs
Have brought about the annual reckoning.
If this austere insociable life
Change not your offer made in heat of blood;

768. *the*] Ff; omitted Q 1. 772. *this in our*] Hanmer; *this our* Q 1; *these are our* Ff, Q 2; *these are your* Tyrwhitt conjecture. 773. *been*] *seen* Tyrwhitt conjecture. 776. *quote*] Hanmer, etc.; *cote, coat, coate* old editions. 788. *the*] Q 1; *their* Ff, Q 2.

771. *bombast*] stuffing of wool for padding clothes. See *Othello*, I. i. 13.

776. *quote*] take them as meaning so.

779. *world-without-end*] Compare Sonnet lvii. Nashe uses the expression in *Foure Letters Confuted* (McKerrow, i. 324), 1592-3: "When I parted with thy brother in Pierce Penilesse, I left him to be tormented world without ende of our Poets and writers about London." Occurs in the Te Deum and in Isaiah xlv. 17, where the Wyclif reading is "everlasting."

781. *dear*] grievous, heartfelt. But no doubt the Princess implies the sense of acceptable, forgivable.

787. *signs*] of the zodiac. This expression for the duration of a year occurs again in *Measure for Measure*, I. ii. 172. Compare *Gesta Grayorum*, 1594 (Malone Soc., ed. Greg, p. 10): "In his Crest, his Government for the twelve days of Christmas was resembled to the Sun's passing the twelve Signs."

If frosts and fasts, hard lodging and thin weeds,
Nip not the gaudy blossoms of your love,
But that it bear this trial and last love;
Then at the expiration of the year,
Come challenge me, challenge me by these deserts,
And, by this virgin palm now kissing thine,
I will be thine; and, till that instant, shut
My woeful self up in a mourning house,
Raining the tears of lamentation
For the remembrance of my father's death.
If this thou do deny, let our hands part;
Neither intitled in the other's heart.

King. If this, or more than this, I would deny,
To flatter up these powers of mine with rest,
The sudden hand of death close up mine eye!
Hence hermit, then—my heart is in thy breast.

[*Ber.* And what to me, my love? and what to me?

Ros. You must be purged to your sins are rack'd:

797. *instant*] Ff, Q 2; *instance* Q 1. 802. *intitled*] Ff 1, 2, 3; *intiled* Q 1; *intituled* F 4. 804. *flatter*] *fetter* Hanmer (Warburton). 806. *hermit*] New (Pollard); *herrite* Q 1; *euer* Ff. 808. *purged to*] *purged to,* Q 1; *purged too,* Ff. *rack'd*] Qq, Ff.; *rank* Rowe.

791. *weeds*] garments. Greene commonly applies the term to a palmer's wear.

793. *last love*] survive as love.

802. *intitled*] having a claim (a legal sense).

804. *flatter up . . . with rest*] indulge in idleness and freedom from cares. If I should refuse you anything for the sake of my selfish comfort.

806. *Hence hermit, then*] The Folio reading is clearly a feeble attempt at emendation. A. W. Pollard's suggestion (*Library*, October 1917) is close to the Quarto and gives us just what the King might be expected to say: "You tell me to be a hermit—very well, I will be; your word to me is law."

807-12. *And what . . . sick*] Rosaline's next speech makes these lines redundant. They are clearly an early draft, somehow left uncancelled by Shakespeare although he had written new lines for Rosaline and Berowne and borrowed from the old for Dumain and Katharine. See Introduction 2.51.

808. *purged . . rack'd*] The Folio punctuation demands a forced sense for *rack'd*, hence Rowe's attractive emendation. *Rank* might be spelt *răcke*. Dover Wilson suggests "that the compositor printed 'to' for 'till' (a common type of error) and that the line should read 'You must be purged till your sins are racked.' The word 'attaint' in the next line seems to make the connection between 'rack' and torture certain." There is no need, however, to alter "to," which still sometimes took the place of "till" even at this date. *N.E.D.* quotes a deposition in a Durham ecclesiastical court, *c.* 1575: "Umphray culd gett no reste of the said Thomas to he had cast hym doon on his bedd." Common earlier.

You are attaint with faults and perjury;
Therefore, if you my favour mean to get,
A twelvemonth shall you spend and never rest
But seek the weary beds of people sick.]

Dum. But what to me, my love? but what to me?
A wife?

Kath. A beard, fair health, and honesty;
With three-fold love I wish you all these three.

Dum. O! shall I say, I thank you, gentle wife?

Kath. Not so, my lord. A twelvemonth and a day
I'll mark no words that smooth-faced wooers say:
Come when the king doth to my lady come;
Then, if I have much love, I'll give you some.

Dum. I'll serve thee true and faithfully till then.

Kath. Yet swear not, lest you be forsworn again.

Long. What says Maria?

Mar. At the twelvemonth's end
I'll change my black gown for a faithful friend.

Long. I'll stay with patience; but the time is long.

Mar. The liker you; few taller are so young.

Ber. Studies my lady? mistress, look on me.
Behold the window of my heart, mine eye,
What humble suit attends thy answer there;
Impose some service on me for thy love.

814. *A wife?* Kath. *A beard*] Camb., New; Kath. *A wife? A beard* Qq, Ff 1, 2, 3; Kath. *A wife, a beard* F 4. 830. *thy*] Q 1; *my* Ff, Q 2.

814. *A wife*] The words were first given to Dumain by Clark and Aldis Wright. Their emendation is the best means of making sense of the Quarto punctuation; that of the fourth Folio suggests an Elizabethan equivalent of our "a house, a wife, and a thousand a year," but the "threefold" of the next line forbids this reading.

817. *A twelvemonth and a day*] "Halliwell gives quotations from Ducange and from Cowell's *Interpreter*, which shows that this term constituted the full legal year both on the Continent and in England. It is found in Chaucer's *Wyf of Bathes Tale*" (Furness). Hence the common expression "a year and a day."

818. *smooth-faced*] Shakespeare has this compound twice elsewhere; of commodity (advantage), in *King John*, II. i. 573; and of peace, in *Richard III.* V. v. 33. He may have met it in Greene's *Menaphon* (Grosart, vi. 41): "Some sweare Love Smooth'd face Love Is sweetest sweete that men can have." It occurs also in *The Troublesome Raigne of King John* (Hazlitt's *Shakes. Lib.* p. 263): "A smooth facte Nunne (for ought I know) is all the Abbott's wealth."

824. *friend*] sweetheart. See line 404 above (note).

829, 830. *suit . . . service*] See note

Ros. Oft have I heard of you, my Lord Berowne,
Before I saw you, and the world's large tongue
Proclaims you for a man replete with mocks;
Full of comparisons and wounding flouts,
Which you on all estates will execute
That lie within the mercy of your wit:
To weed this wormwood from your fruitful brain,
And there withal to win me, if you please,
Without the which I am not to be won,
You shall this twelve month term from day to day,
Visit the speechless sick, and still converse
With groaning wretches; and your task shall be,
With all the fierce endeavour of your wit
To enforce the pained impotent to smile.

Ber. To move wild laughter in the throat of death?
It cannot be; it is impossible:
Mirth cannot move a soul in agony.

Ros. Why, that's the way to choke a gibing spirit,
Whose influence is begot of that loose grace
Which shallow laughing hearers give to fools.
A jest's prosperity lies in the ear
Of him that hears it, never in the tongue
Of him that makes it: then, if sickly ears,
Deaf'd with the clamours of their own dear groans,
Will hear your idle scorns, continue then,
And I will have you and that fault withal;
But if they will not, throw away that spirit,
And I shall find you empty of that fault,
Right joyful of your reformation.

Ber. A twelvemonth! well, befall what will befall,
I'll jest a twelvemonth in an hospital.

837. *fruitful*] Ff, *fructful* Q 1. 854. *dear*] *dere* Johnson conjecture; *drear* Jackson conjecture; *dire* Collier MS. 855. *then*] *them* Rann conjecture, Dyce.

at line 276. This recognized phrase in courtship occurs in *The Shepherdess Felismena*, in Yonge's trans. of Montmayor's *Diana* (*Shakes. Lib.* p. 289, ed. 1875), 1598: "He should never have got any other guerdon of his sutes and services, but onely to see and to be seene, and sometimes to speake to his Mistresse." A term in Feudalism primarily.

835. *all estates*] people of all sorts.

843. *fierce*] ardent, eager.

854. *dear*] heartfelt; see line 781 (note), and compare Sonnet xxxvii. 3: "fortune's dearest spite."

860. *befall . . . befall*] Compare

Prin. [*To the King.*] Ay, sweet my lord; and so I take my leave.
King. No, madam; we will bring you on your way.
Ber. Our wooing doth not end like an old play;
Jack hath not Jill: these ladies' courtesy
Might well have made our sport a comedy.
King. Come, sir, it wants a twelvemonth and a day,
And then 'twill end.
Ber. That's too long for a play.

Re-enter ARMADO.

Arm. Sweet majesty, vouchsafe me,—
Prin. Was not that Hector?
Dum. The worthy knight of Troy.
Arm. I will kiss thy royal finger, and take leave. I am a votary; I have vowed to Jaquenetta to hold the plough for her sweet love three year. But, most esteemed greatness, will you hear the dialogue that

874. *year*] *yeare* Q 1; *years* Ff, Q 2.

"befall what may befall" (*2 Henry VI.* III. ii. 402, and *Titus Andronicus,* v. i. 57). Similar to "hap what will," "come what come may," both of which occur in Greene's *Carde of Fancie,* 1587.

863. *bring you on your way*] conduct, accompany you on your way. The expression occurs again in *Winter's Tale,* IV. iii. 122; and in *Measure for Measure,* I. i. 62. It is close to the "bring me forward" of *Everyman,* line 290.

865. *Jack . . . Jill*] an old saying, occurring in Heywood's *Dialogue,* 1546 (Dyce); and see Sharman's edition of Heywood's *Proverbs,* p. 100. And earlier, in Skelton's *Magnyfycence* (Dyce, i. 234), 1515: "What avayleth lordshyp, yourselfe for to kyll, With care and with thought, howe Jack shall have Gyl." Gosson has "Every John and his Joan" (*Schoole of Abuse,* 1579).

872. *royal finger*] See above, v. i. 98.

873, 874. *hold the plough*] See note at lines 713-15 above.

875. *dialogue*] This use of "dialogue" is not included by *New Eng. Dict.* amongst "dialogues set as musical compositions," the earliest example being from J. Playford, 1653. In *The Queen's Entertainment at the Earl of Hertford's,* 1591 (Nichols' *Progresses,* iii. 113), there is a song of a similar structure between "Dem" (and) and "Resp" (onse), with an echo to take up the closing syllables of each quatrain. It is "The Song presented by Nereus on the water, sung dialogue-wise, everie fourth verse answered with two Echoes." Shakespeare's bird-notes replace the already stale echo device. Apart from such musical examples, the prose "dialogue," in which the two sides of an argument were stated by opposing characters, was a favourite form, particularly in religious controversy. The fashion was set by Erasmus and the German protestants, who were much translated and imitated in such English examples as the *Proper Dyalogue betweene a*

the two learned men have compiled in praise of the owl and the cuckoo? it should have followed in the end of our show.

King. Call them forth quickly; we will do so.

Arm. Holla! approach.

Re-enter HOLOFERNES, NATHANIEL, MOTH, COSTARD, *and others.*

This side is *Hiems*, Winter, this *Ver*, the Spring; the one maintained by the owl, the other by the cuckoo. *Ver*, begin.

THE SONG.

Spring. When daisies pied and violets blue
And lady-smocks all silver-white
And cuckoo-buds of yellow hue
Do paint the meadows with delight,

Re-enter . . .] *Enter all* Qq, Ff. 885, 886. Theobald; the order is 886, 885 in Qq, Ff. 886. *cuckoo-buds*] *cowslip-buds* Farmer conjecture; *crocus-buds* Whalley conjecture. 887. *with delight*] *much bedight* Warburton.

Gentillman and a Husbandman (1530). Equivalent terms were "debate" and "dispute," as in Robert Greene's *A Quip for an Upstart Courtier, or a Quaint Dispute between Velvet-breeches and Cloth-breeches.* Armado's dialogue is presumably the "antic" forecast, in case the play "fadge" not, in v. i. 141.

880. *Holla*] "a shout to excite attention" (*New Eng. Dict.*); "a call to a person to come near" (Schmidt). Compare Gascoigne, *The Steel Glas* (Arber, p. 72), 1577: "But holla; here, I see a wondrous sight, I see a swarme of Saints within my glasse. . . . What should they be (my lord), what should they be?"

882. *the one . . . the other*] the two sides in the debate. See line 875.

884. *When daisies pied*, etc.] Furness writes: "Whalley speaks of this song 'which gave so much pleasure to the Town, and was in everybody's mouth about seven years ago.' This must have been about 1740. Genest records no production of *Love's Labour's Lost* at or about this date, or in fact at any date. But we know that this song was introduced into *As You Like It*; which Genest says, was acted in November, 1740, for the first time for forty years. It had an unusual run of twenty-five nights."

885–6. *lady-smocks . . . cuckoo-buds*] Commentators have long argued as to what these flowers might be. In *Review of English Studies*, III (new series), pp. 117–29 J. W. Lever has shown that Shakespeare took them not from nature but from the first edition of Gerard's *Herball* (1597). This describes six varieties of "water Cresses or Cuckow flowers." To all but one Gerard, a native of Cheshire, also applies the purely local name of "Ladie smockes." The fifth variety, "Milke white Ladie smockes," is said to have yellowish flowers, to grow "in moist medowes" and to bloom "when the Cuckowe doth begin to sing her

The cuckoo then, on every tree,
Mocks married men ; for thus sings he,
Cuckoo ;
Cuckoo, cuckoo : O word of fear,
Unpleasing to a married ear !

When shepherds pipe on oaten straws,
And merry larks are ploughman's clocks,
When turtles tread, and rooks, and daws,
And maidens bleach their summer smocks,
The cuckoo then, on every tree,
Mocks married men ; for thus sings he,
Cuckoo ;
Cuckoo, cuckoo : O word of fear,
Unpleasing to a married ear !

Winter. When icicles hang by the wall,
And Dick the shepherd blows his nail,
And Tom bears logs into the hall,
And milk comes frozen home in pail,

pleasant notes without stammering." All this Shakespeare takes over. Gerard's "fower leaves of a yellowish colour" (meaning the pale-green calyx ?) becoming the impossible "cuckoo-buds of yellow hue."

888, 889. *cuckoo . . . thus sings he*] The quibble on cuckold reappears in *Merry Wives of Windsor*, II. i. 124. This special nastiness of the cuckoo is first found in the poems of T. Howell (1568) who calls it a "slanderous bird" ; but that it brings bad luck is a superstition as old as Pliny.

893. *pipe on oaten straws*] Compare T. Watson, *Eclogue upon Death of Walsingham* (Arber, p. 163), 1590 : "An humble style befitts a simple swain, My Muse shall pipe but on an oaten quill." And Golding's *Ovid*, i. 842 : "Some good plaine soule that had some flocke to feede And as he went he pyped still upon an Oten Reede" (1567). Spenser speaks of the shepherd's "oaten pipe" in *Shepheard'sCalendar* for January (1579).

894. *larks . . . clocks*] "rise with the lark" occurs in Lyly's *Euphues and his England* (Arber, p. 229), 1580 ; and "up with the lark" in Greene's *Never Too Late* (Grosart, viii. 124).

903. *blows his nail*] wait patiently while one has nothing to do. Schmidt says "to warm his hands," an accidental property of the saying, arising out of idleness in cold. The expression occurs again as descriptive of listlessness in *3 Henry VI.* II. v. 3. A few examples must be quoted : "hee was driven to daunce attendaunce without doores and blowe his nailes" (North, *Doni's Philosophie* [edited Jacobs, p. 231], 1570) ; "who sate all the while with the Porter, blowing his nailes" (*Jests of George Peele* [Hazlitt's repr. p. 276], 1607) ; Cotgrave explains this in v. *ceincture :* "pull straws, pluck daisies, pick rushes, or blow their fingers ; generally the phrase imports an idle and lazie fashion, or posture." In verses by Campion from Davison's *Poetical Rhapsodie*, 1611 (quoted by Nichols, iii. 350), cold is specified : "But in their brests, where Love his Court should hold, Poor Cupid sits, and blows his nailes for cold."

When blood is nipp'd, and ways be foul,
Then nightly sings the staring owl,
Tu-whit ;
Tu-who, a merry note,
While greasy Joan doth keel the pot.

When all aloud the wind doth blow,
And coughing drowns the parson's saw,
And birds sit brooding in the snow,
And Marian's nose looks red and raw,
When roasted crabs hiss in the bowl,
Then nightly sings the staring owl,
Tu-whit ;
Tu-who, a merry note,
While greasy Joan doth keel the pot.

The words of Mercury are harsh after the songs of Apollo. [*Exeunt.*

906. *foul*] *fall* Q 1 ; *full* Q 1 (Dev.). 908, 909. *Tu-whit ; Tu-who*] Qq, Ff : *Tu-who ; Tu-whit, to-who* Capell. 920, 921. *The words . . . Apollo*] In Q 1 printed in larger type, without any speech-heading ; Ff add *You that way : we this way* and heading Brag. (Armado).

908, 909. *Tu-whit ; Tu-who*] Holt White refers to Lyly's *Mother Bombie* (written *ante* 1590), III. iv. : "To whit, to who, the owle does cry ; Phip, phip, the sparrowes as they fly." Nashe has it in the Song of Ver in *Summer's Last Will* (1592). Compare, again, Lyly's *Endymion*, III. iii. : "There appeared in my sleep a goodly owle, who sitting upon my shoulder, cried twit, twit, and before mine eyes presented her-selfe the expresse image of Dipsas. I marvailed what the owle said till at last, I perceived twit, twit, to it, to it."

910. *keel the pot*] cool the pot, as a cook does by "stirring, skimming, or pouring on something cold, in order to prevent it boiling over" (*New Eng. Dict.*). Steevens quotes from Marston's *What You Will* (opening of the play), 1607 : "Faith, Doricus, thy brain boils ; keel it, keel it, or all the fat's in the fire." Skeat has a note on "keel" in his edition of *Piers the Plowman* (ii. 270). He quotes "Kelyn, or make colde, *frigefacio*" (*Prompt. Parvulorum*).

915. *crabs*] crab-apples. See *A Midsummer Night's Dream*, II. i. 48. Nares quotes from the old song in *Gammer Gurton's Needle*, Act ii. : "I cannot eat but little meat . . . I love no roast but a nut-brown toast, Or a crab laid in the fire." Steevens refers to Nashe's *Summer's Last Will* (McKerrow, iii, 281), 1592 : "Loves no good deeds, and hateth talke, But sitteth in a corner turning Crabbes, Or coughing o'er a warmed pot of Ale"—into which the wild apples were put when roasted. And Malone's remark that "What is called lamb's wool is produced" is confirmed by Peele, *Old Wives Tale* (ed. Bullen, i. 306), 1595 : "Lay a crab in the fire to roast for lamb's wool" (spice and sugar being added).

915, 916. *bowl . . . owl*] For the rhyme see IV. i. 138 (note).

920, 921. *Mercury . . . Apollo*] The larger type of the Quarto may reflect a different hand in the manu-script. On this assumption Dover Wilson suggests that the line is a mere reader's comment on the play as a whole. The Folio addition was perhaps made by the stage-manager to ensure a tidy *Exeunt.*